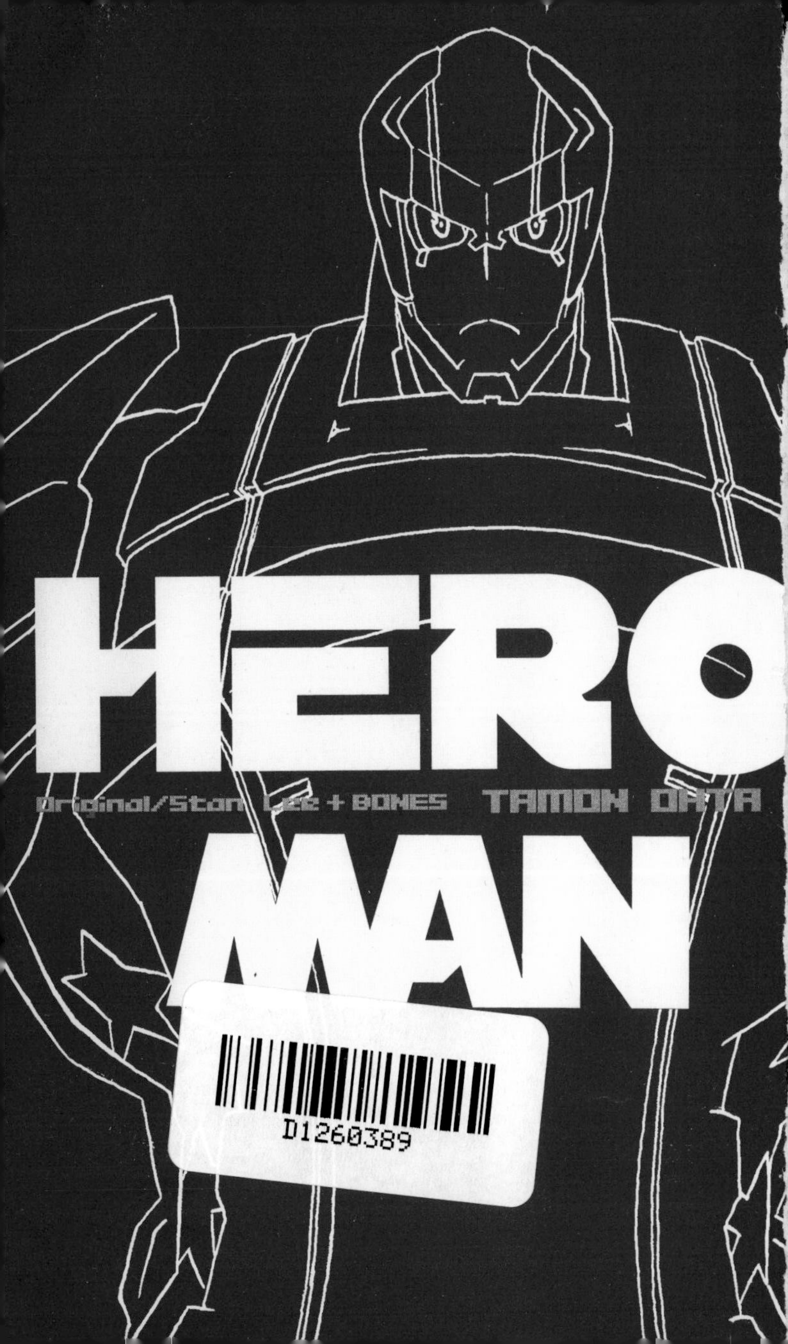

HERO MAN

Original/Stan Lee + BONES TAMON OHTA

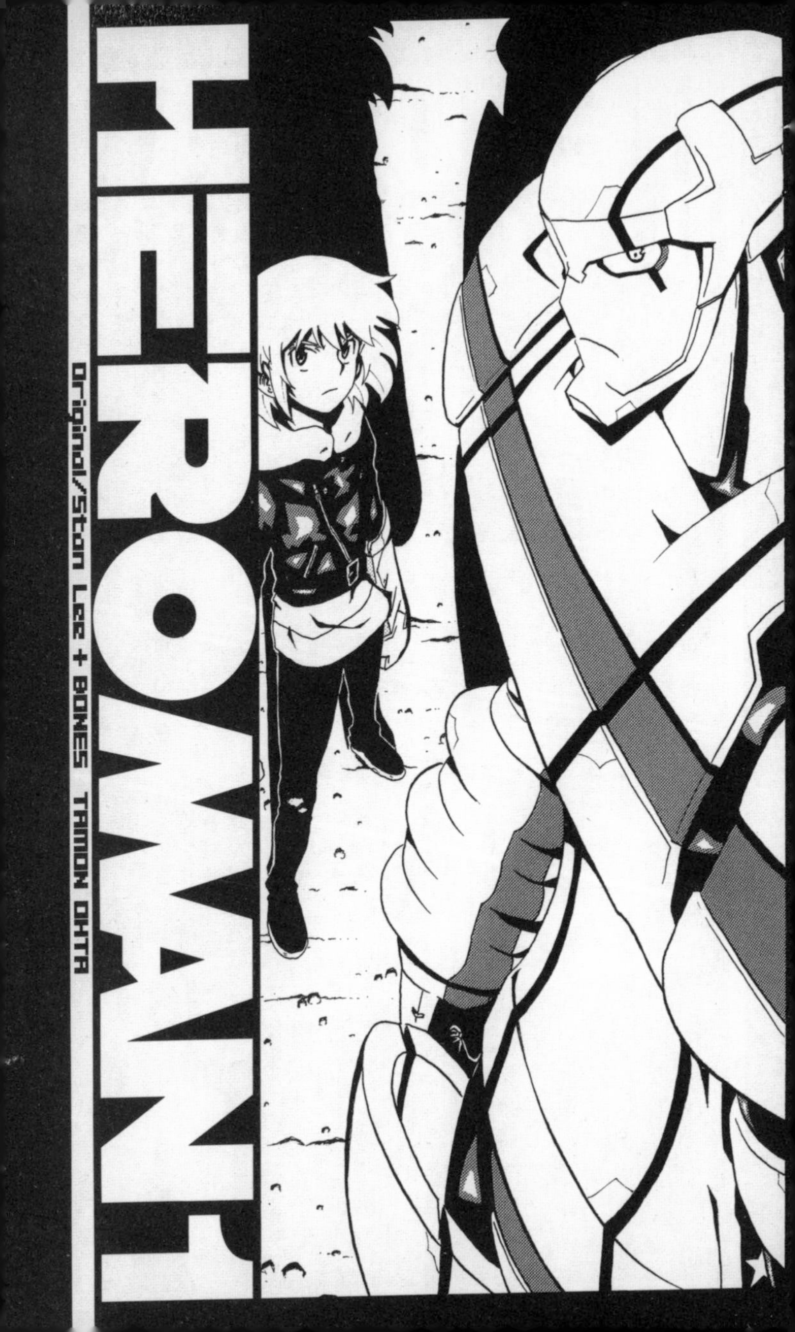
HEROMAN
Original/Stan Lee + BONES TAMON OHTA

HEROMAN
01 › contents

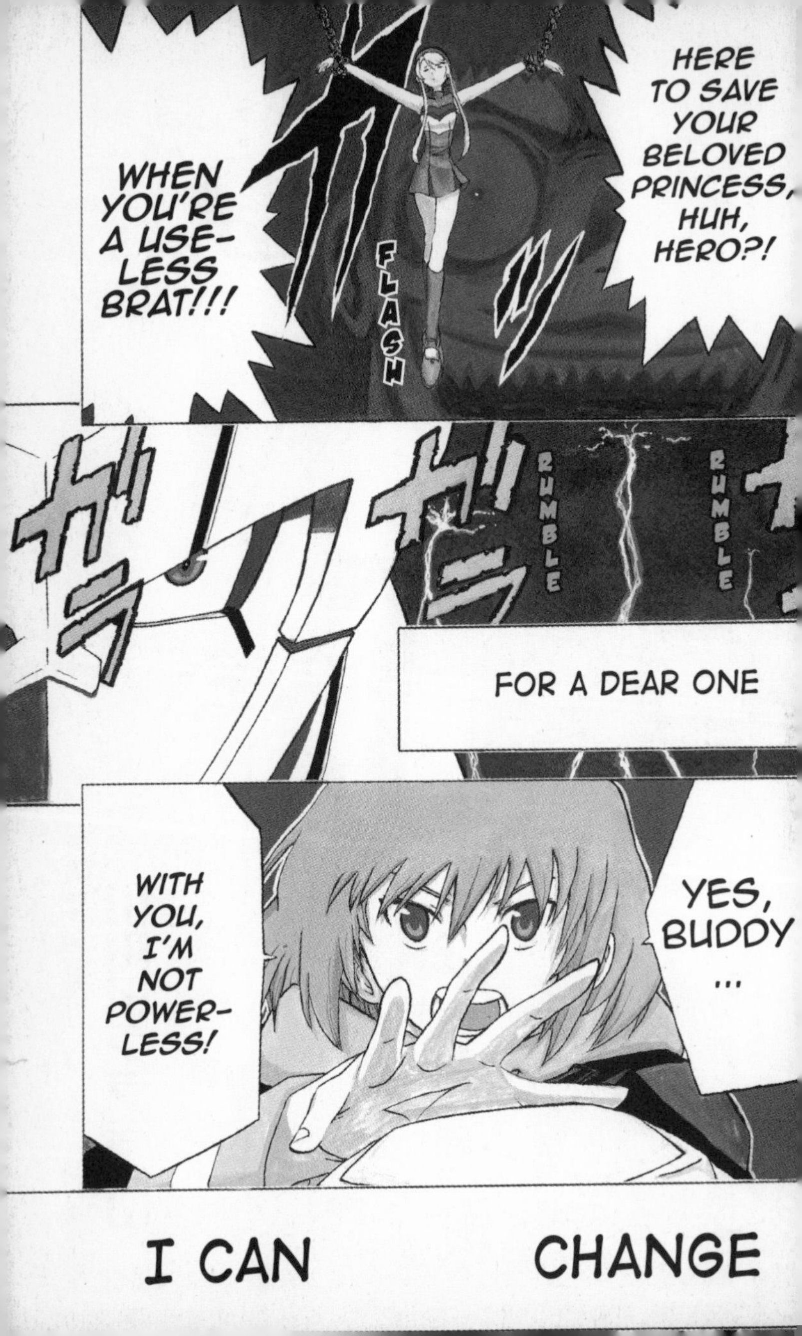
HERE TO SAVE YOUR BELOVED PRINCESS, HUH, HERO?!
FLASH
WHEN YOU'RE A USE-LESS BRAT!!!
RUMBLE
RUMBLE
FOR A DEAR ONE
YES, BUDDY ...
WITH YOU, I'M NOT POWER-LESS!
I CAN CHANGE

#01 BEGINNING

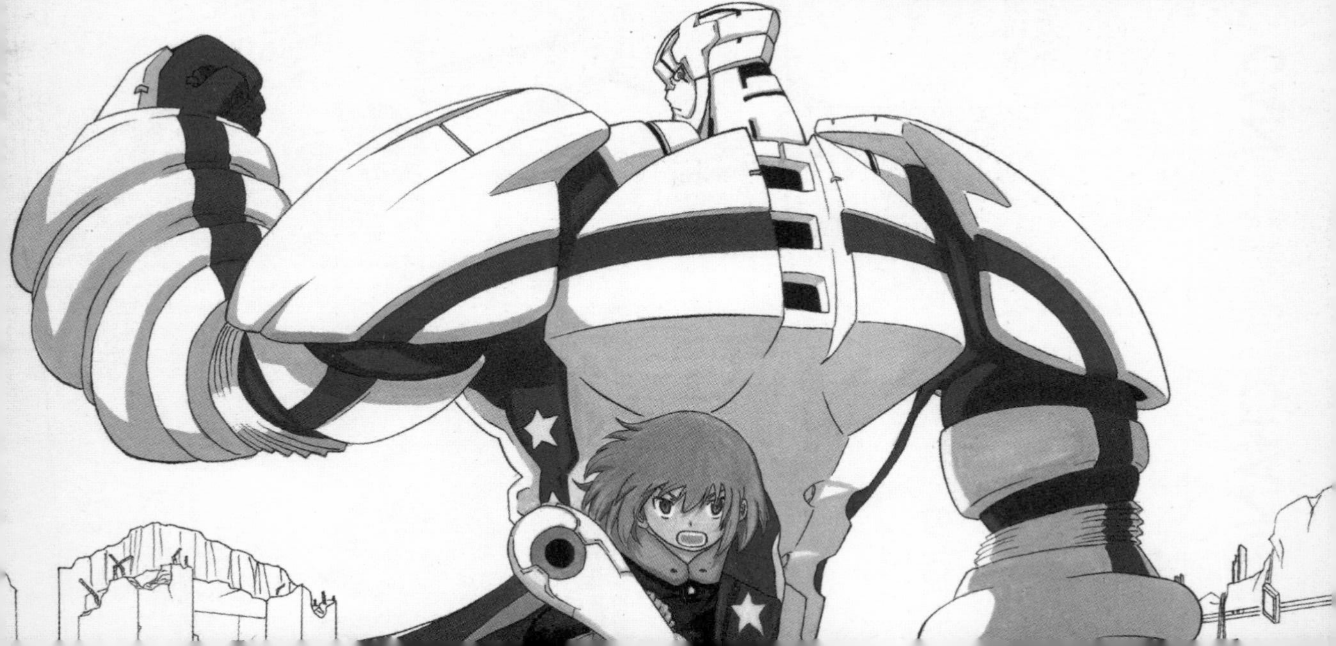

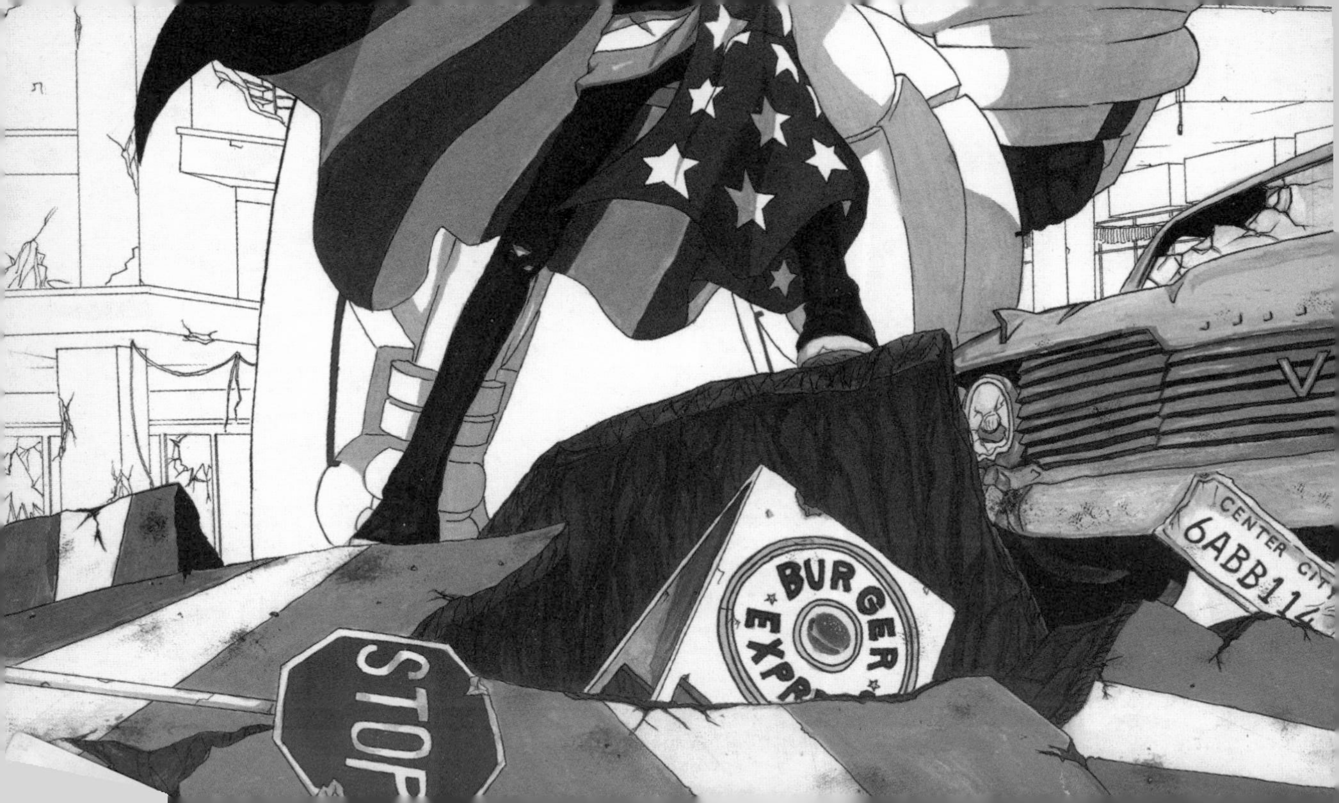
STOP
BURGER EXPR
CENTER CITY
6ABB114

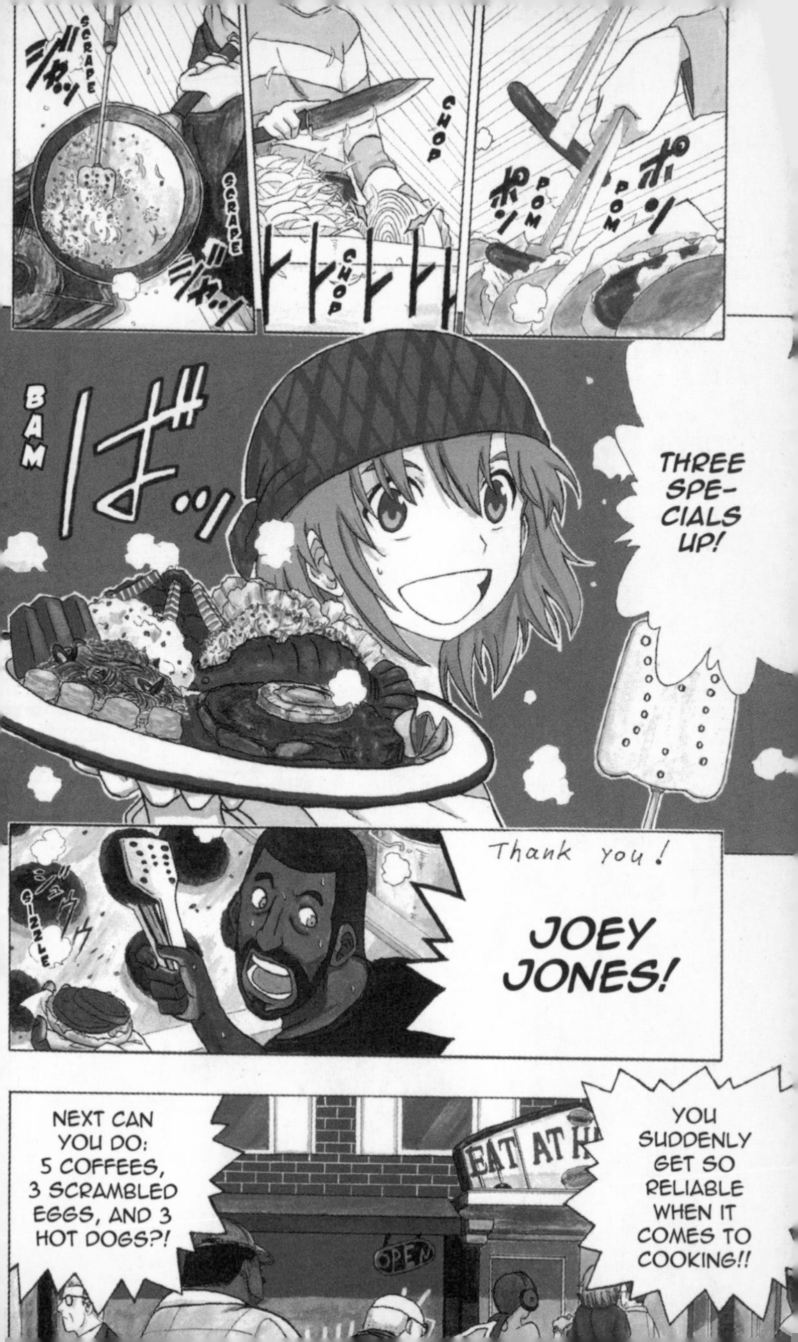

ポッ
POM
ポッ
POM
CHOP
トトトトト
CHOP
SCRAPE
ジャッ
SCRAPE
ジャッ
THREE SPE-CIALS UP!
BAM
ばっ
Thank you!
JOEY JONES!
SIZZLE
YOU SUDDENLY GET SO RELIABLE WHEN IT COMES TO COOKING!!
EAT AT
OPEN
NEXT CAN YOU DO: 5 COFFEES, 3 SCRAMBLED EGGS, AND 3 HOT DOGS?!

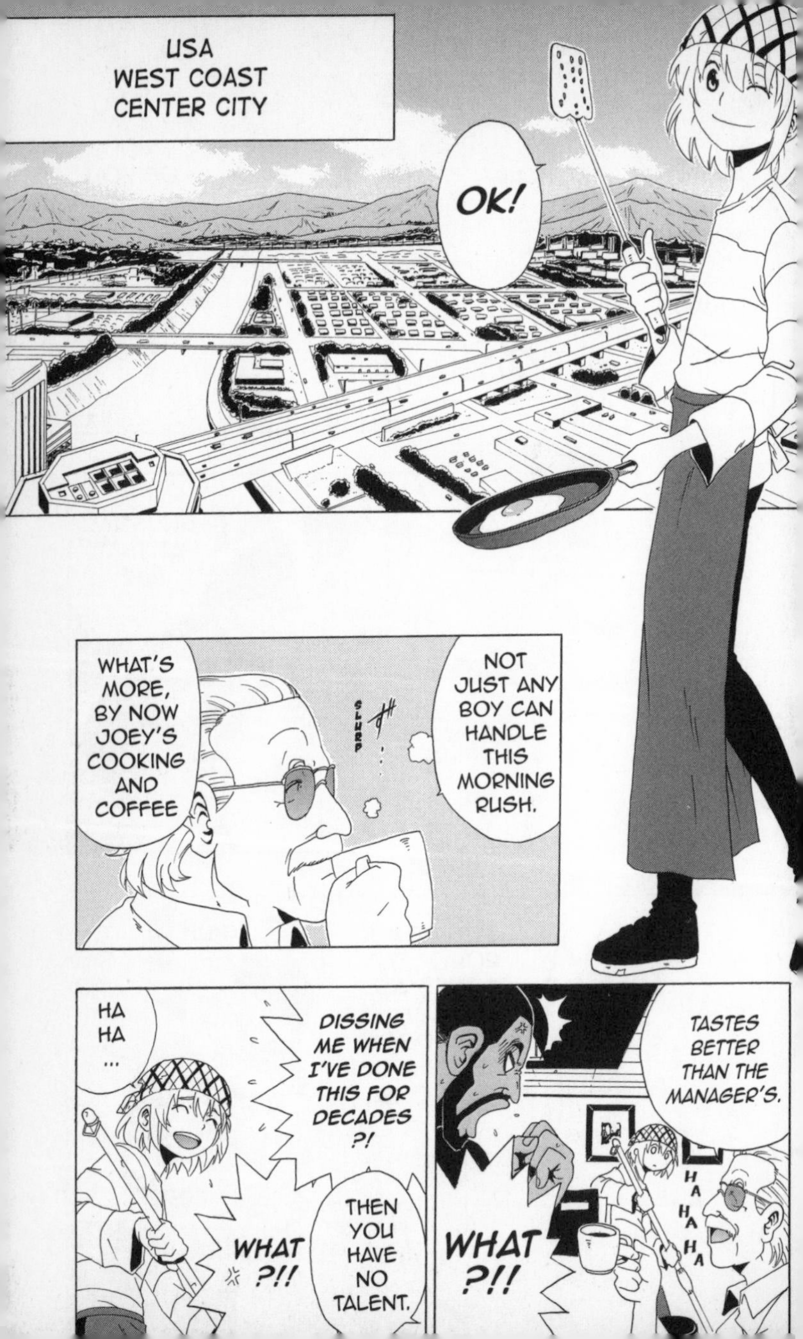
USA WEST COAST CENTER CITY
OK!
NOT JUST ANY BOY CAN HANDLE THIS MORNING RUSH.
SLURP
WHAT'S MORE, BY NOW JOEY'S COOKING AND COFFEE
TASTES BETTER THAN THE MANAGER'S.
HA HA HA HA
WHAT ?!!
DISSING ME WHEN I'VE DONE THIS FOR DECADES ?!
HA HA ...
THEN YOU HAVE NO TALENT.
WHAT ?!!

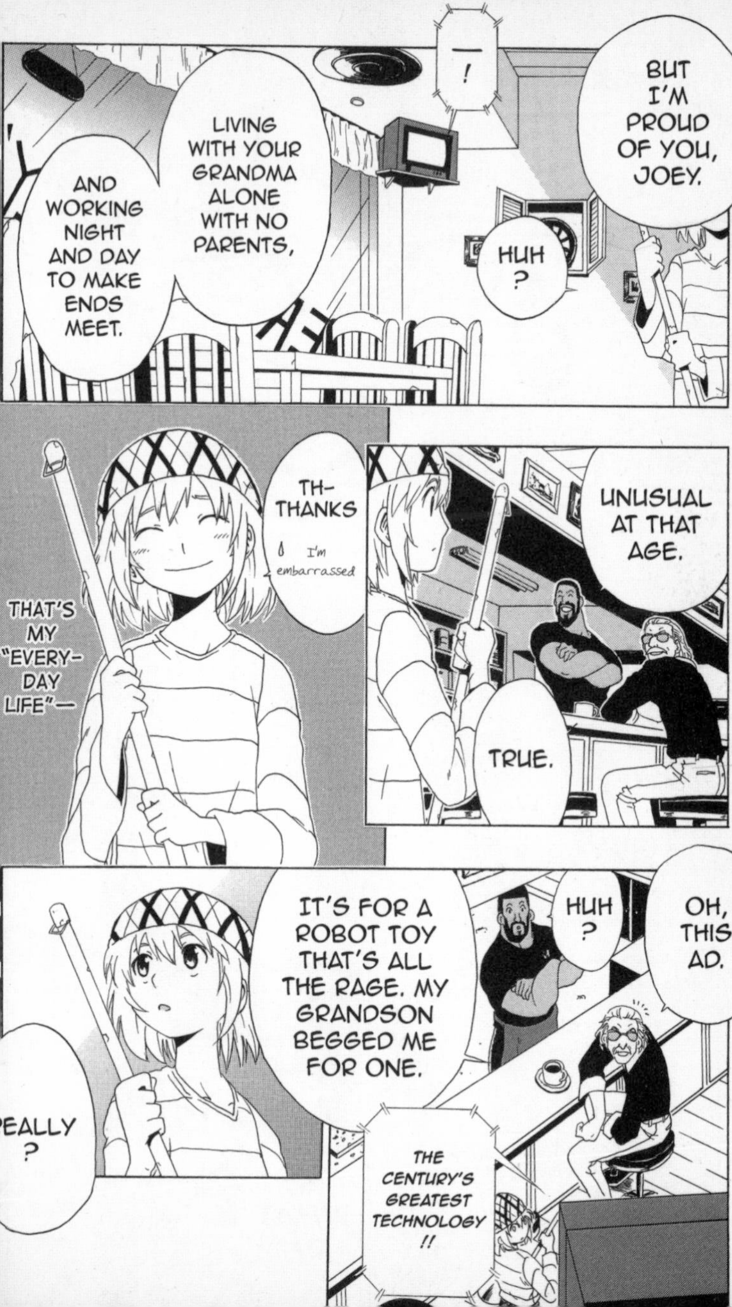
BUT I'M PROUD OF YOU, JOEY.
—!
HUH?
LIVING WITH YOUR GRANDMA ALONE WITH NO PARENTS,
AND WORKING NIGHT AND DAY TO MAKE ENDS MEET.
UNUSUAL AT THAT AGE.
TRUE.
TH-THANKS
I'm embarrassed
THAT'S MY "EVERY-DAY LIFE"—
OH, THIS AD.
HUH?
IT'S FOR A ROBOT TOY THAT'S ALL THE RAGE. MY GRANDSON BEGGED ME FOR ONE.
THE CENTURY'S GREATEST TECHNOLOGY!!
EALLY?

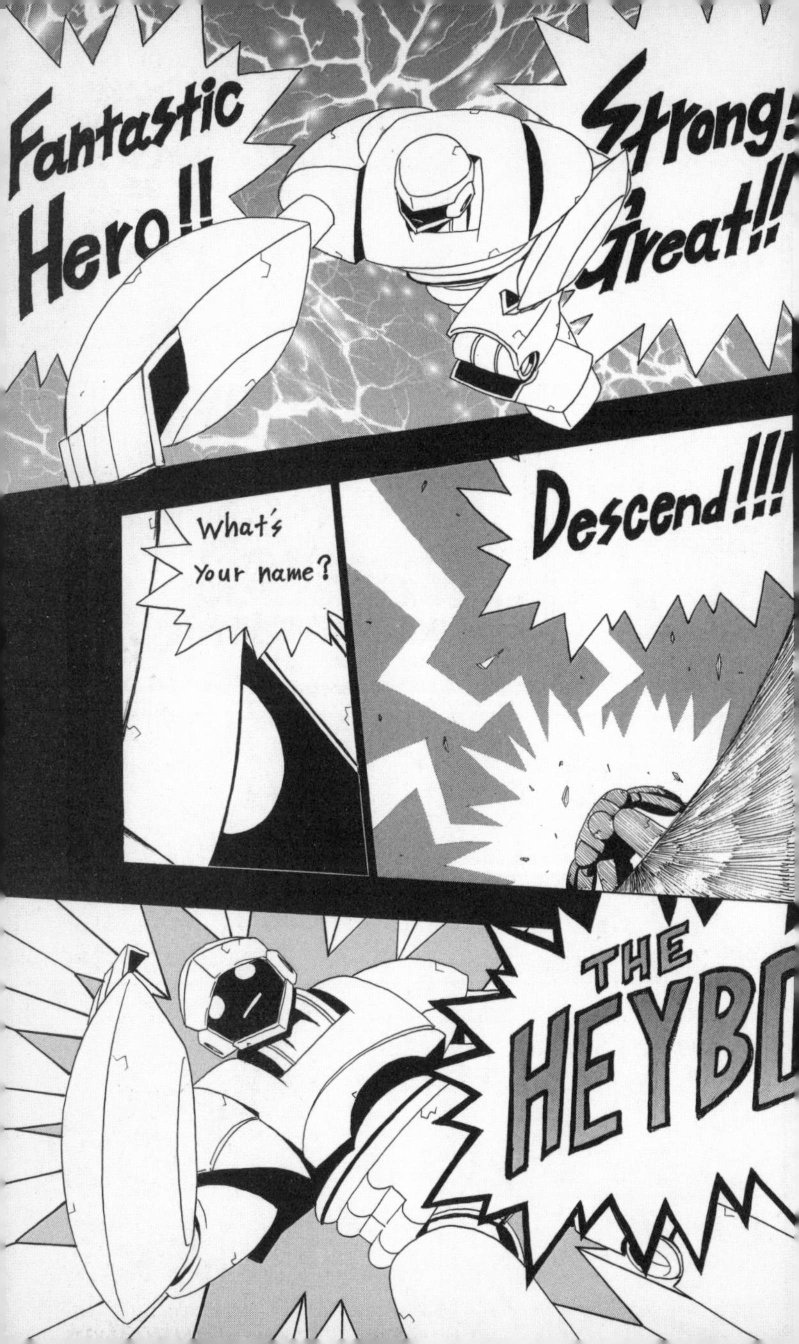
Strong! Great!!
Fantastic Hero!!
Descend!!!
What's your name?
THE
HEYBO

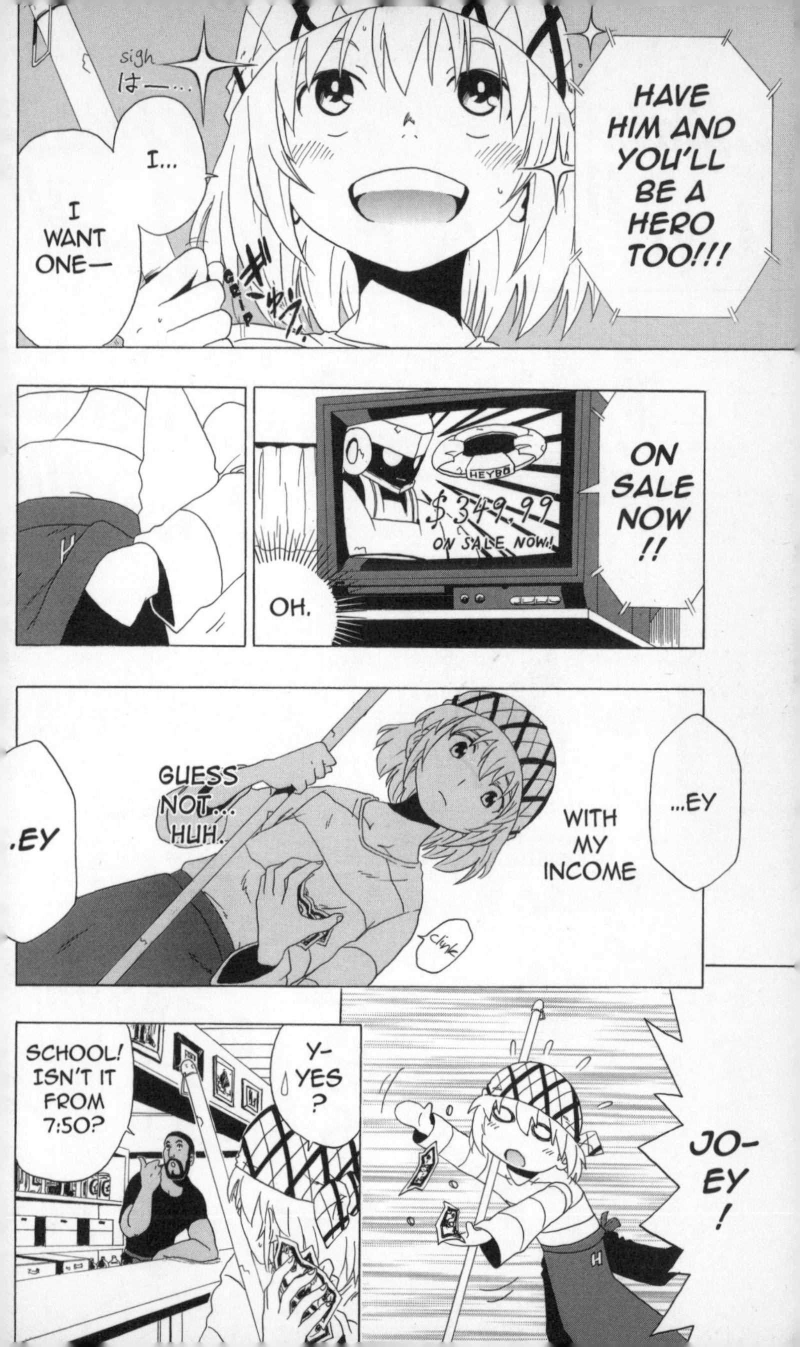

HAVE HIM AND YOU'LL BE A HERO TOO!!!
sigh
は―…
I...
I WANT ONE―
GRIP
ギュッ
ON SALE NOW !!
HEYBO
$349.99
ON SALE NOW!
OH.
...EY
WITH MY INCOME
GUESS NOT... HUH.
.EY
clink
JO-EY!
Y- YES ?
SCHOOL! ISN'T IT FROM 7:50?

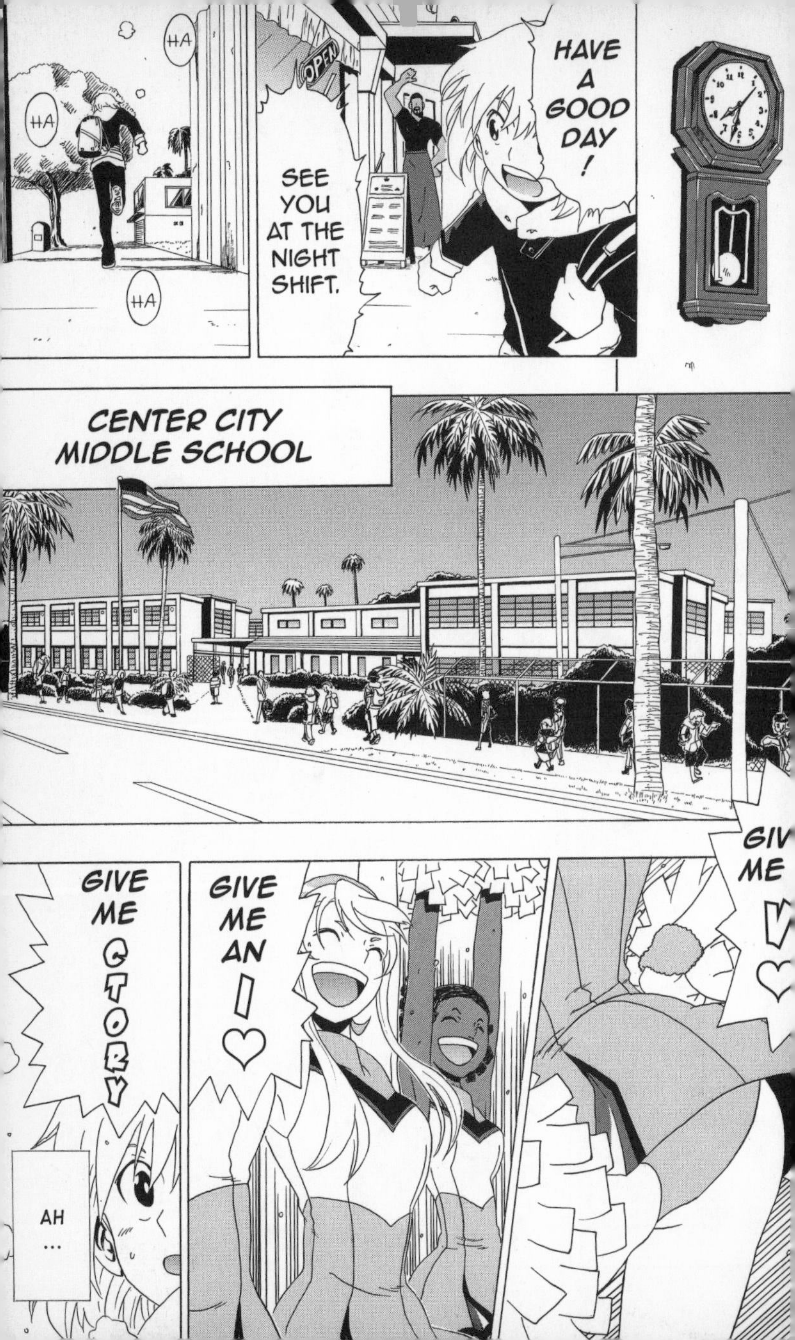
HAVE A GOOD DAY!
SEE YOU AT THE NIGHT SHIFT.
HA
HA
HA
CENTER CITY MIDDLE SCHOOL
GIV ME V ♥
GIVE ME AN I ♥
GIVE ME CTORY
AH ...

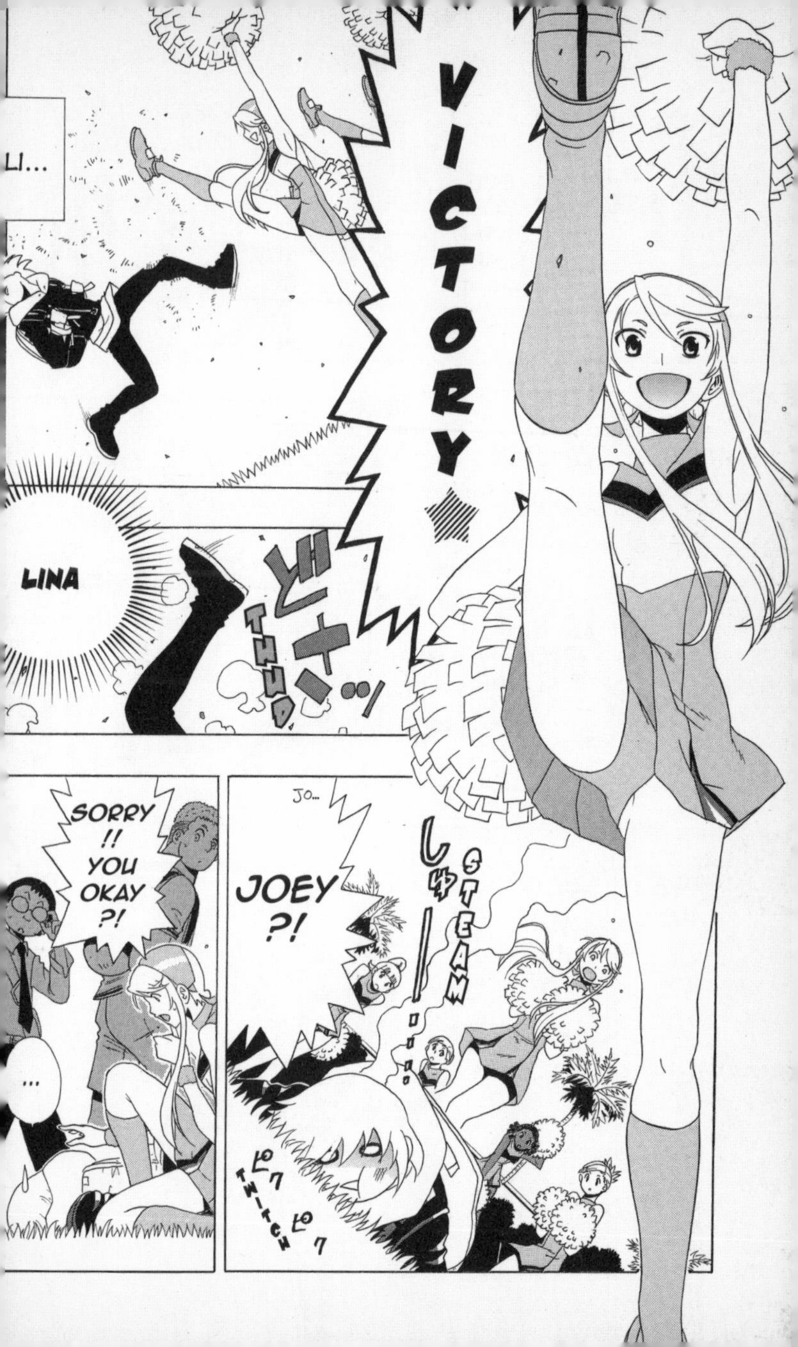
VICTORY
LI...
LINA
THUD
JO...
JOEY ?!
STEAM
TWITCH
SORRY !! YOU OKAY ?!
...

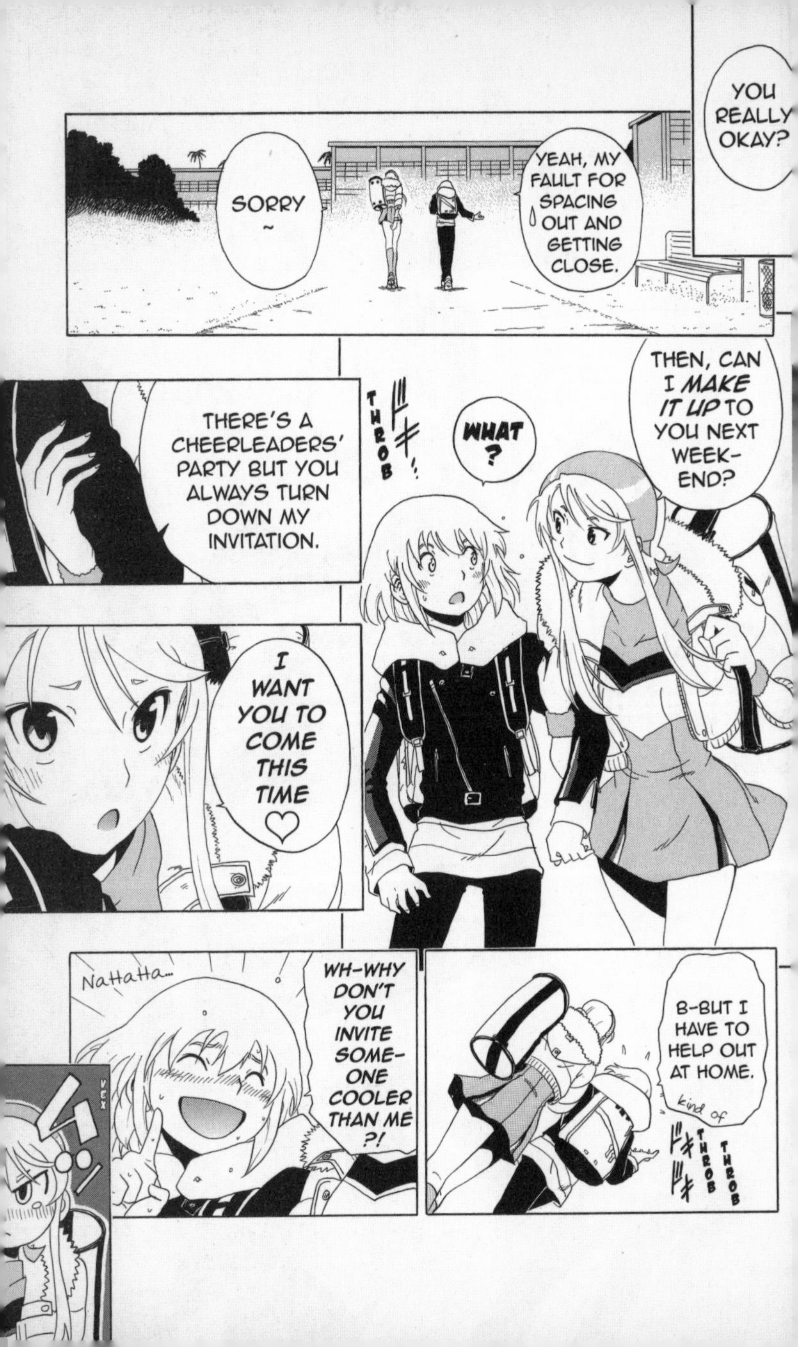
YOU REALLY OKAY?
YEAH, MY FAULT FOR SPACING OUT AND GETTING CLOSE.
SORRY ~
THEN, CAN I *MAKE IT UP* TO YOU NEXT WEEK-END?
WHAT?
THROB
THERE'S A CHEERLEADERS' PARTY BUT YOU ALWAYS TURN DOWN MY INVITATION.
I WANT YOU TO COME THIS TIME ♡
B-BUT I HAVE TO HELP OUT AT HOME.
kind of
THROB THROB
WH-WHY DON'T YOU INVITE SOME-ONE COOLER THAN ME ?!
NaHaHa...
VEX

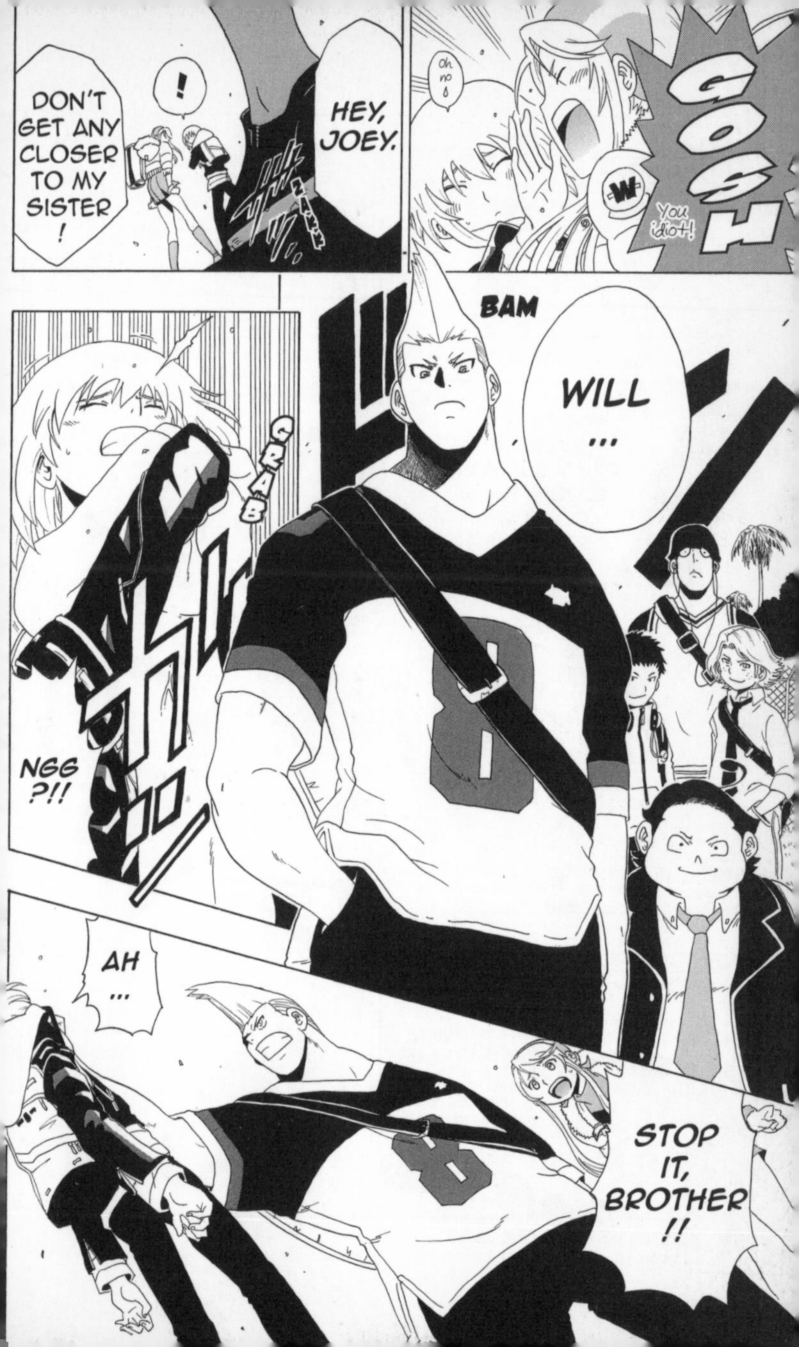
GOSH
W
oh no
You idiot!
HEY, JOEY.
!
DON'T GET ANY CLOSER TO MY SISTER!
BAM
WILL ...
GRAB
NGG ?!!
STOP IT, BROTHER !!
AH ...

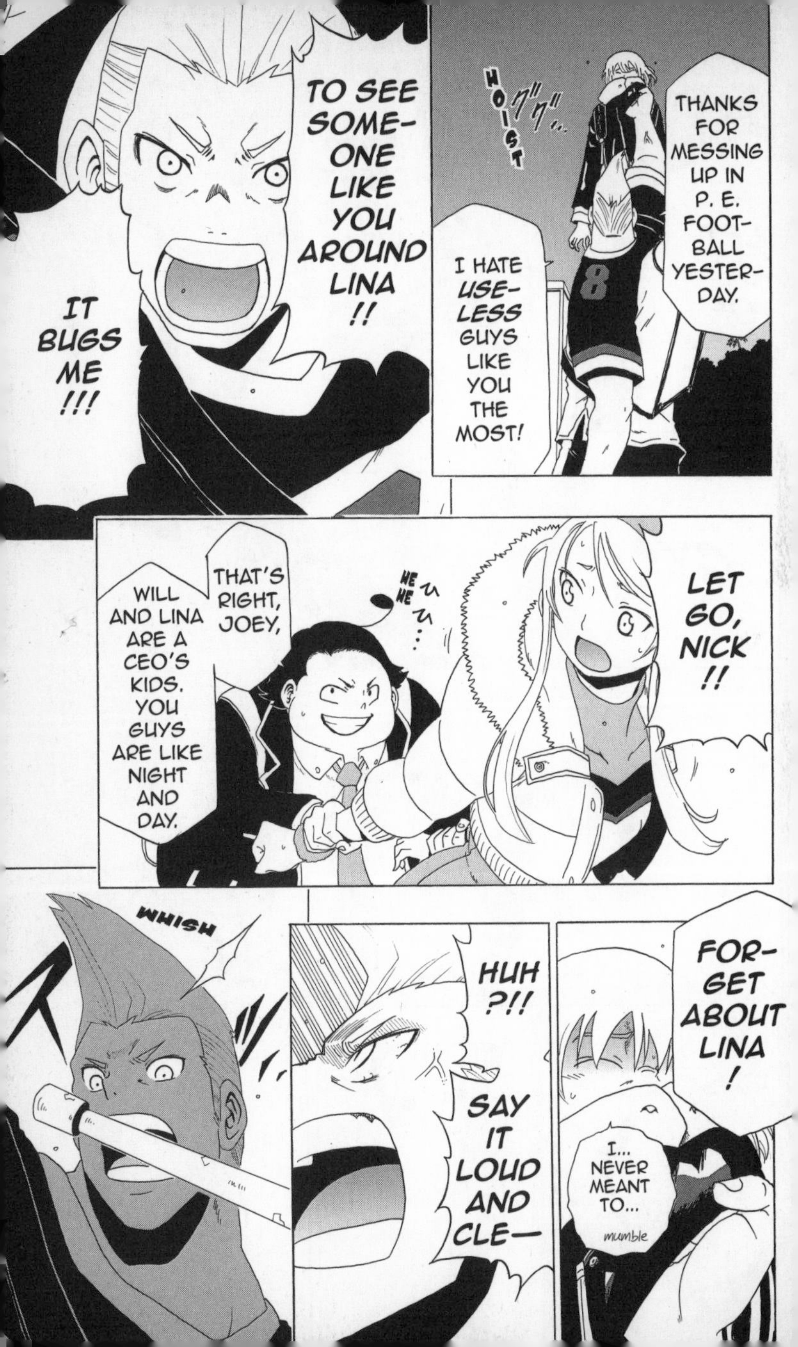
THANKS FOR MESSING UP IN P. E. FOOTBALL YESTERDAY.
HOIST
I HATE USELESS GUYS LIKE YOU THE MOST!
TO SEE SOMEONE LIKE YOU AROUND LINA!!
IT BUGS ME!!!
LET GO, NICK!!
HE HE...
THAT'S RIGHT, JOEY,
WILL AND LINA ARE A CEO'S KIDS. YOU GUYS ARE LIKE NIGHT AND DAY.
FORGET ABOUT LINA!
I... NEVER MEANT TO...
mumble
HUH?!!
SAY IT LOUD AND CLE—
WHISH

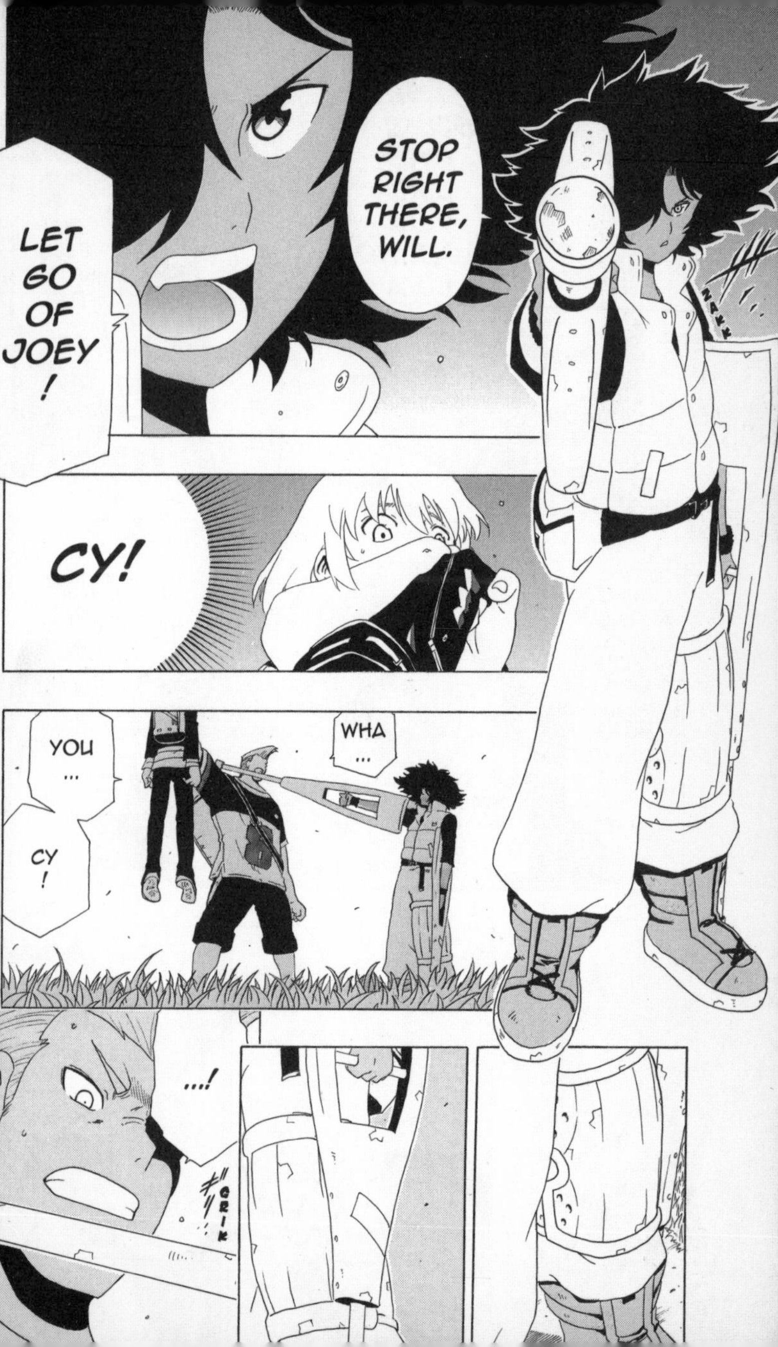
NAKK
STOP RIGHT THERE, WILL.
LET GO OF JOEY!
CY!
WHA...
YOU...
CY!
...!
GRIK

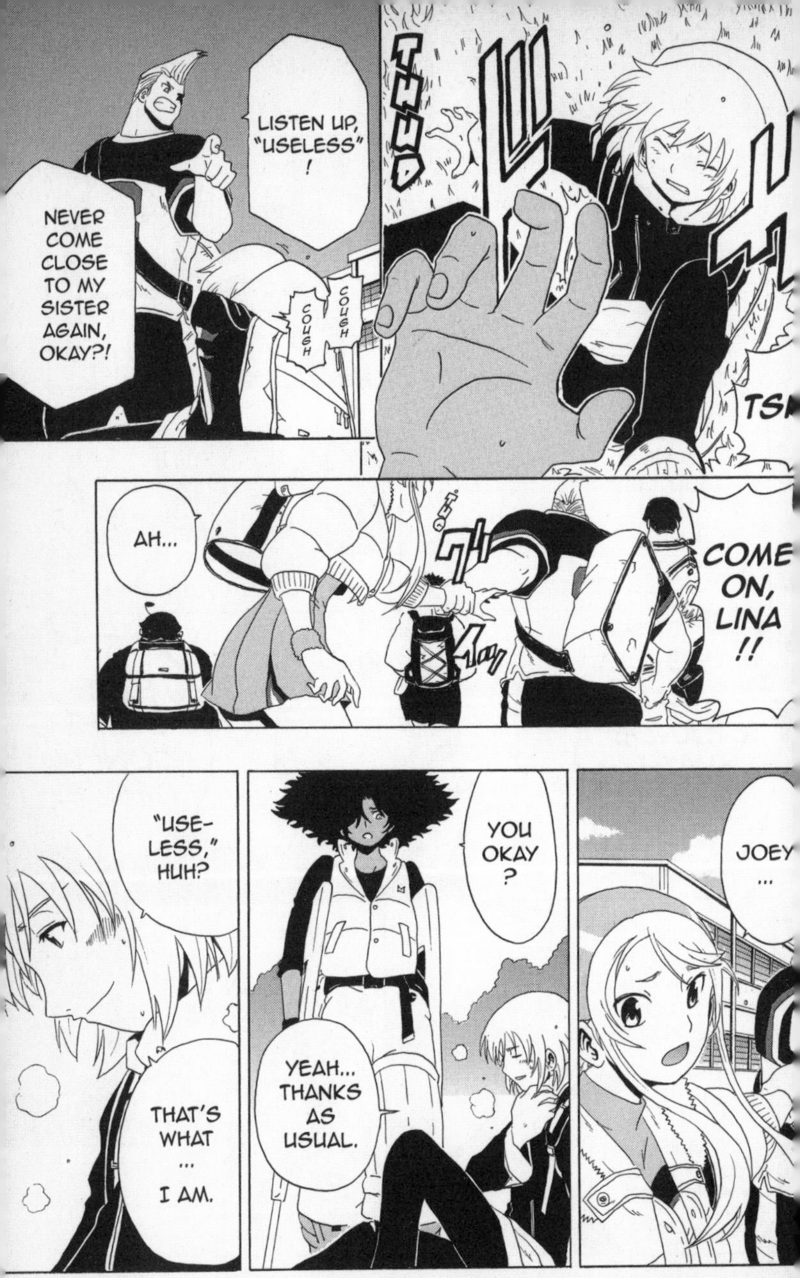

LISTEN UP, "USELESS"!
NEVER COME CLOSE TO MY SISTER AGAIN, OKAY?!
COUGH COUGH
COME ON, LINA!!
AH...
JOEY...
YOU OKAY?
YEAH... THANKS AS USUAL.
"USE-LESS," HUH?
THAT'S WHAT ... I AM.

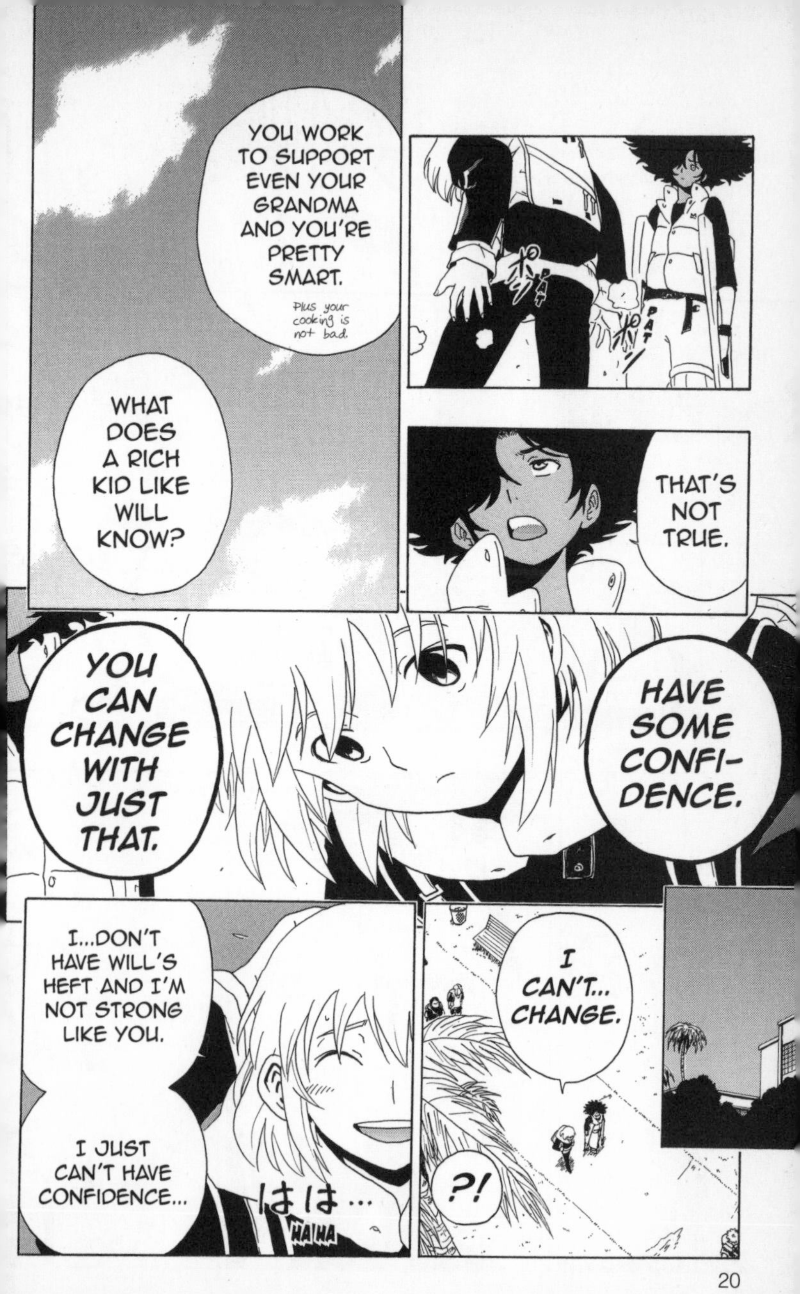
PAT
PAT
THAT'S NOT TRUE.
YOU WORK TO SUPPORT EVEN YOUR GRANDMA AND YOU'RE PRETTY SMART.
Plus your cooking is not bad.
WHAT DOES A RICH KID LIKE WILL KNOW?
HAVE SOME CONFI-DENCE.
YOU CAN CHANGE WITH JUST THAT.
I CAN'T... CHANGE.
?!
I...DON'T HAVE WILL'S HEFT AND I'M NOT STRONG LIKE YOU.
I JUST CAN'T HAVE CONFIDENCE...
はは…
HA HA

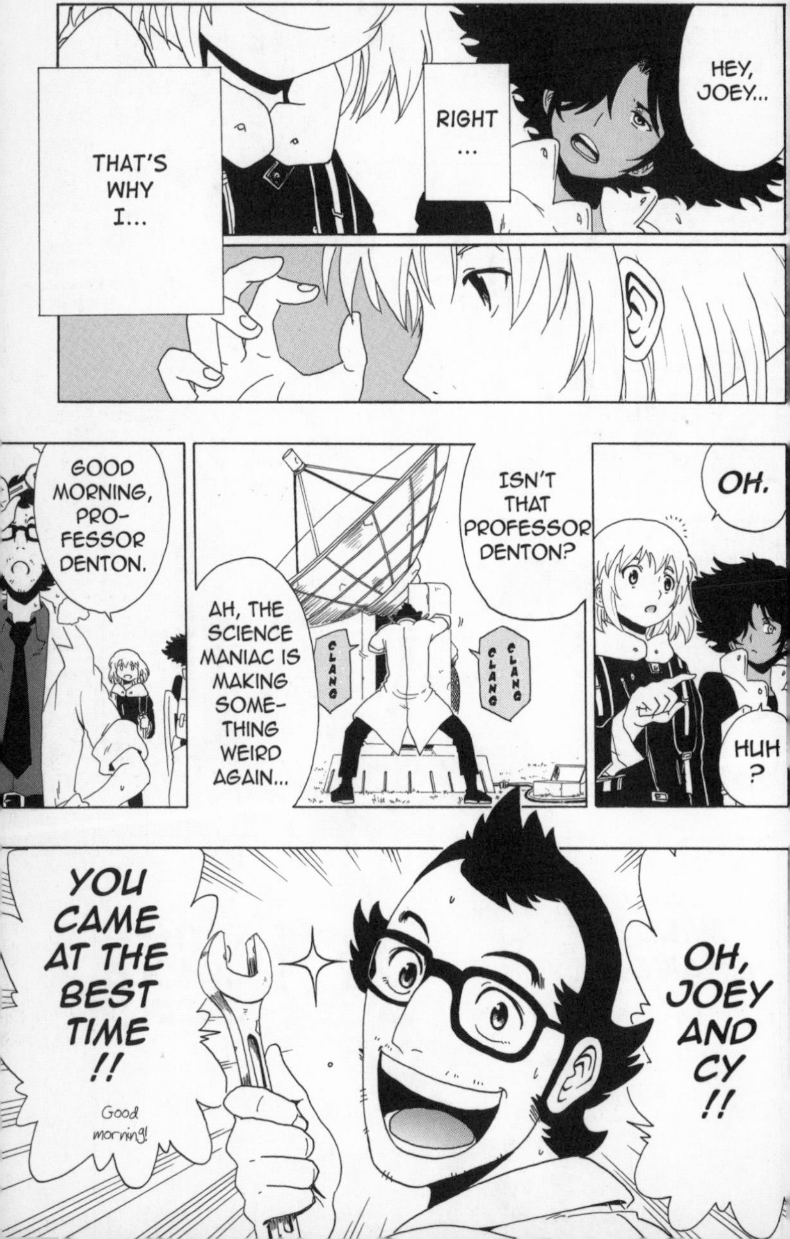
HEY, JOEY...
RIGHT ...
THAT'S WHY I...
OH.
HUH ?
ISN'T THAT PROFESSOR DENTON?
CLANG CLANG
CLANG
AH, THE SCIENCE MANIAC IS MAKING SOME-THING WEIRD AGAIN...
GOOD MORNING, PRO-FESSOR DENTON.
OH, JOEY AND CY !!
YOU CAME AT THE BEST TIME !!
Good morning!

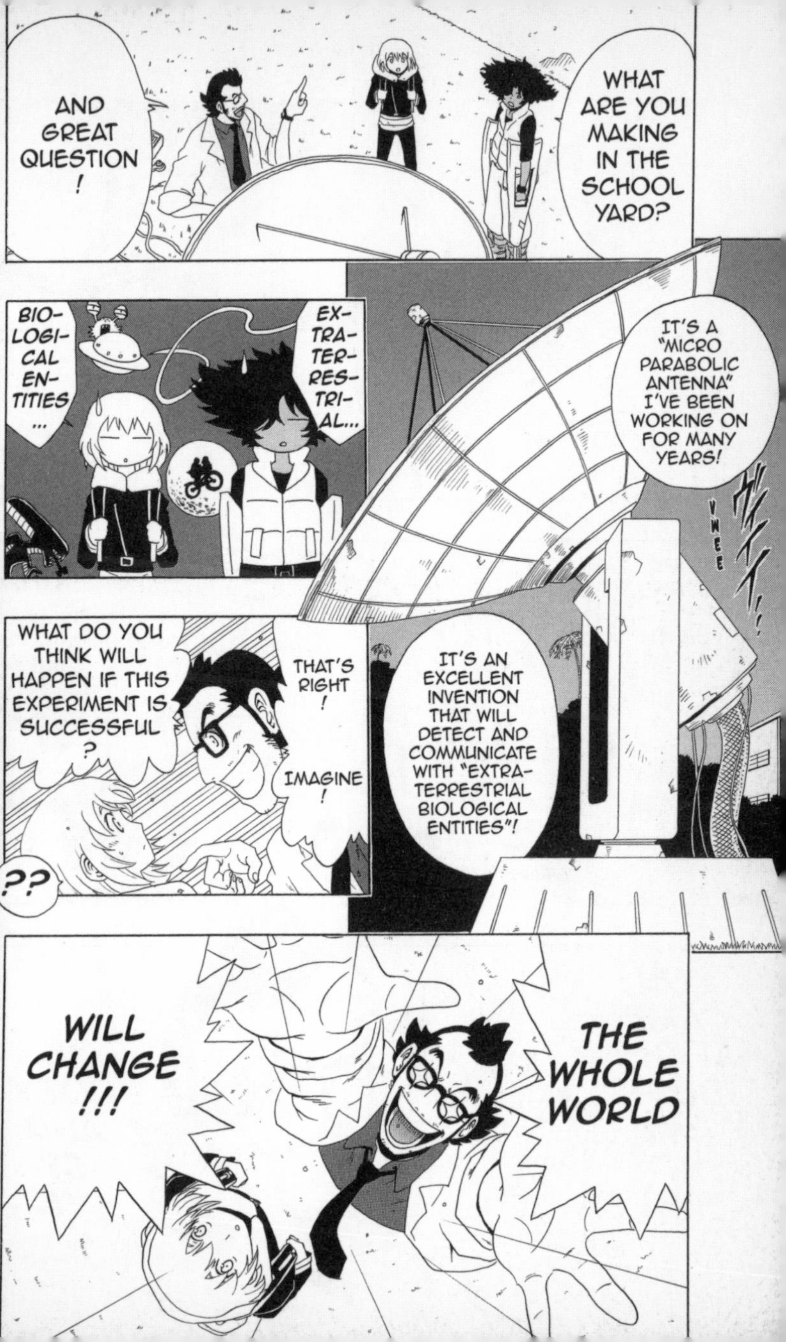
WHAT ARE YOU MAKING IN THE SCHOOL YARD?
AND GREAT QUESTION!
IT'S A "MICRO PARABOLIC ANTENNA" I'VE BEEN WORKING ON FOR MANY YEARS!
VWEE
IT'S AN EXCELLENT INVENTION THAT WILL DETECT AND COMMUNICATE WITH "EXTRA-TERRESTRIAL BIOLOGICAL ENTITIES"!
EX-TRA-TER-RES-TRI-AL...
BIO-LOGI-CAL EN-TITIES...
THAT'S RIGHT!
IMAGINE!
WHAT DO YOU THINK WILL HAPPEN IF THIS EXPERIMENT IS SUCCESSFUL?
??
THE WHOLE WORLD
WILL CHANGE!!!

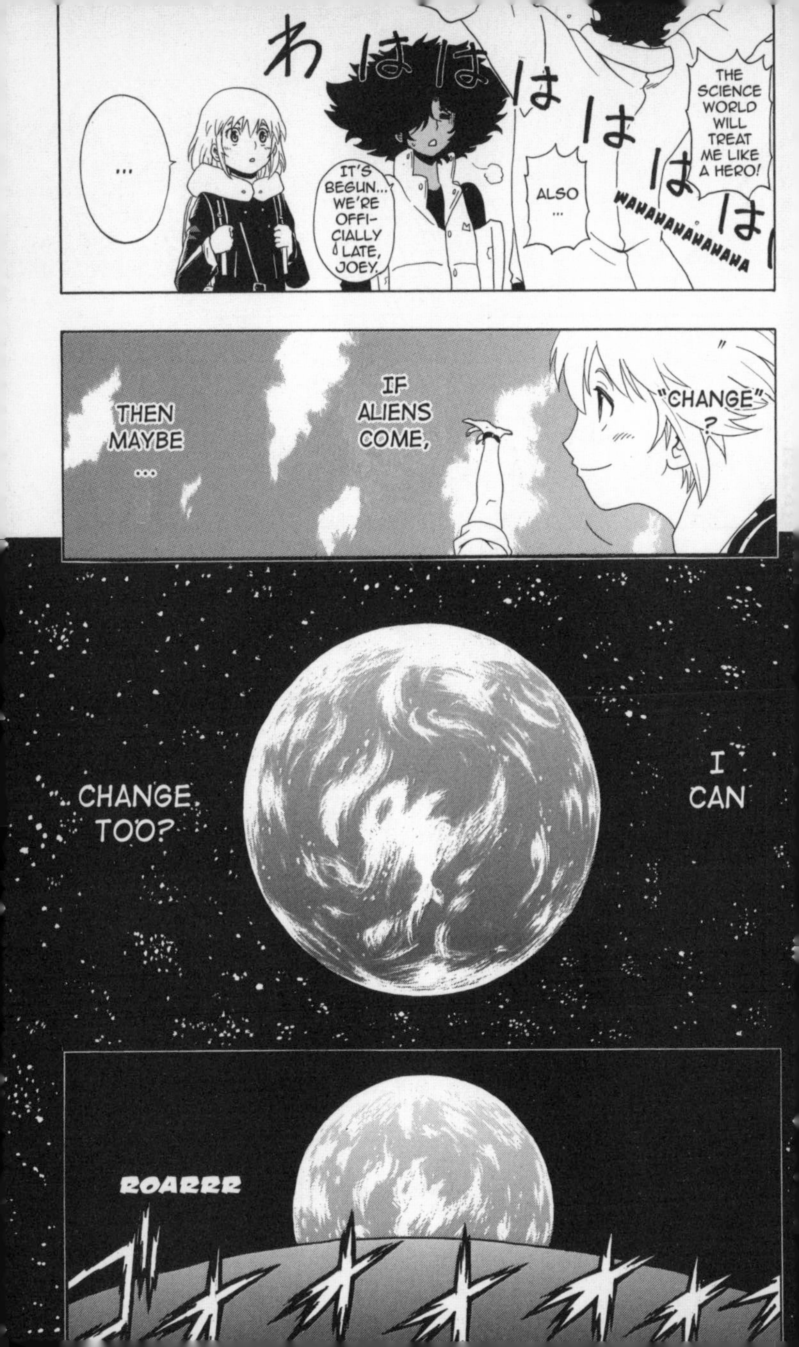
THE SCIENCE WORLD WILL TREAT ME LIKE A HERO!
わははははは
WAHAHAHAHAHAHAHA
ALSO ...
IT'S BEGUN... WE'RE OFFICIALLY LATE, JOEY.
...
"CHANGE"?
IF ALIENS COME,
THEN MAYBE ...
I CAN
CHANGE TOO?
ROARRR

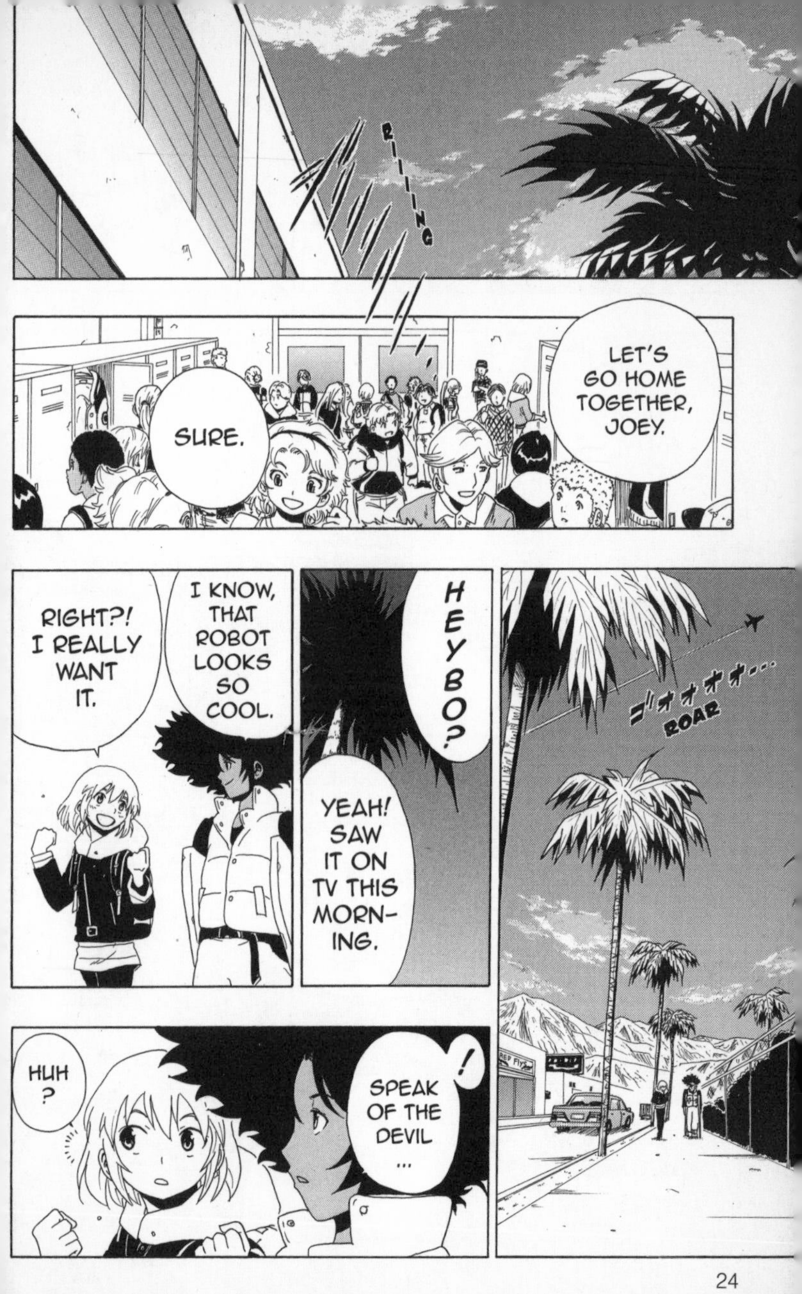
RIIIING
LET'S GO HOME TOGETHER, JOEY.
SURE.
ゴオオオオ...
ROAR
HEYBO?
YEAH! SAW IT ON TV THIS MORN-ING.
I KNOW, THAT ROBOT LOOKS SO COOL.
RIGHT?! I REALLY WANT IT.
!
SPEAK OF THE DEVIL ...
HUH ?

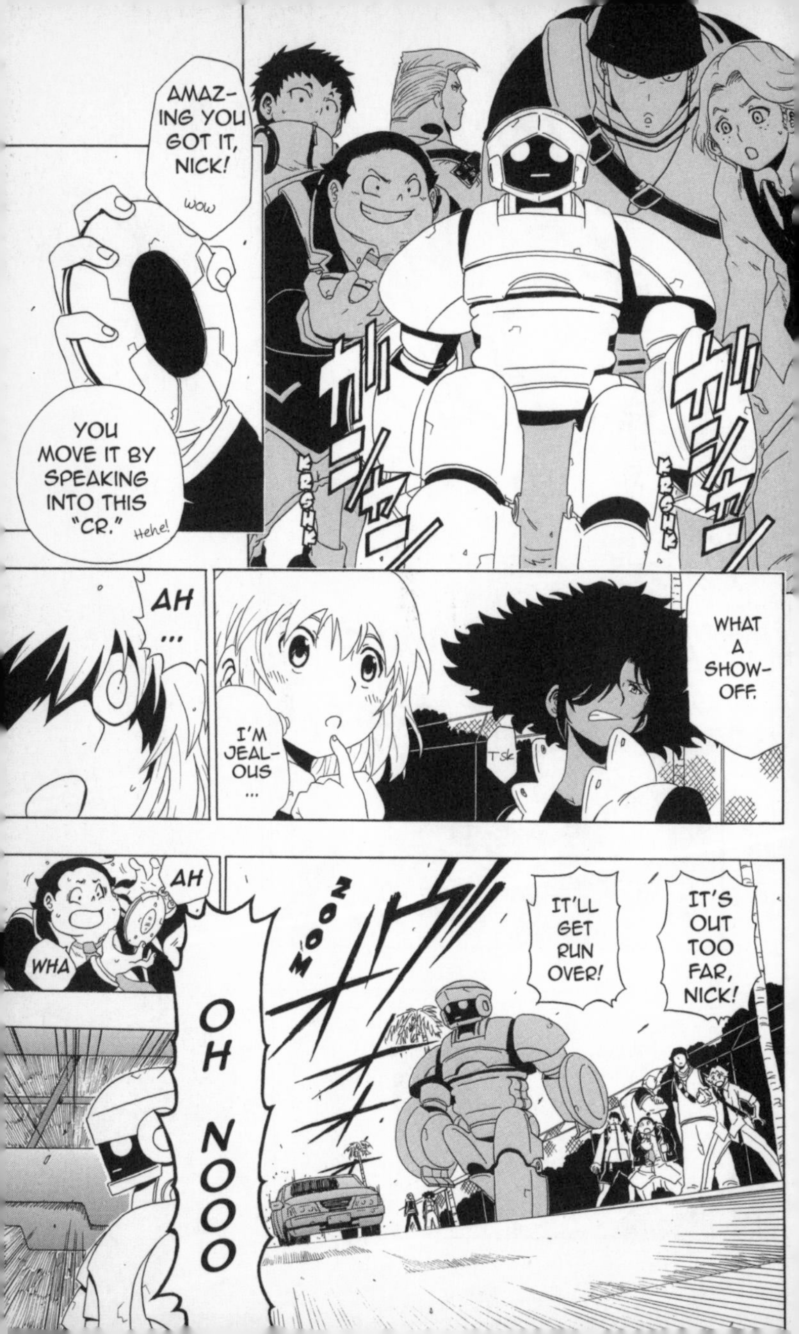
KRSHK
KRSHK
AMAZING YOU GOT IT, NICK!
WOW
YOU MOVE IT BY SPEAKING INTO THIS "CR."
Hehe!
WHAT A SHOW-OFF.
Tsk
I'M JEALOUS...
AH...
IT'S OUT TOO FAR, NICK!
IT'LL GET RUN OVER!
ZOOOM
AH
WHA
OH NOOO

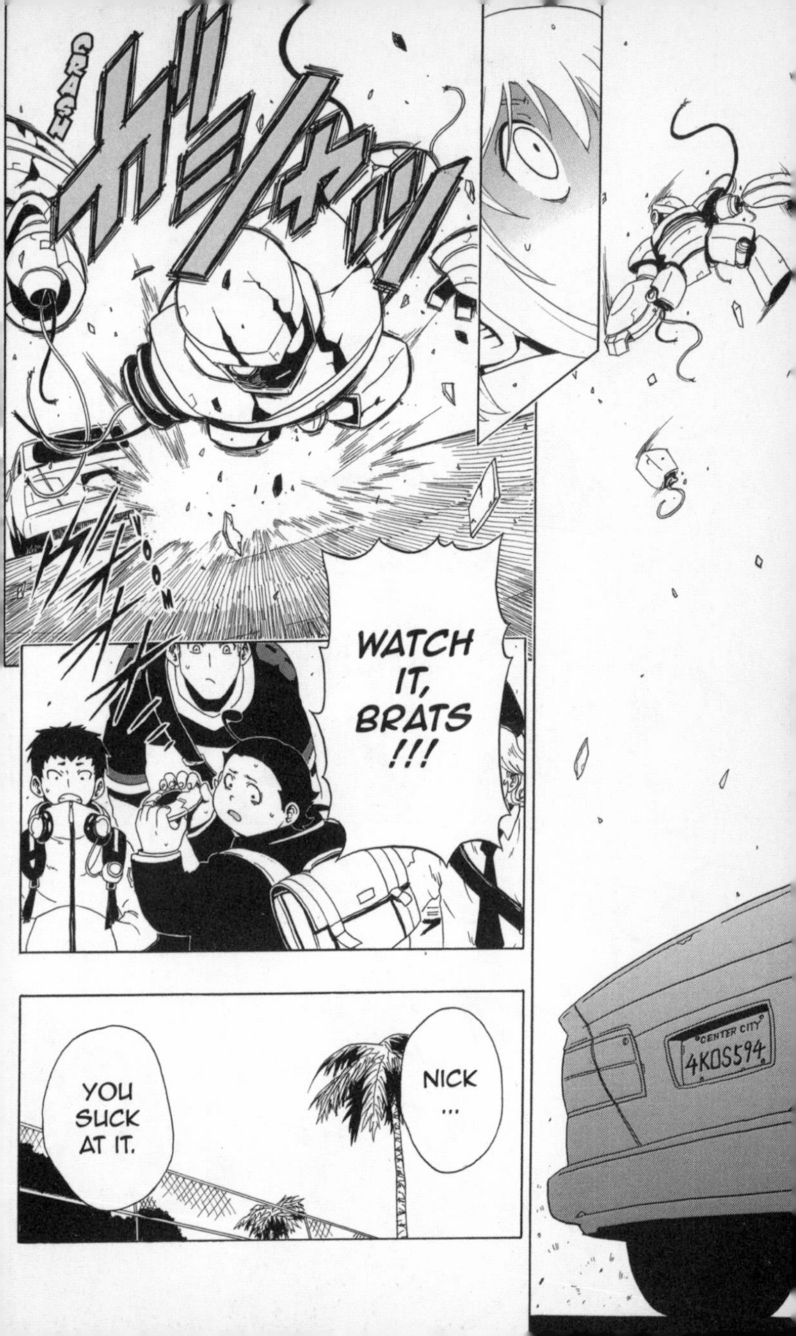
CENTER CITY
4KOS594
CRASH
VOOM
WATCH IT, BRATS!!!
NICK...
YOU SUCK AT IT.

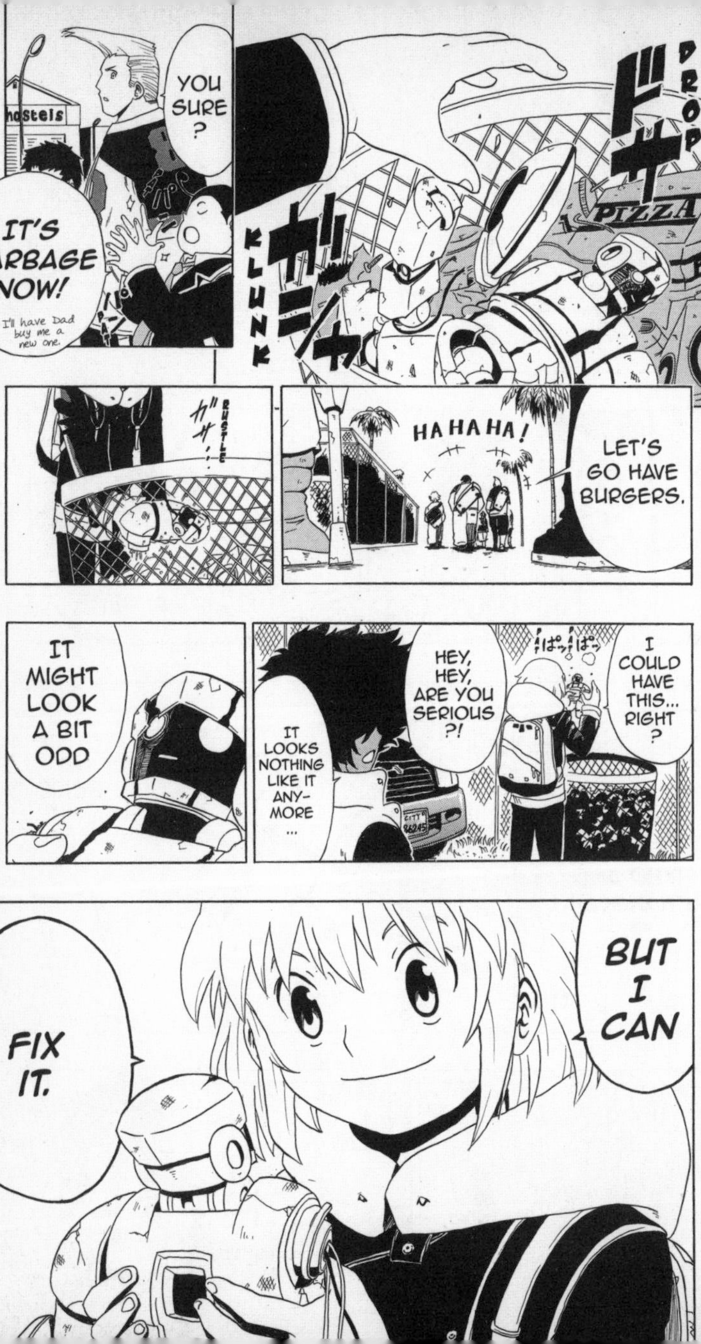
DROP
PIZZA
KLUNK
YOU SURE?
IT'S GARBAGE NOW!
I'll have Dad buy me a new one.
LET'S GO HAVE BURGERS.
HA HA HA!
RUSTLE
I COULD HAVE THIS... RIGHT?
HEY, HEY, ARE YOU SERIOUS?!
IT LOOKS NOTHING LIKE IT ANYMORE...
IT MIGHT LOOK A BIT ODD
BUT I CAN
FIX IT.

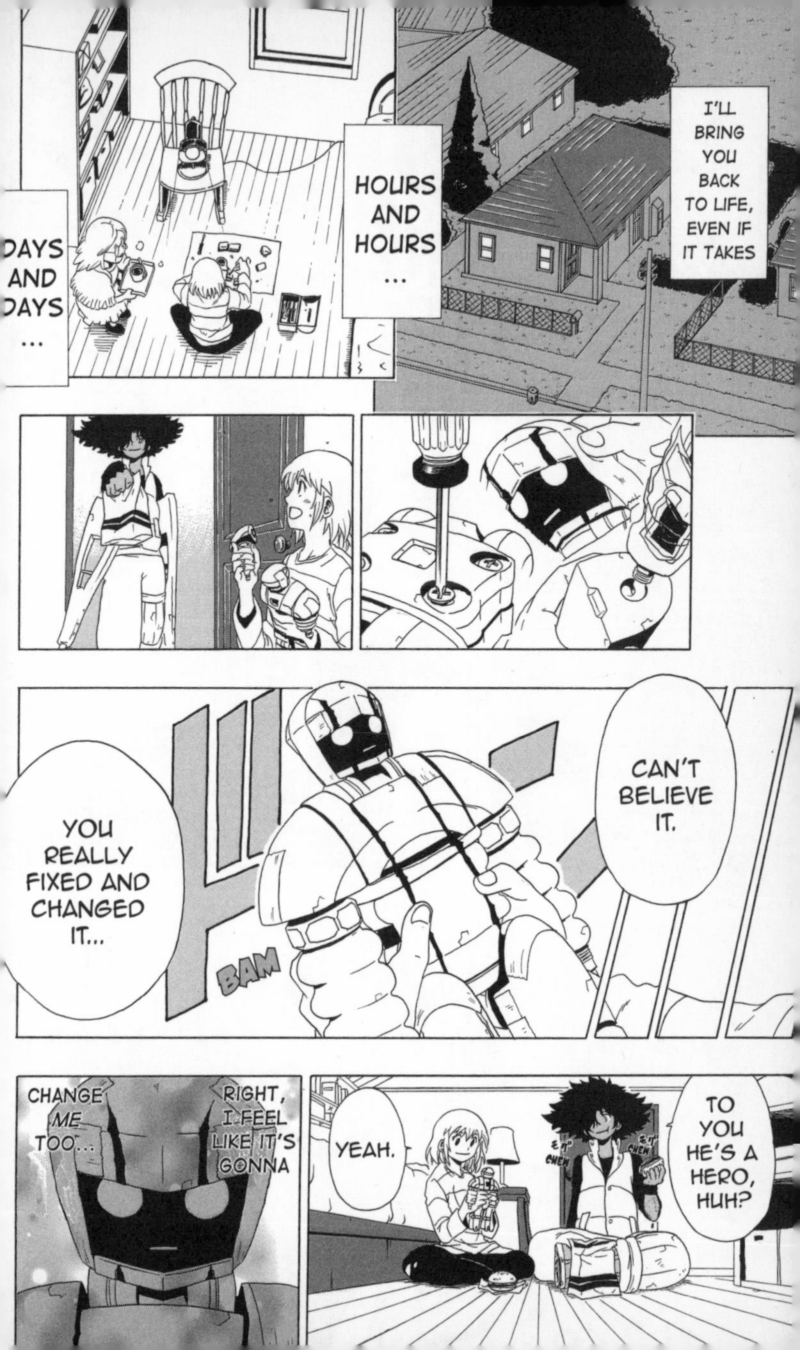
I'LL BRING YOU BACK TO LIFE, EVEN IF IT TAKES
HOURS AND HOURS ...
DAYS AND DAYS ...
CAN'T BELIEVE IT.
YOU REALLY FIXED AND CHANGED IT...
BAM
TO YOU HE'S A HERO, HUH?
CHEW
CHEW
YEAH.
RIGHT, I FEEL LIKE IT'S GONNA
CHANGE *ME* TOO...

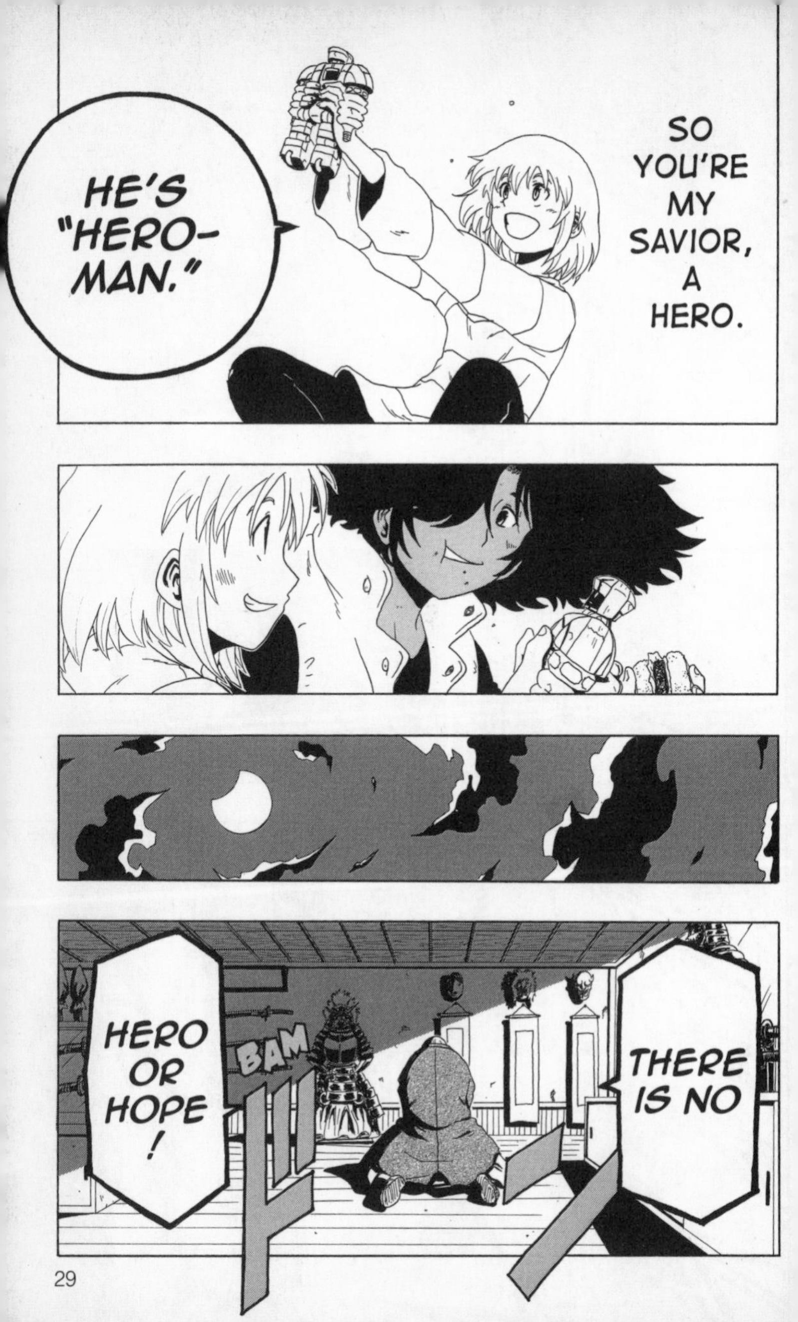
SO YOU'RE MY SAVIOR, A HERO.
HE'S "HERO-MAN."
THERE IS NO
BAM
HERO OR HOPE!

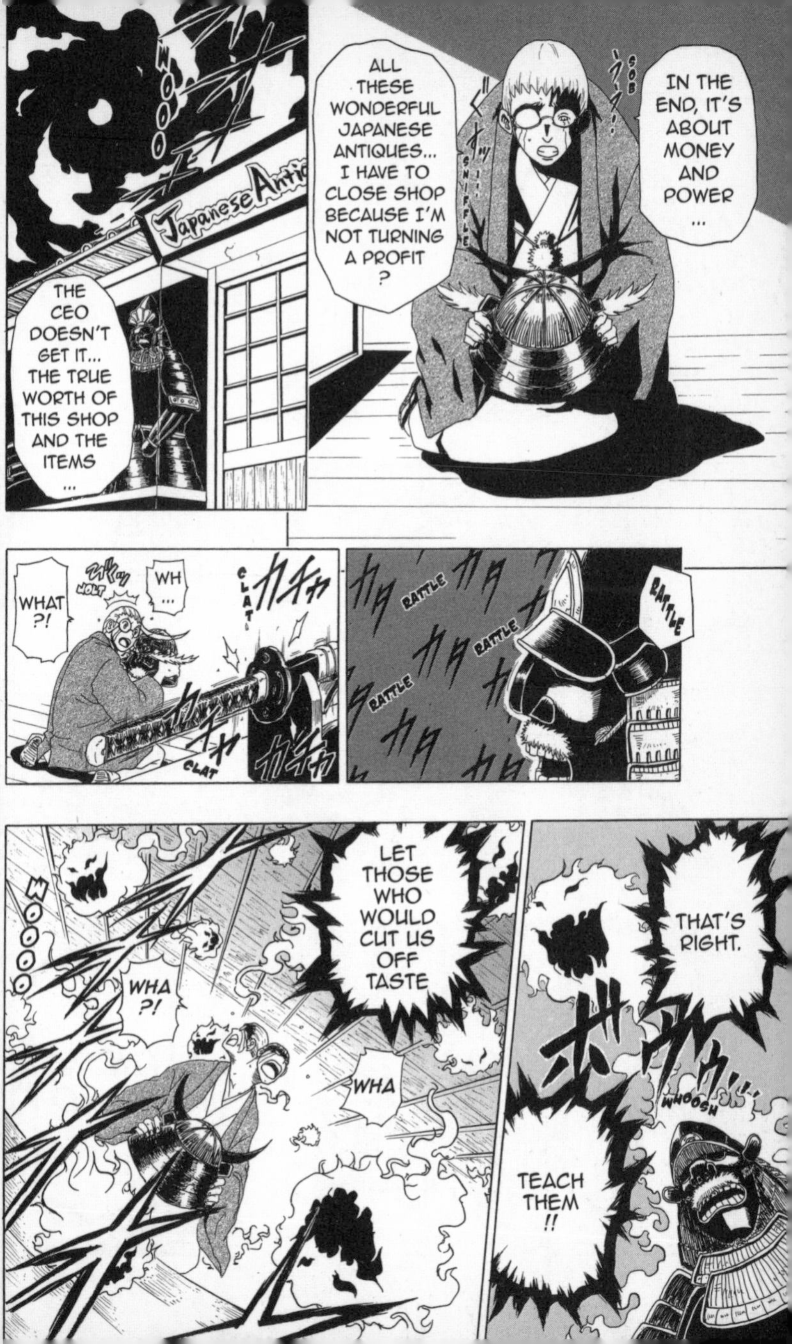
SOB
SNIFFLE
IN THE END, IT'S ABOUT MONEY AND POWER ...
ALL THESE WONDERFUL JAPANESE ANTIQUES... I HAVE TO CLOSE SHOP BECAUSE I'M NOT TURNING A PROFIT ?
WOOOO
Japanese Anti
THE CEO DOESN'T GET IT... THE TRUE WORTH OF THIS SHOP AND THE ITEMS ...
RATTLE
RATTLE
RATTLE
RATTLE
CLAT
WH ...
JOLT
WHAT ?!
CLAT
THAT'S RIGHT.
WHOOSH
TEACH THEM !!
LET THOSE WHO WOULD CUT US OFF TASTE
WOOOO
WHA ?!
WHA

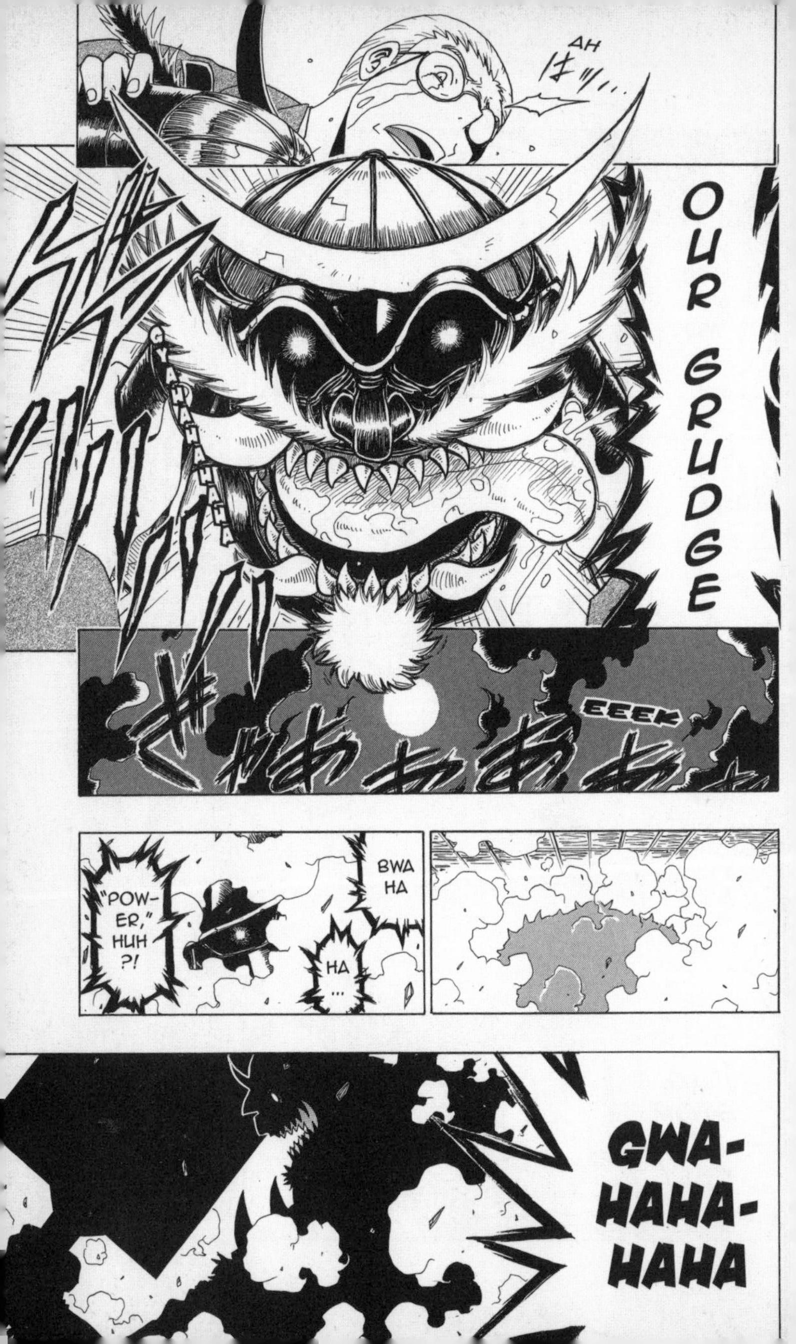
AH
OUR GRUDGE
GYAHAHAHAHAHA
EEEK
BWA HA
HA ...
"POW-ER," HUH ?!
GWA-HAHA-HAHA

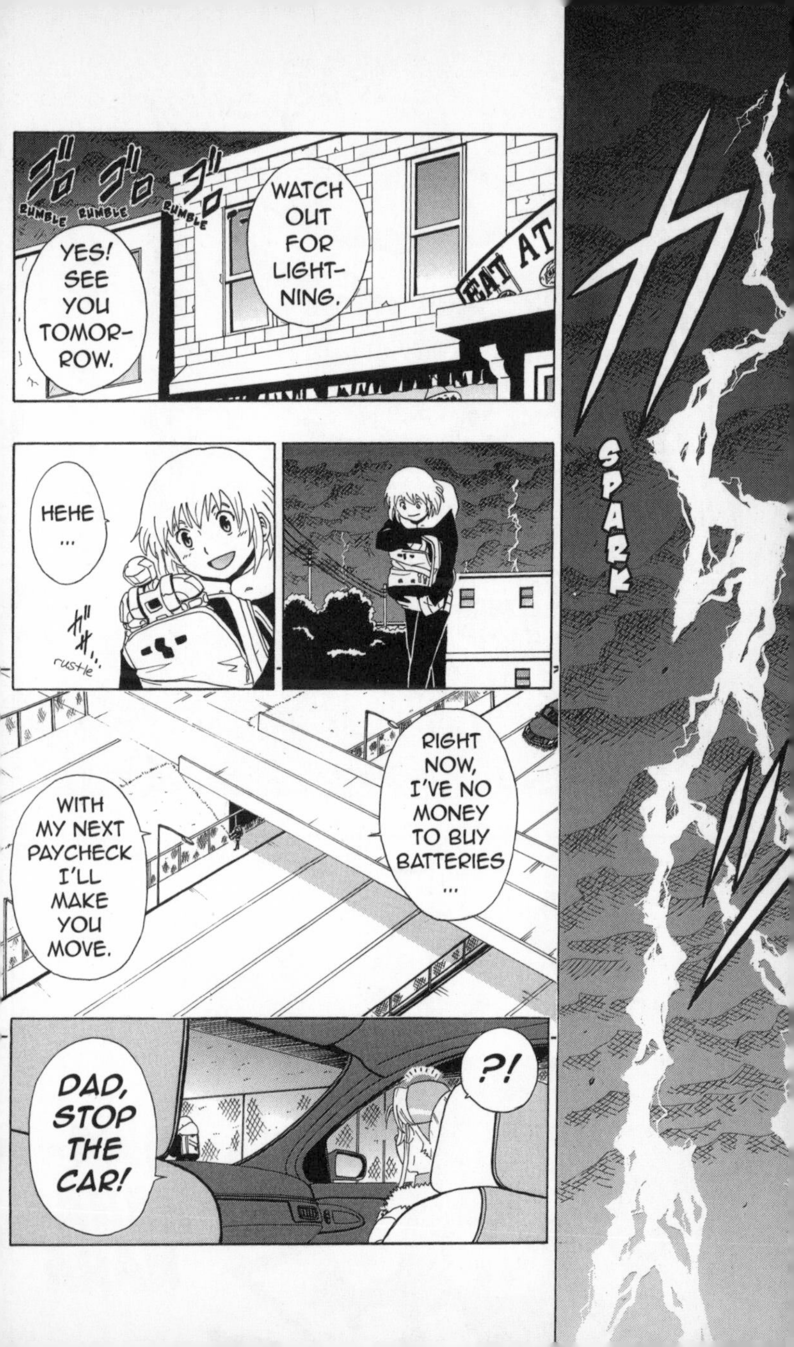
SPARK
RUMBLE RUMBLE RUMBLE
EAT AT
WATCH OUT FOR LIGHT-NING.
YES! SEE YOU TOMOR-ROW.
HEHE ...
rustle
RIGHT NOW, I'VE NO MONEY TO BUY BATTERIES ...
WITH MY NEXT PAYCHECK I'LL MAKE YOU MOVE.
?!
DAD, STOP THE CAR!

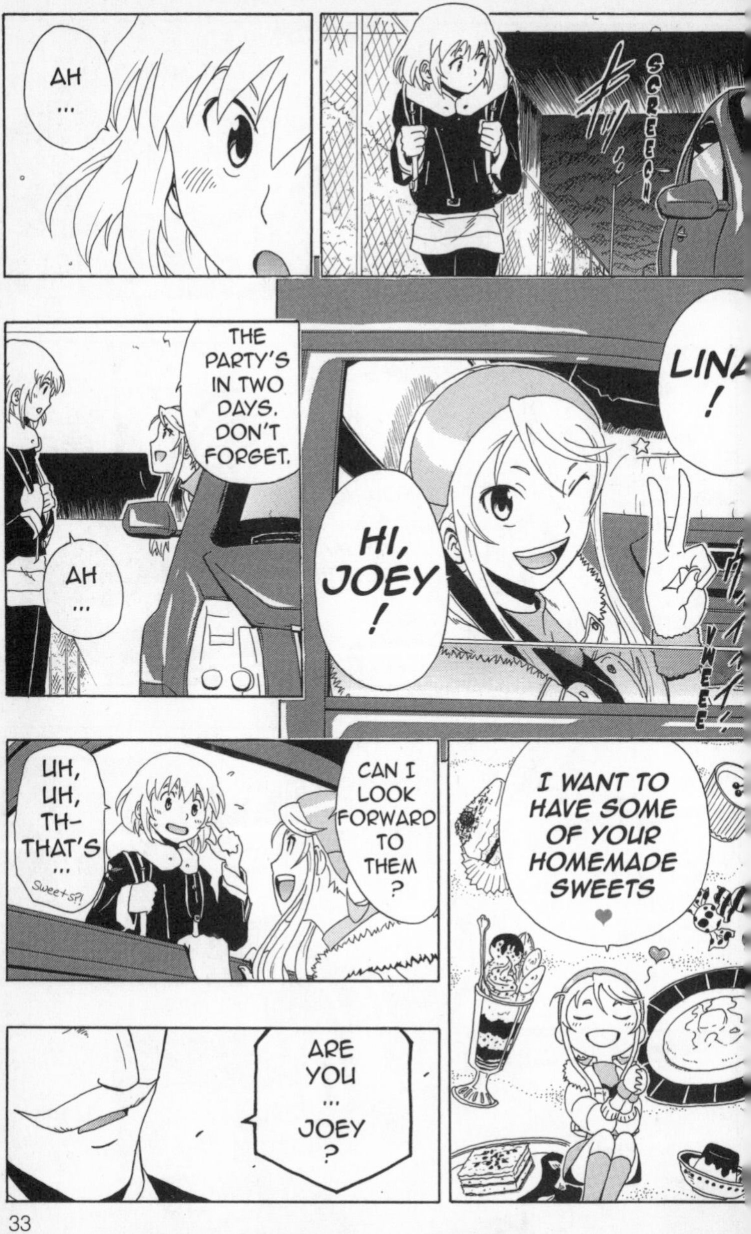

SCREECH
AH ...
LINA !
HI, JOEY !
VWEEE
THE PARTY'S IN TWO DAYS. DON'T FORGET.
AH ...
I WANT TO HAVE SOME OF YOUR HOMEMADE SWEETS ♥
CAN I LOOK FORWARD TO THEM ?
UH, UH, TH-THAT'S ...
Sweets?!
ARE YOU ... JOEY ?

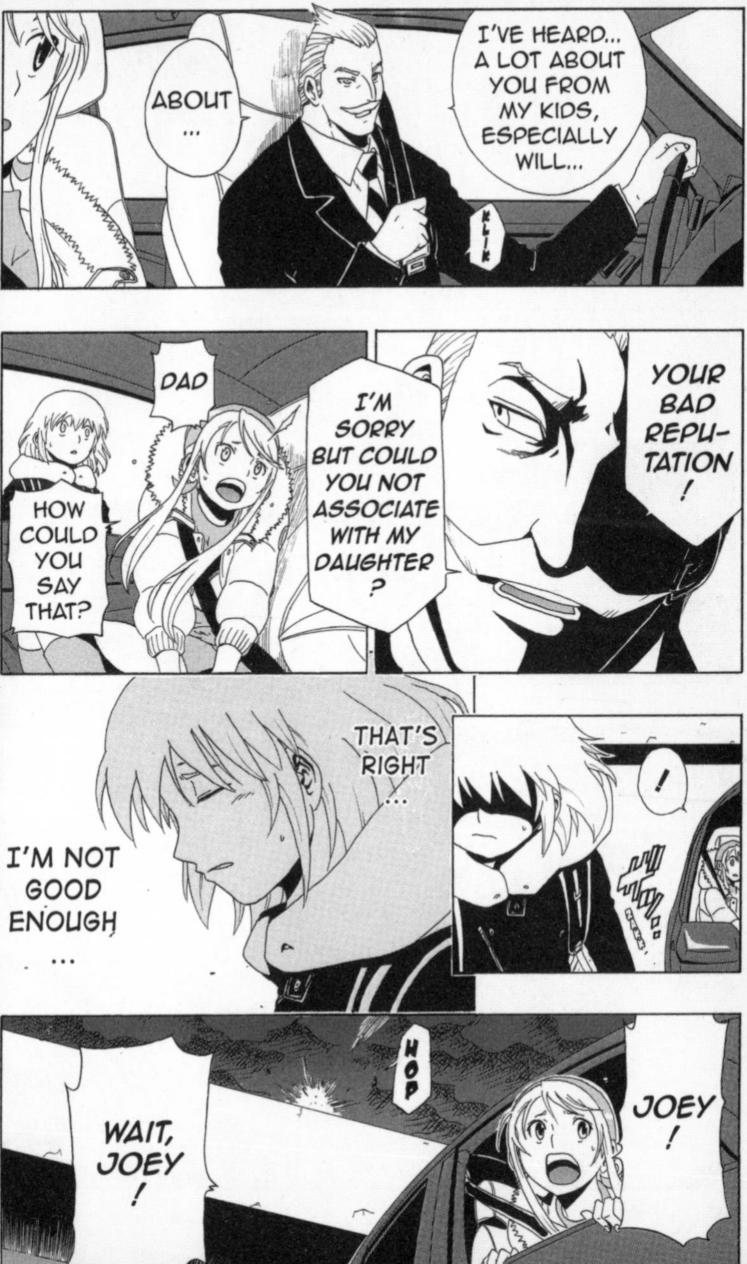
I'VE HEARD... A LOT ABOUT YOU FROM MY KIDS, ESPECIALLY WILL...
KLIK
ABOUT ...
YOUR BAD REPU-TATION !
I'M SORRY BUT COULD YOU NOT ASSOCIATE WITH MY DAUGHTER ?
DAD
HOW COULD YOU SAY THAT?
!
THAT'S RIGHT ...
I'M NOT GOOD ENOUGH ...
JOEY !
HOP
WAIT, JOEY !

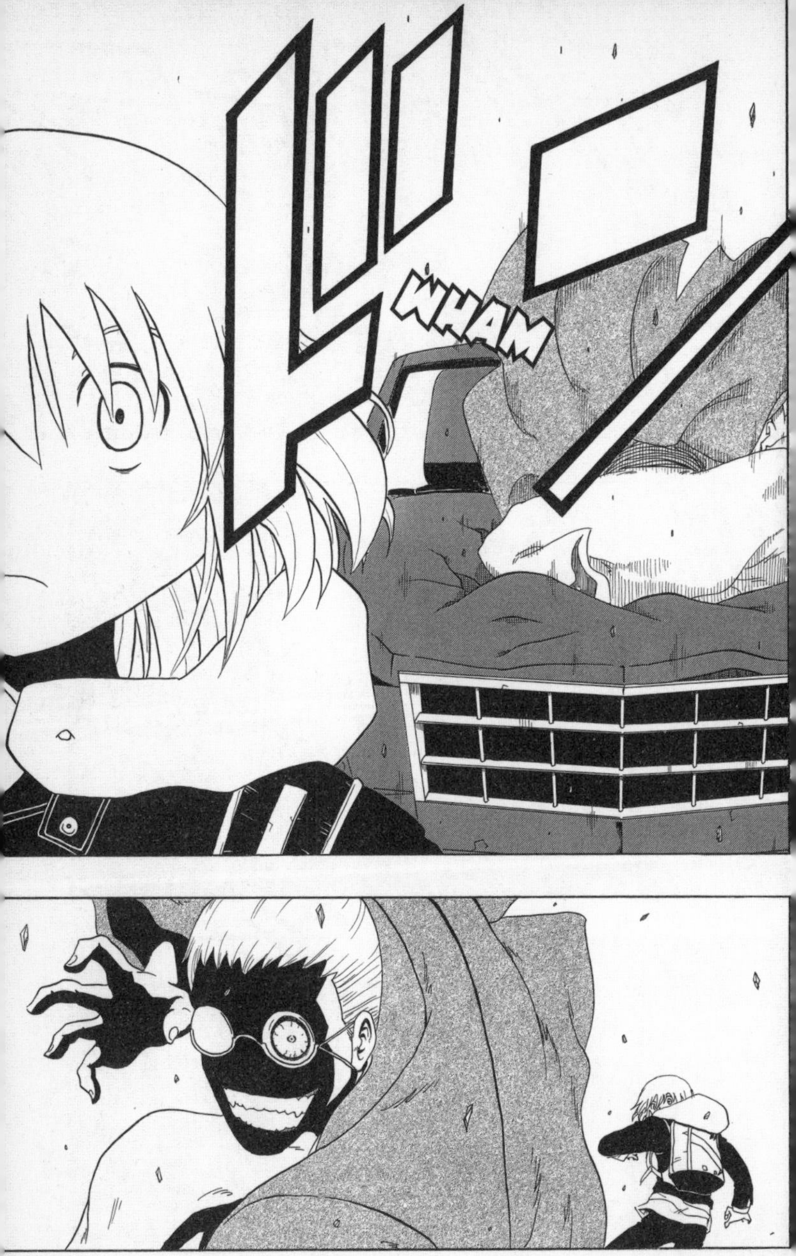
WHAM

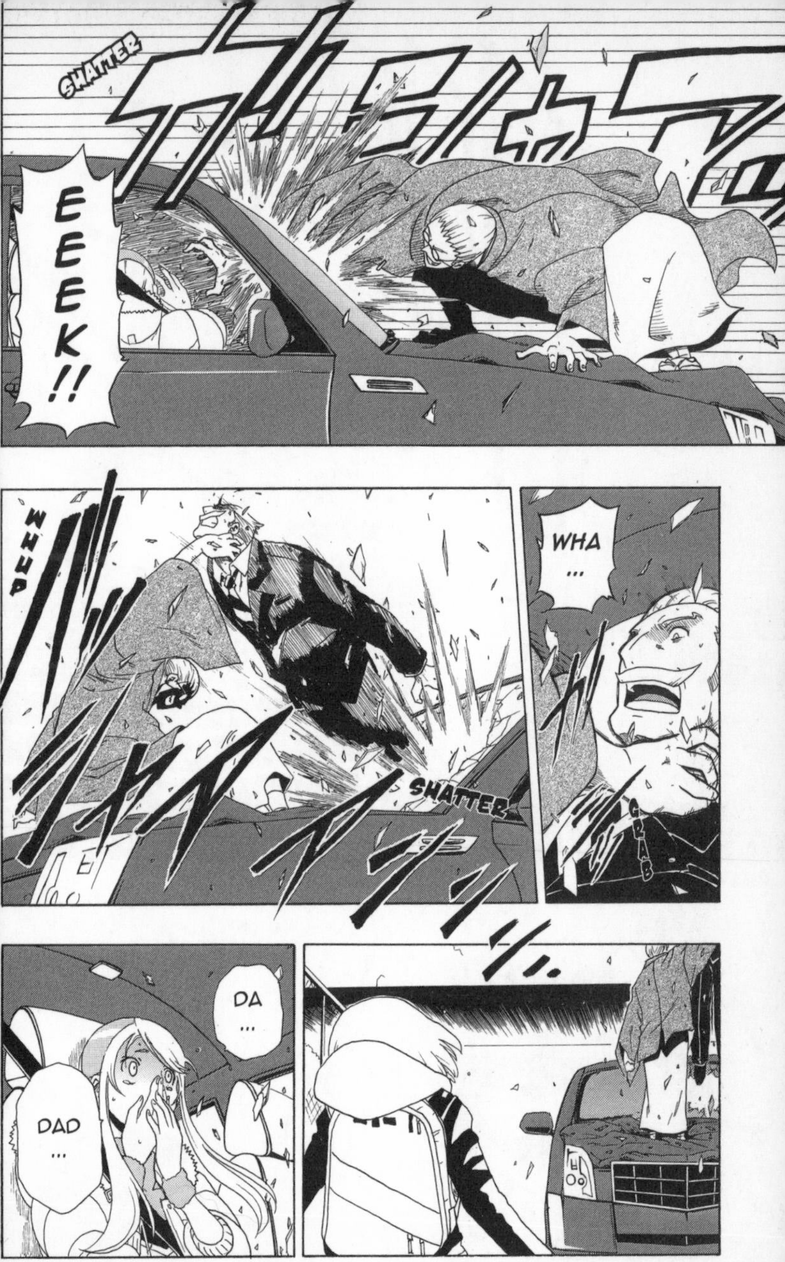
SHATTER
EEEEK!!
WHA ...
GRAB
WHUP
SHATTER
DA ...
DAD ...

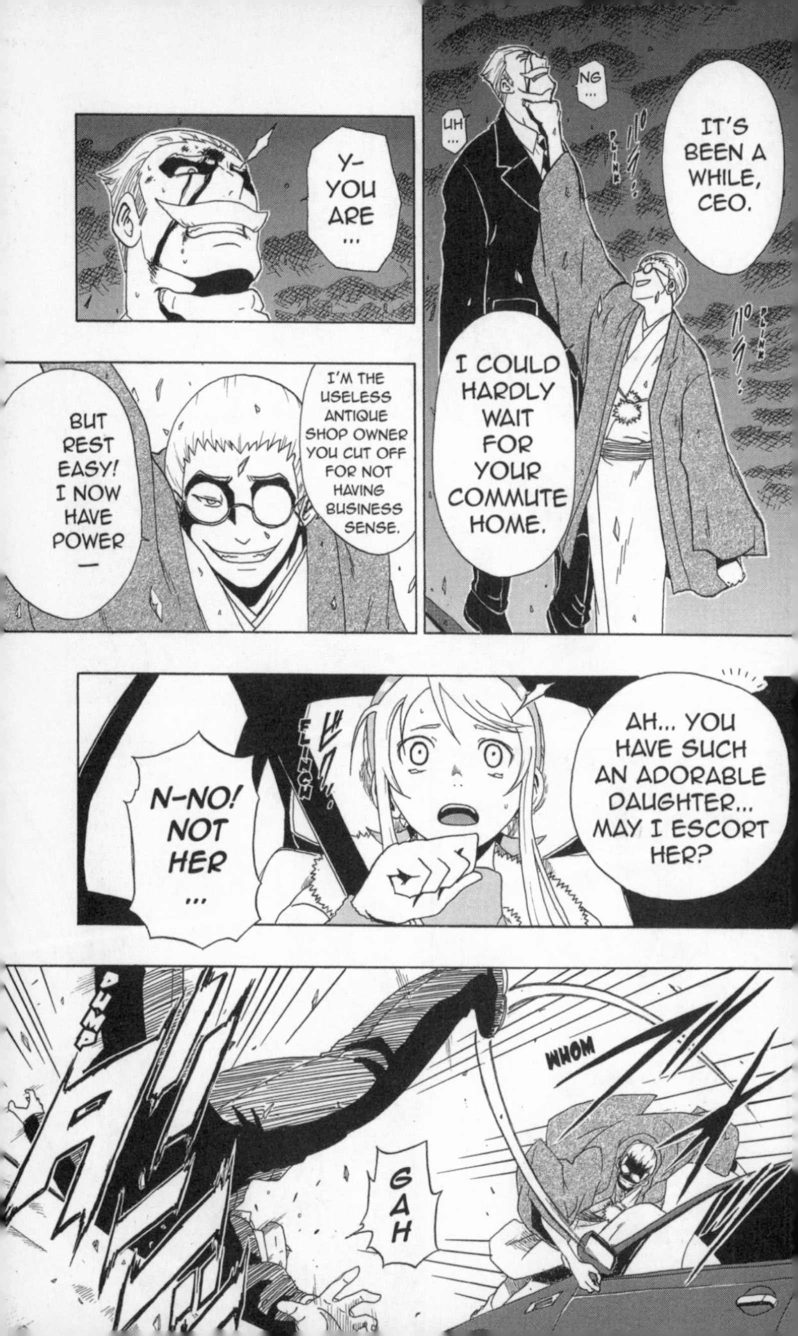
IT'S BEEN A WHILE, CEO.
NG ...
UH ...
PLINK
I COULD HARDLY WAIT FOR YOUR COMMUTE HOME.
PLINK
Y-YOU ARE ...
I'M THE USELESS ANTIQUE SHOP OWNER YOU CUT OFF FOR NOT HAVING BUSINESS SENSE.
BUT REST EASY! I NOW HAVE POWER —
AH... YOU HAVE SUCH AN ADORABLE DAUGHTER... MAY I ESCORT HER?
FLINCH
N-NO! NOT HER ...
WHOM
GAH
DUMP

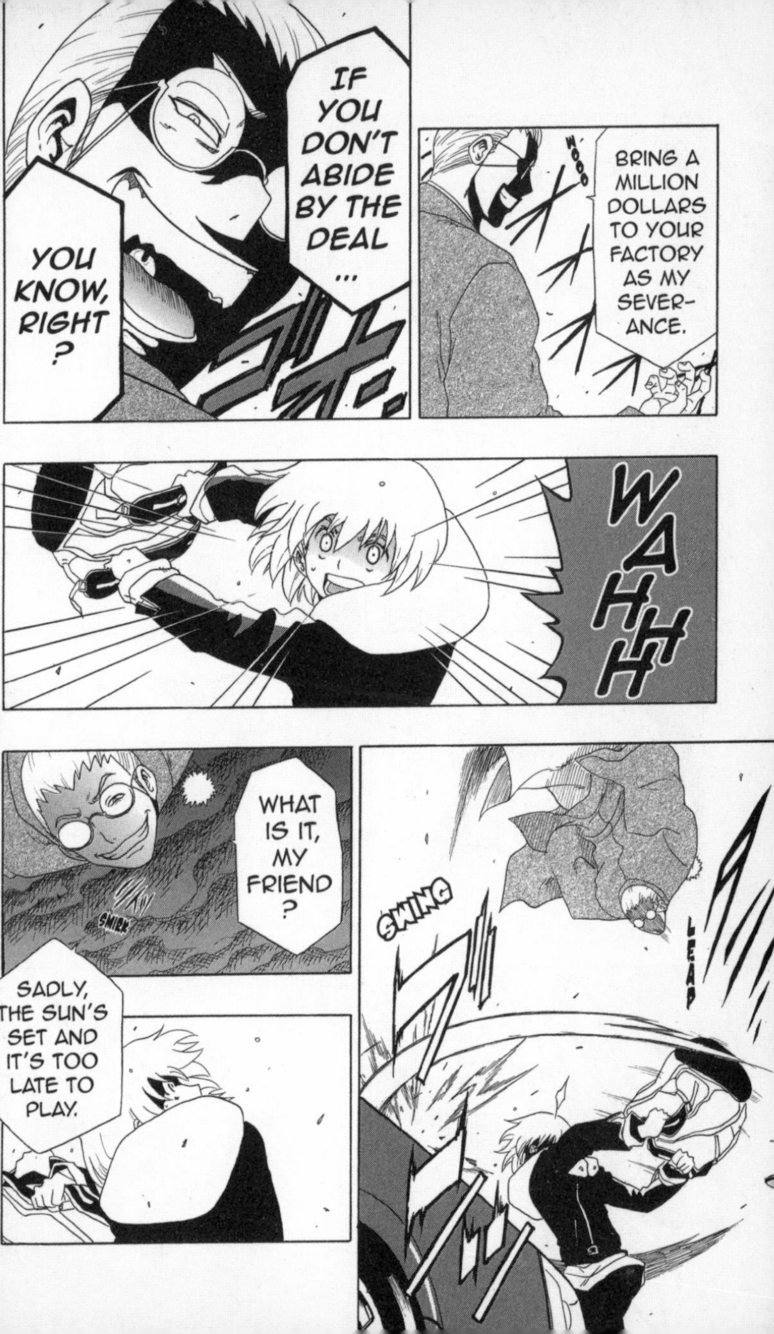
WOOO
BRING A MILLION DOLLARS TO YOUR FACTORY AS MY SEVERANCE.
IF YOU DON'T ABIDE BY THE DEAL...
YOU KNOW, RIGHT?
WAHHH
LEAP
SWING
WHAT IS IT, MY FRIEND?
SMIRK
SADLY, THE SUN'S SET AND IT'S TOO LATE TO PLAY.

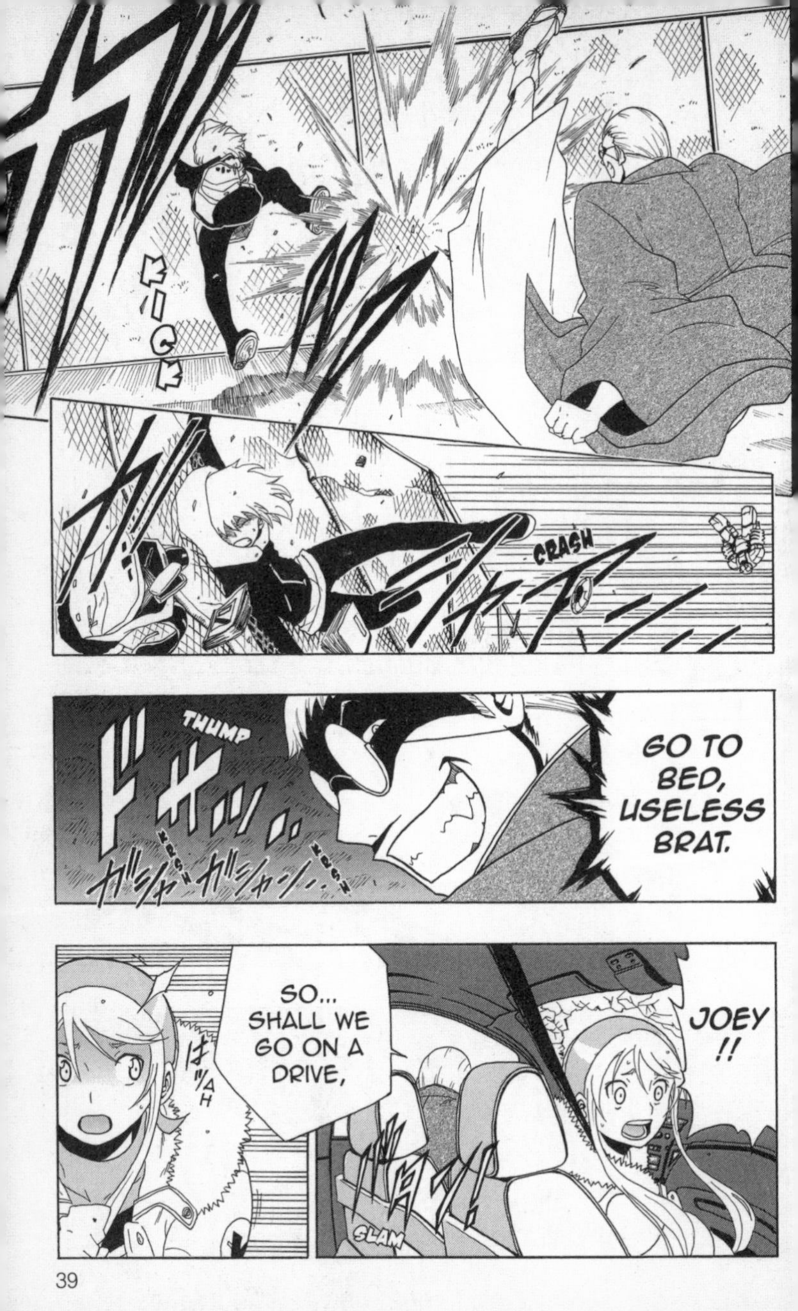
KICK
CRASH
GO TO BED, USELESS BRAT.
THUMP
KRSH
KRSH
JOEY !!
SO... SHALL WE GO ON A DRIVE,
AH
SLAM

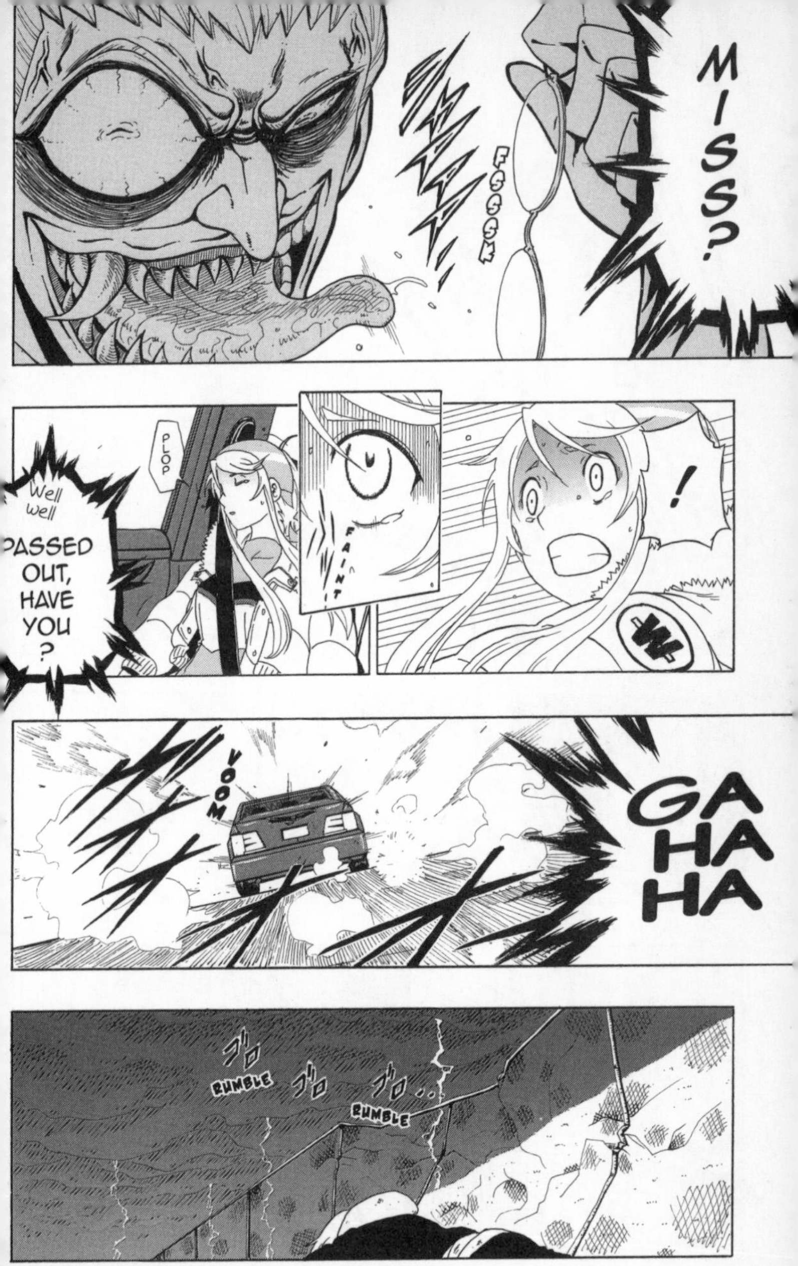
MISS?
FSSSK
!
FAINT
PLOP
Well Well
PASSED OUT, HAVE YOU?
GA HA HA HA
VOOM
ゴロ
RUMBLE
ゴロ
ゴロ..
RUMBLE

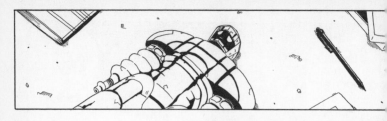

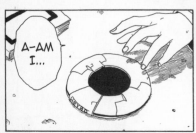

A-AM I...

USELESS ...

AFTER ALL ?!

GRAB

CHANGE ?!

I CAN'T —

RISE

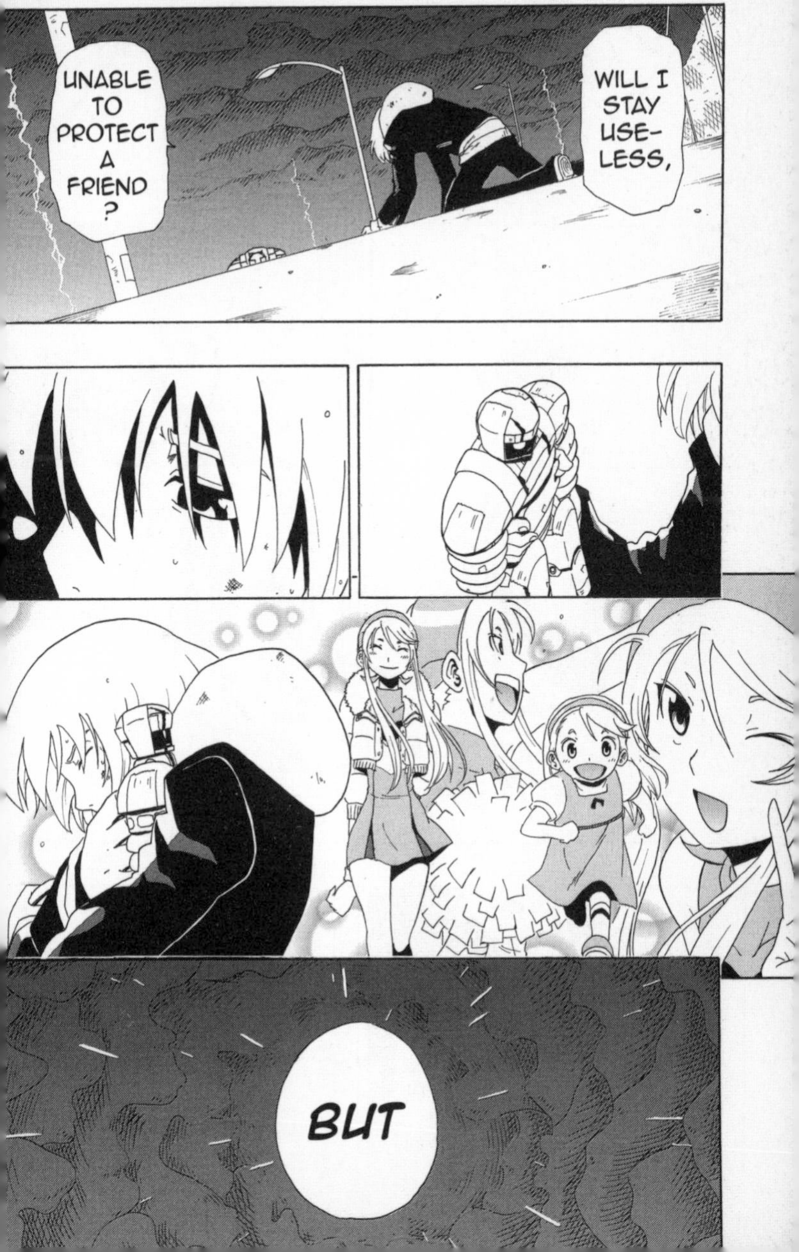
WILL I STAY USE-LESS,
UNABLE TO PROTECT A FRIEND ?
BUT

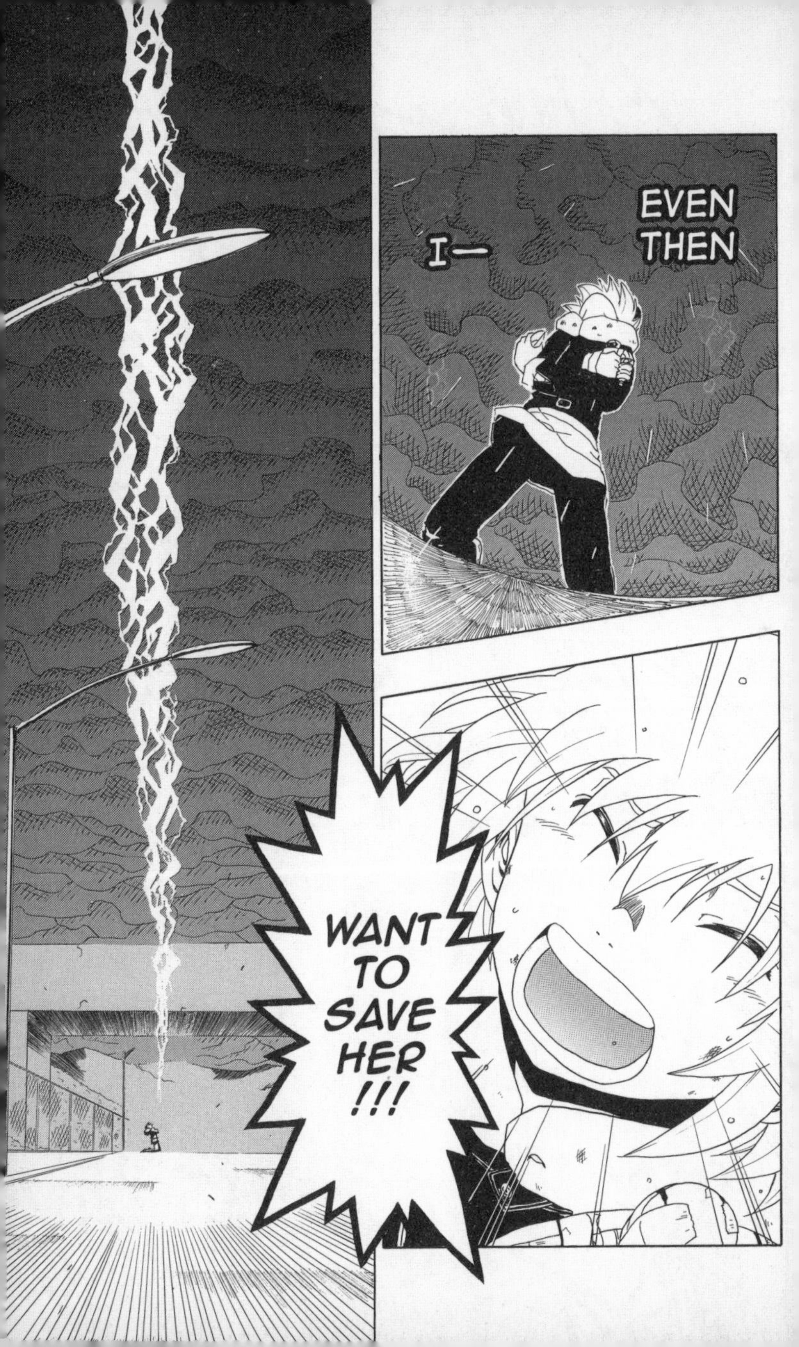
EVEN THEN
I—
WANT TO SAVE HER!!!

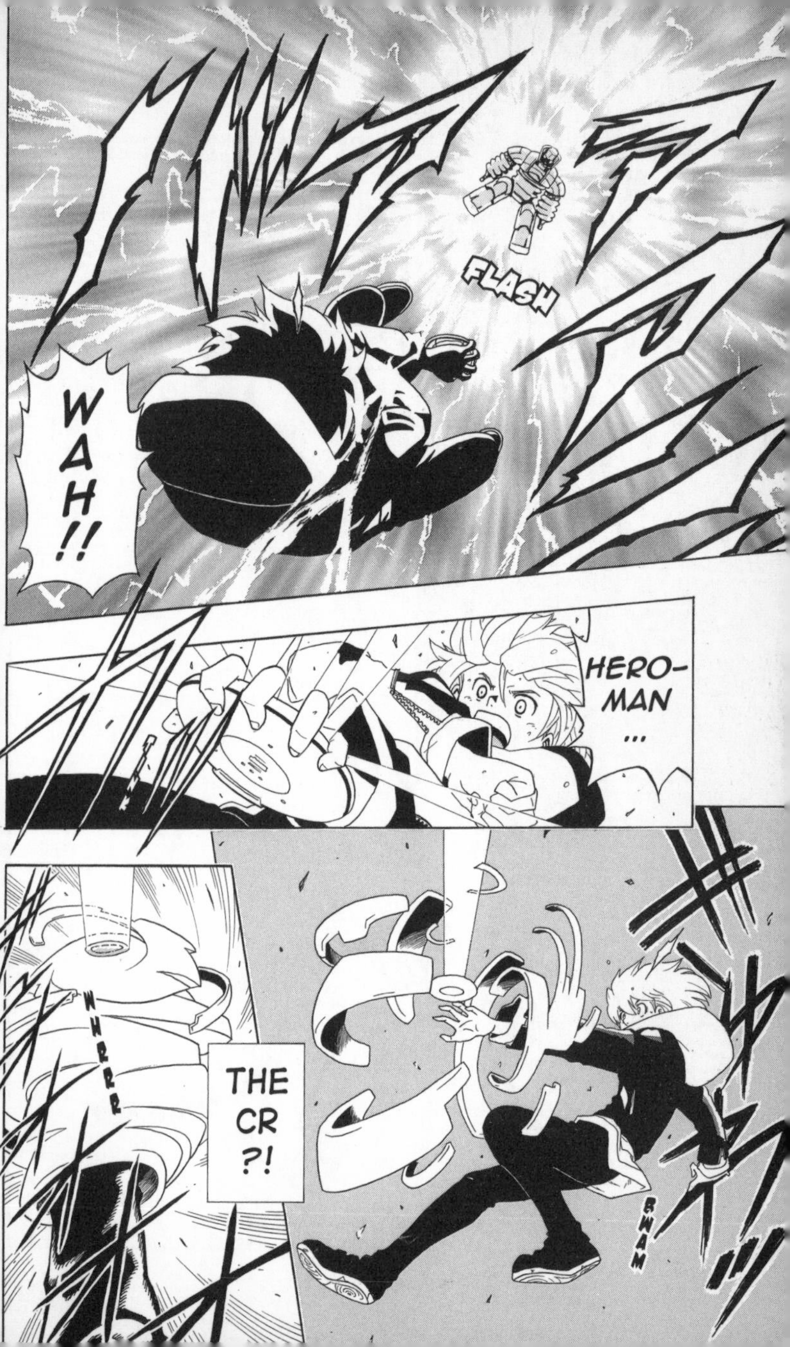
FLASH
WAH!!
HERO-MAN ...
BWAM
THE CR ?!
WHRRR

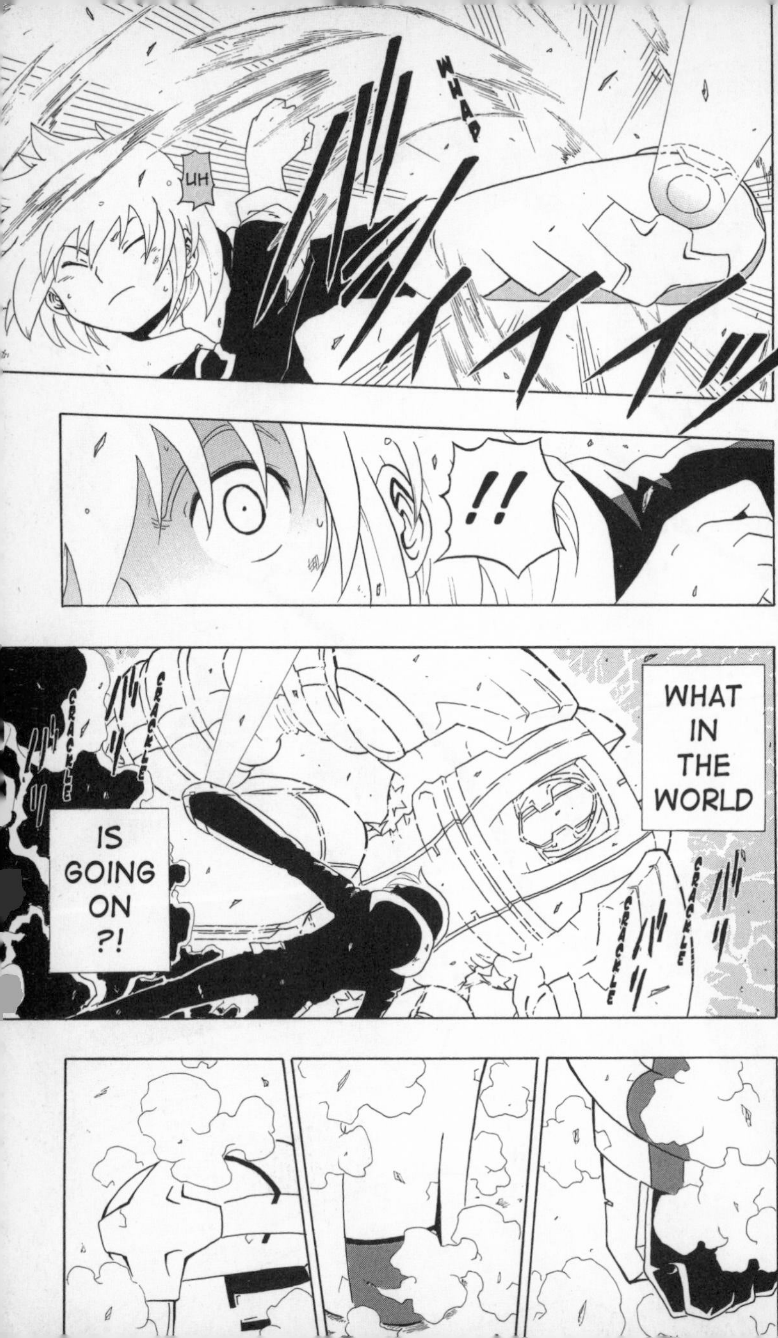
WHAP
UH
!!
WHAT IN THE WORLD
CRACKLE
CRACKLE
IS GOING ON?!
CRACKLE
CRACKLE

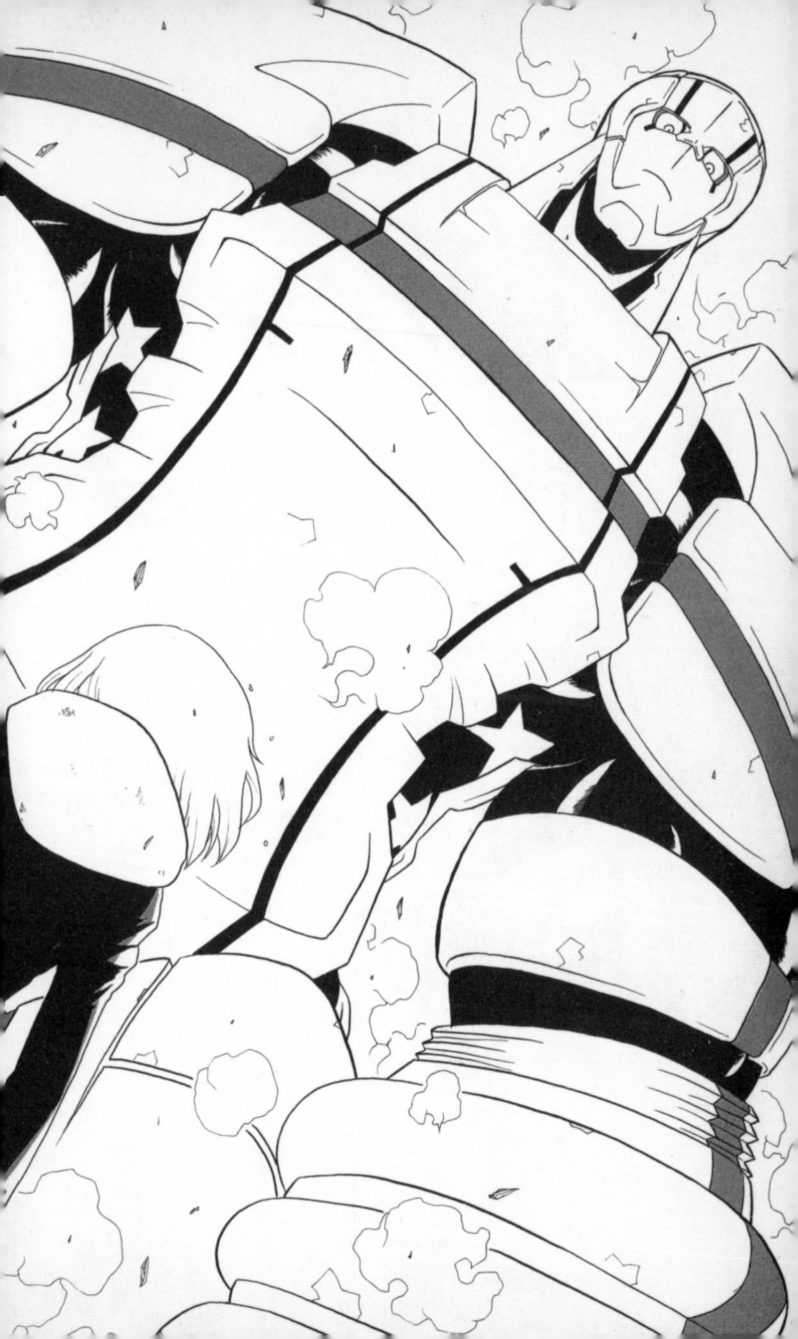

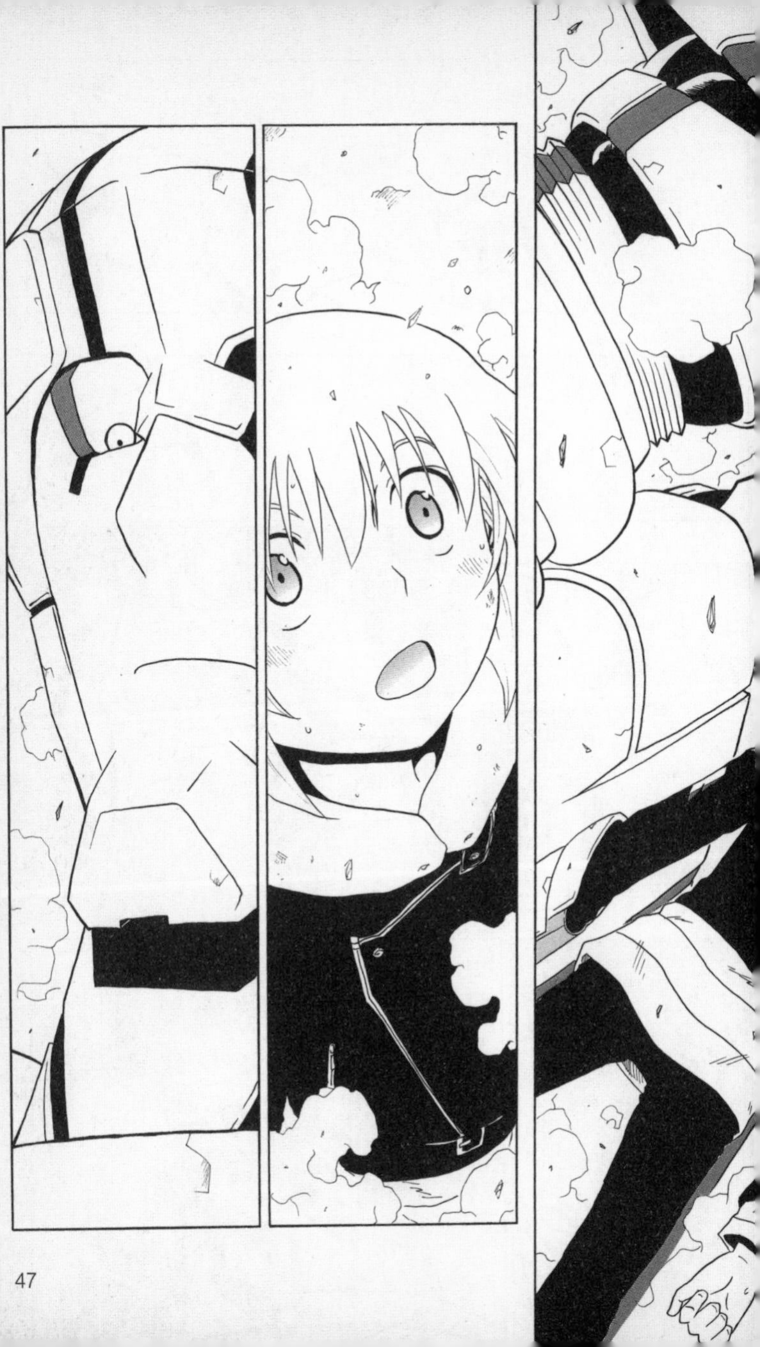

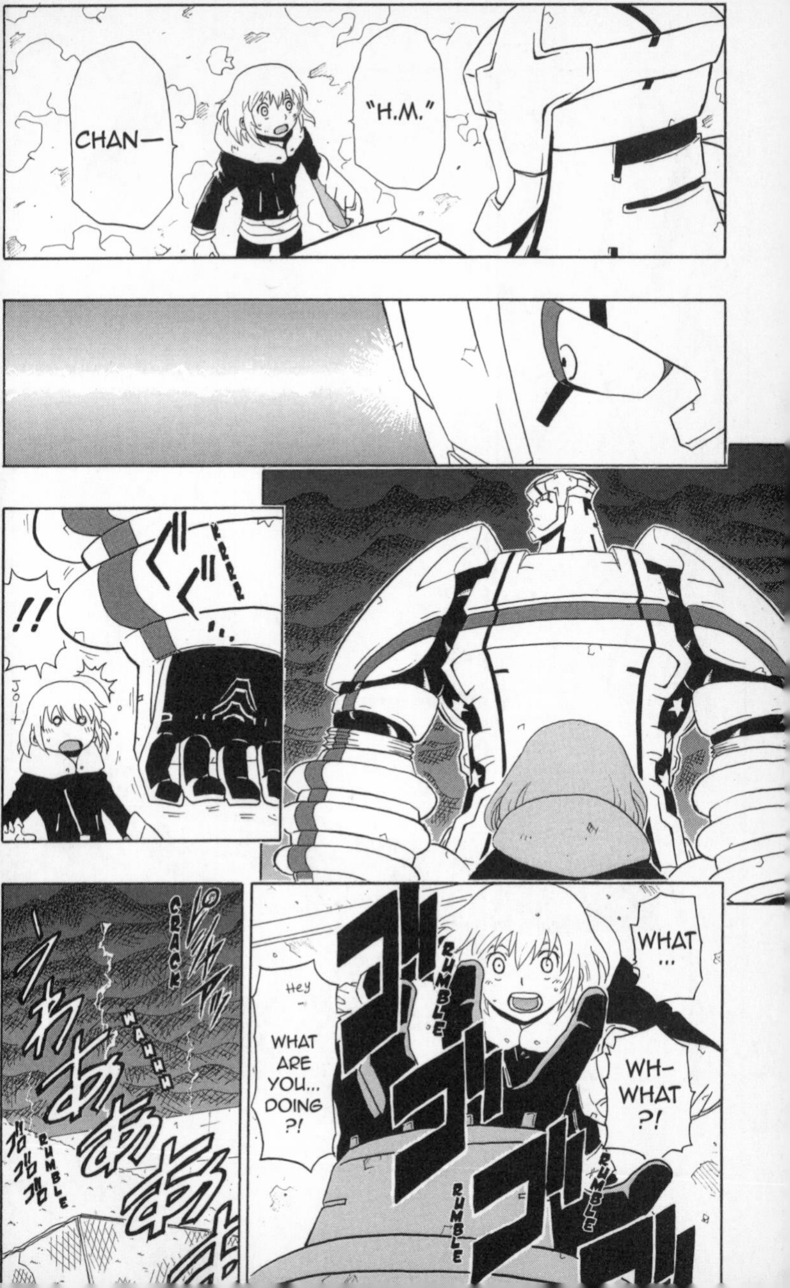
"H.M."
CHAN—
KRRRR
!!
Jolt
WHAT...
RUMBLE
Hey—
WHAT ARE YOU... DOING?!
WH- WHAT?!
RUMBLE
RUMBLE
CRACK
WAHHH
RUMBLE

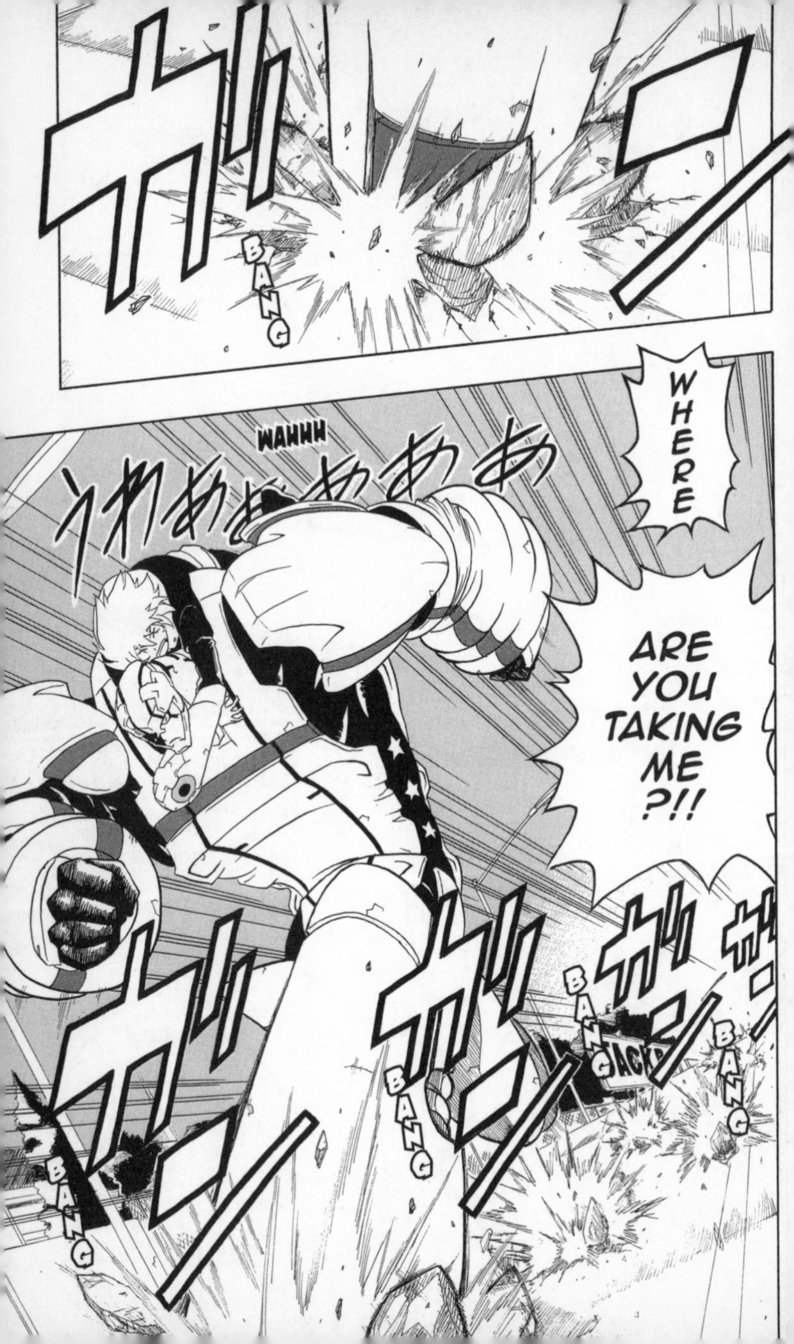
BANG
WHERE
ARE YOU TAKING ME ?!!
WAHHH
BANG
BANG
BANG
BANG

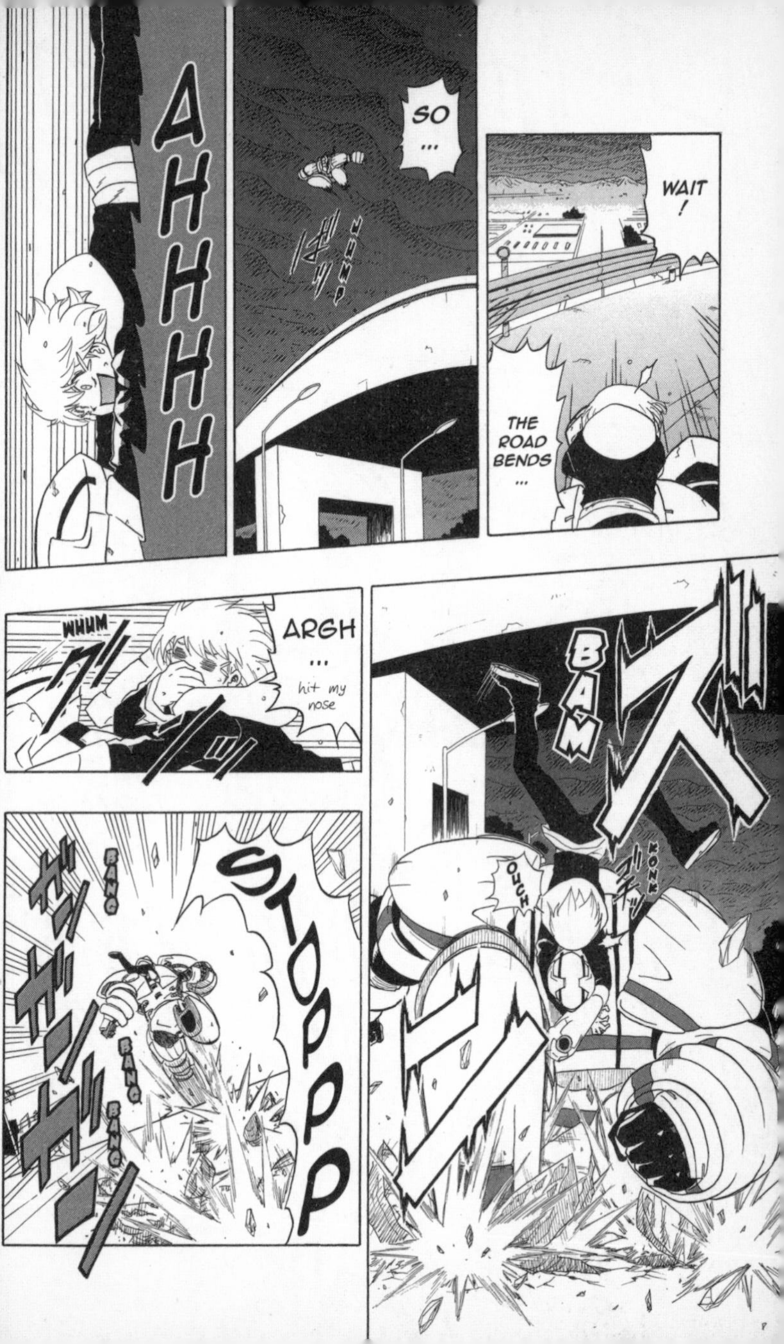
WAIT!
THE ROAD BENDS...
SO...
JUMP
AHHHHH
BAM
KONK
OUCH
ARGH... hit my nose
WHUM
STOPPP
BANG
BANG
BANG

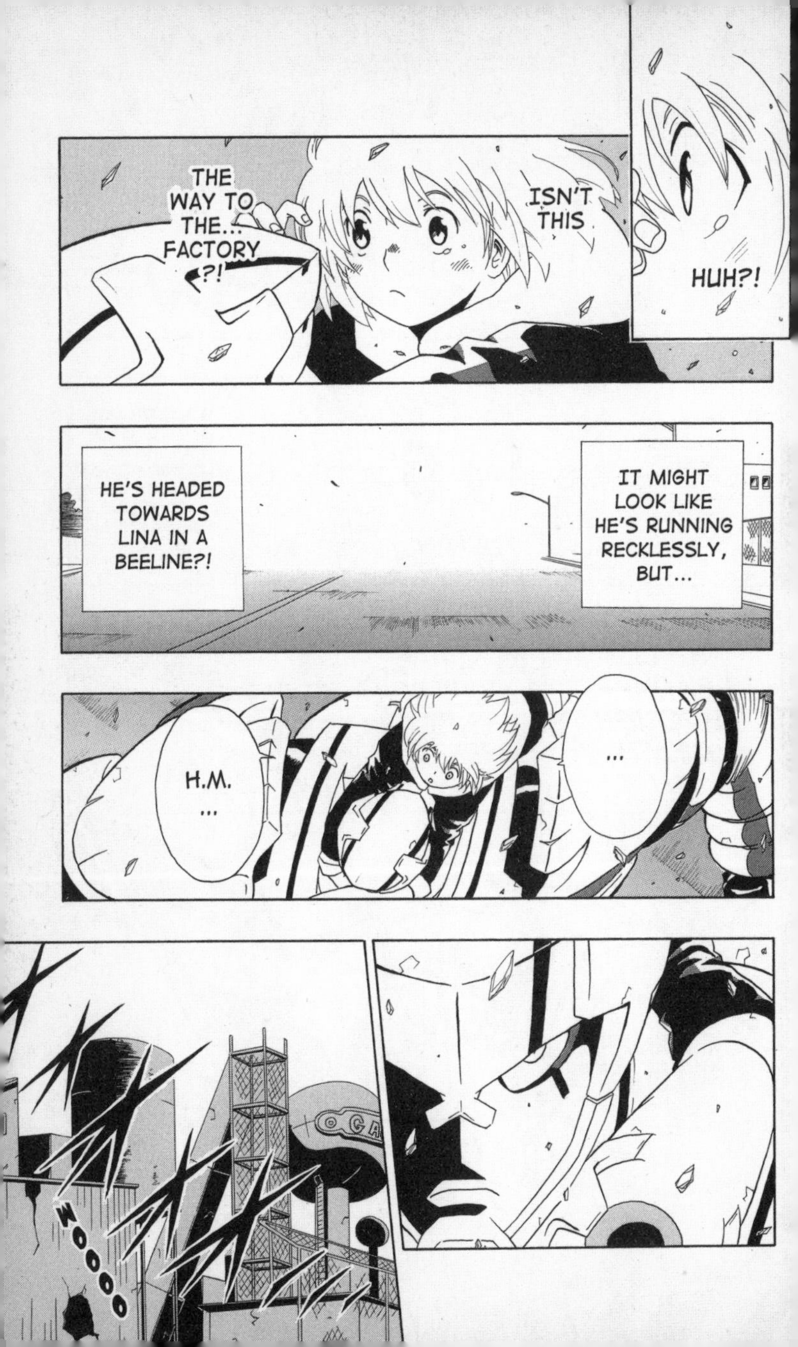
HUH?!
ISN'T THIS
THE WAY TO THE... FACTORY ?!
IT MIGHT LOOK LIKE HE'S RUNNING RECKLESSLY, BUT...
HE'S HEADED TOWARDS LINA IN A BEELINE?!
...
H.M. ...
WOOOO

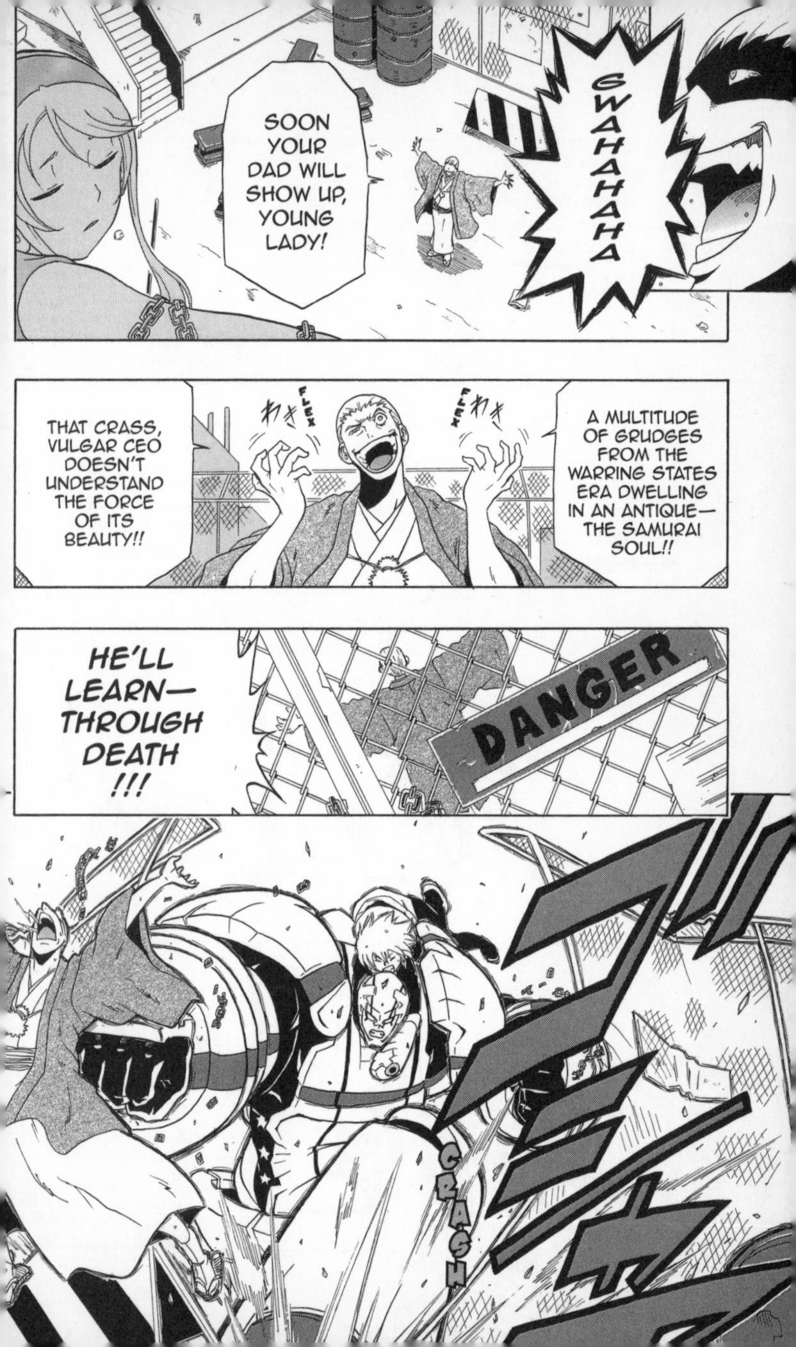
GWAHAHAHA
SOON YOUR DAD WILL SHOW UP, YOUNG LADY!
A MULTITUDE OF GRUDGES FROM THE WARRING STATES ERA DWELLING IN AN ANTIQUE— THE SAMURAI SOUL!!
FLEX
FLEX
THAT CRASS, VULGAR CEO DOESN'T UNDERSTAND THE FORCE OF ITS BEAUTY!!
HE'LL LEARN— THROUGH DEATH !!!
DANGER
CRASH

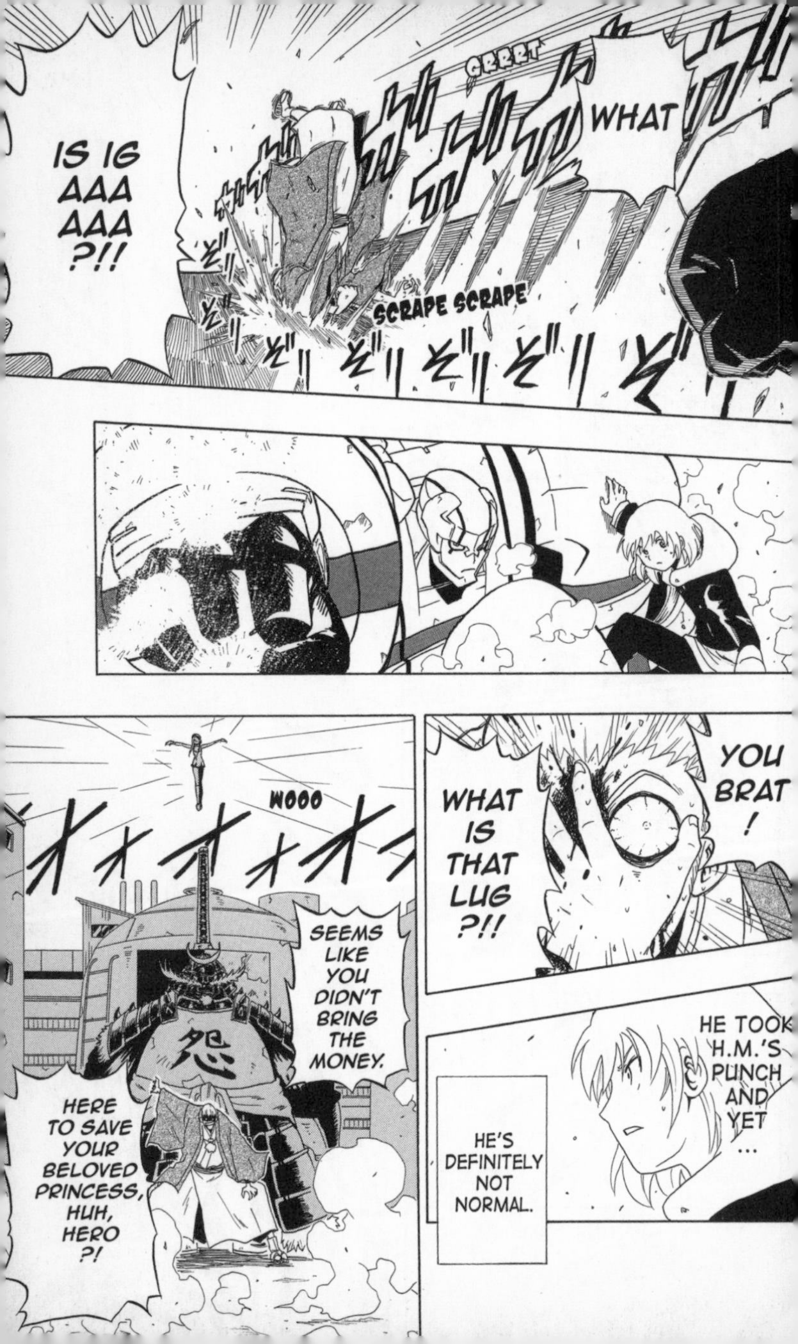
WHAT
GRRRT
SCRAPE SCRAPE
IS IG AAAAAA?!!
YOU BRAT!
WHAT IS THAT LUG?!!
HE TOOK H.M.'S PUNCH AND YET...
HE'S DEFINITELY NOT NORMAL.
WOOO
SEEMS LIKE YOU DIDN'T BRING THE MONEY.
HERE TO SAVE YOUR BELOVED PRINCESS, HUH, HERO?!

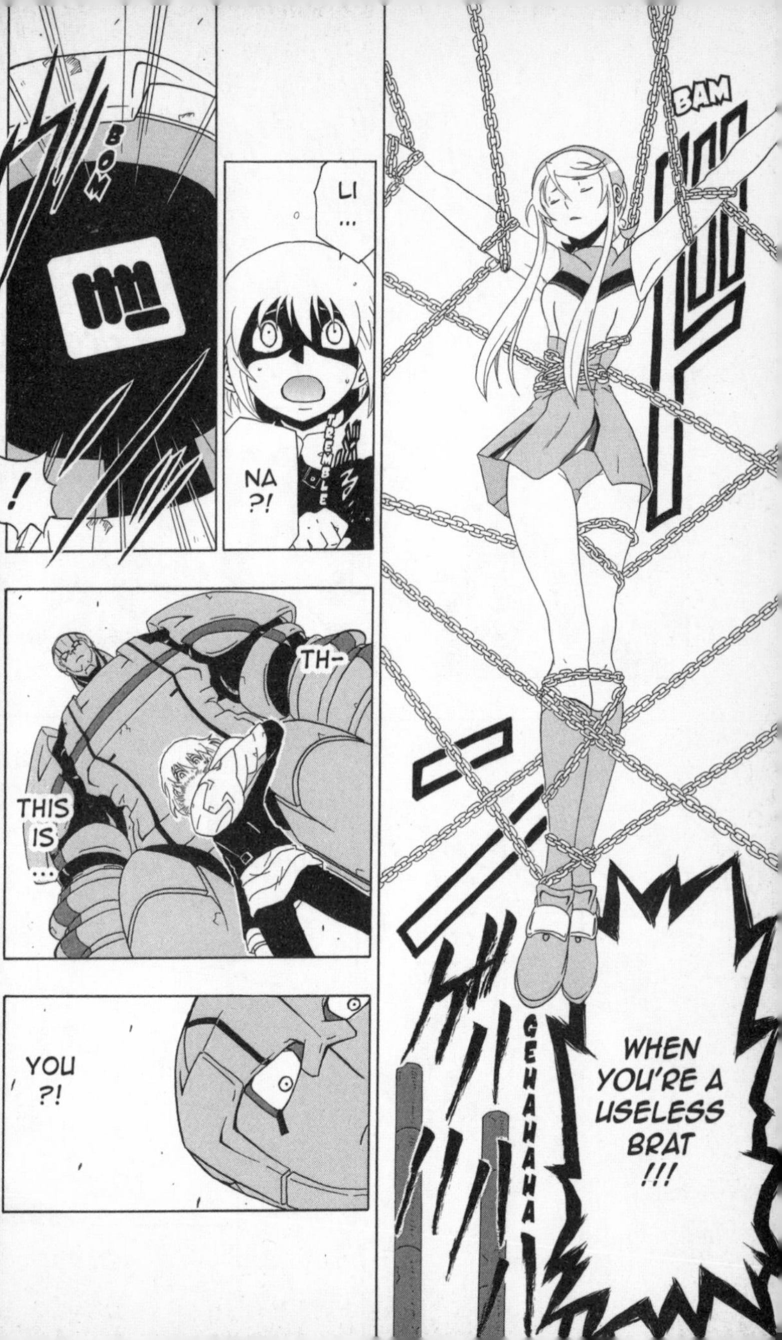

BAM
WHEN YOU'RE A USELESS BRAT !!!
GEHAHAHA
LI ...
TREMBLE
NA ?!
BOM
!
TH-
THIS IS ...
YOU ?!

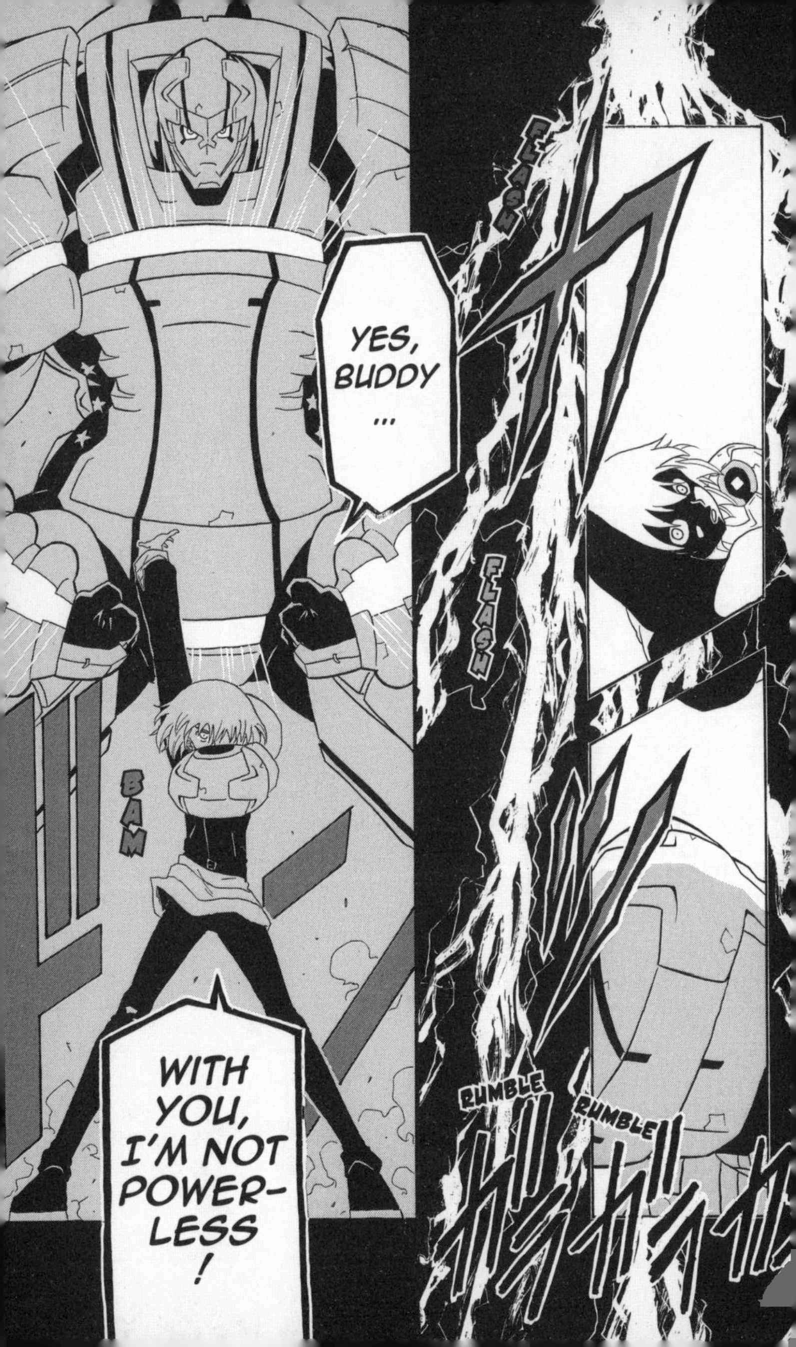
FLASH
FLASH
RUMBLE
RUMBLE
YES, BUDDY ...
BAM
WITH YOU, I'M NOT POWER-LESS !

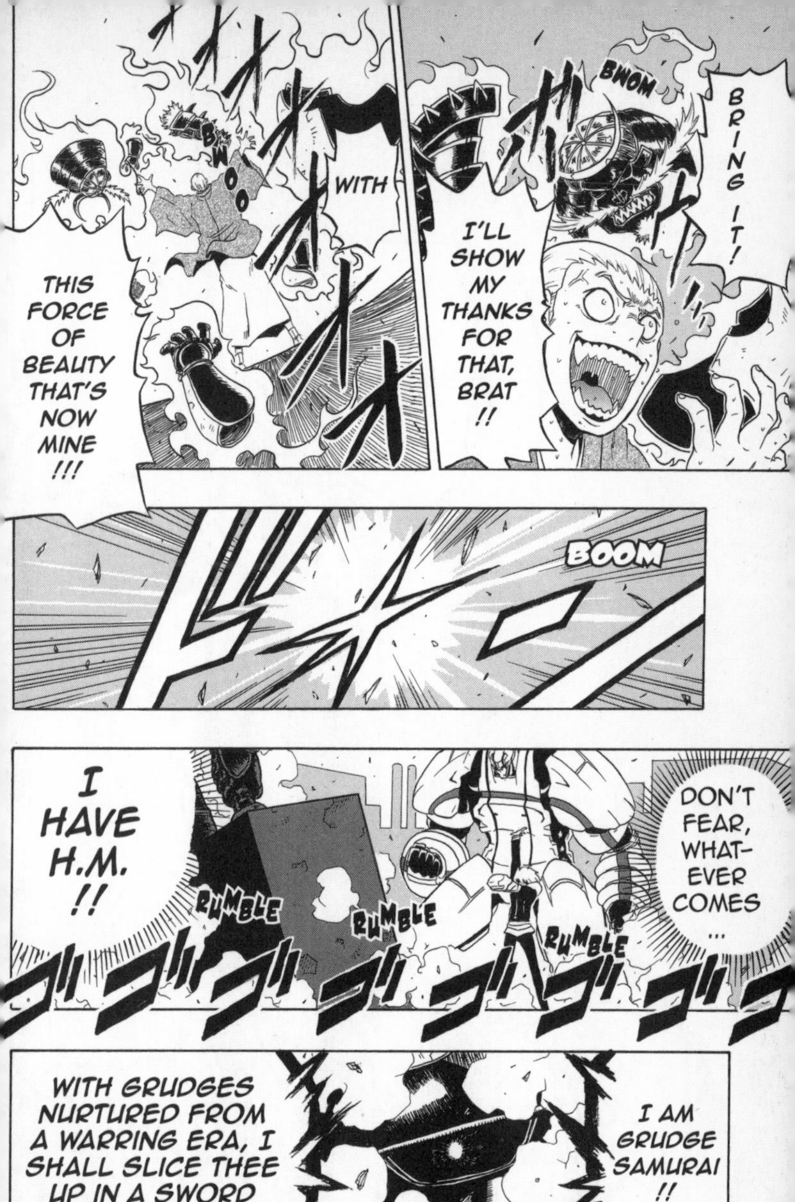
BRING IT!
BWOM
I'LL SHOW MY THANKS FOR THAT, BRAT!!
WITH
BWOOO
THIS FORCE OF BEAUTY THAT'S NOW MINE!!!
BOOM
DON'T FEAR, WHATEVER COMES...
RUMBLE
RUMBLE
RUMBLE
I HAVE H.M.!!
I AM GRUDGE SAMURAI!!
WITH GRUDGES NURTURED FROM A WARRING ERA, I SHALL SLICE THEE UP IN A SWORD DANCE OF HATE!!

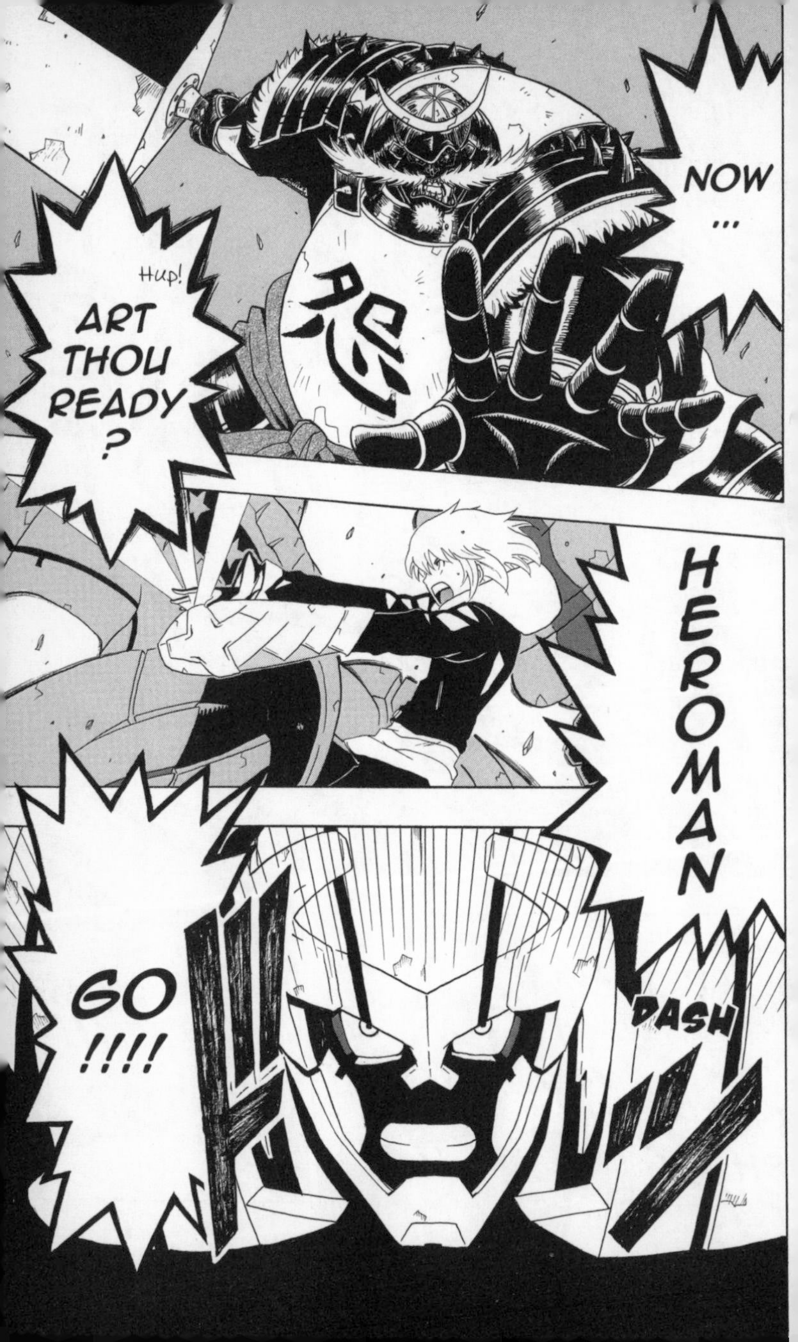

NOW ...
Hup!
ART THOU READY ?
HEROMAN
GO !!!!
DASH

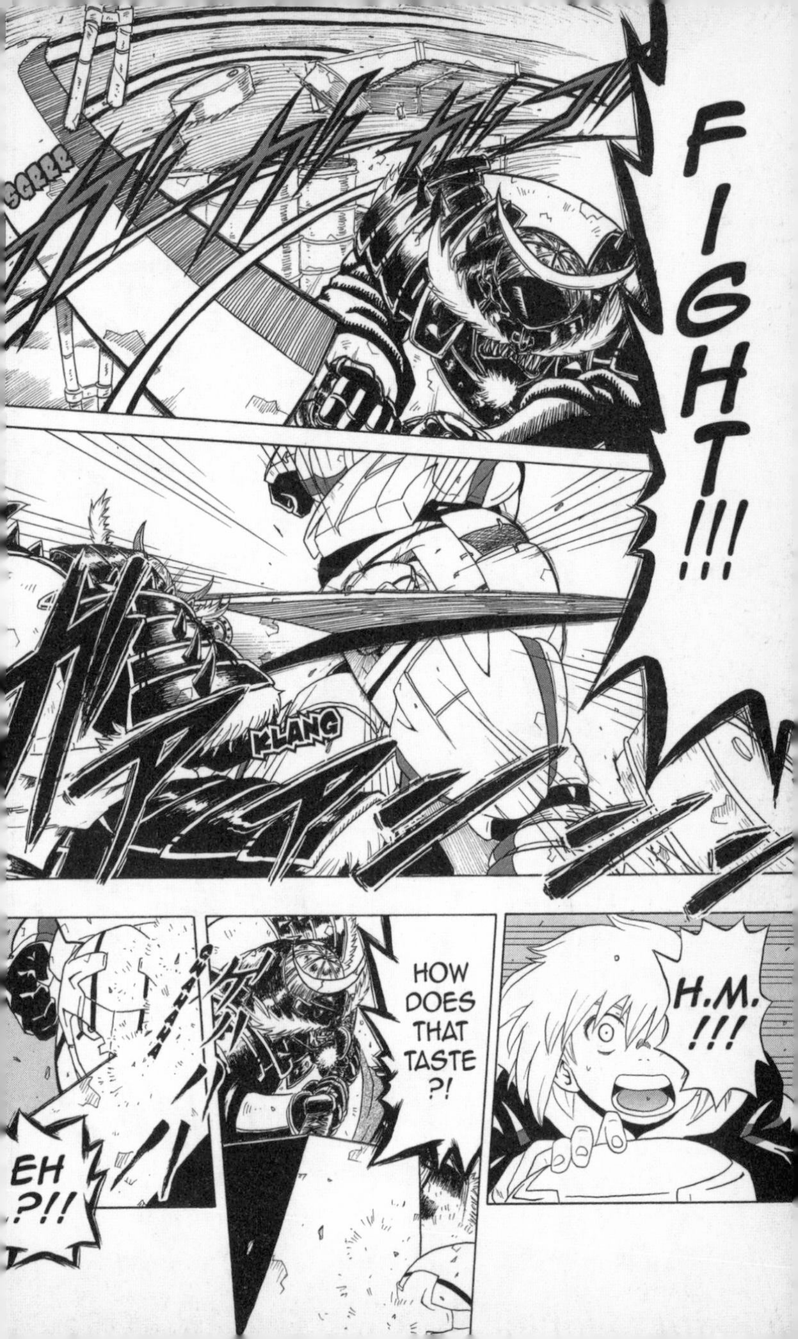
FIGHT!!!
SGRRR
KLANG
H.M.!!!
HOW DOES THAT TASTE?!
GWAHAHAHA
EH?!!

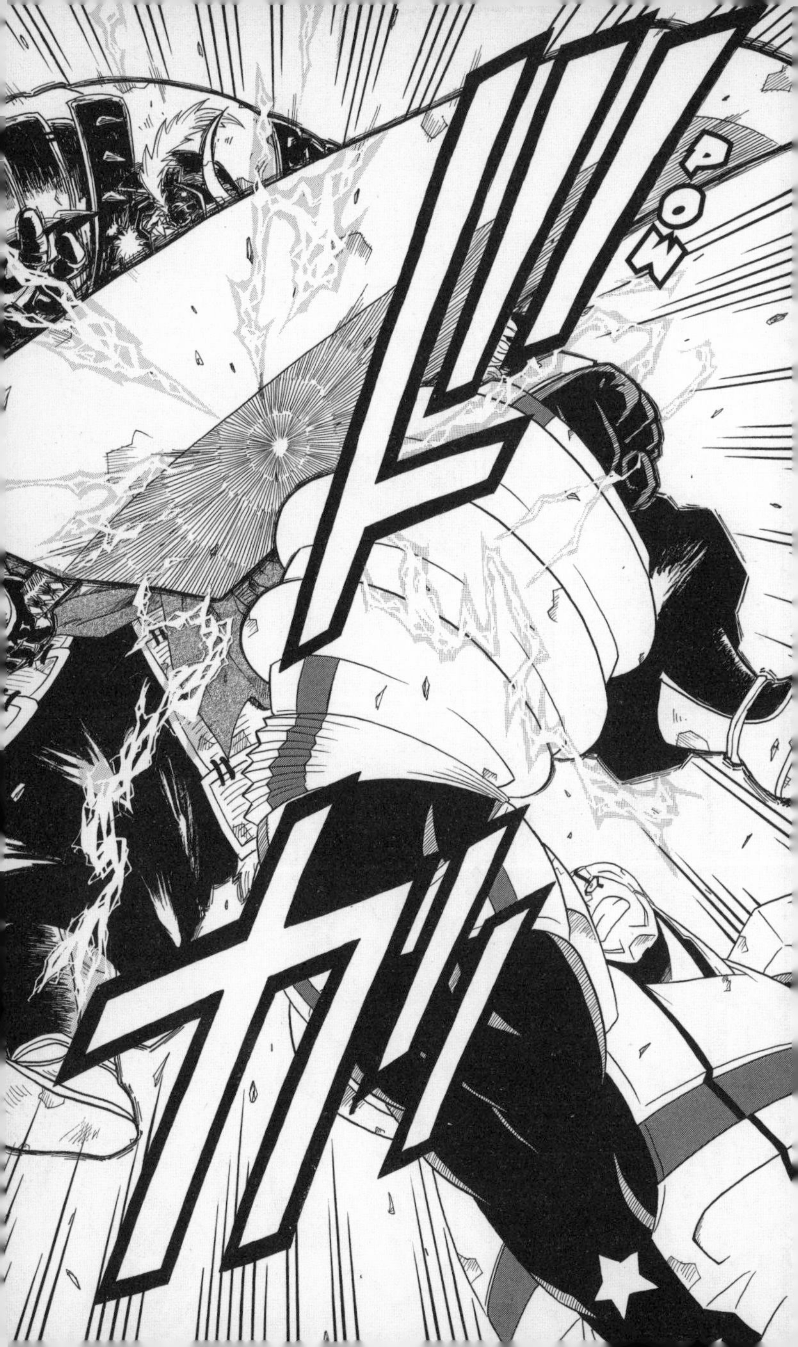
POW

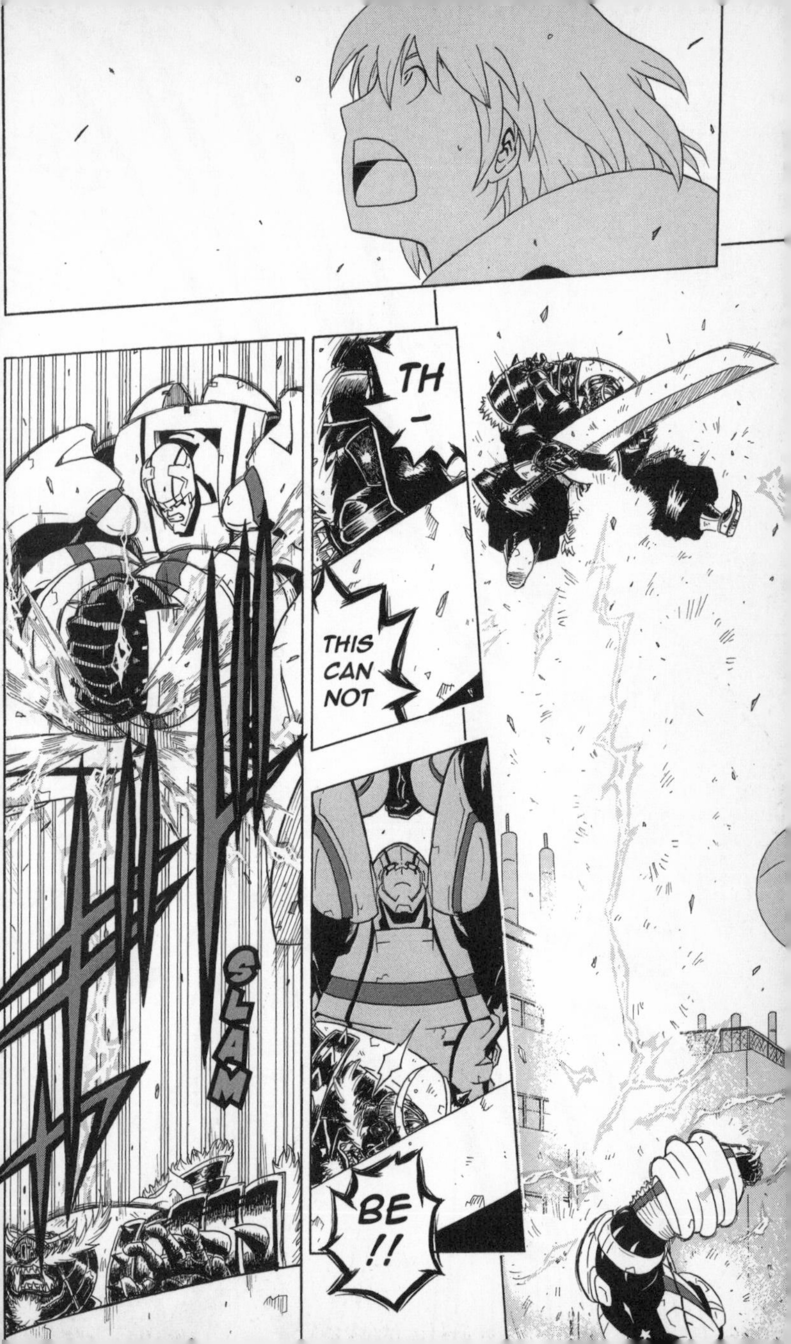
TH
–
THIS CAN NOT
BE !!
SLAM

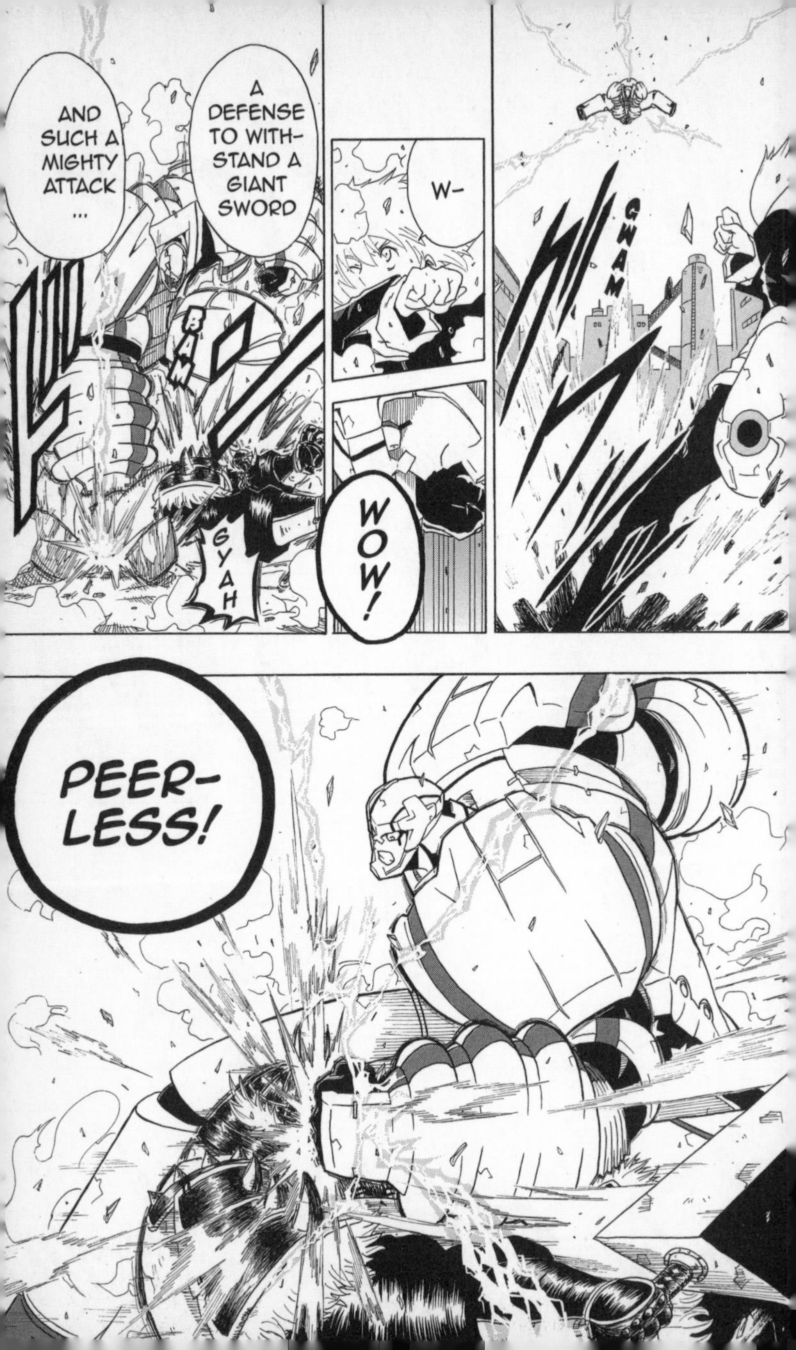
GWAM
W-
WOW!
A DEFENSE TO WITH-STAND A GIANT SWORD
AND SUCH A MIGHTY ATTACK ...
BAM
GYAH
PEER-LESS!

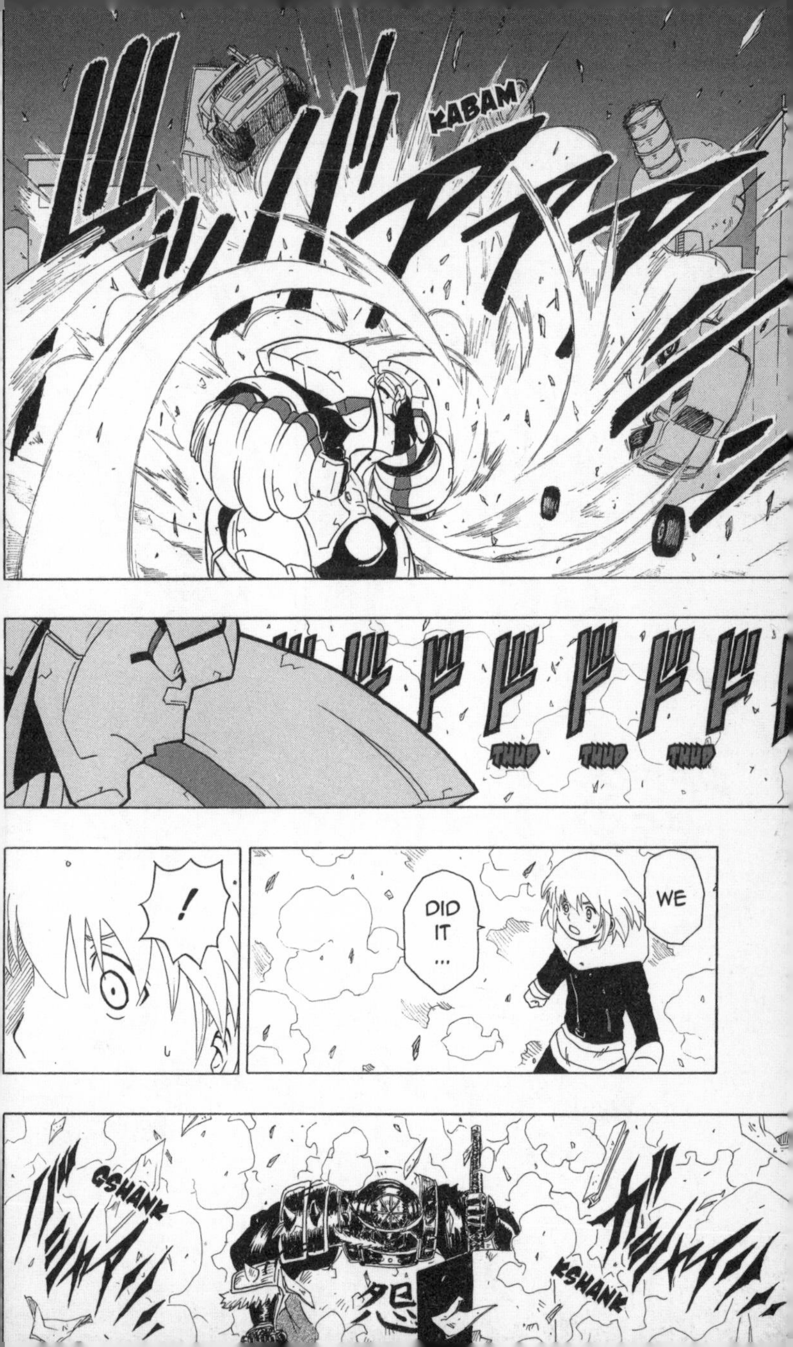
KABAM
THUD
THUD
THUD
WE
DID IT ...
!
KSHANK
GSHANK

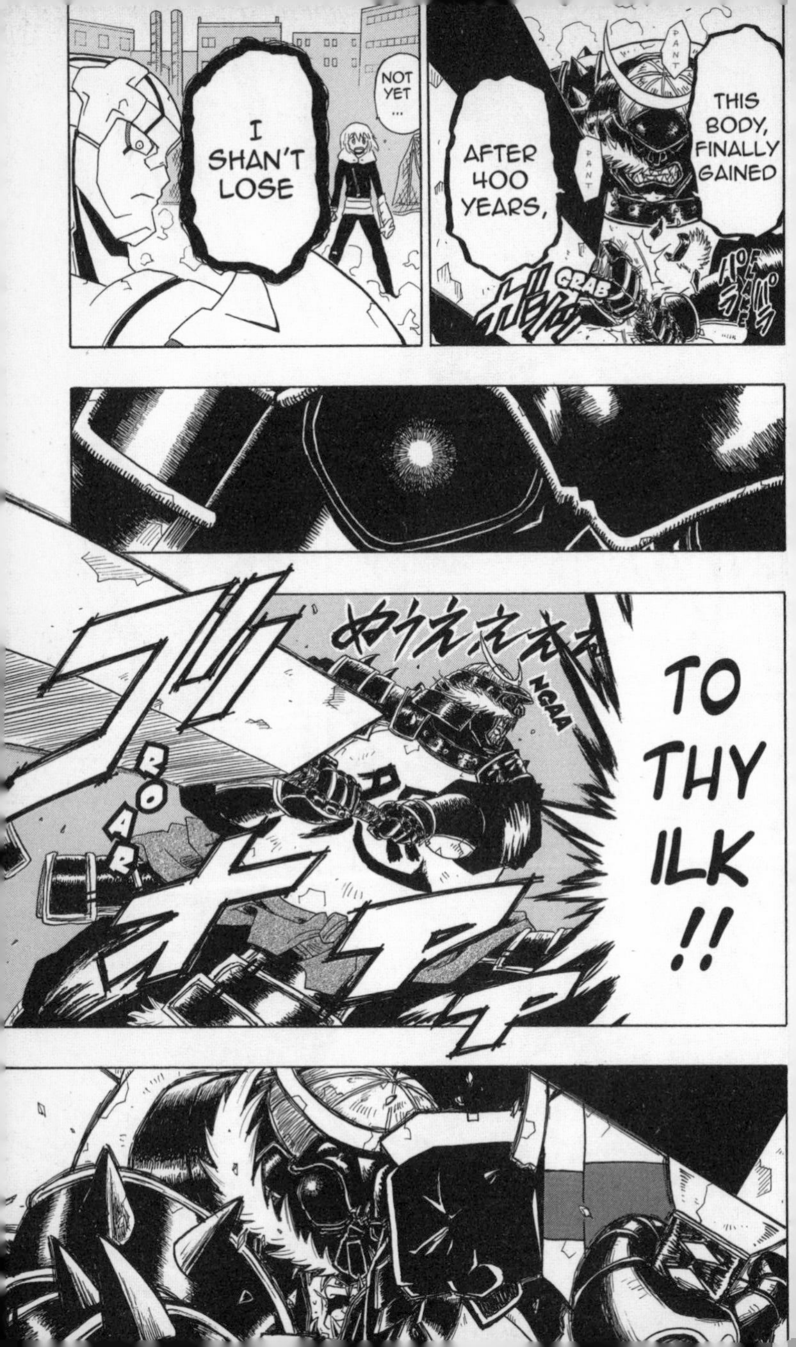
PANT
THIS BODY, FINALLY GAINED
PANT
AFTER 400 YEARS,
GRAB
NOT YET ...
I SHAN'T LOSE
TO THY ILK!!
NGAA
ROAR

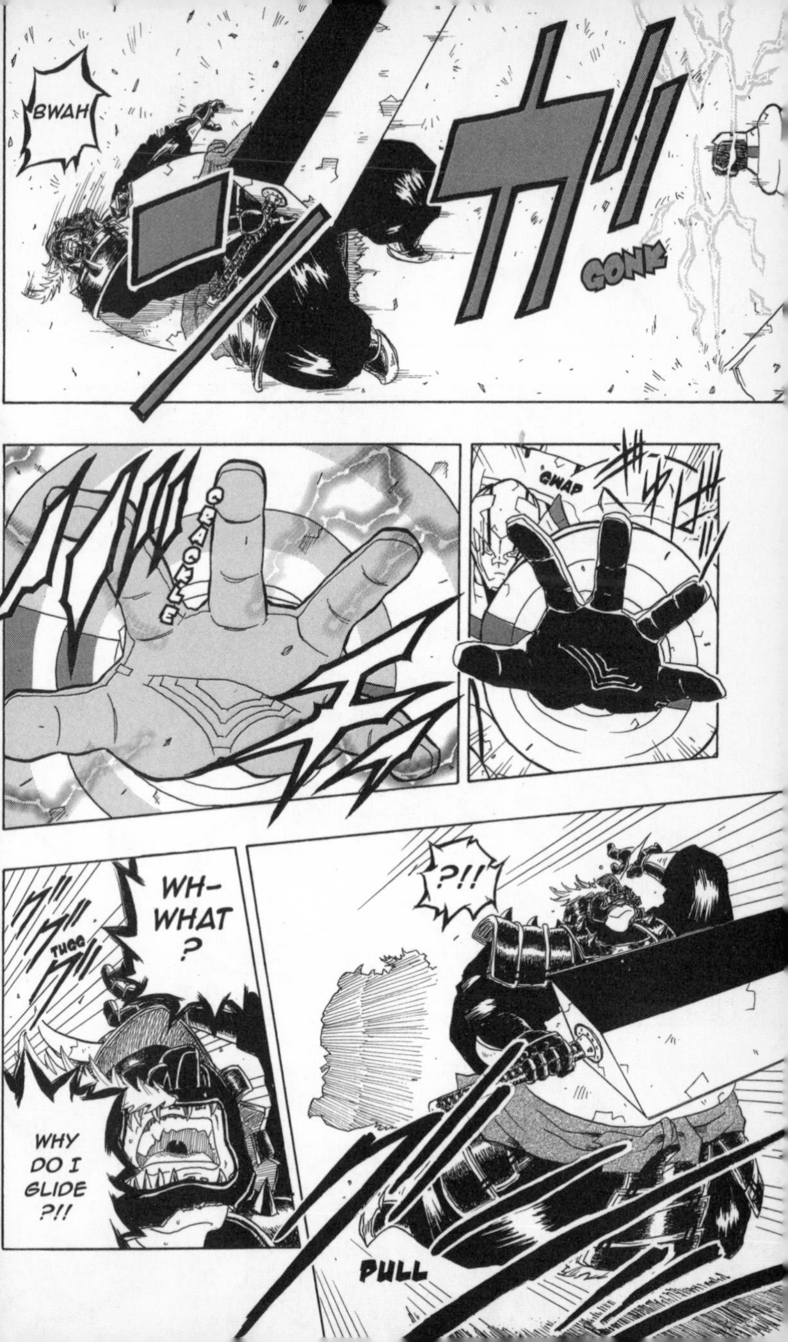
BWAH
GONK
CRACKLE
GWAP
WH-WHAT?
TUGG
?!!
WHY DO I GLIDE?!!
PULL

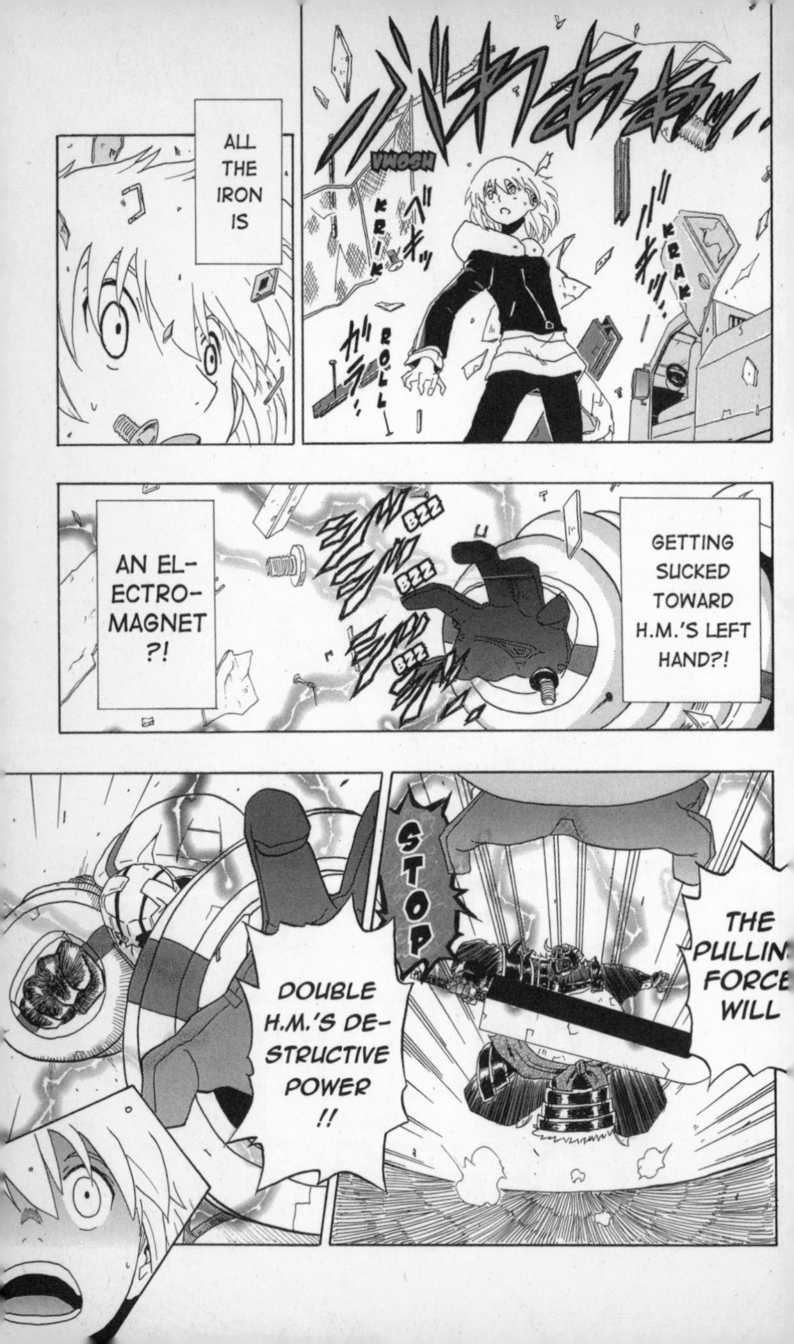

KRAK
VMOSH
KRIK
ROLL
ALL THE IRON IS
GETTING SUCKED TOWARD H.M.'S LEFT HAND?!
BZZ
BZZ
BZZ
AN EL-ECTRO-MAGNET ?!
THE PULLIN FORCE WILL
STOP
DOUBLE H.M.'S DE-STRUCTIVE POWER !!

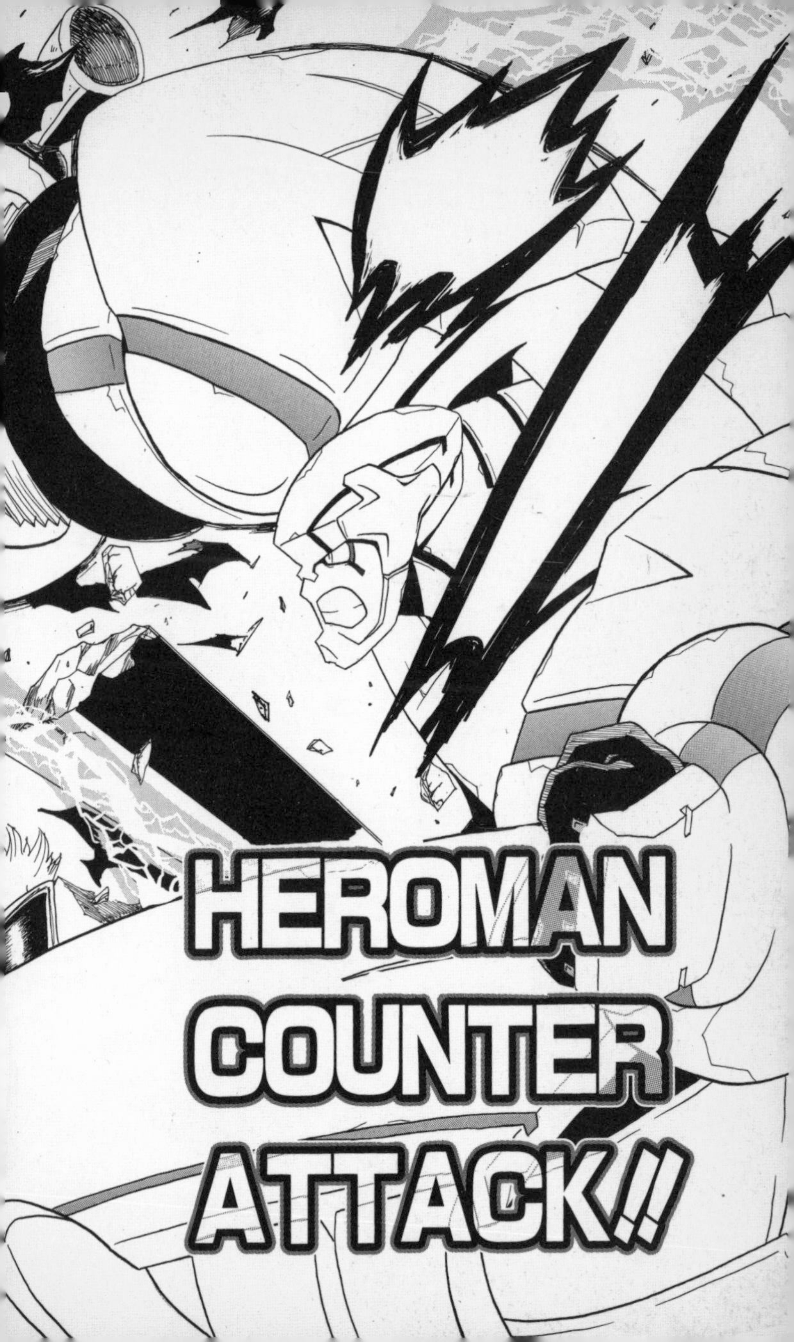
HEROMAN
COUNTER
ATTACK!!

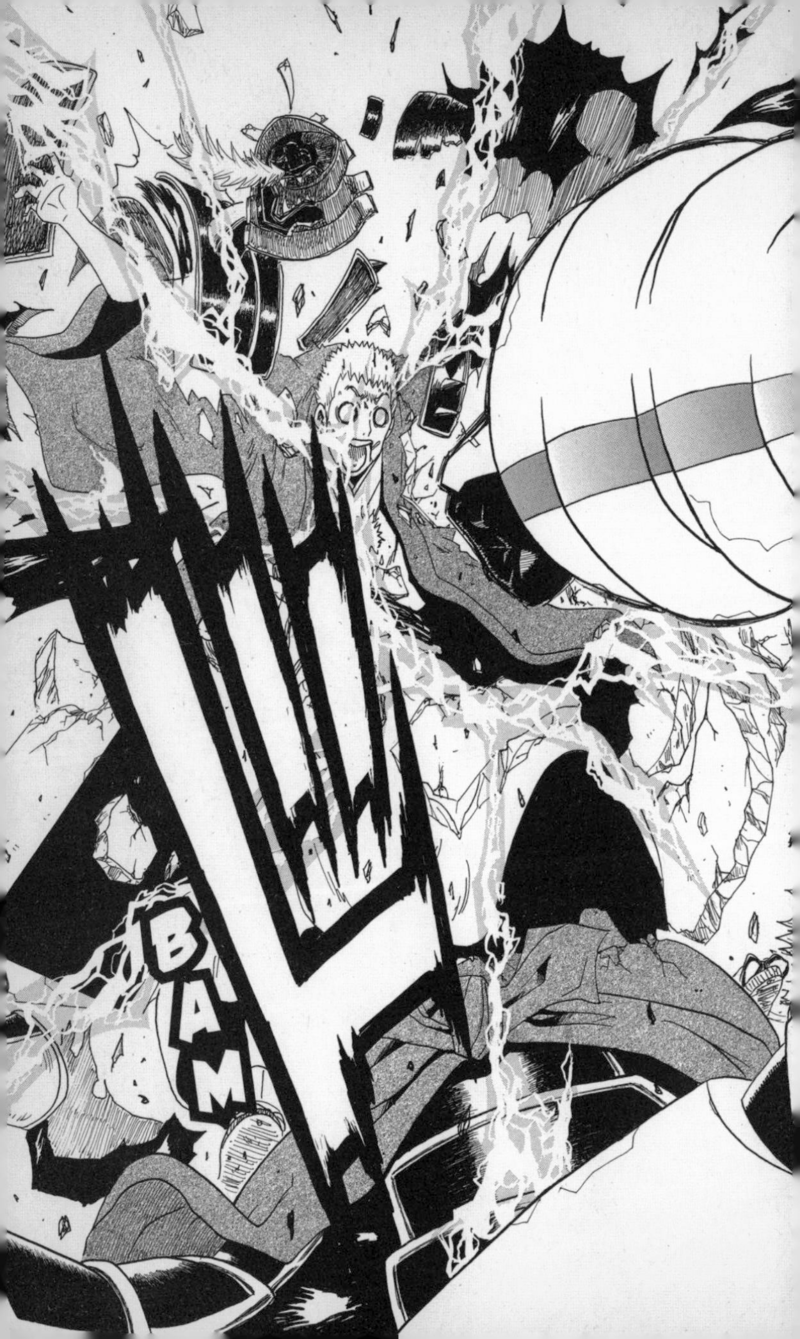
BAM

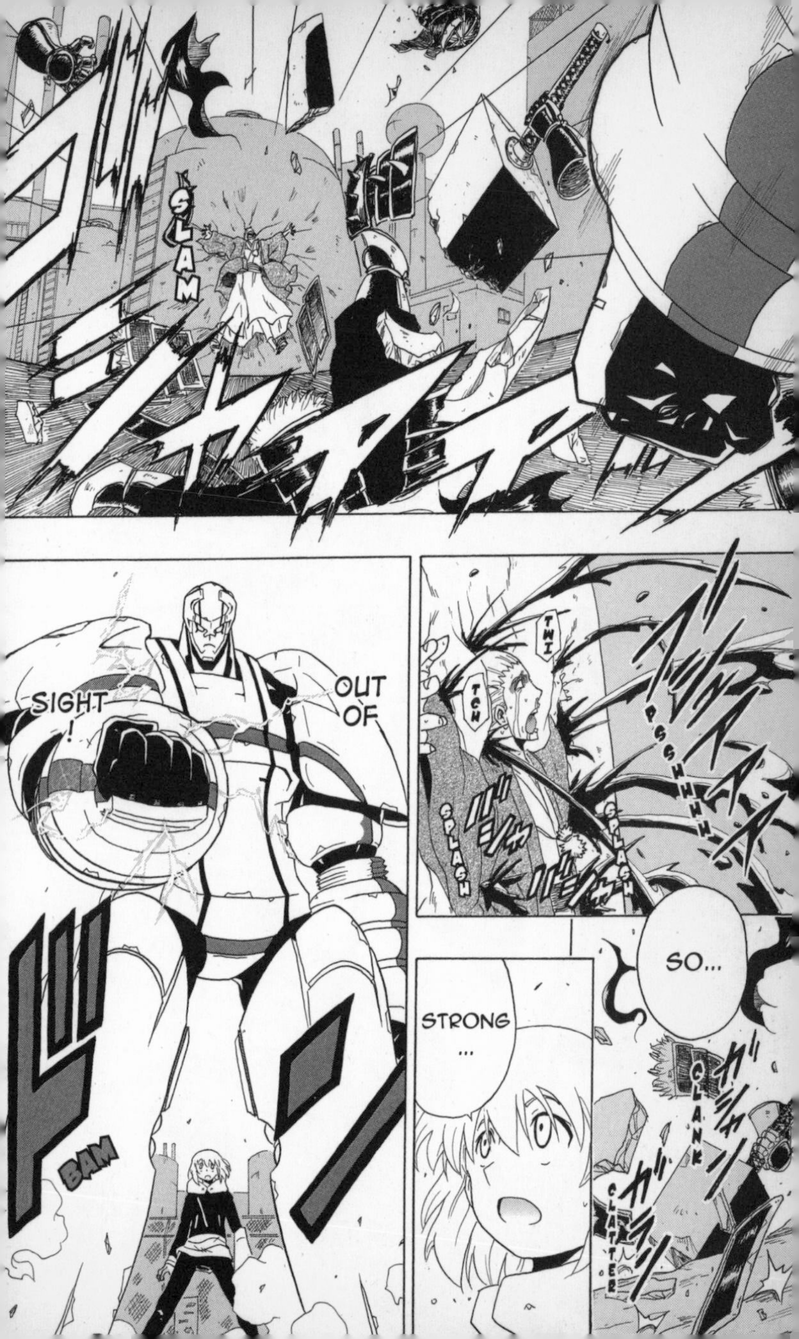
SLAM
TWI
TCH
PSSHHHH
SPLASH
SPLASH
OUT OF
SIGHT!
BAM
SO...
STRONG...
CLANK
CLATTER

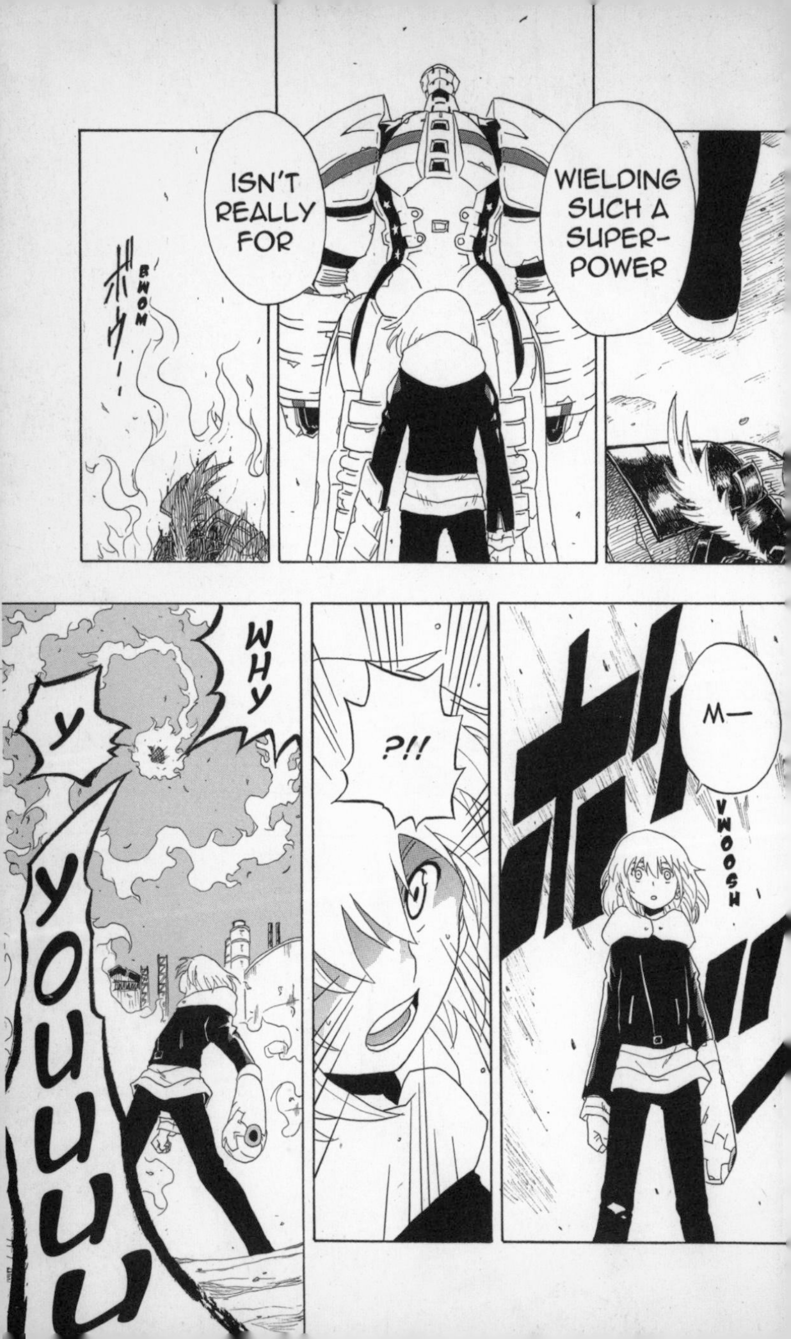
WIELDING SUCH A SUPER-POWER
ISN'T REALLY FOR
BWOM
M—
VWOOSH
?!!
WHY
Y
YOUUUU

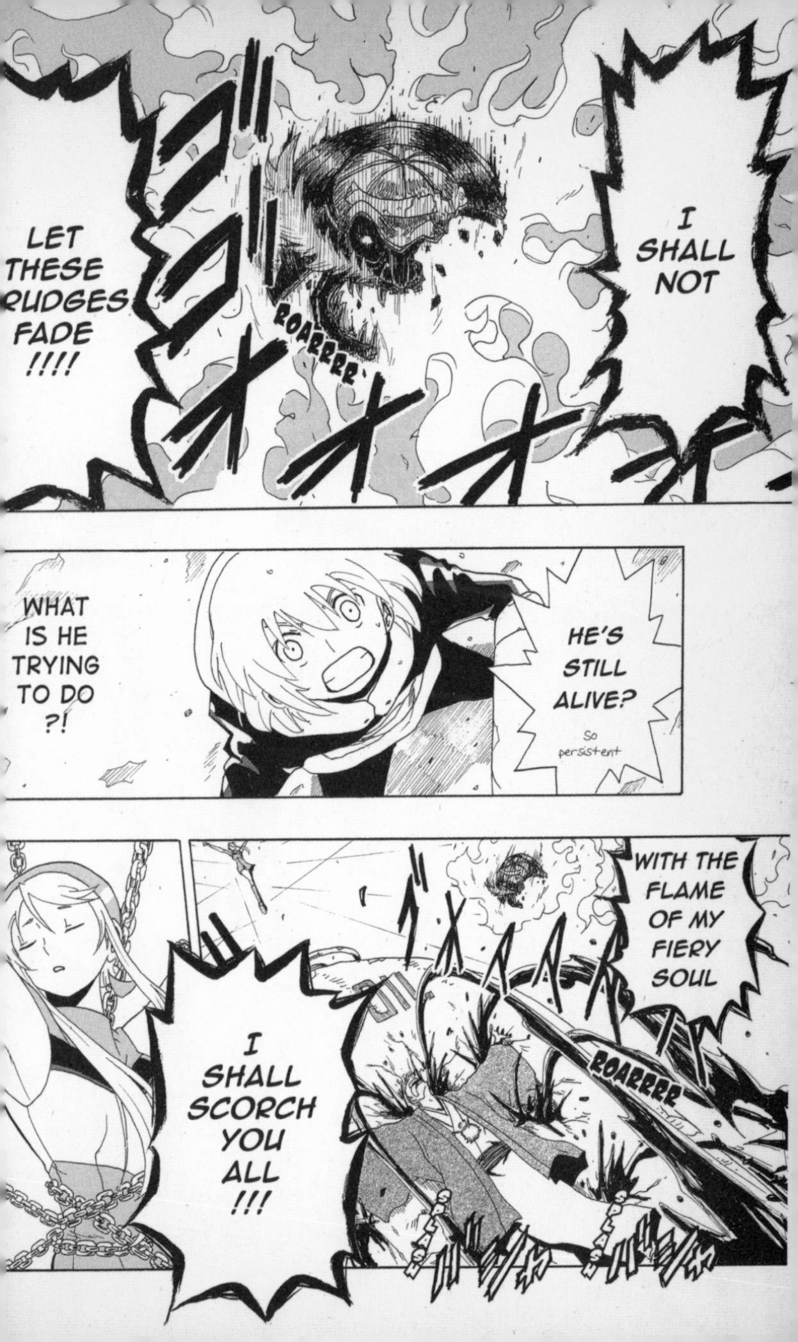
I SHALL NOT
ROARRRR
LET THESE RUDGES FADE !!!!
HE'S STILL ALIVE?
So persistent
WHAT IS HE TRYING TO DO ?!
WITH THE FLAME OF MY FIERY SOUL
ROARRRR
I SHALL SCORCH YOU ALL !!!
SPLASH
SPLASH

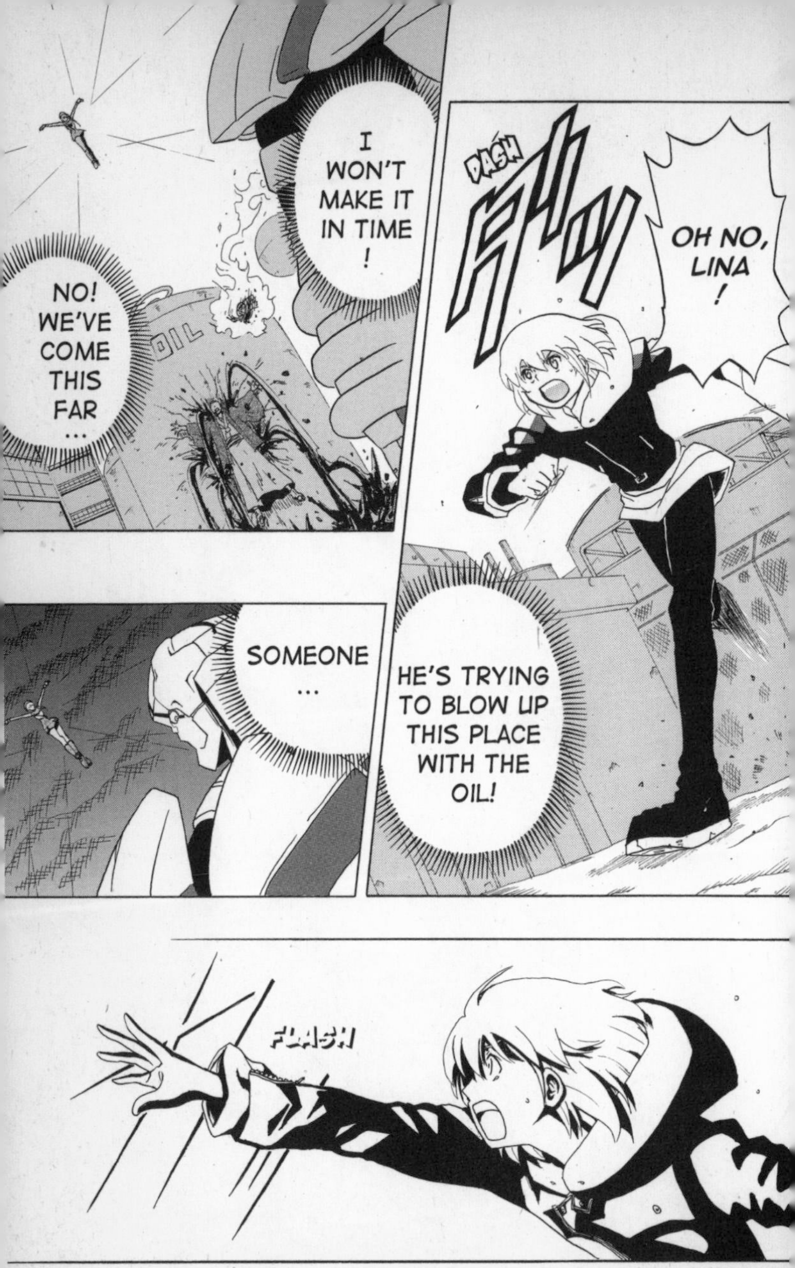
DASH
OH NO, LINA!
HE'S TRYING TO BLOW UP THIS PLACE WITH THE OIL!
I WON'T MAKE IT IN TIME!
NO! WE'VE COME THIS FAR...
OIL
SOMEONE...
FLASH

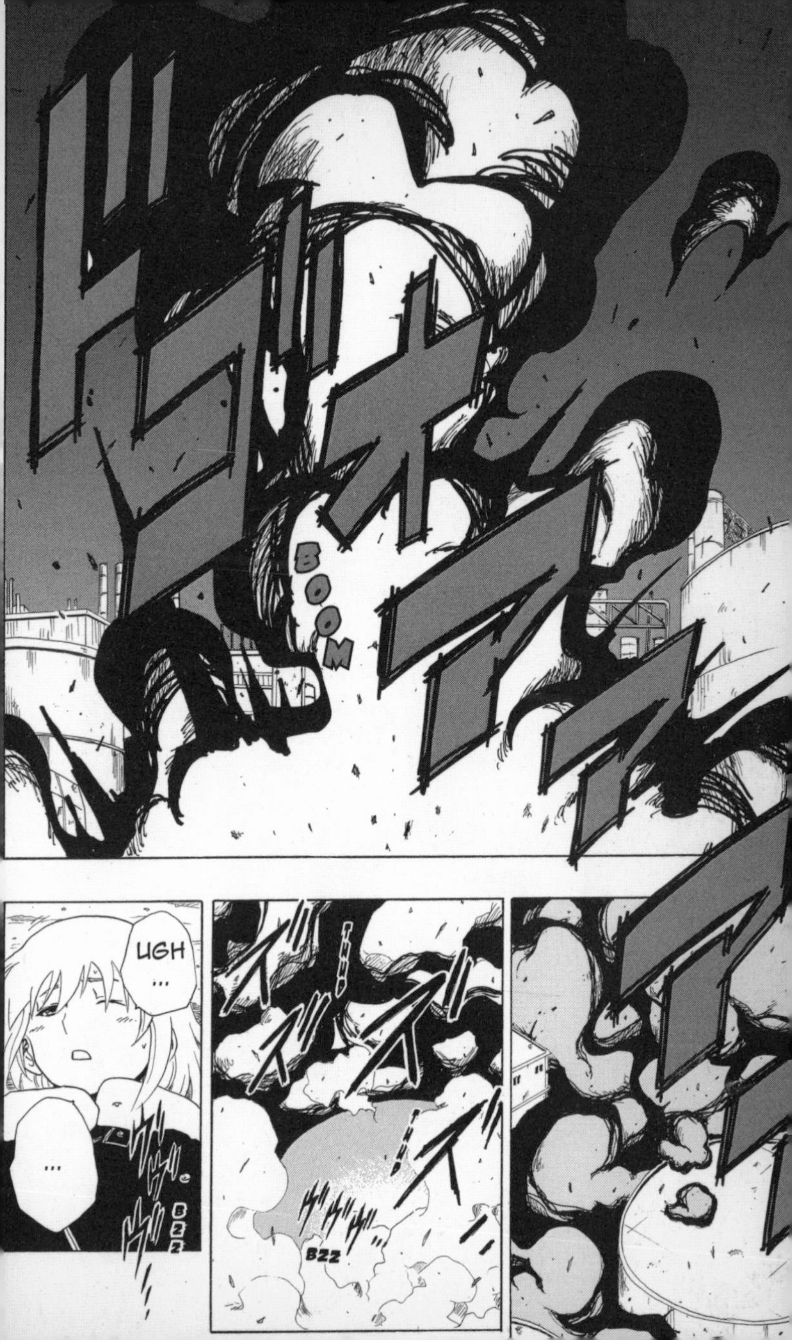
BOOM
THUD
THUD
BZZ
UGH
...
...
BZZ

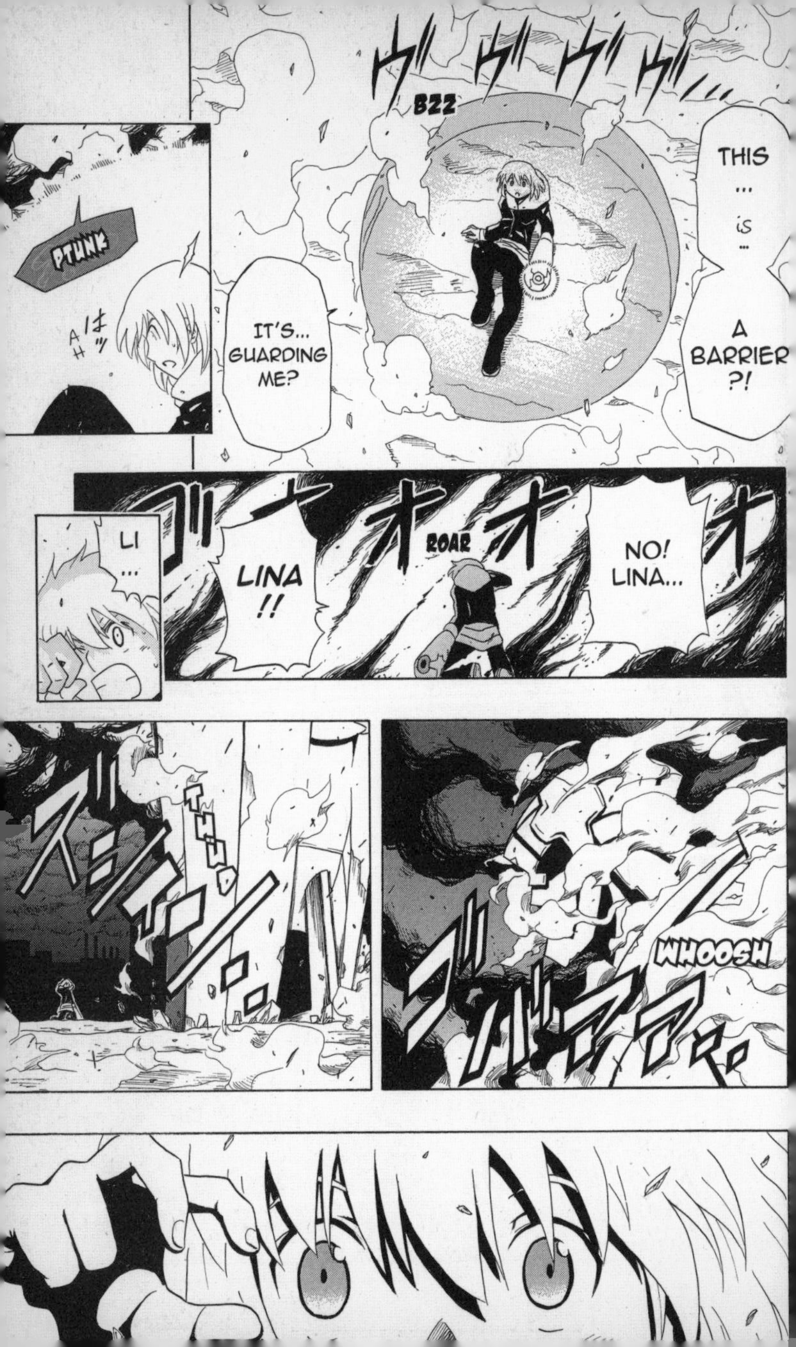
BZZ
THIS... IS... A BARRIER ?!
IT'S... GUARDING ME?
PTUNK
はッ
AH
ROAR
NO! LINA...
LINA !!
LI ...
WHOOSH
THUD

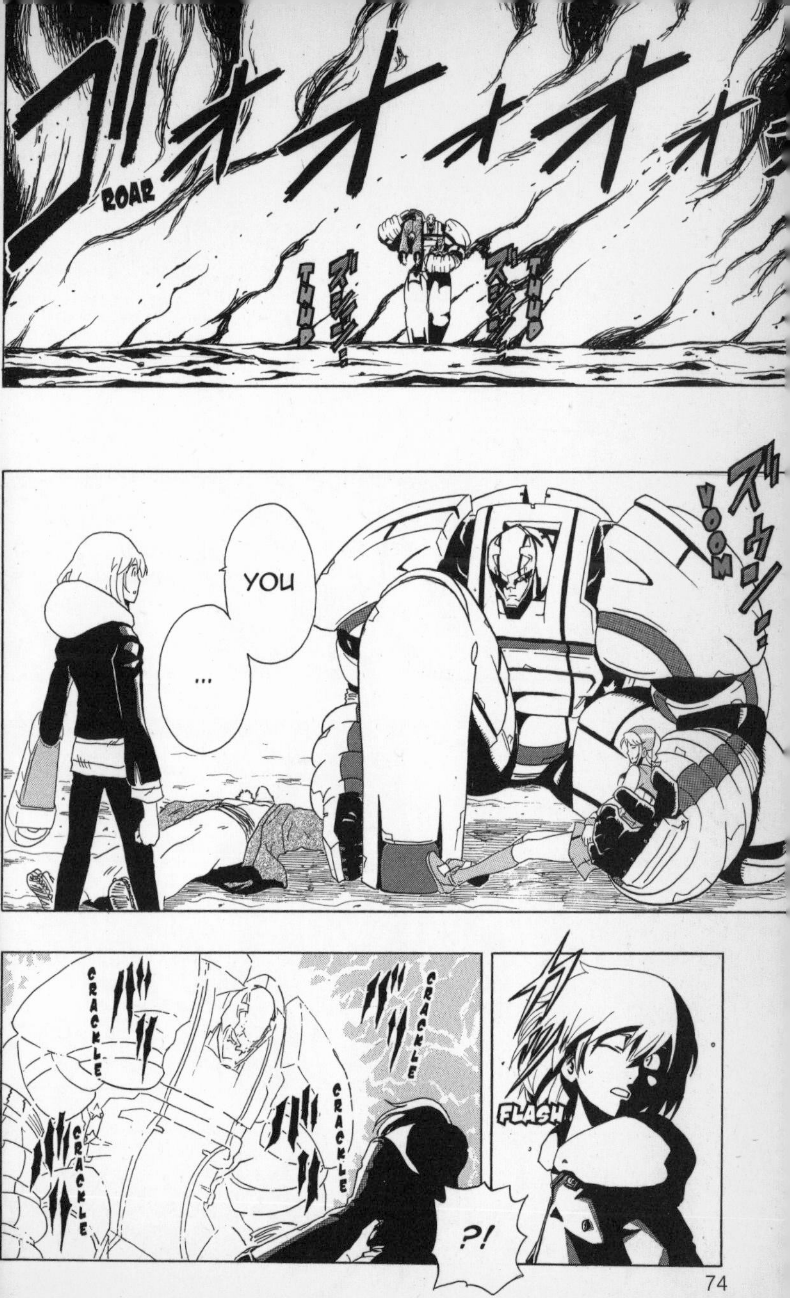
ROAR
THUD
THUD
VOOM
YOU
...
FLASH
?!
CRACKLE
CRACKLE
CRACKLE
CRACKLE

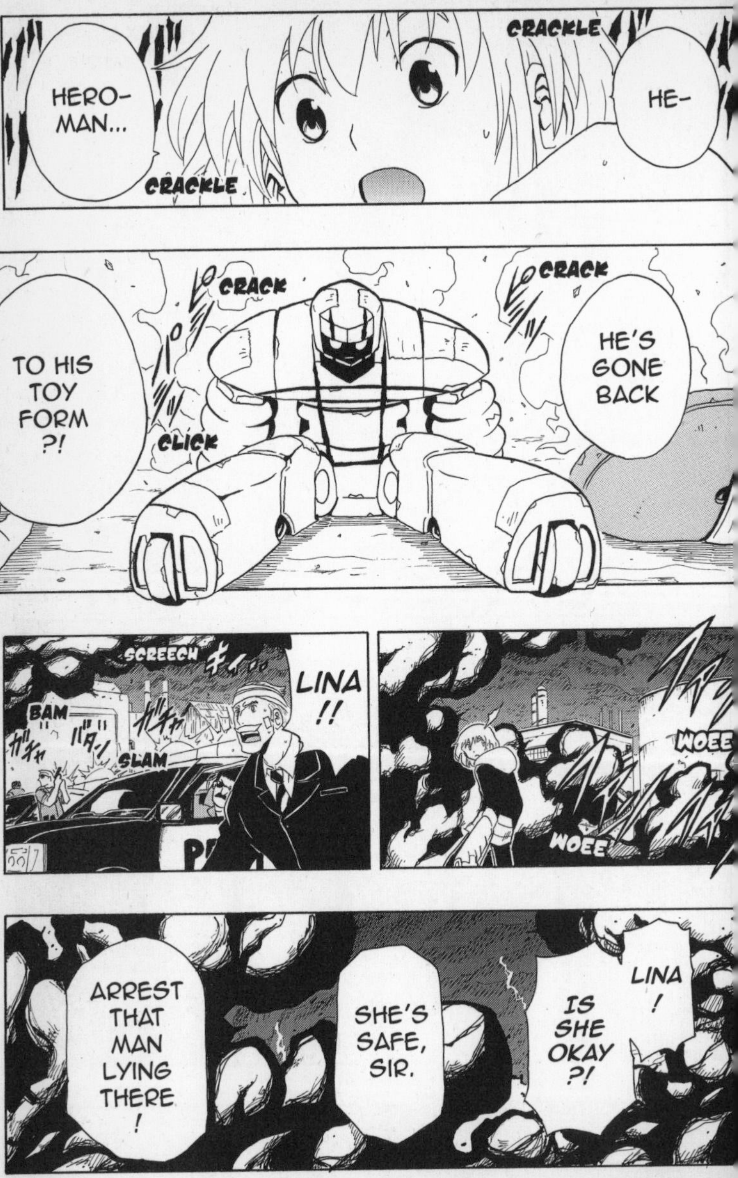
CRACKLE
HE-
HERO-MAN...
CRACKLE
CRACK
HE'S GONE BACK
CRACK
TO HIS TOY FORM ?!
CLICK
WOEE
WOEE
LINA !!
SCREECH
BAM
SLAM
LINA !
IS SHE OKAY ?!
SHE'S SAFE, SIR.
ARREST THAT MAN LYING THERE !

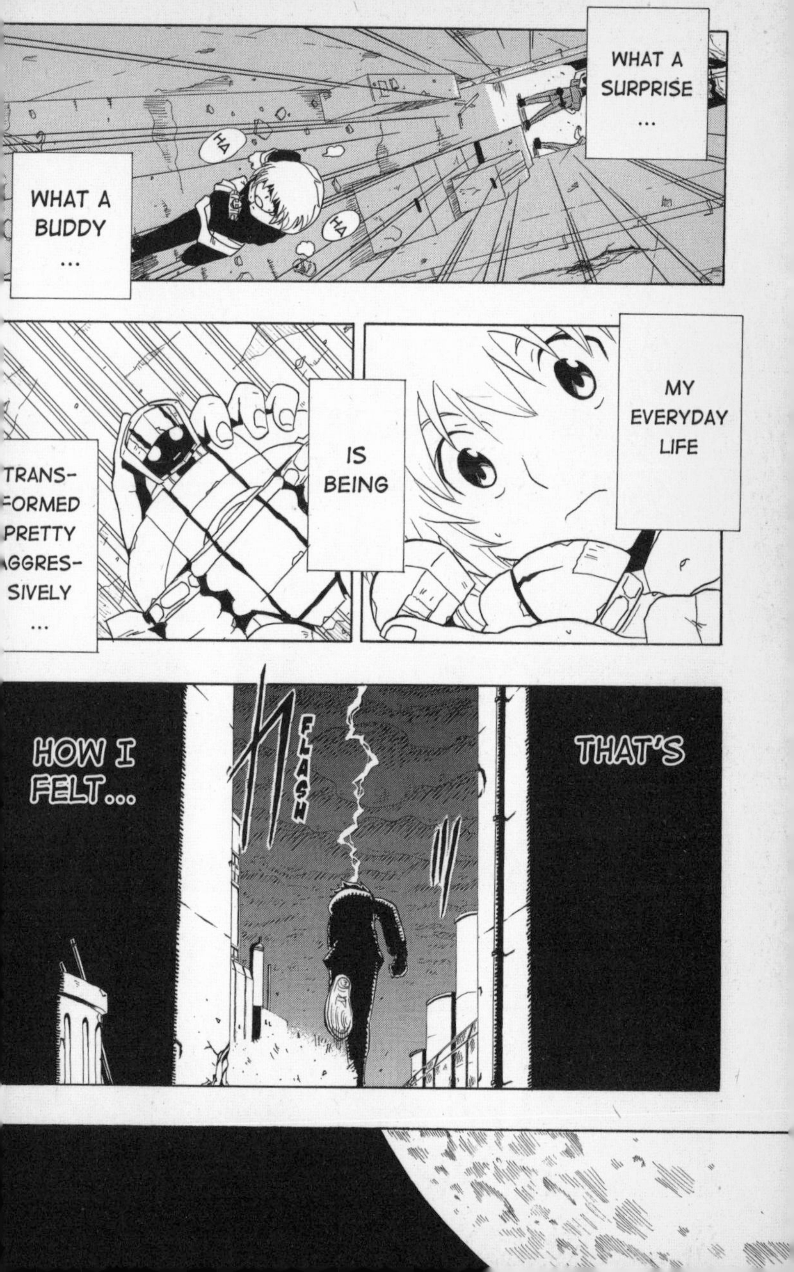
WHAT A SURPRISE ...
HA
HA
WHAT A BUDDY ...
MY EVERYDAY LIFE
IS BEING
TRANS-FORMED PRETTY AGGRES-SIVELY ...
THAT'S
FLASH
HOW I FELT...

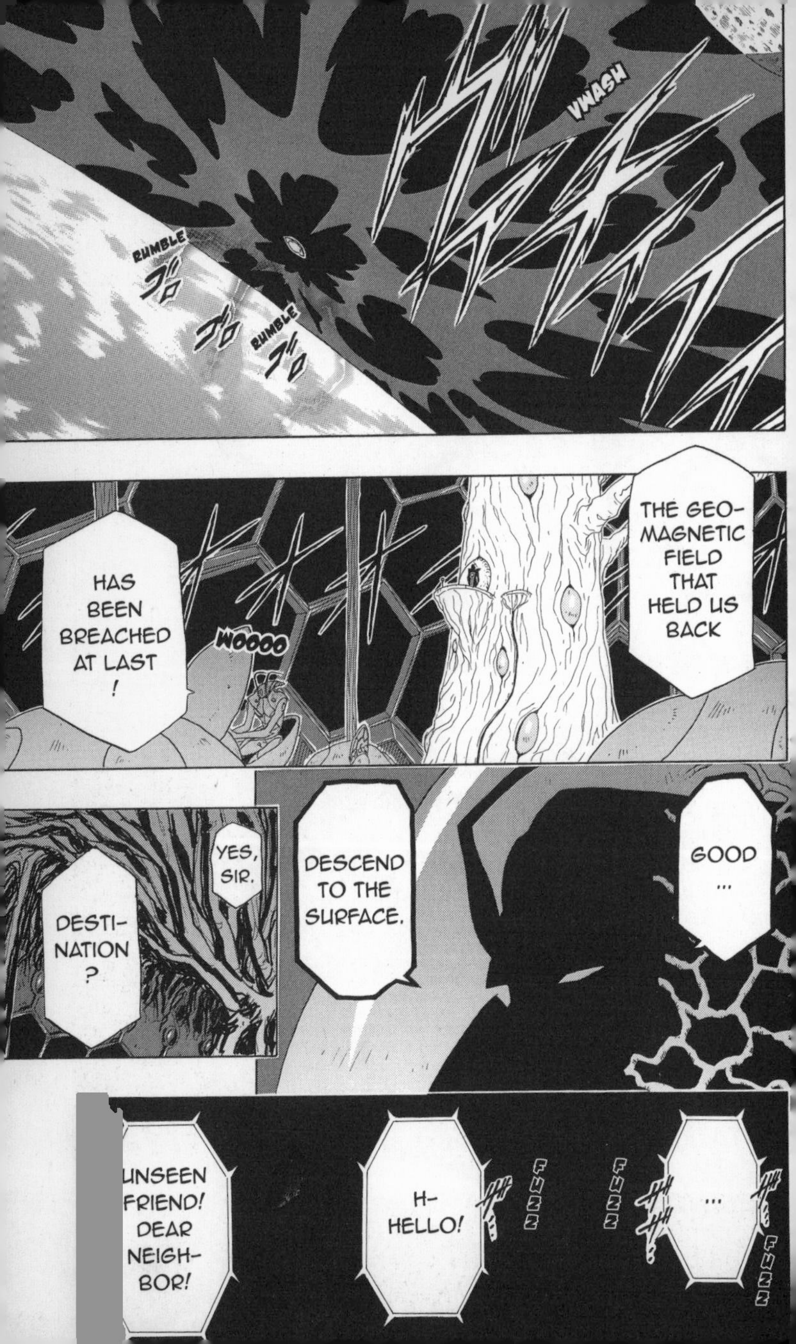
VWASH
RUMBLE
ゴロ
ゴロ
RUMBLE
ゴロ
THE GEO-MAGNETIC FIELD THAT HELD US BACK
WOOOO
HAS BEEN BREACHED AT LAST!
GOOD...
DESCEND TO THE SURFACE.
YES, SIR.
DESTINATION?
...
FUZZ
FUZZ
FUZZ
H-HELLO!
UNSEEN FRIEND! DEAR NEIGHBOR!

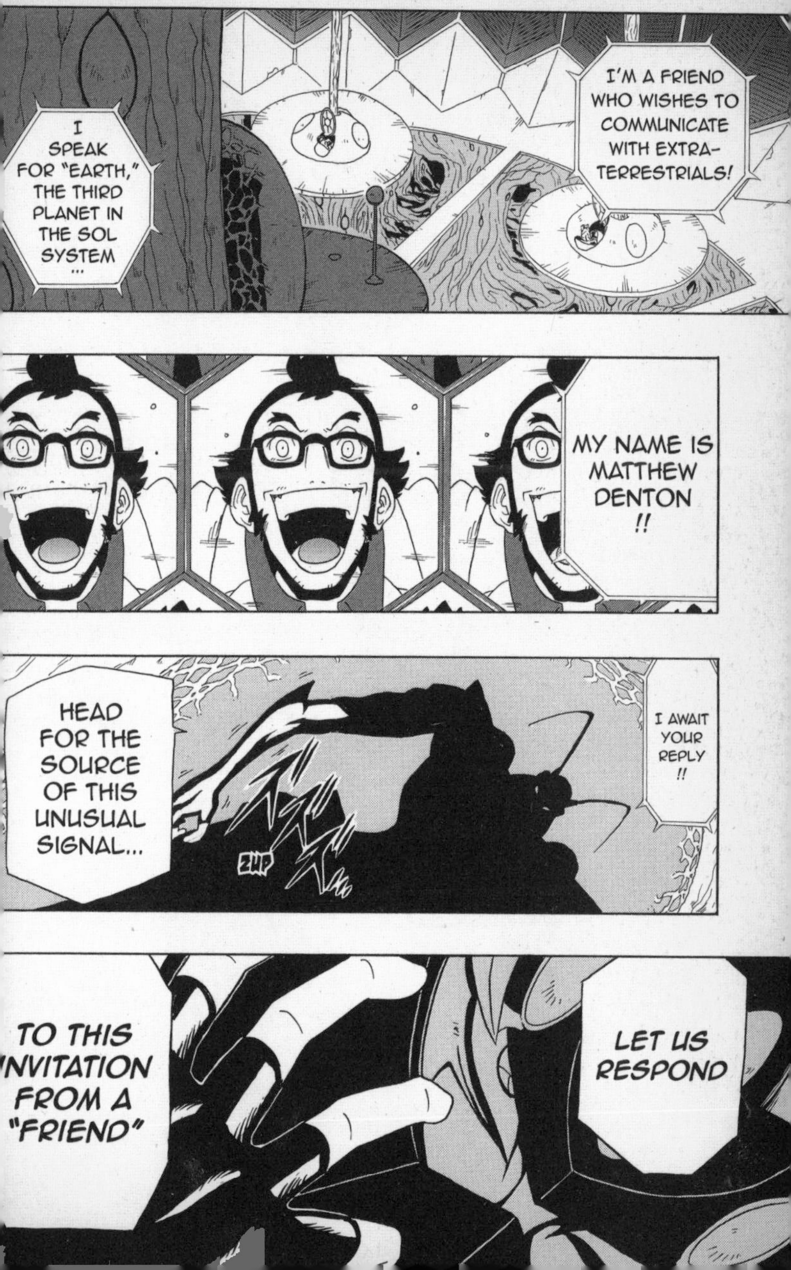
I'M A FRIEND WHO WISHES TO COMMUNICATE WITH EXTRA-TERRESTRIALS!
I SPEAK FOR "EARTH," THE THIRD PLANET IN THE SOL SYSTEM ...
MY NAME IS MATTHEW DENTON !!
I AWAIT YOUR REPLY !!
HEAD FOR THE SOURCE OF THIS UNUSUAL SIGNAL...
ZUP
LET US RESPOND
TO THIS INVITATION FROM A "FRIEND"

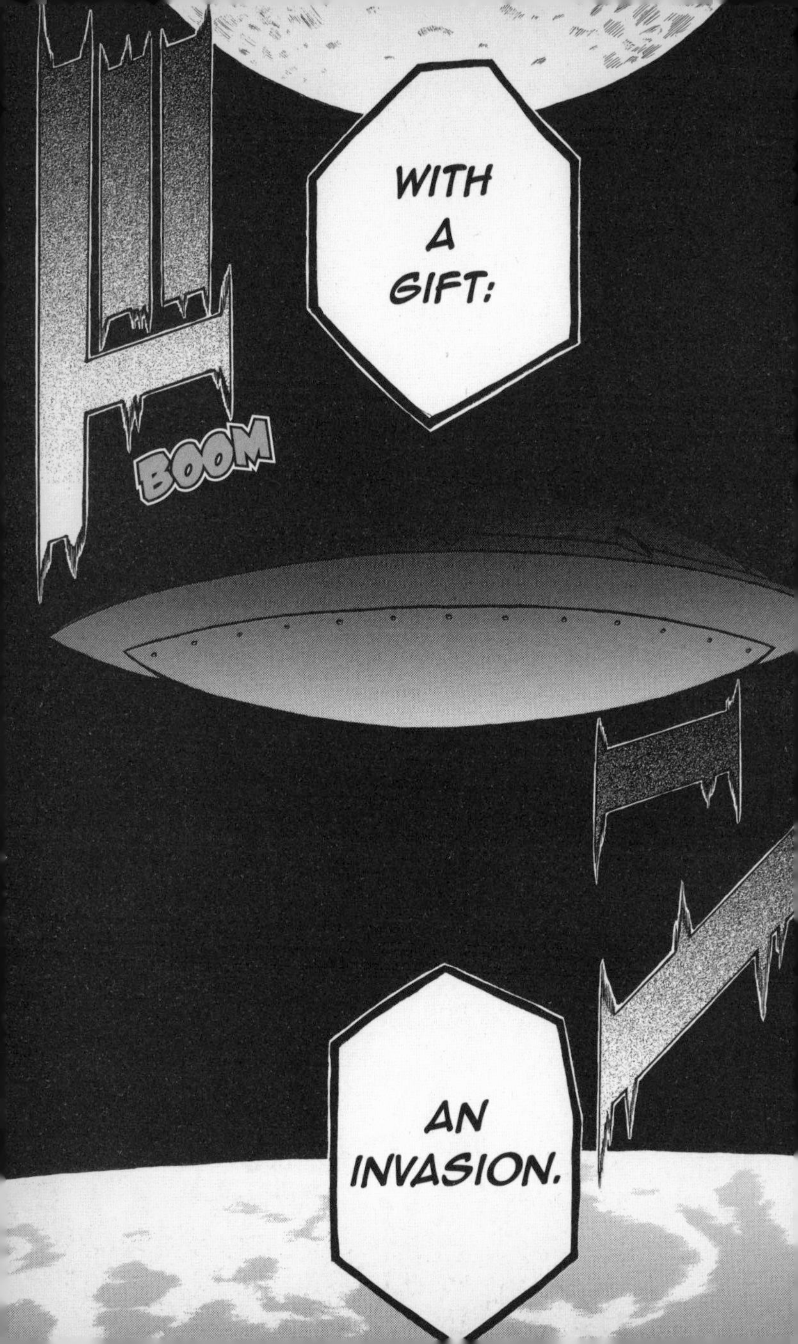
WITH A GIFT:
BOOM
AN INVASION.

HEROMAN

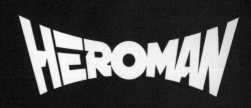

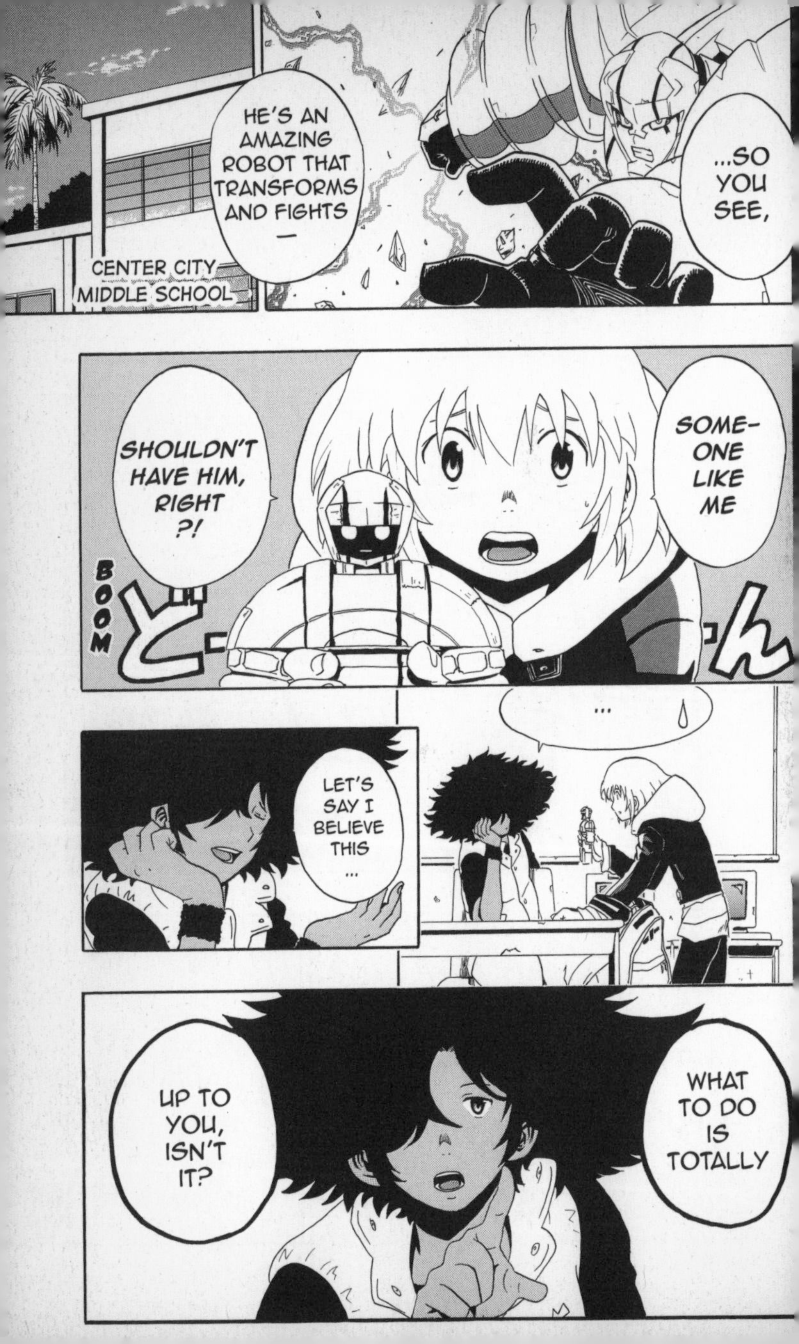
...SO YOU SEE,
HE'S AN AMAZING ROBOT THAT TRANSFORMS AND FIGHTS —
CENTER CITY MIDDLE SCHOOL
SOME-ONE LIKE ME
SHOULDN'T HAVE HIM, RIGHT ?!
BOOM
...
LET'S SAY I BELIEVE THIS ...
WHAT TO DO IS TOTALLY
UP TO YOU, ISN'T IT?

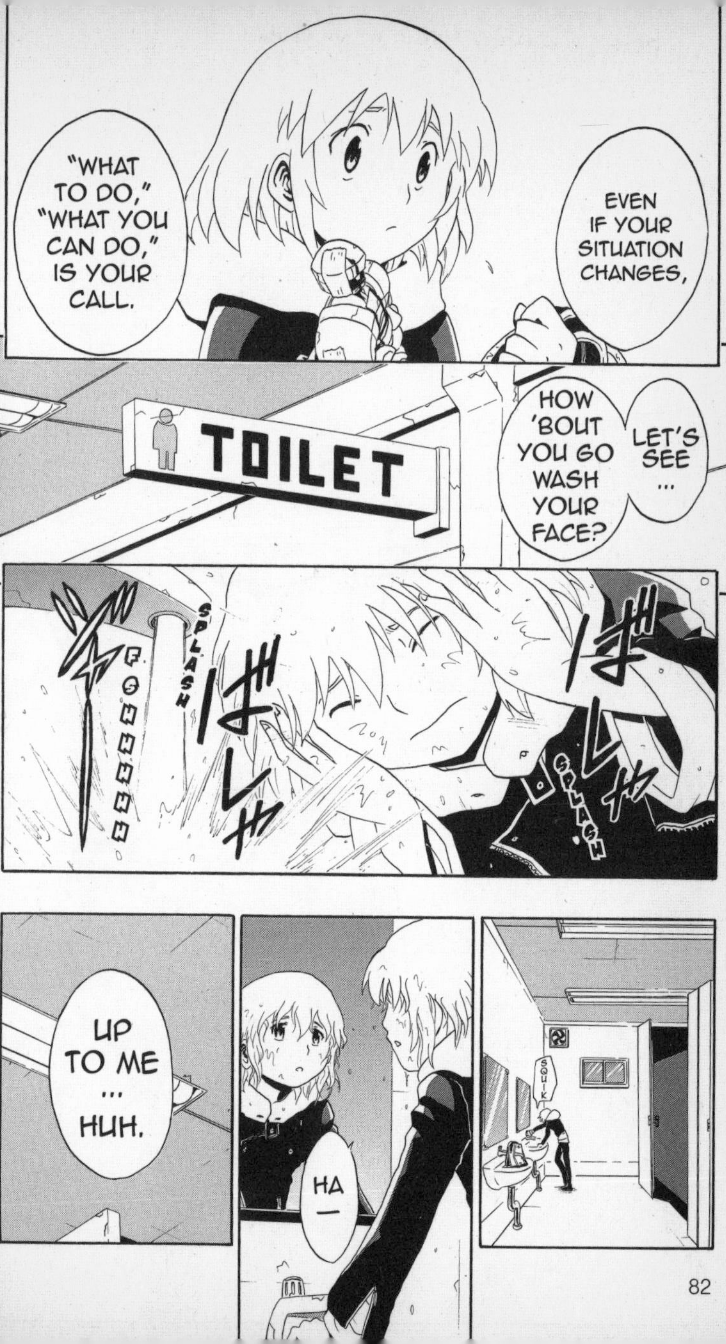
EVEN IF YOUR SITUATION CHANGES,
"WHAT TO DO," "WHAT YOU CAN DO," IS YOUR CALL.
LET'S SEE ...
HOW 'BOUT YOU GO WASH YOUR FACE?
TOILET
ばしゃ
SPLASH
ばしゃ
SPLASH
FSHHHHHHHH
SQUIK
HA —
UP TO ME ... HUH.

#02 CONTACT

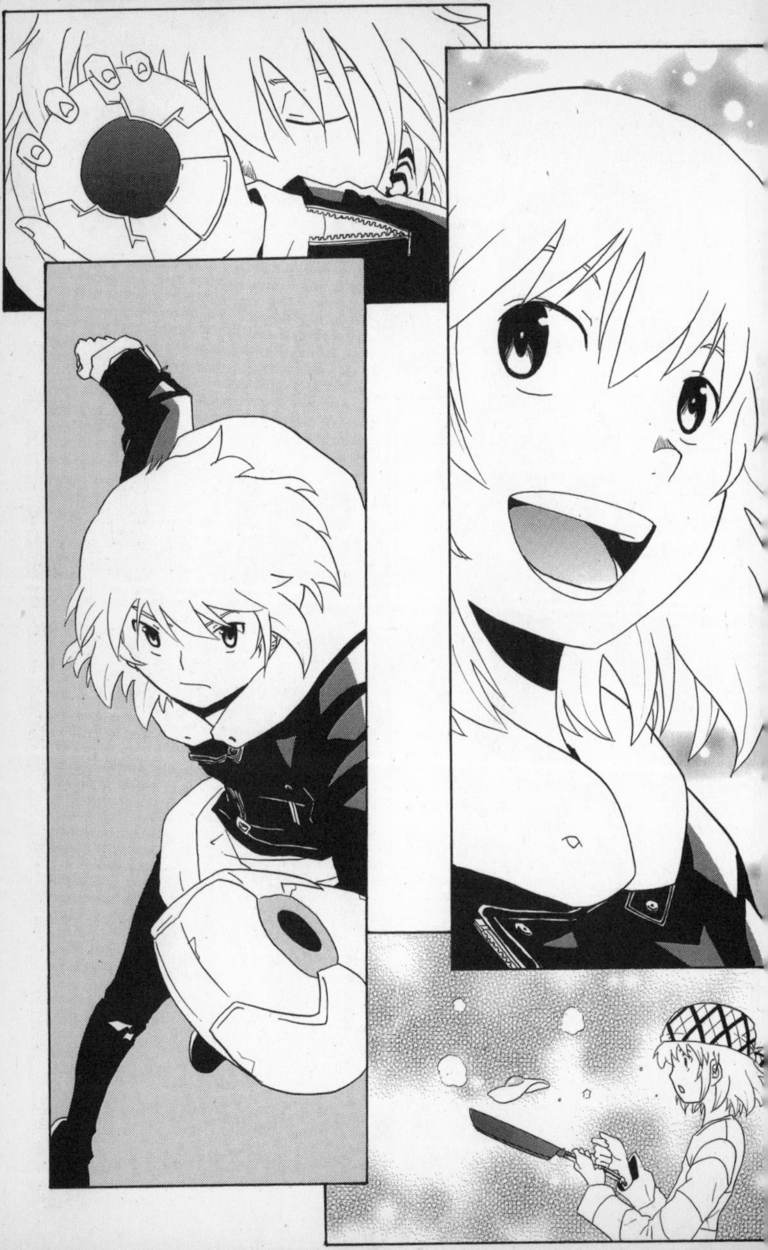

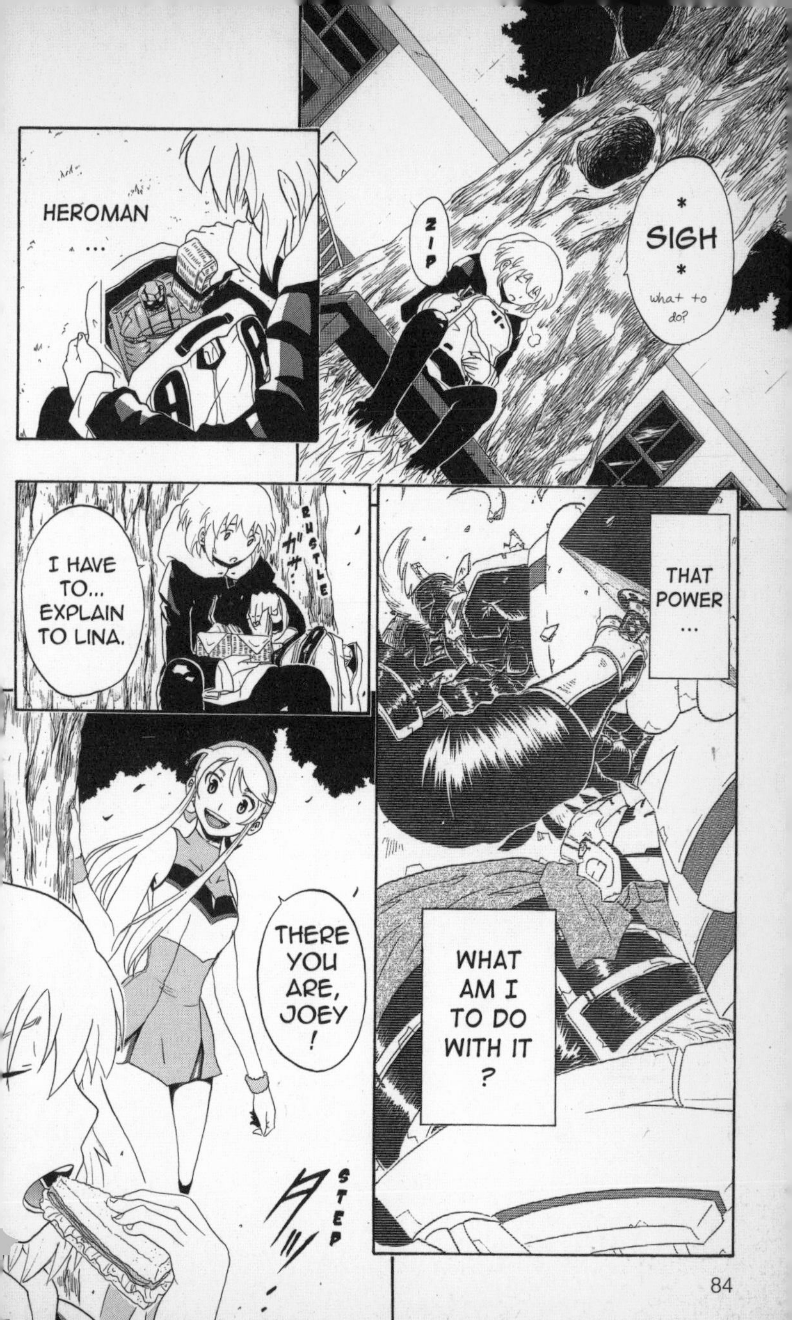
* SIGH *
what to do?
ZIP
HEROMAN ...
THAT POWER ...
WHAT AM I TO DO WITH IT ?
I HAVE TO... EXPLAIN TO LINA.
ガサ RUSTLE
THERE YOU ARE, JOEY !
STEP

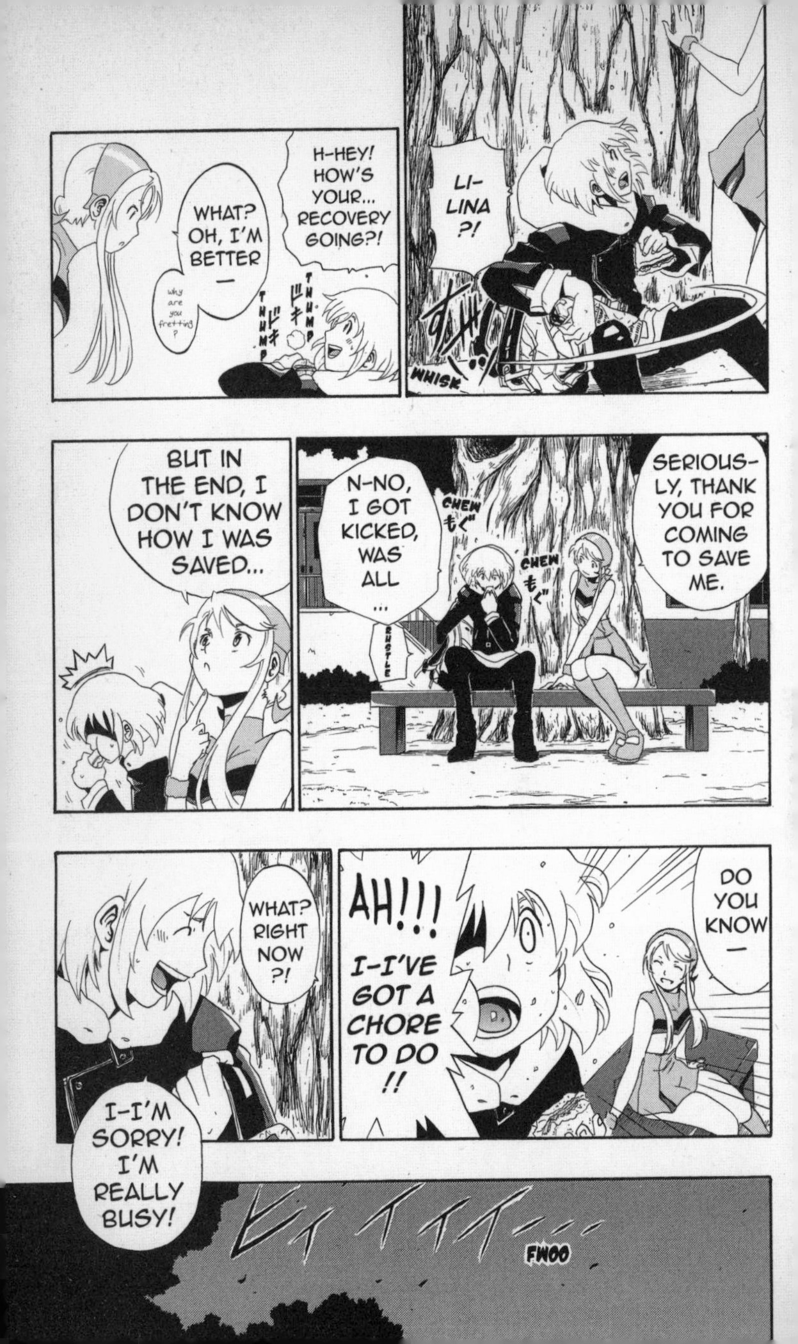
LI-LINA?!
WHISK
H-HEY! HOW'S YOUR... RECOVERY GOING?!
THUMP THUMP
WHAT? OH, I'M BETTER —
why are you fretting?
SERIOUSLY, THANK YOU FOR COMING TO SAVE ME.
CHEW
CHEW
N-NO, I GOT KICKED, WAS ALL...
RUSTLE
BUT IN THE END, I DON'T KNOW HOW I WAS SAVED...
DO YOU KNOW —
AH!!!
I-I'VE GOT A CHORE TO DO!!
WHAT? RIGHT NOW?!
I-I'M SORRY! I'M REALLY BUSY!
FWOO

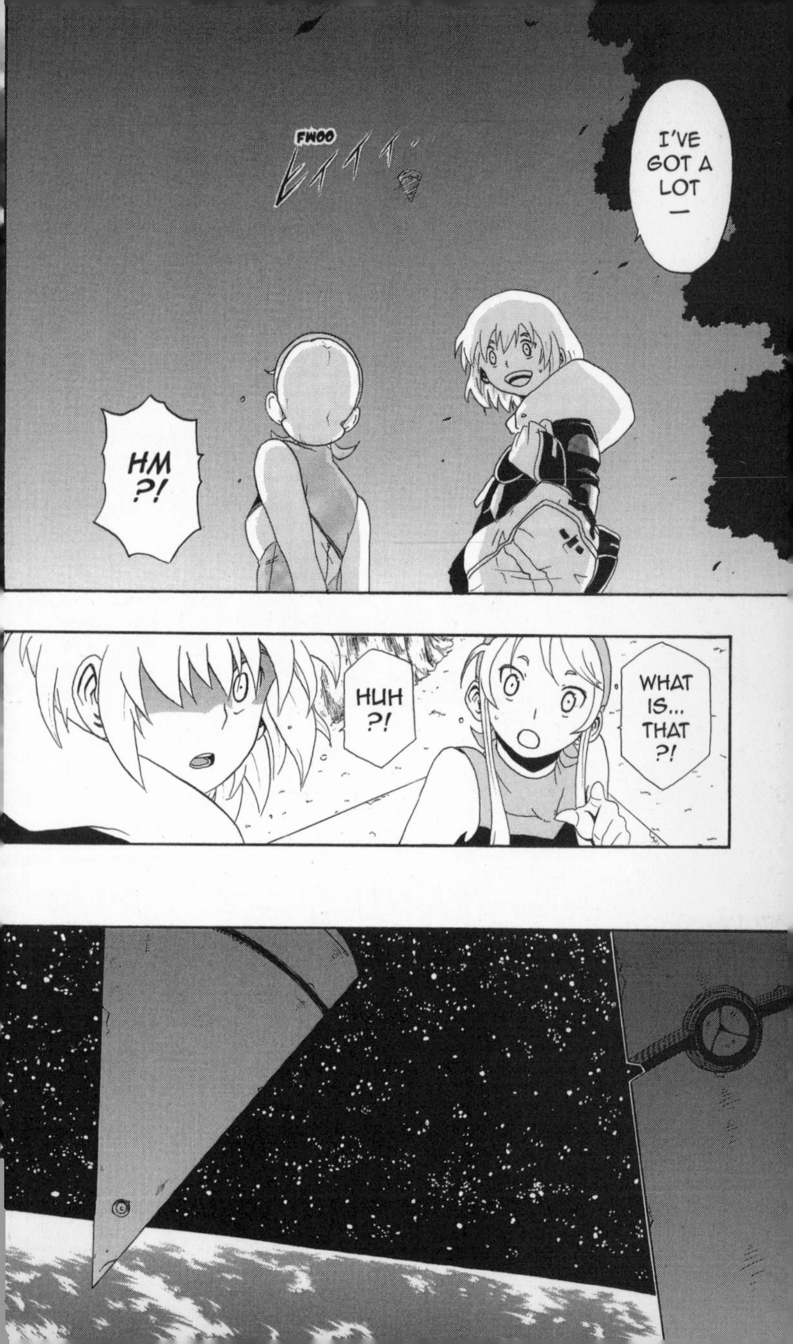
I'VE GOT A LOT —
FWOO
HM ?!
WHAT IS... THAT ?!
HUH ?!

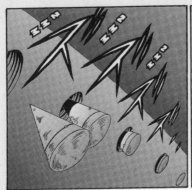

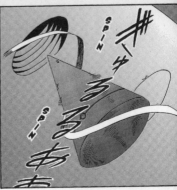

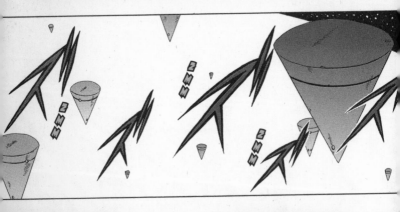

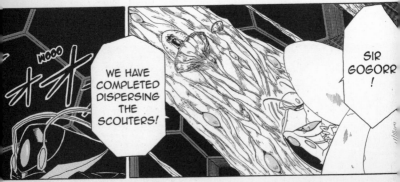

SPIN
SPIN
ZMM
ZMM
ZMM
ZMM
ZMM
ZMM
SIR GOGORR!
WE HAVE COMPLETED DISPERSING THE SCOUTERS!
WOOO

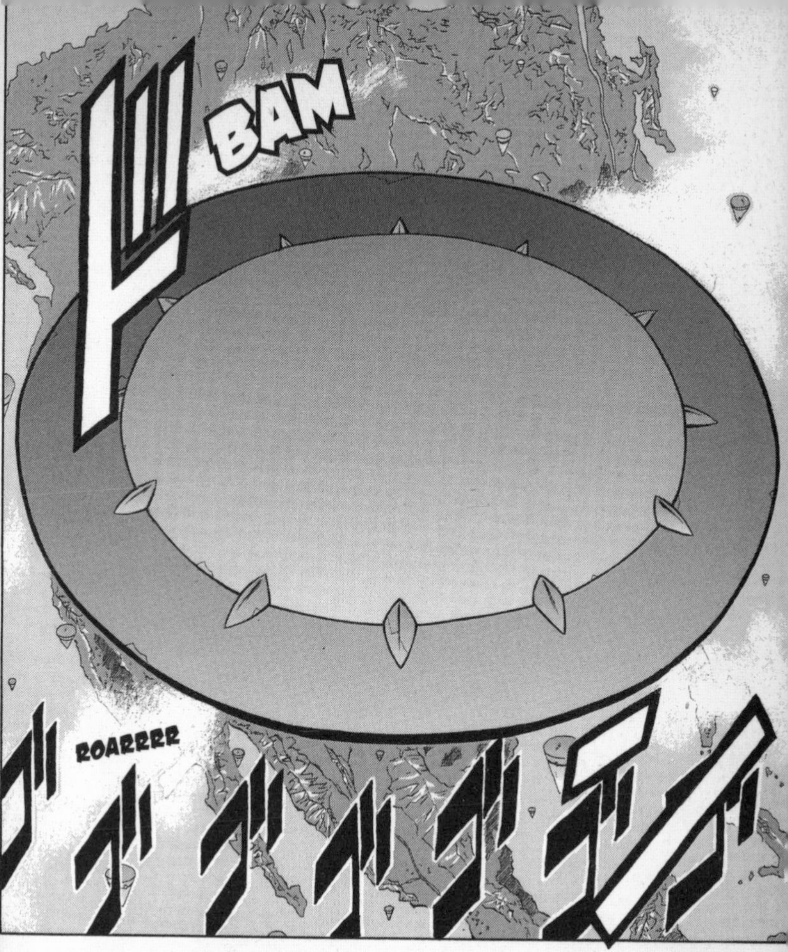
BAM
ROARRRR

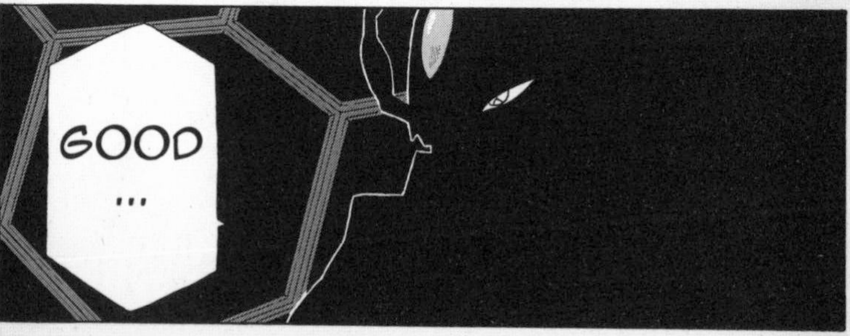
GOOD
...

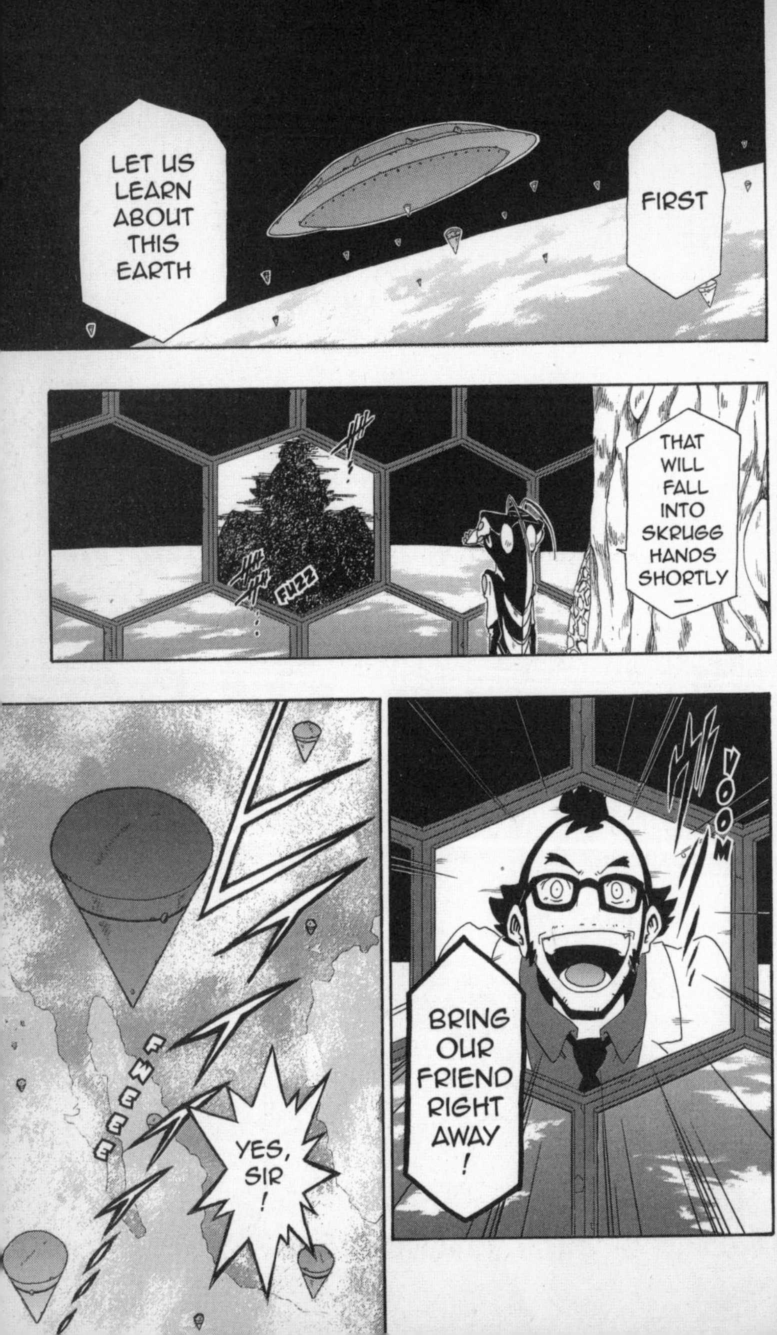
FIRST
LET US LEARN ABOUT THIS EARTH
THAT WILL FALL INTO SKRUGG HANDS SHORTLY —
FUZZ
VOOOM
BRING OUR FRIEND RIGHT AWAY!
YES, SIR!
FWEEEE

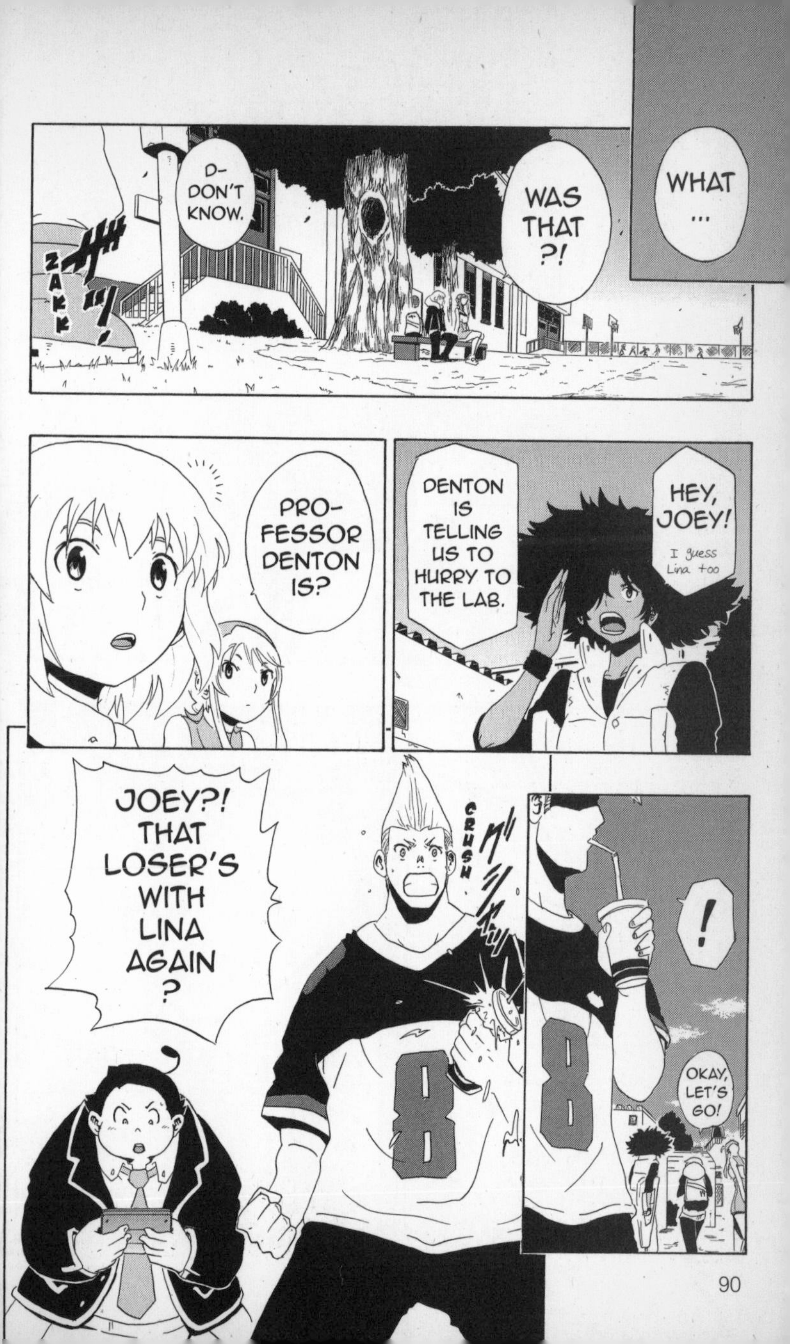

WHAT ...
WAS THAT ?!
D- DON'T KNOW.
ZAKK
HEY, JOEY!
I guess Lina too
DENTON IS TELLING US TO HURRY TO THE LAB.
PRO-FESSOR DENTON IS?
!
OKAY, LET'S GO!
CRUSH
JOEY?! THAT LOSER'S WITH LINA AGAIN ?

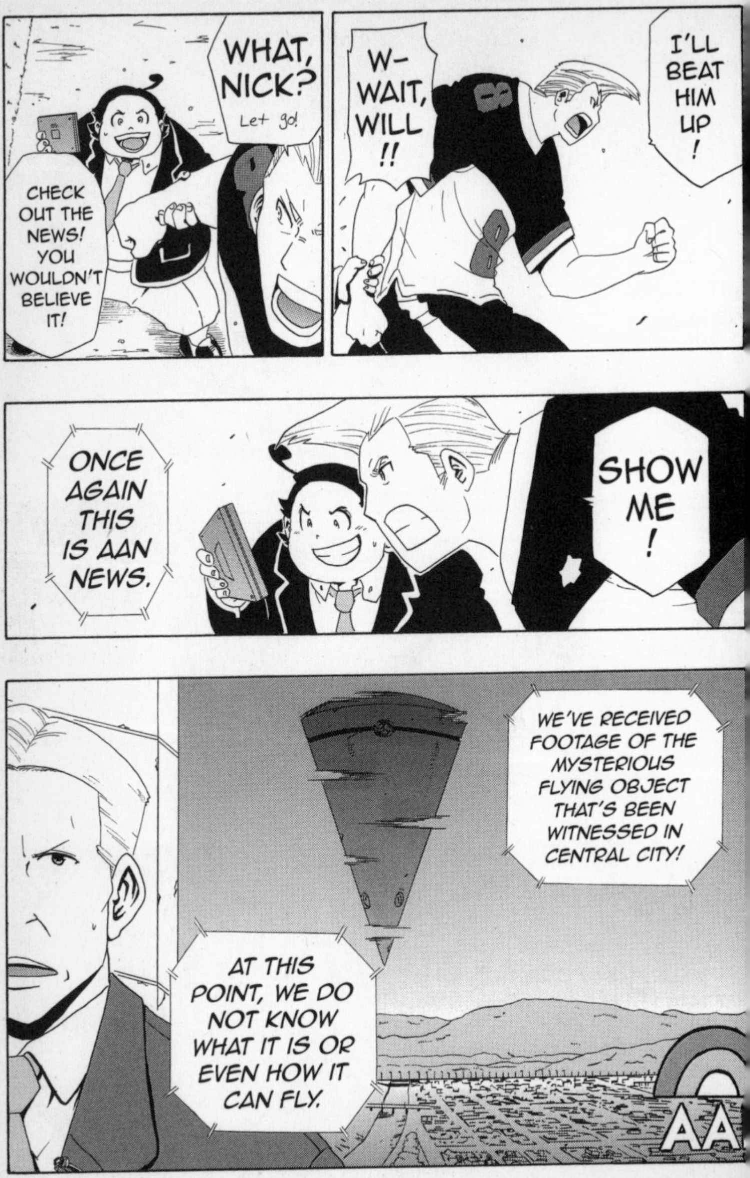
I'LL BEAT HIM UP!
W-WAIT, WILL!!
WHAT, NICK?
Let go!
CHECK OUT THE NEWS! YOU WOULDN'T BELIEVE IT!
SHOW ME!
ONCE AGAIN THIS IS AAN NEWS.
WE'VE RECEIVED FOOTAGE OF THE MYSTERIOUS FLYING OBJECT THAT'S BEEN WITNESSED IN CENTRAL CITY!
AT THIS POINT, WE DO NOT KNOW WHAT IT IS OR EVEN HOW IT CAN FLY.
AA

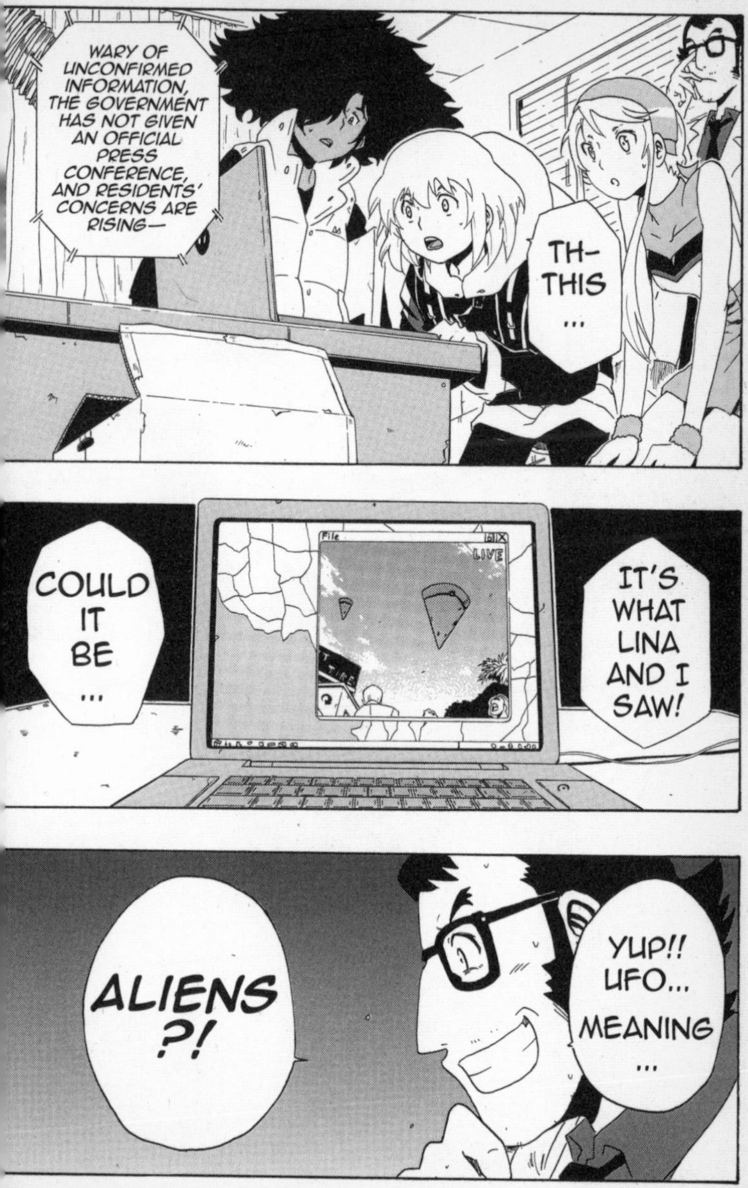
WARY OF UNCONFIRMED INFORMATION, THE GOVERNMENT HAS NOT GIVEN AN OFFICIAL PRESS CONFERENCE, AND RESIDENTS' CONCERNS ARE RISING—
TH-THIS ...
IT'S WHAT LINA AND I SAW!
File
LIVE
COULD IT BE ...
YUP!! UFO... MEANING ...
ALIENS ?!

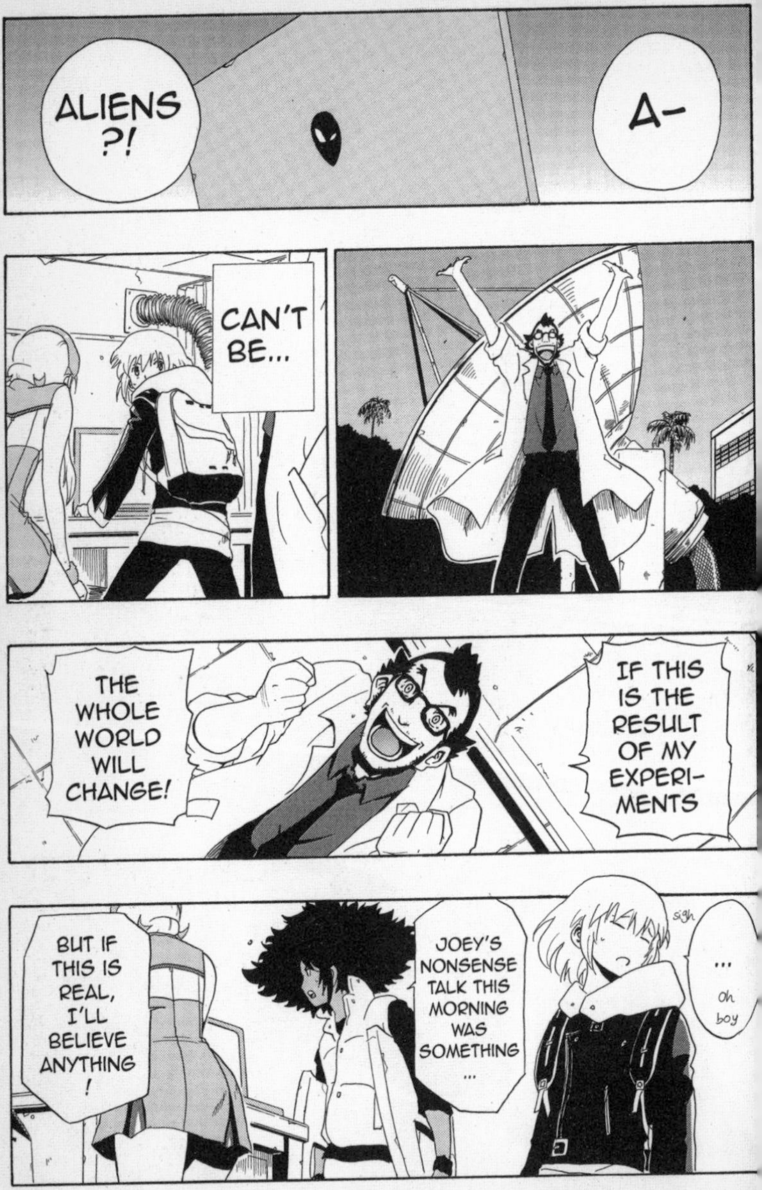
A-
ALIENS ?!
CAN'T BE...
IF THIS IS THE RESULT OF MY EXPERIMENTS
THE WHOLE WORLD WILL CHANGE!
sigh
... oh boy
JOEY'S NONSENSE TALK THIS MORNING WAS SOMETHING ...
BUT IF THIS IS REAL, I'LL BELIEVE ANYTHING!

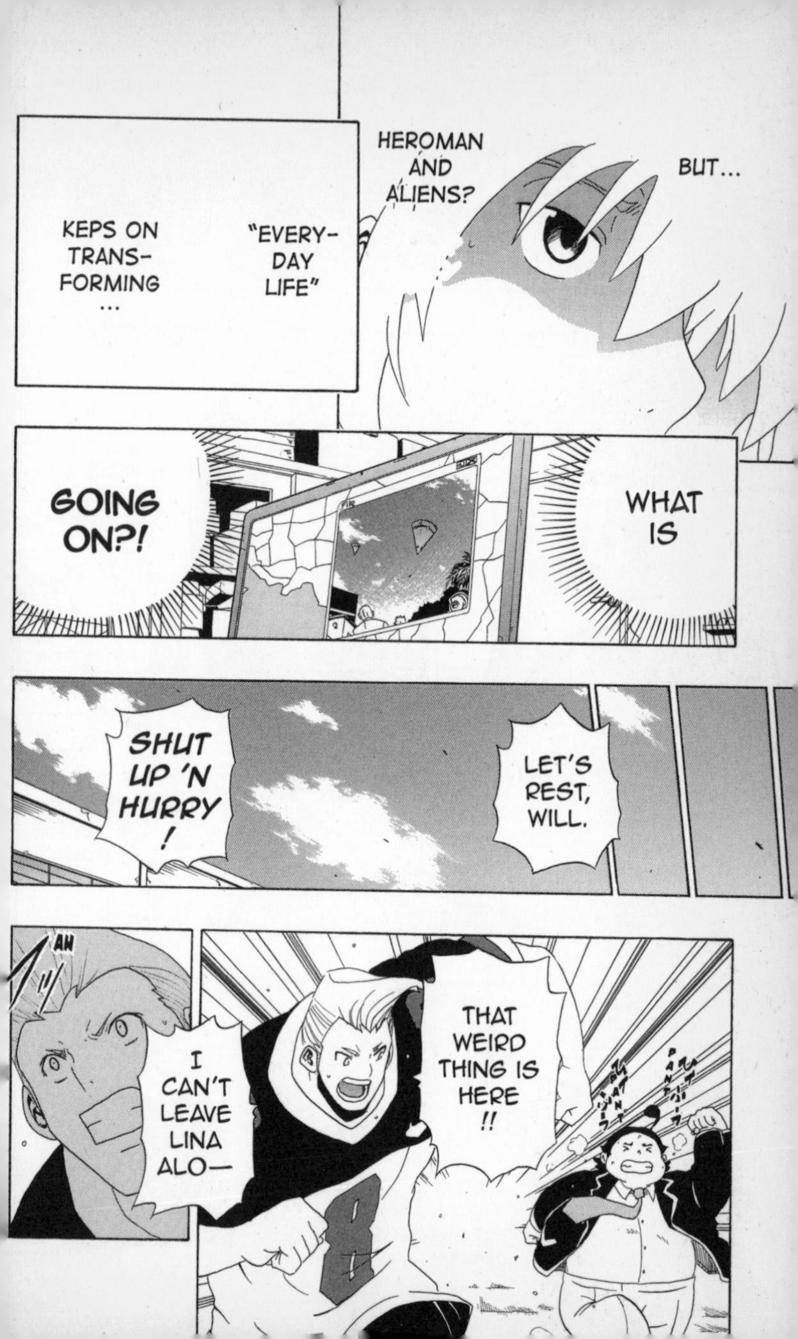
HEROMAN AND ALIENS?
BUT...
"EVERY-DAY LIFE"
KEPS ON TRANS-FORMING ...
WHAT IS
GOING ON?!
LET'S REST, WILL.
SHUT UP 'N HURRY!
THAT WEIRD THING IS HERE!!
AH
I CAN'T LEAVE LINA ALO—

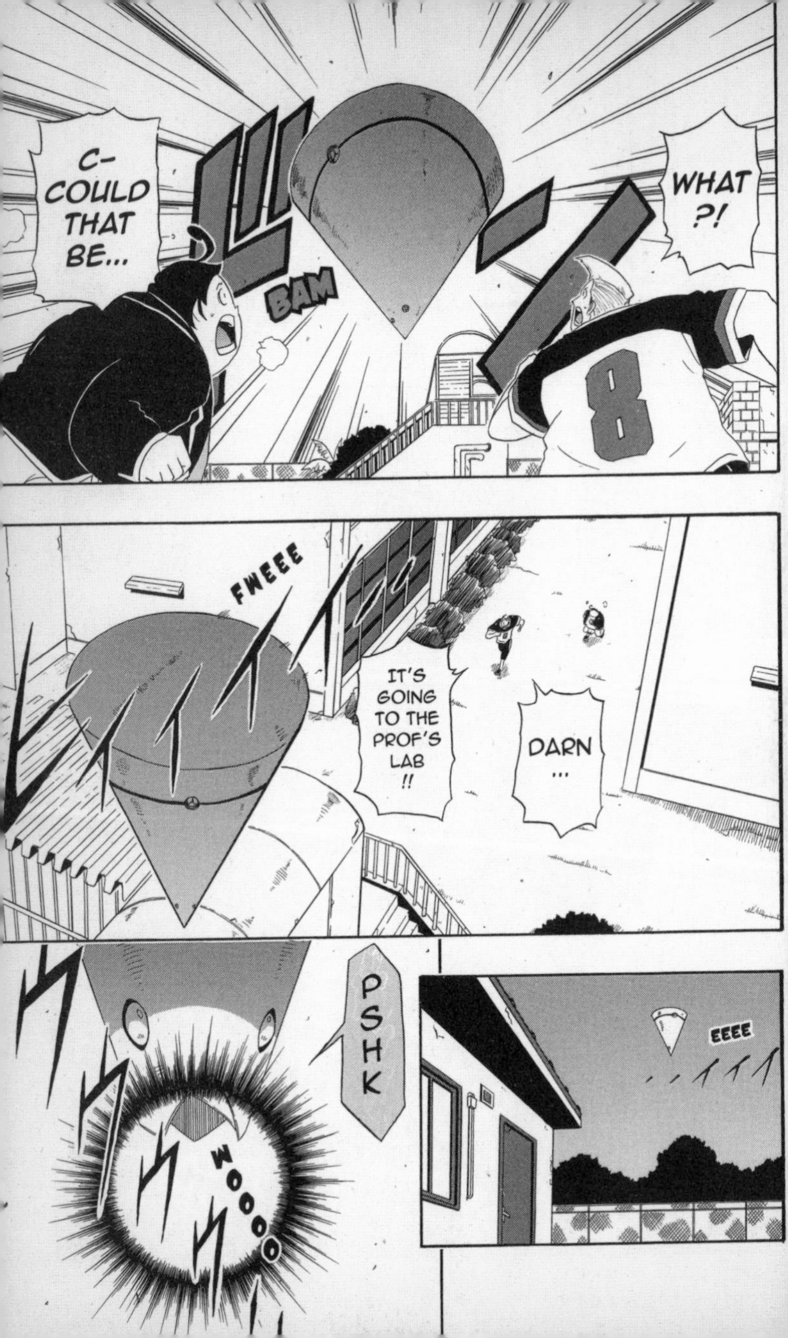
WHAT ?!
C-COULD THAT BE...
BAM
FWEEE
IT'S GOING TO THE PROF'S LAB !!
DARN ...
EEEE
PSHK
WOOOO

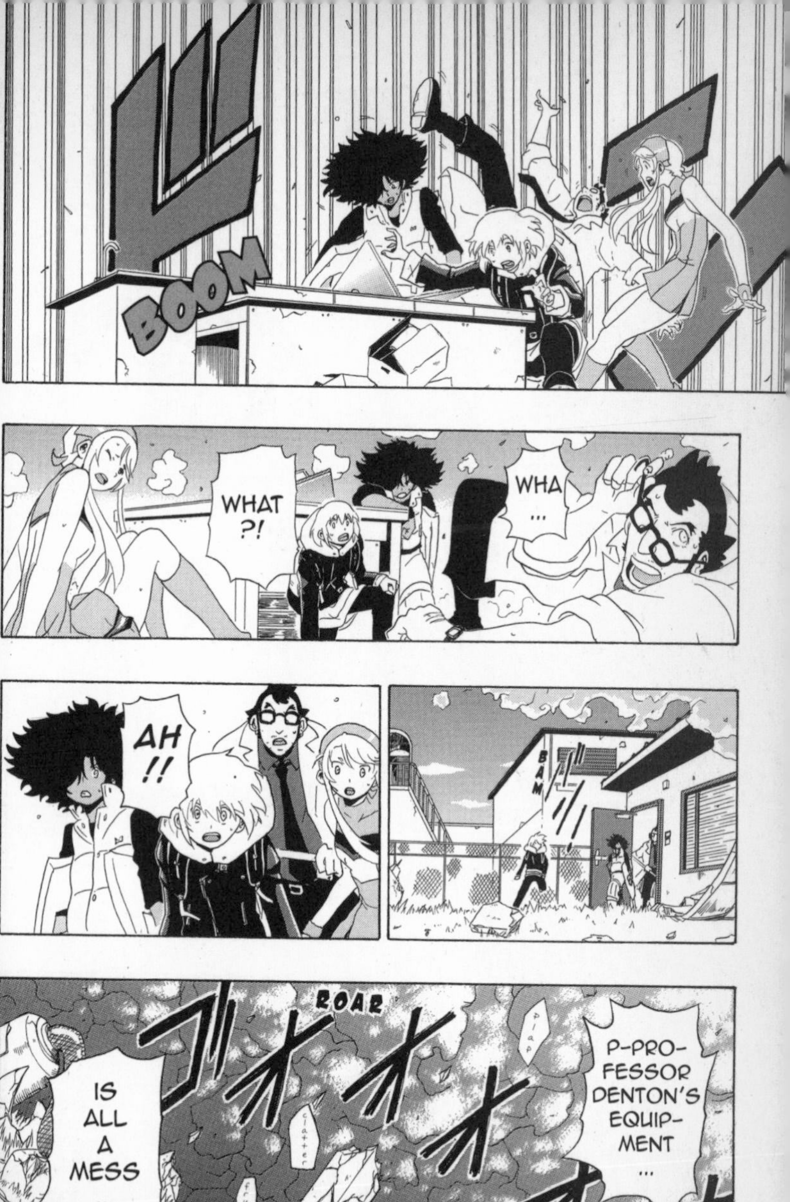
BOOM
WHA ...
WHAT ?!
BAM
AH !!
ROAR
P-PRO-FESSOR DENTON'S EQUIP-MENT ...
plap
clatter
frump
IS ALL A MESS ...

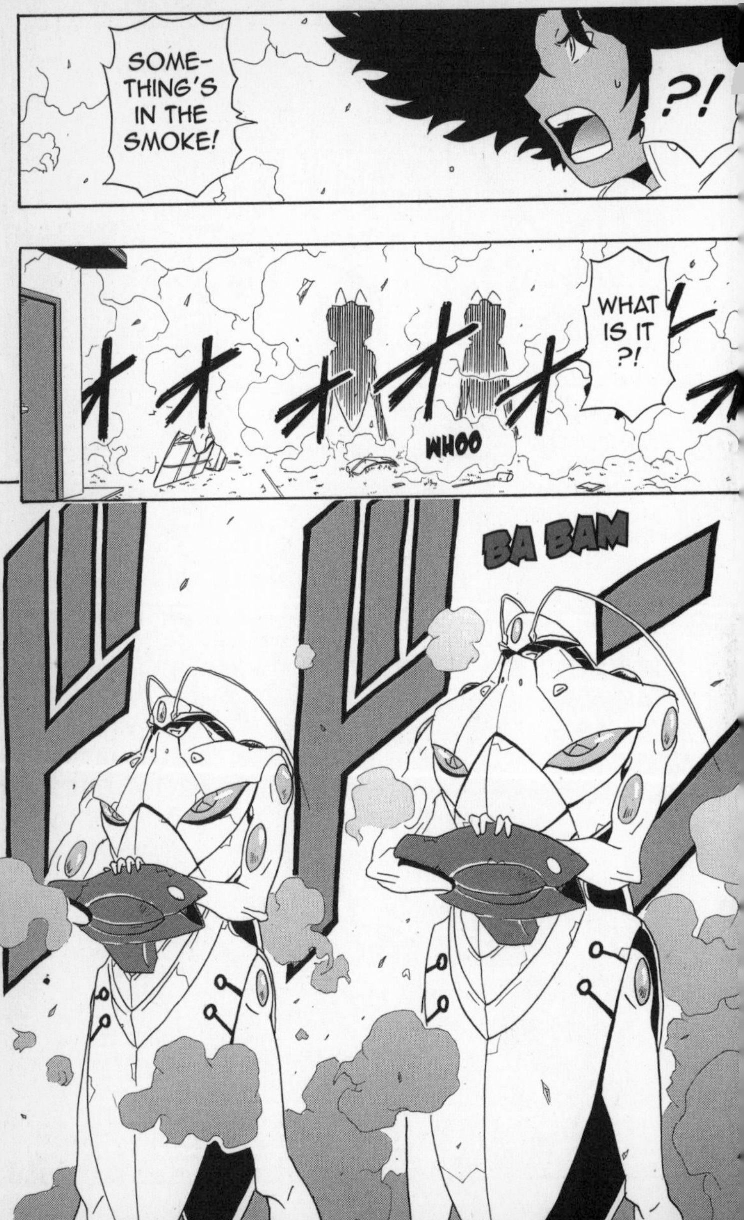
?!
SOME-THING'S IN THE SMOKE!
WHAT IS IT ?!
WHOO
BA BAM

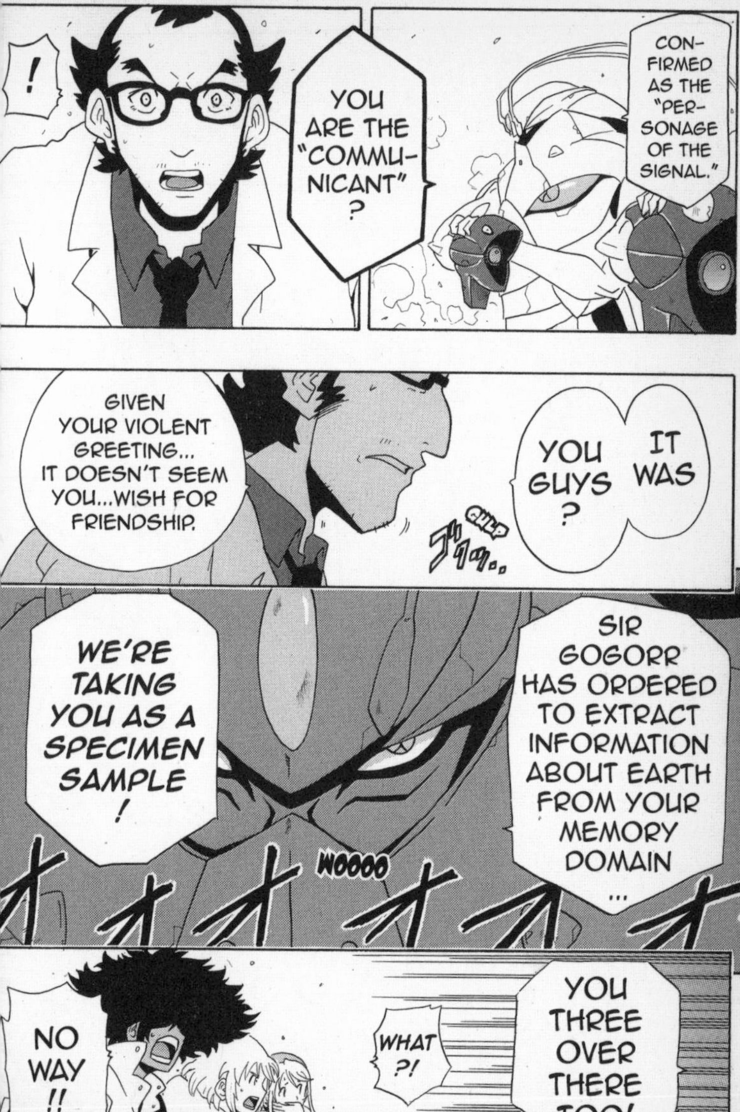
CON-FIRMED AS THE "PER-SONAGE OF THE SIGNAL."
YOU ARE THE "COMMU-NICANT"?
!
IT WAS YOU GUYS?
GULP
GIVEN YOUR VIOLENT GREETING... IT DOESN'T SEEM YOU...WISH FOR FRIENDSHIP.
SIR GOGORR HAS ORDERED TO EXTRACT INFORMATION ABOUT EARTH FROM YOUR MEMORY DOMAIN...
WE'RE TAKING YOU AS A SPECIMEN SAMPLE!
WOOOO
YOU THREE OVER THERE TOO!
WHAT?!
NO WAY!!

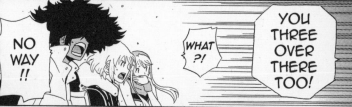

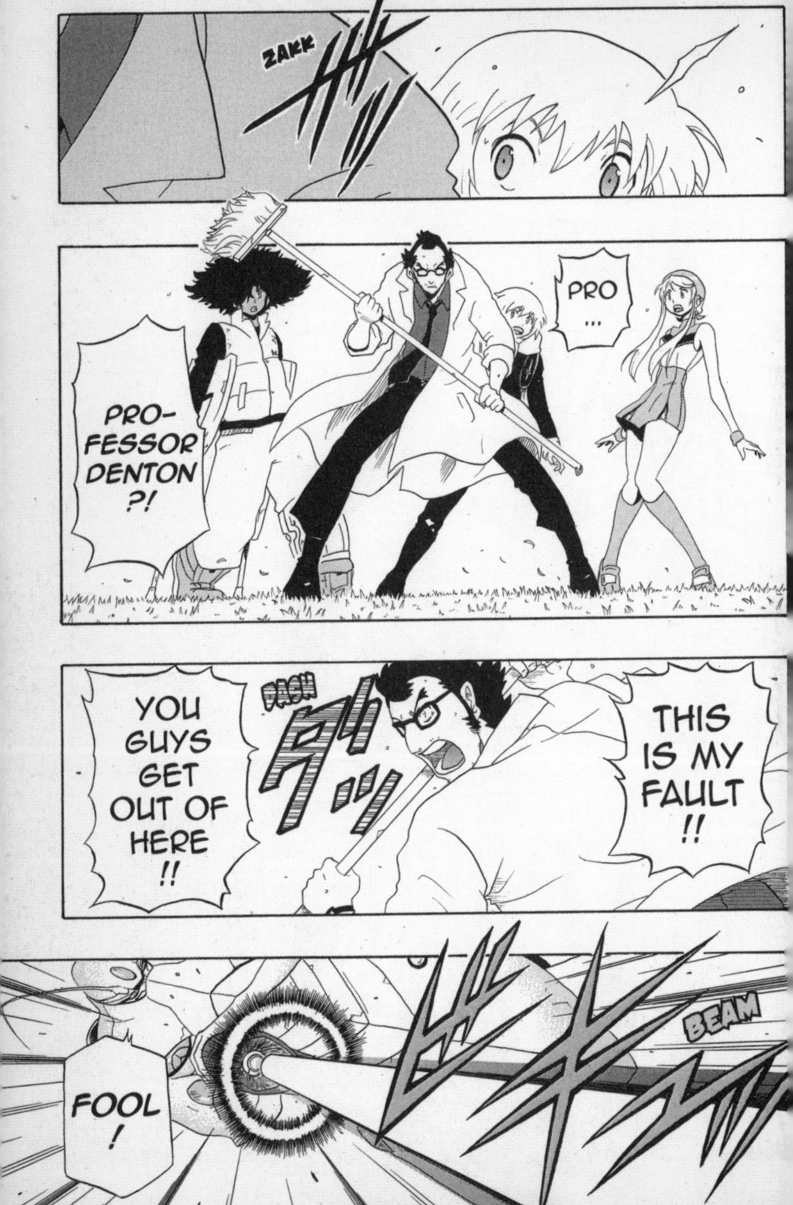
ZAKK
PRO ...
PRO-FESSOR DENTON ?!
THIS IS MY FAULT !!
DASH
YOU GUYS GET OUT OF HERE !!
BEAM
FOOL !

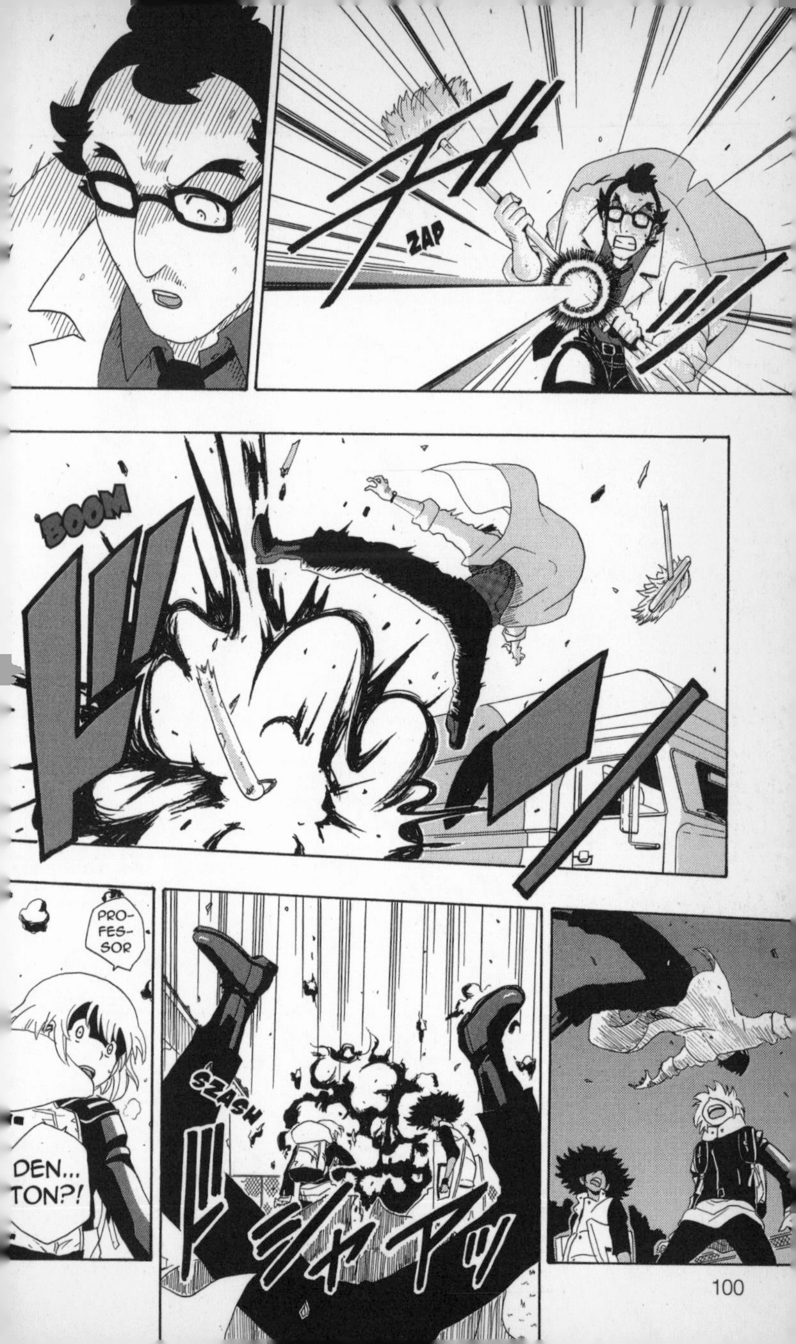
ZAP
BOOM
SZASH
シャアッ
PRO-FES-SOR
DEN... TON?!

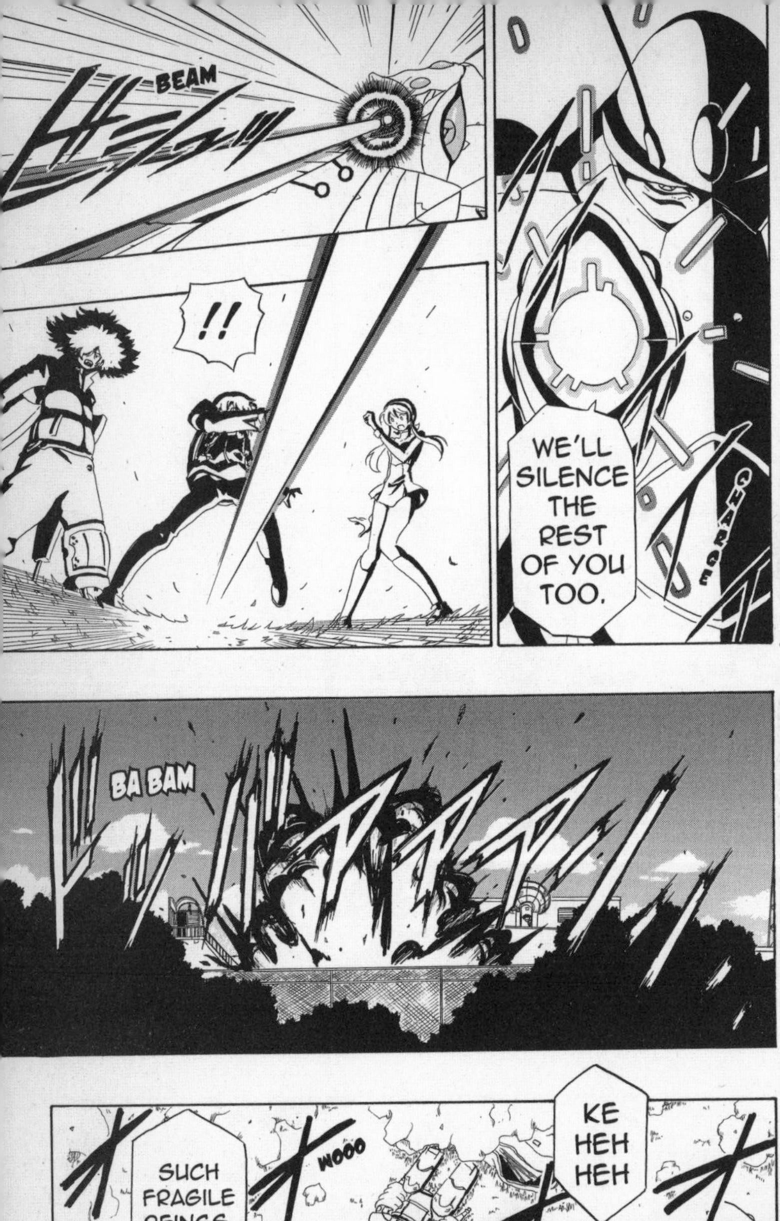
WE'LL SILENCE THE REST OF YOU TOO.
CHARGE
BEAM
!!
BA BAM
KE HEH HEH
WOOO
SUCH FRAGILE BEINGS.

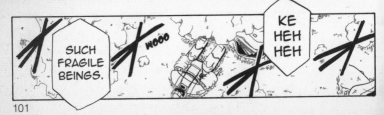

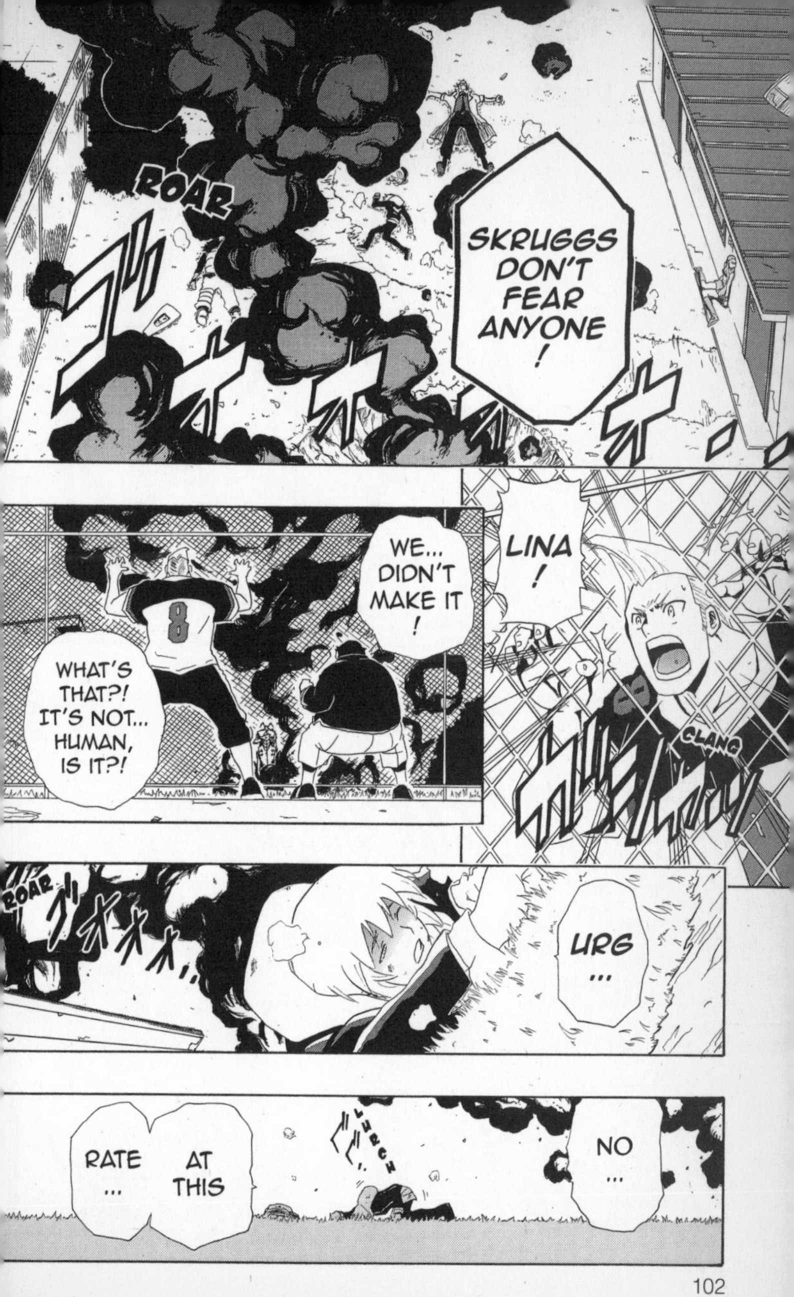
SKRUGGS DON'T FEAR ANYONE!
ROAR
LINA!
CLANG
WE... DIDN'T MAKE IT!
WHAT'S THAT?! IT'S NOT... HUMAN, IS IT?!
URG...
ROAR
NO...
LURCH
AT THIS
RATE...

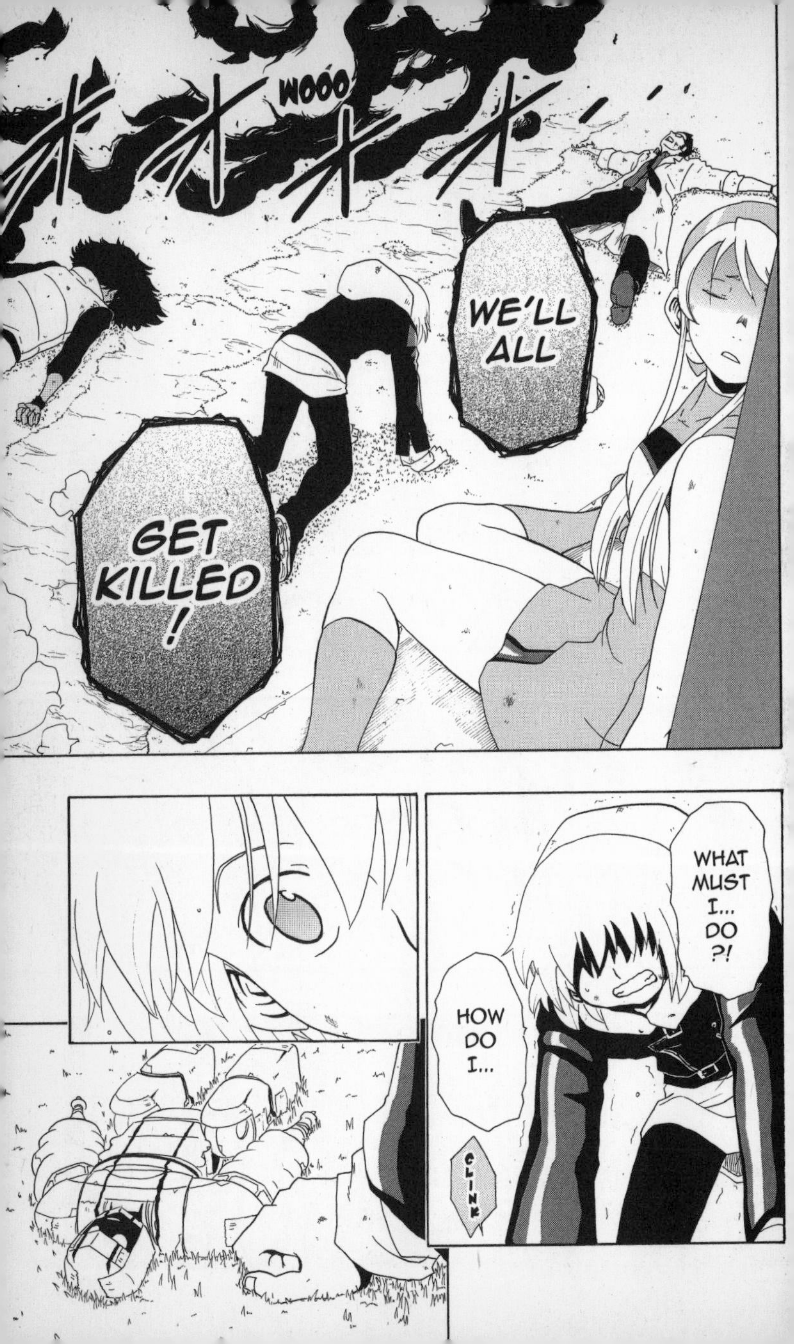
WOOO
WE'LL ALL
GET KILLED!
WHAT MUST I... DO?!
HOW DO I...
CLINK

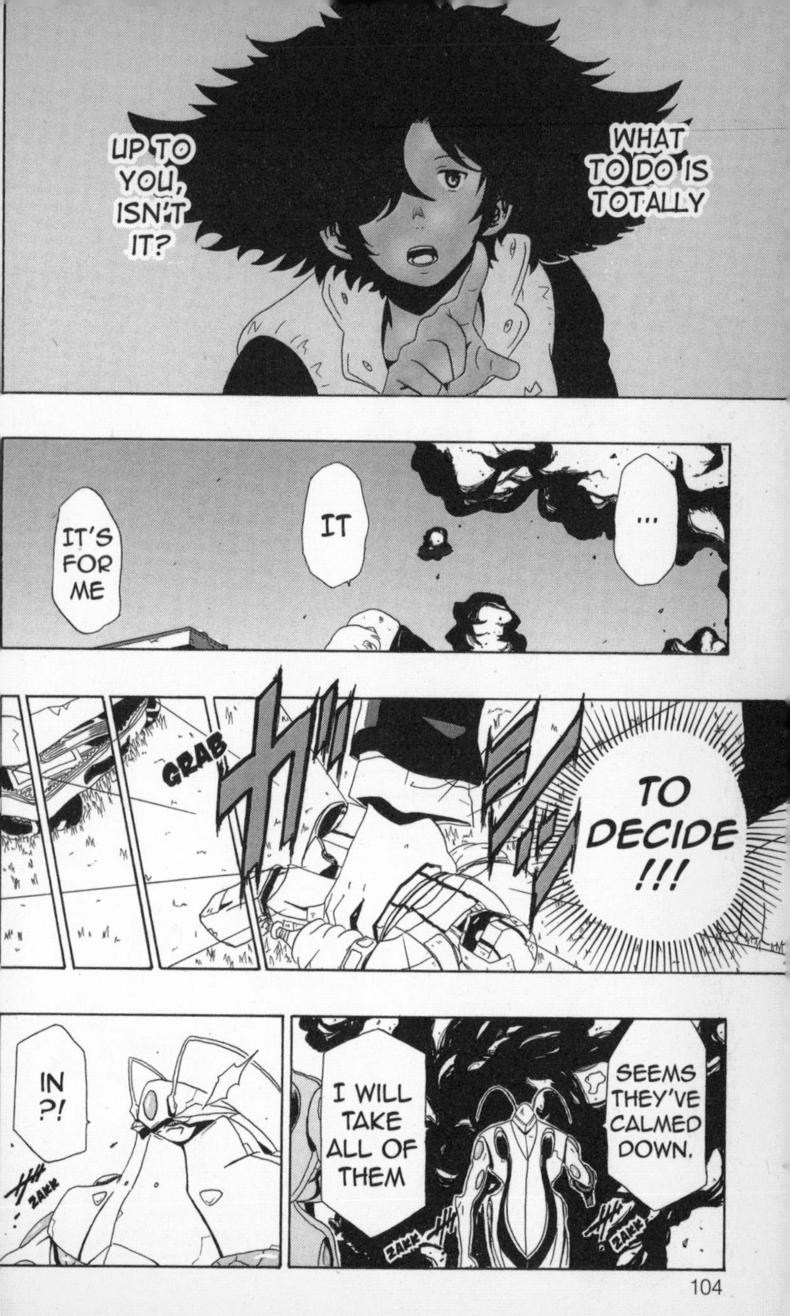
WHAT TO DO IS TOTALLY
UP TO YOU, ISN'T IT?
...
IT
IT'S FOR ME
TO DECIDE !!!
GRAB
SEEMS THEY'VE CALMED DOWN.
I WILL TAKE ALL OF THEM
ZAKK
ZAKK
IN ?!
ZAKK

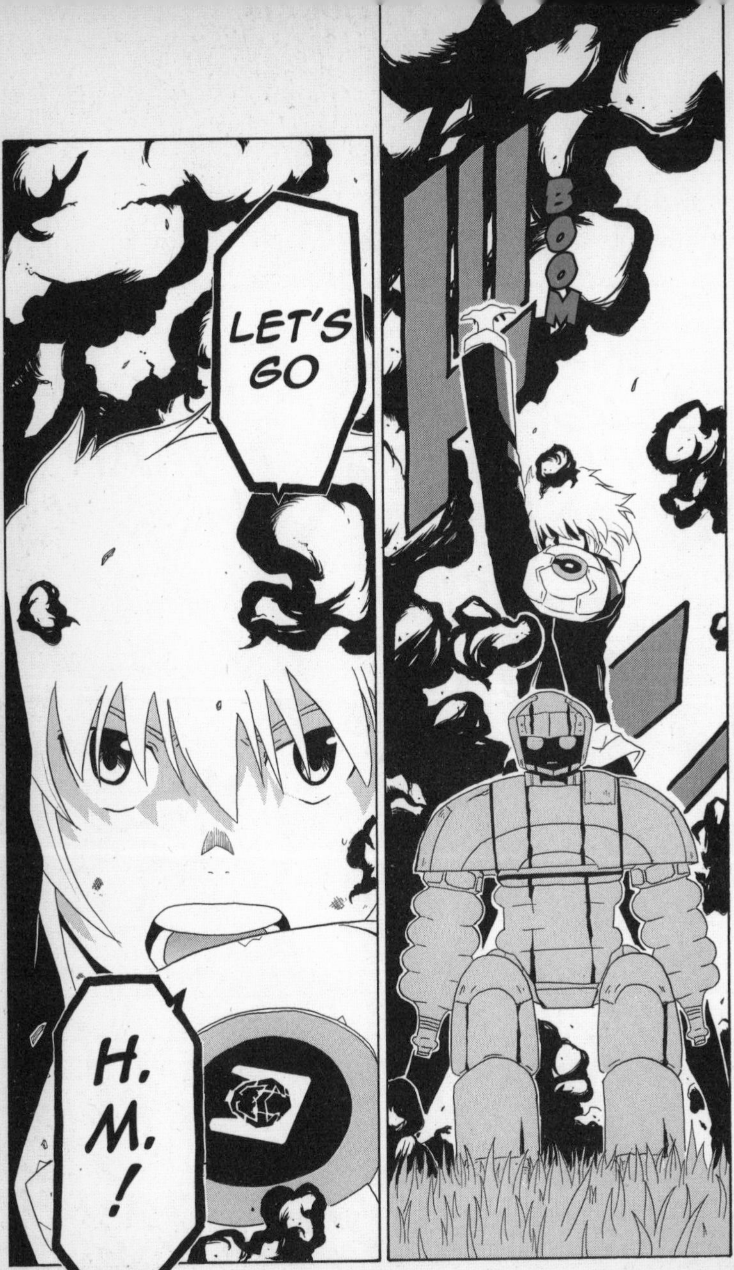
BOOM
LET'S GO
H.M.!

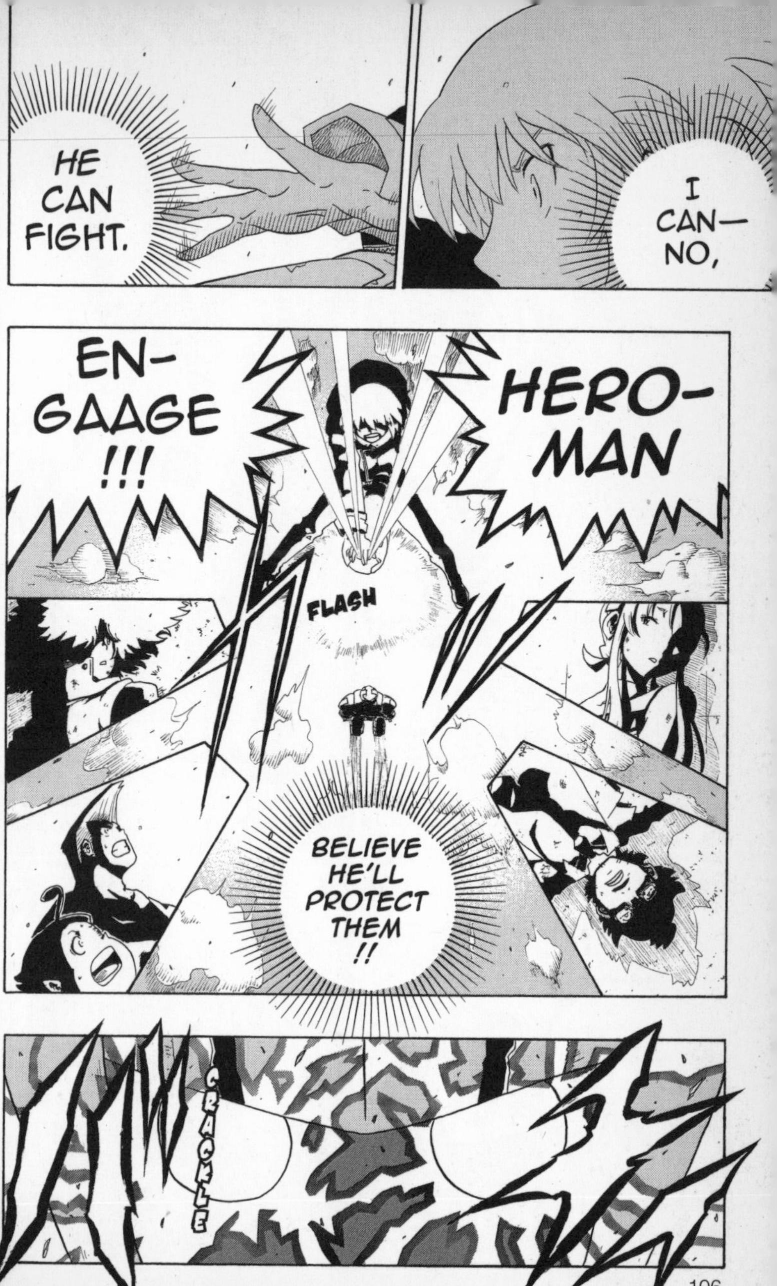
I CAN— NO,
HE CAN FIGHT.
HERO-MAN
EN-GAAGE!!!
FLASH
BELIEVE HE'LL PROTECT THEM!!
CRACKLE

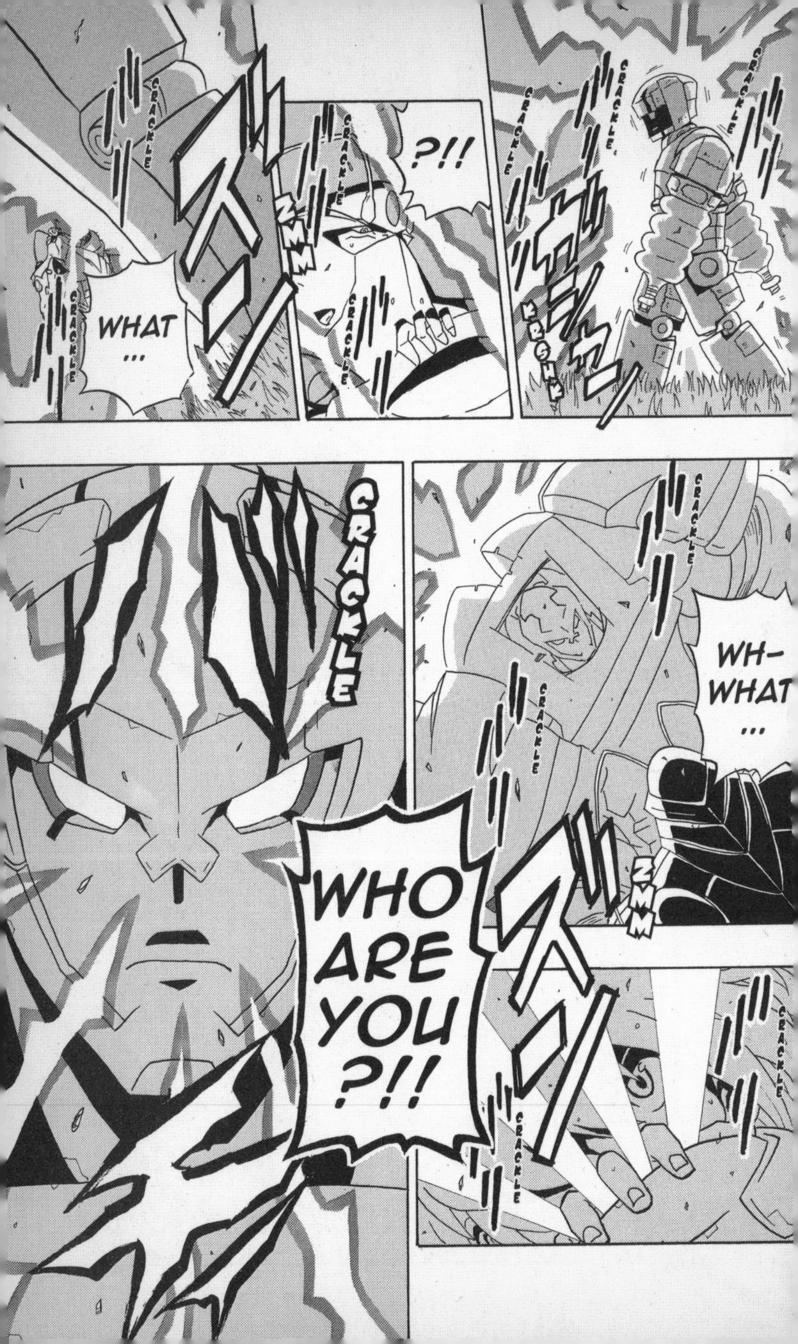
CRACKLE
CRACKLE
CRACKLE
KRSHK
?!!
CRACKLE
ZMMM
CRACKLE
CRACKLE
WHAT ...
CRACKLE
CRACKLE
WH-WHAT ...
CRACKLE
ZMMM
CRACKLE
CRACKLE
CRACKLE
WHO ARE YOU ?!!

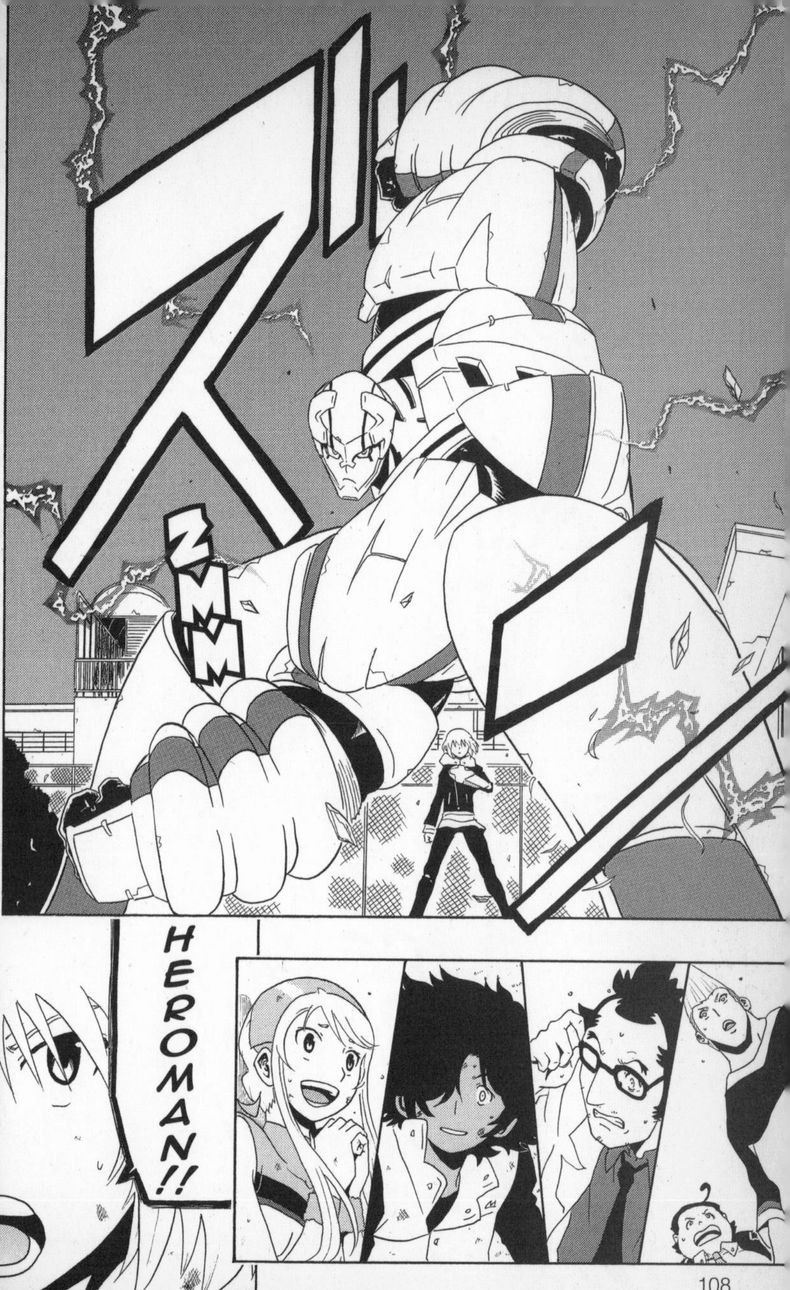

ZMMM
HEROMAN!!

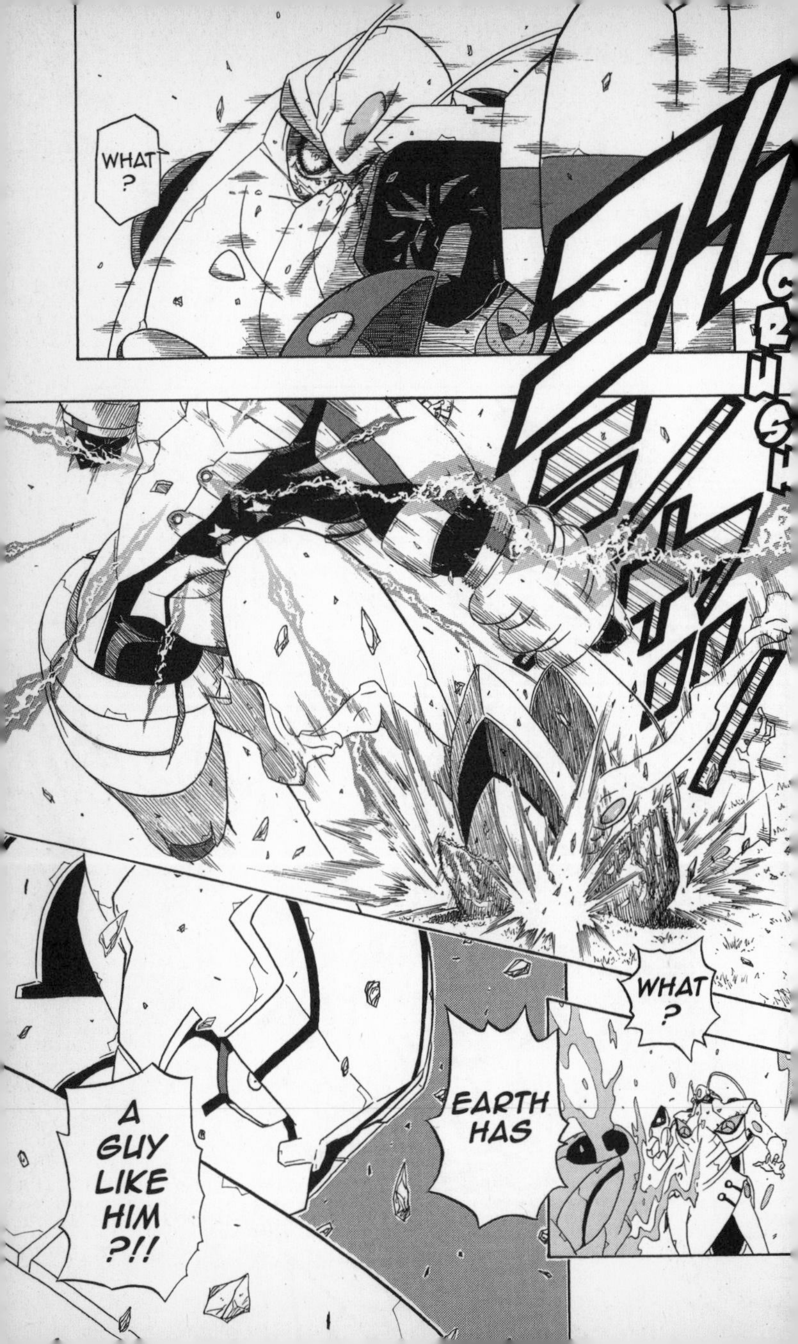
WHAT ?
CRUSH
WHAT ?
EARTH HAS
A GUY LIKE HIM ?!!

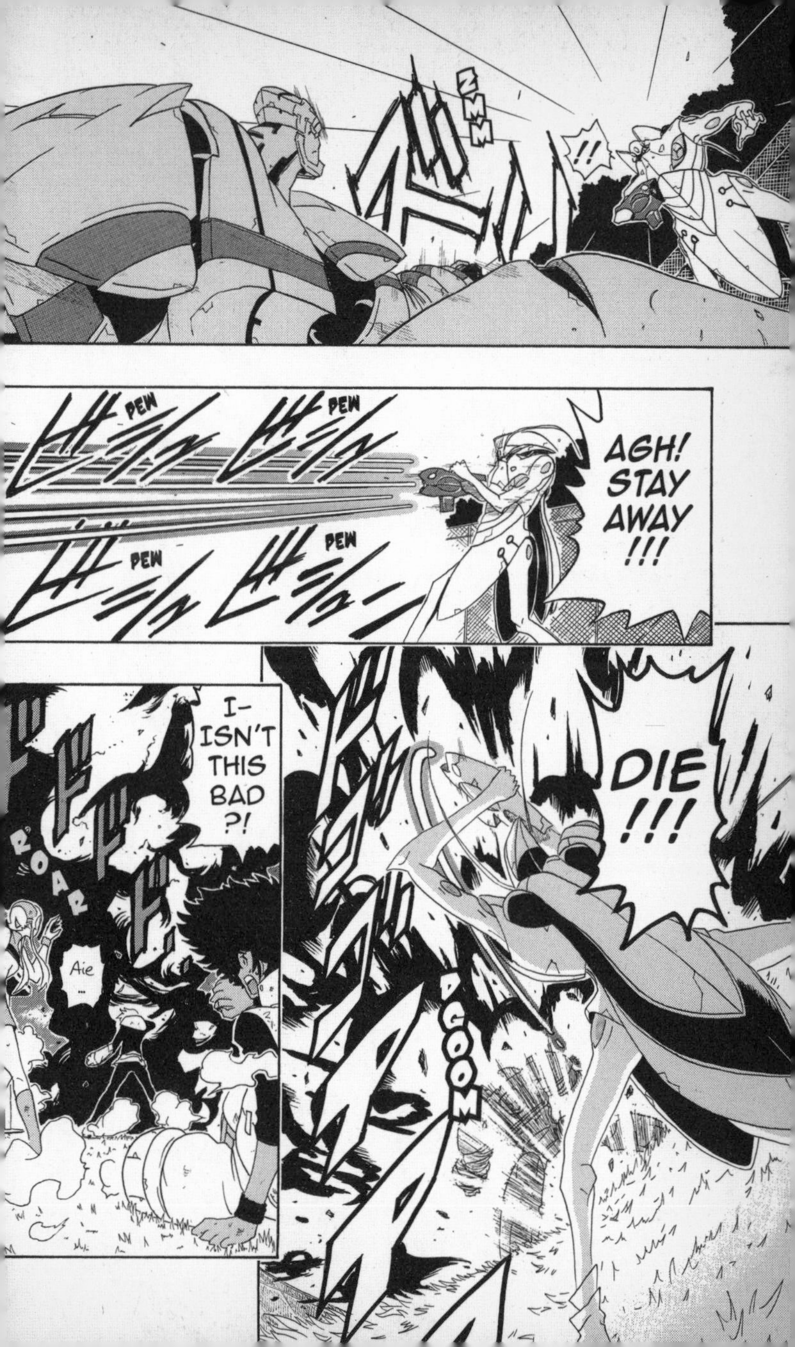
ZMMM
!!
PEW
PEW
PEW
PEW
AGH! STAY AWAY !!!
DIE !!!
DGOOM
I- ISN'T THIS BAD ?!
ROAR
Aie ...

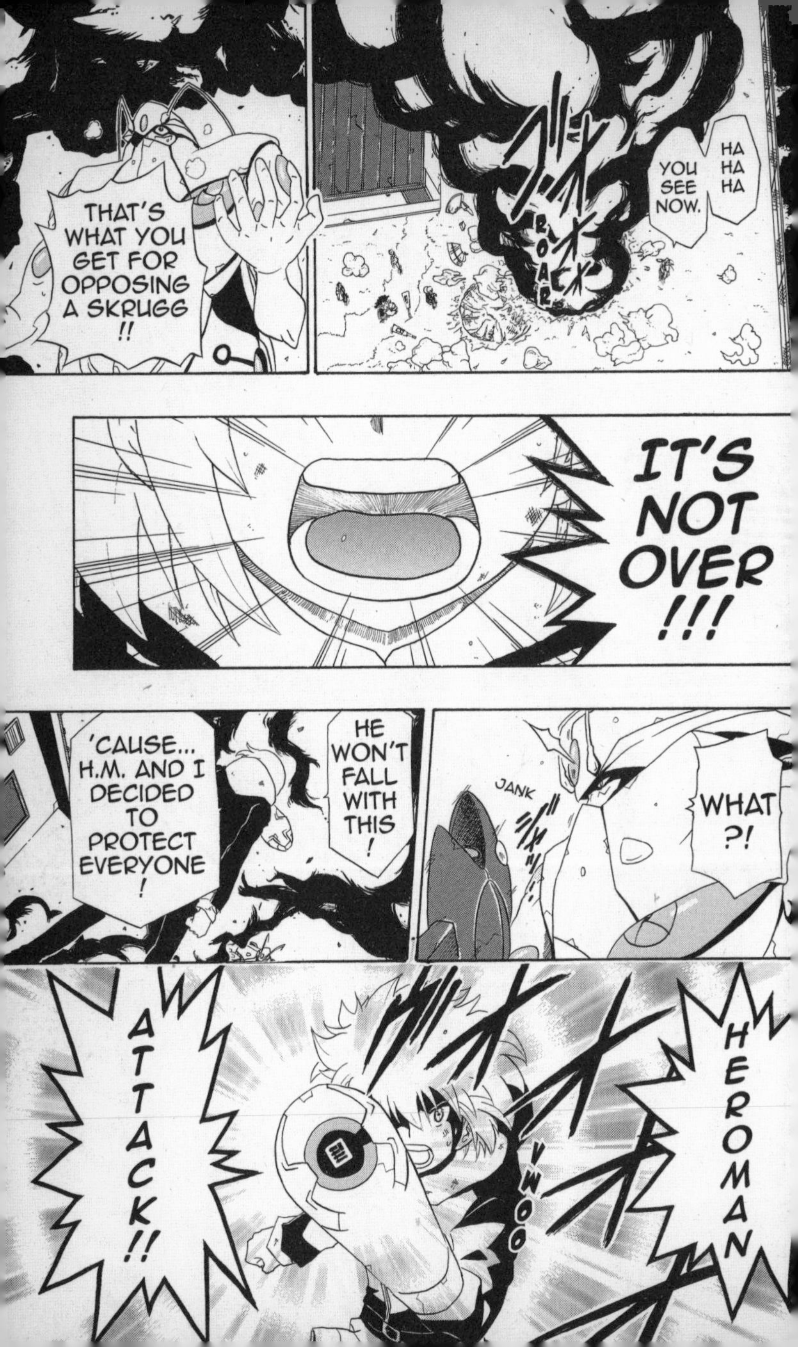
HA HA HA
YOU SEE NOW.
ROAR
THAT'S WHAT YOU GET FOR OPPOSING A SKRUGG!!
IT'S NOT OVER!!!
WHAT?!
JANK
HE WON'T FALL WITH THIS!
'CAUSE... H.M. AND I DECIDED TO PROTECT EVERYONE!
HEROMAN
VWOOO
ATTACK!!

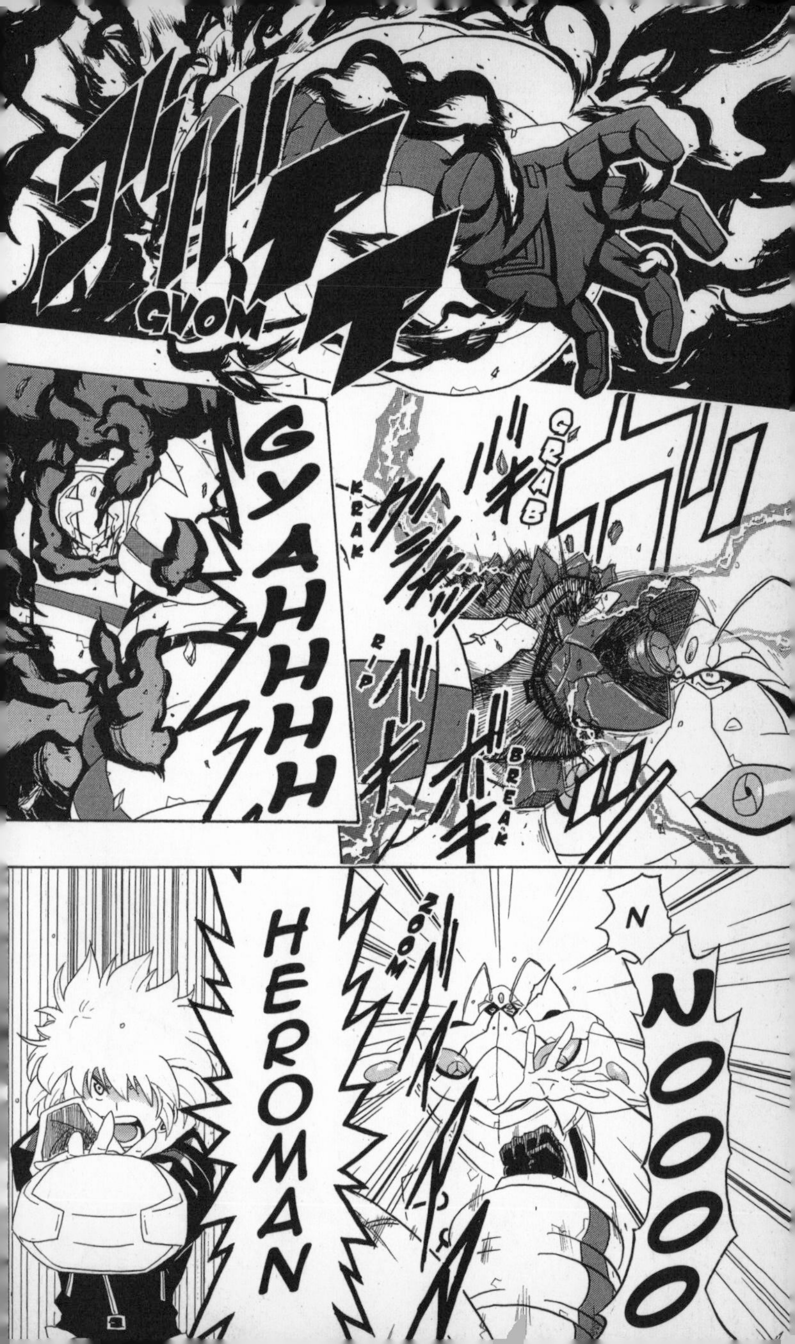
GVOM
GRAB
KRAK
RIP
BREAK
GYAHHHH
N
NOOOO
ZOOM
HEROMAN

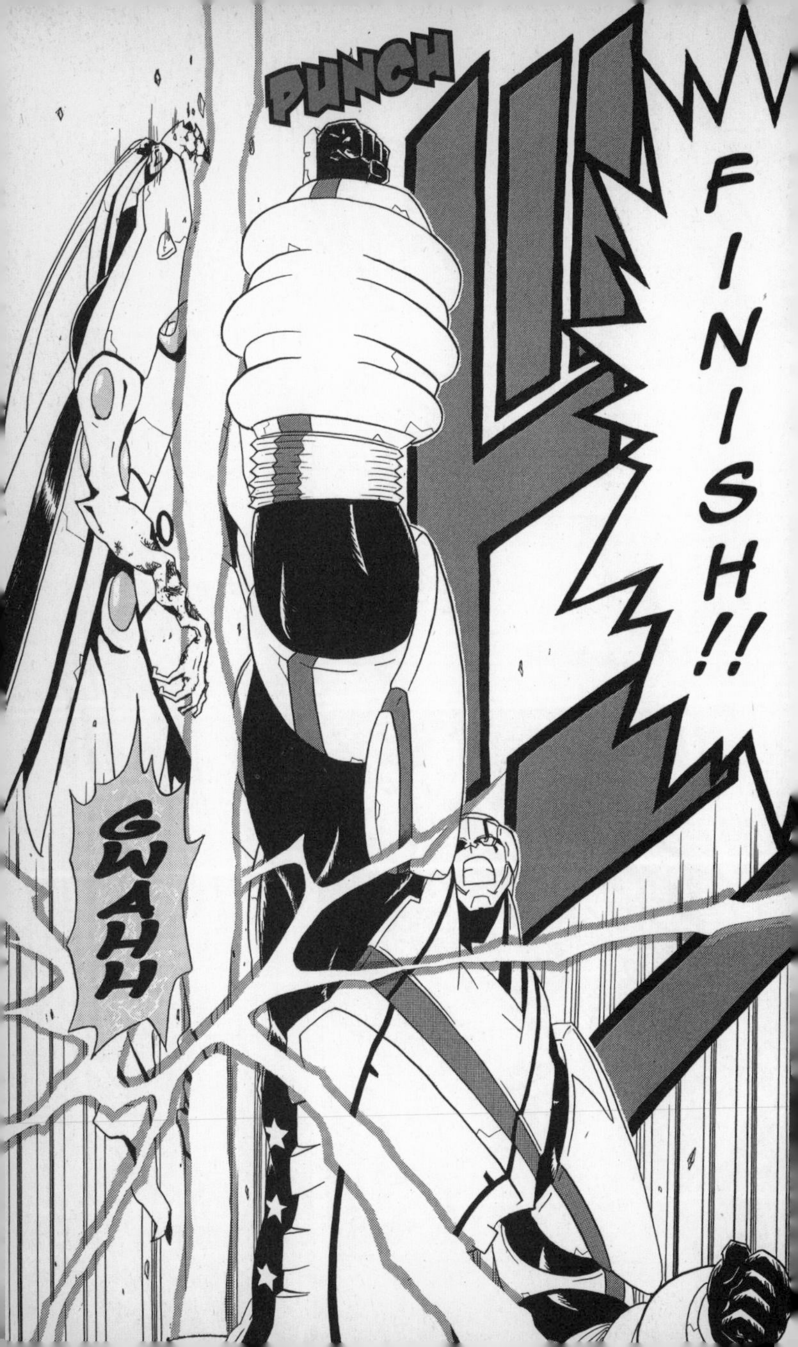
FINISH!!
PUNCH
GWAHH

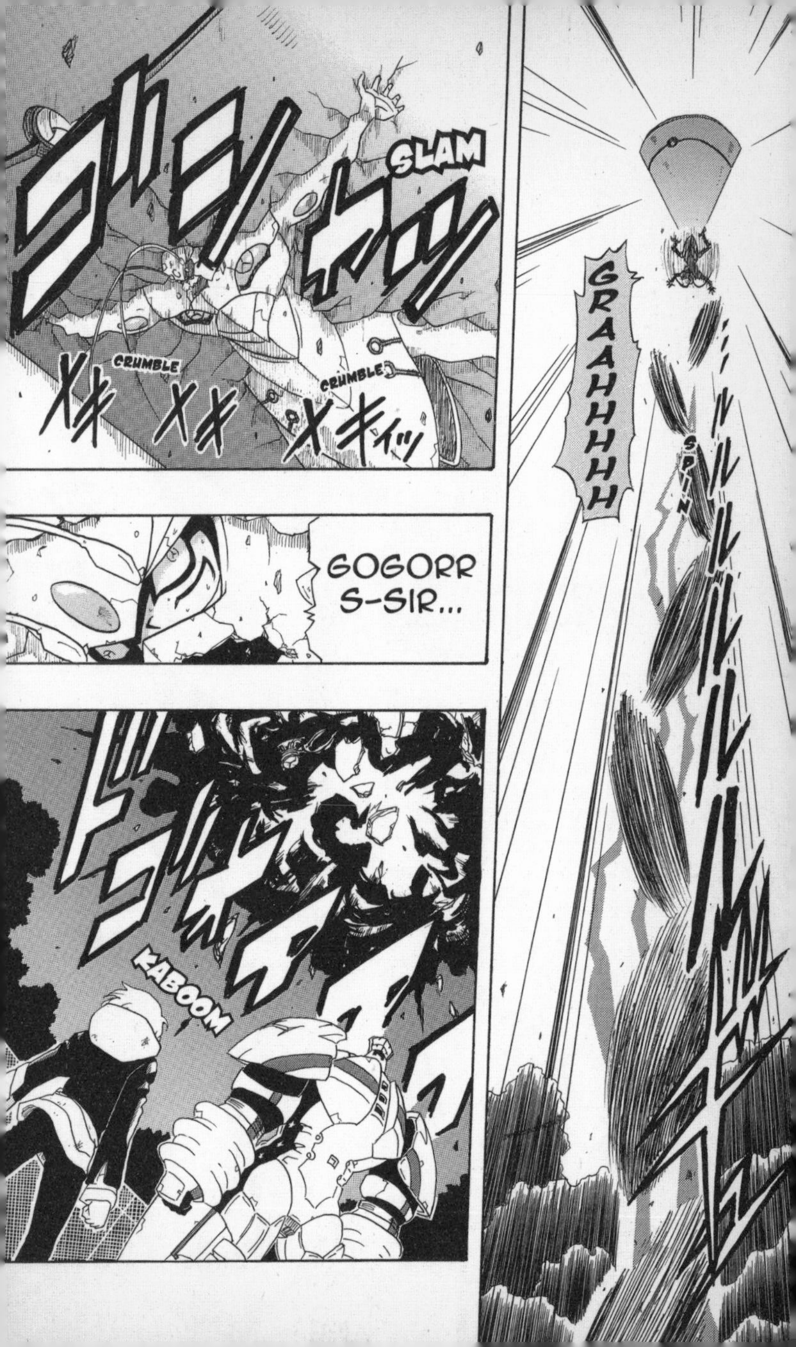
GRAAHHHHH
SPIN
SLAM
CRUMBLE
CRUMBLE
GOGORR S-SIR...
KABOOM

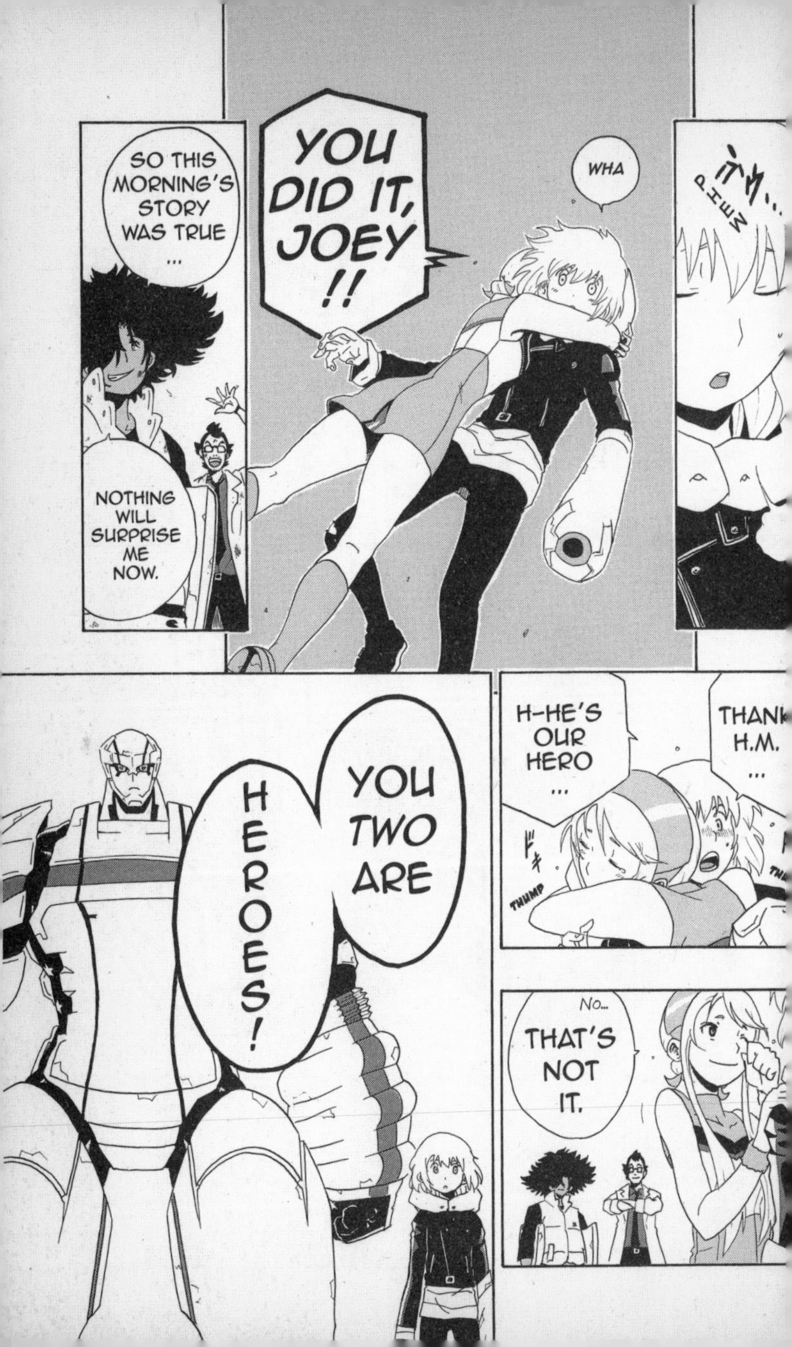
ホッ...
PHEW
WHA
YOU DID IT, JOEY!!
SO THIS MORNING'S STORY WAS TRUE ...
NOTHING WILL SURPRISE ME NOW.
THANK H.M. ...
H-HE'S OUR HERO ...
ドキ
THUMP
No...
THAT'S NOT IT.
YOU TWO ARE HEROES!

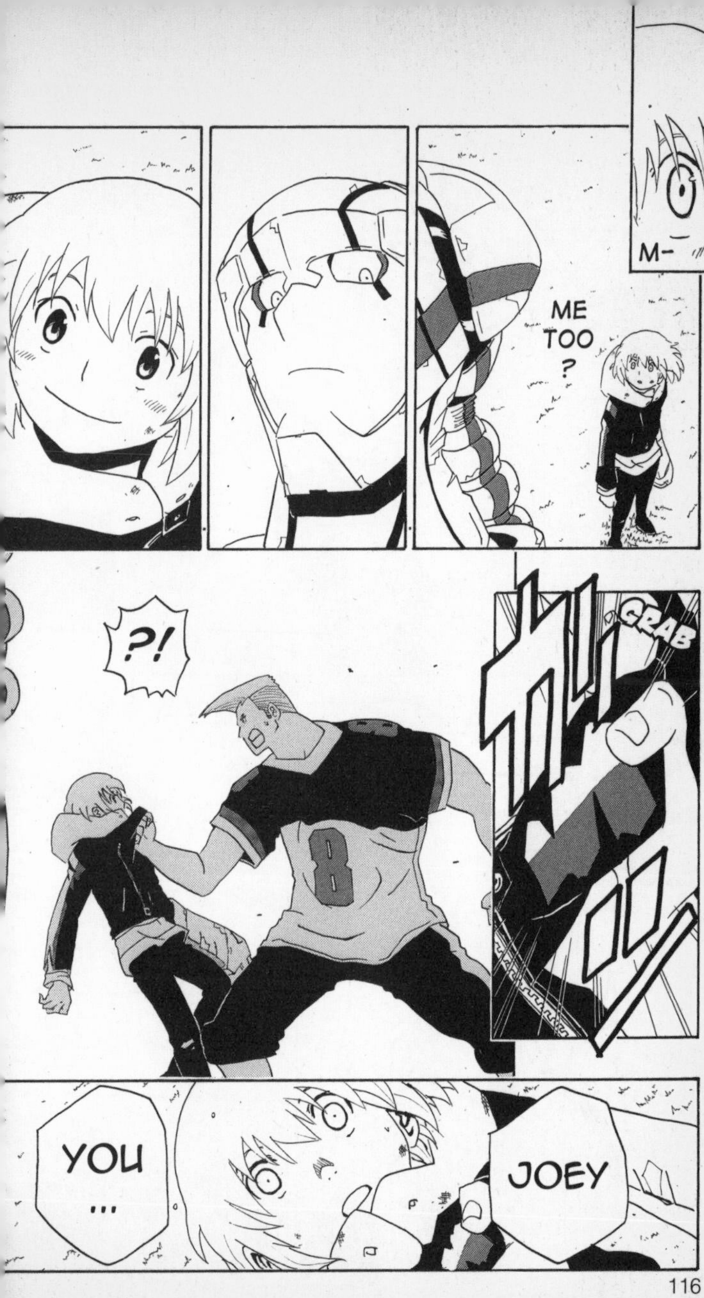
M-
ME TOO ?
GRAB
?!
JOEY
YOU ...

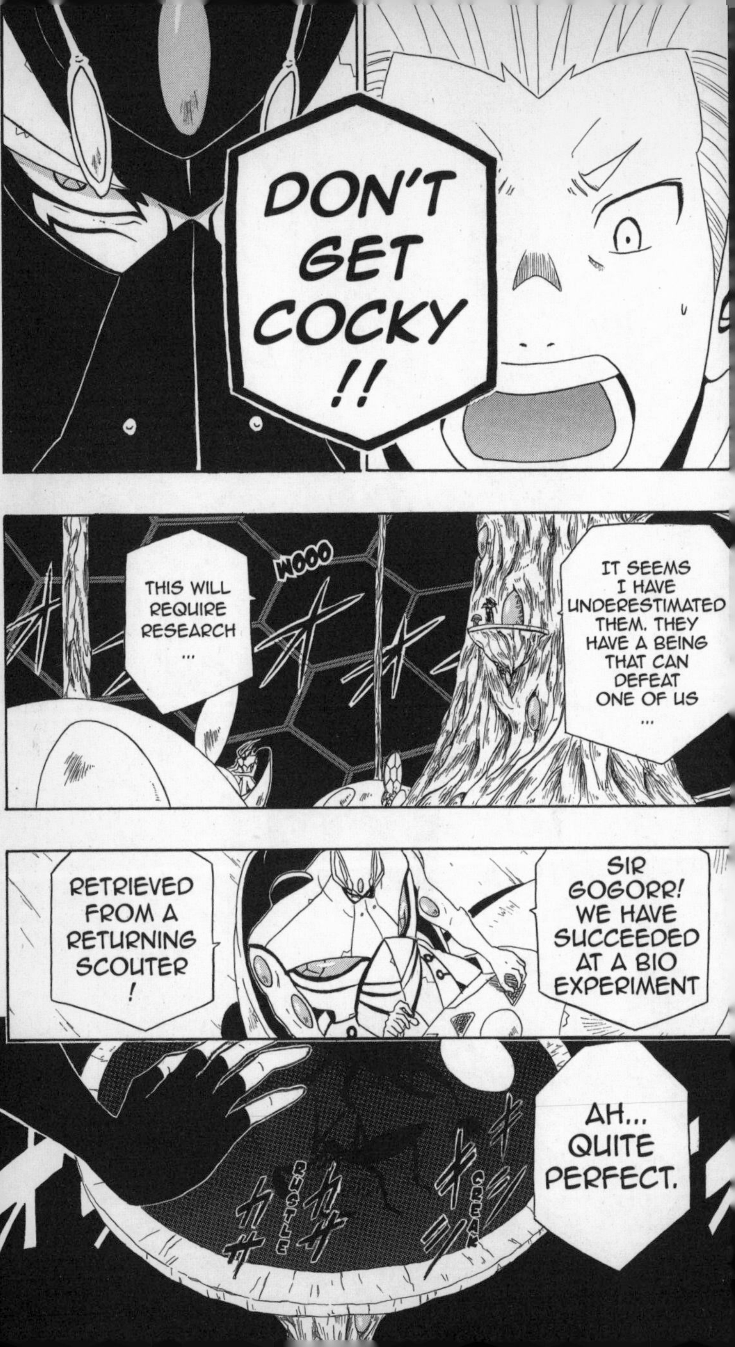
DON'T GET COCKY !!
IT SEEMS I HAVE UNDERESTIMATED THEM. THEY HAVE A BEING THAT CAN DEFEAT ONE OF US ...
WOOO
THIS WILL REQUIRE RESEARCH ...
SIR GOGORR! WE HAVE SUCCEEDED AT A BIO EXPERIMENT
RETRIEVED FROM A RETURNING SCOUTER !
AH... QUITE PERFECT.
CREAK
RUSTLE

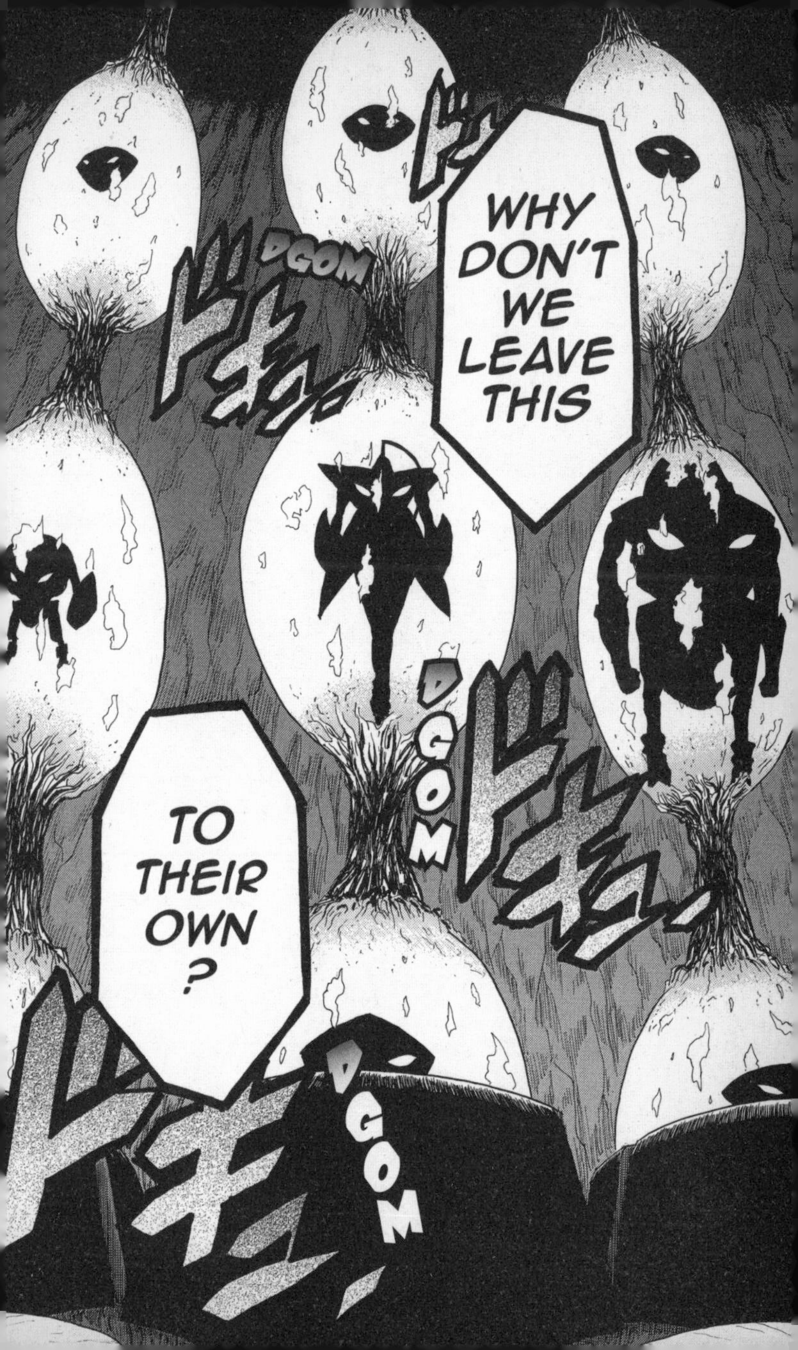
WHY DON'T WE LEAVE THIS
DGOM
DGOM
TO THEIR OWN ?
DGOM

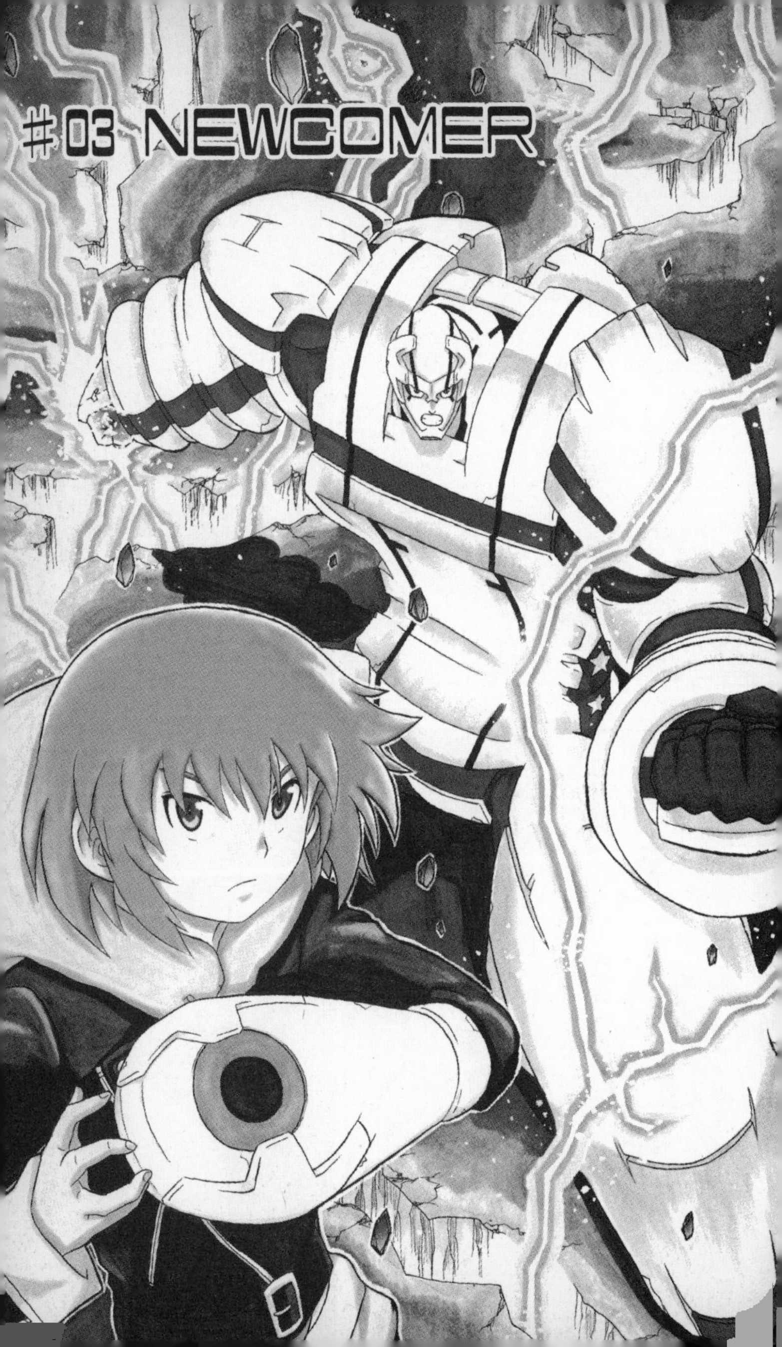
#03 NEWCOMER

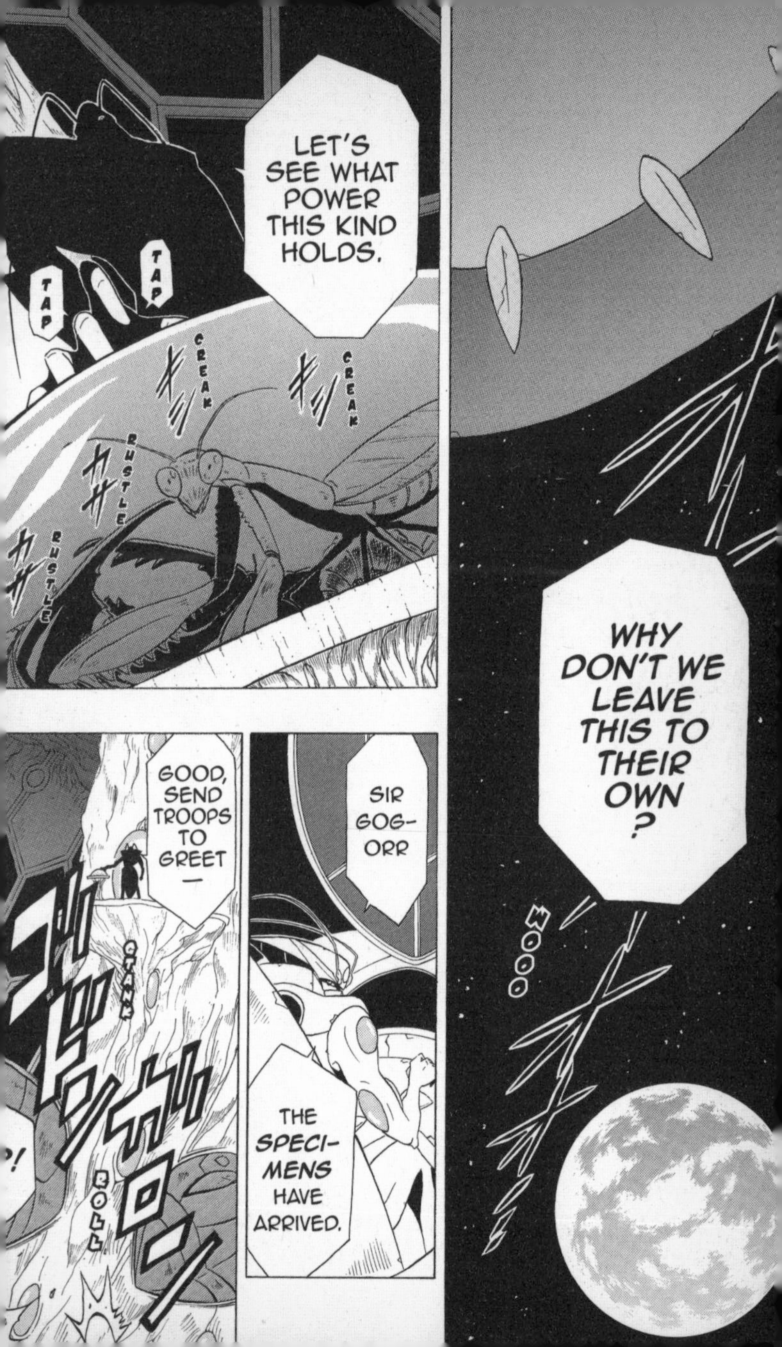
WHY DON'T WE LEAVE THIS TO THEIR OWN?
WOOOO
LET'S SEE WHAT POWER THIS KIND HOLDS.
TAP
TAP
CREAK
CREAK
RUSTLE
RUSTLE
SIR GOG-ORR
THE SPECIMENS HAVE ARRIVED.
GOOD, SEND TROOPS TO GREET—
CLANK
ROLL

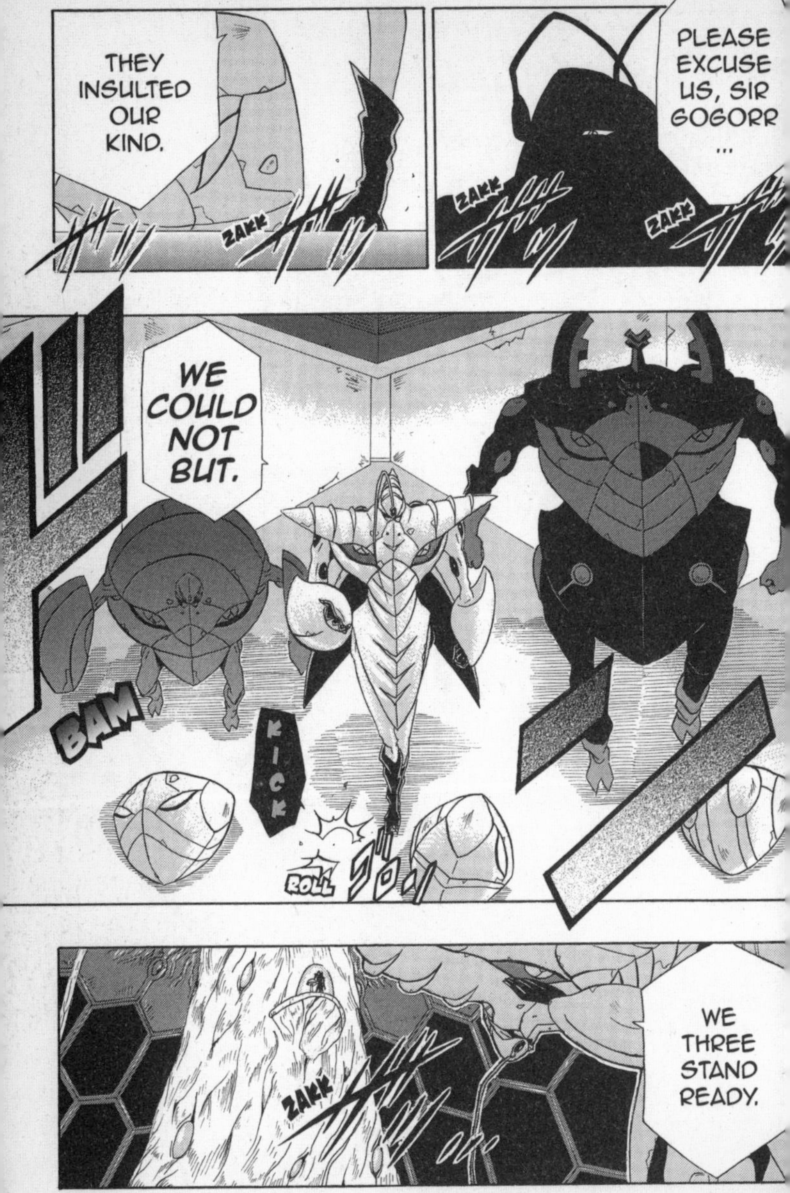

PLEASE EXCUSE US, SIR GOGORR ...
ZAKK
ZAKK
THEY INSULTED OUR KIND.
ZAKK
WE COULD NOT BUT.
BAM
KICK
ROLL
WE THREE STAND READY.
ZAKK

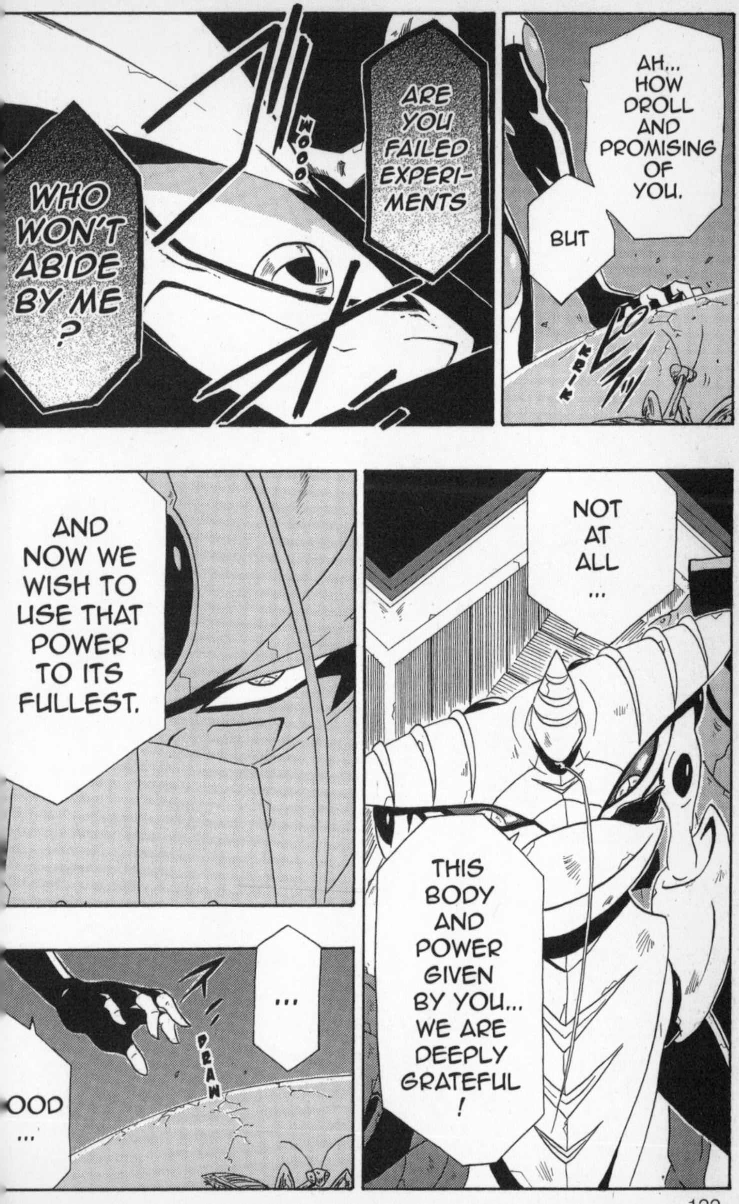
AH... HOW DROLL AND PROMISING OF YOU.
BUT
KRIK
ARE YOU FAILED EXPERI-MENTS
WOOO
WHO WON'T ABIDE BY ME ?
NOT AT ALL ...
THIS BODY AND POWER GIVEN BY YOU... WE ARE DEEPLY GRATEFUL !
AND NOW WE WISH TO USE THAT POWER TO ITS FULLEST.
...
DRAW
OOD ...

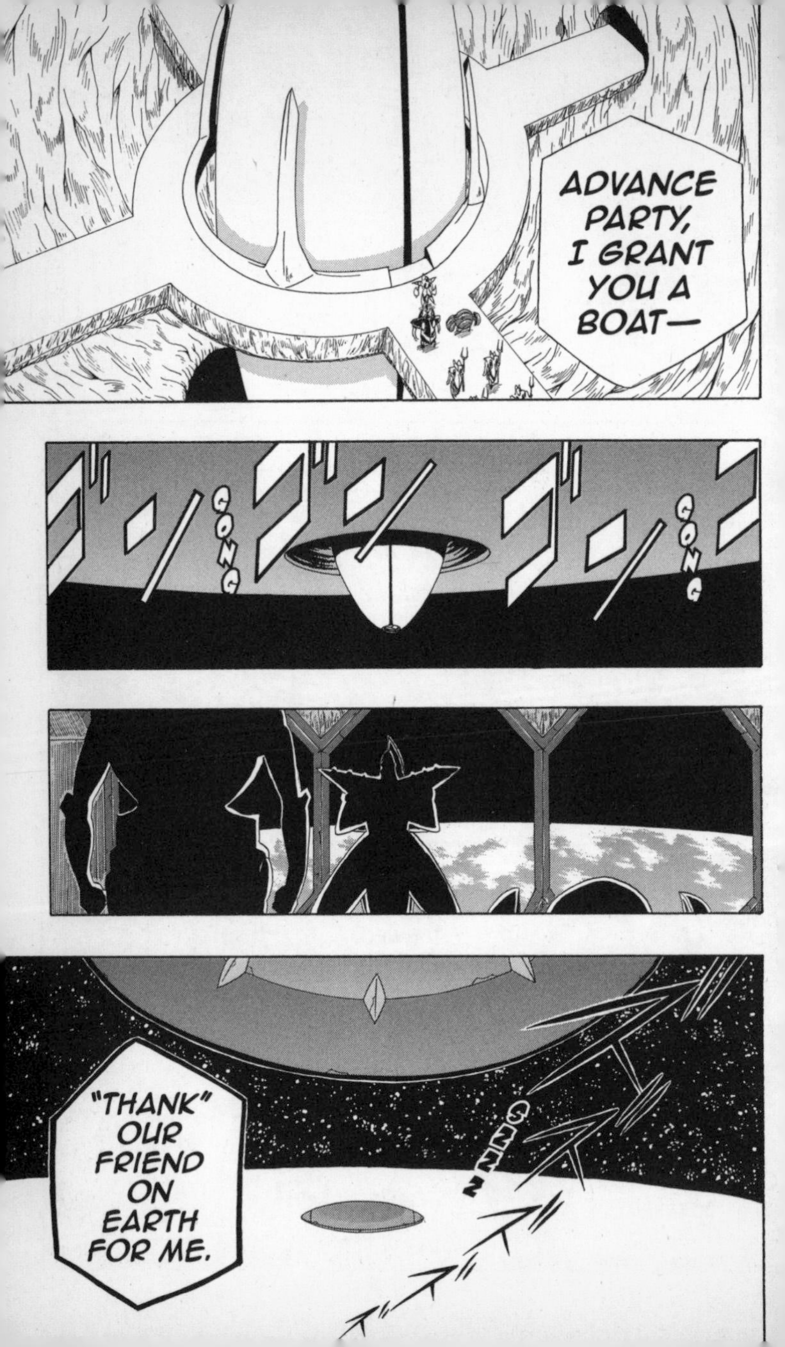
ADVANCE PARTY, I GRANT YOU A BOAT—
GONG
GONG
SZZZ
"THANK" OUR FRIEND ON EARTH FOR ME.

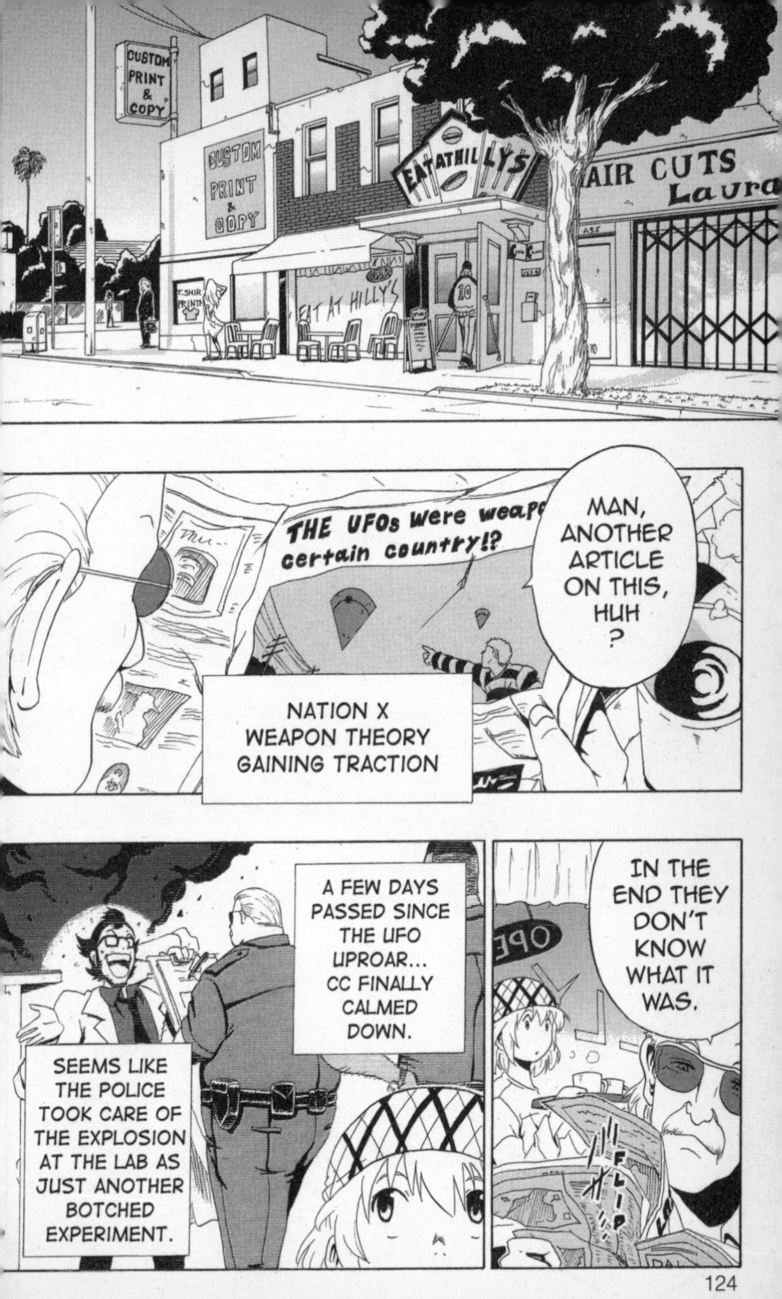
CUSTOM PRINT & COPY
CUSTOM PRINT & COPY
EAT AT HILLY'S
HAIR CUTS
EAT AT HILLY'S
MAN, ANOTHER ARTICLE ON THIS, HUH?
THE UFOs were weap
certain country!?
NATION X WEAPON THEORY GAINING TRACTION
IN THE END THEY DON'T KNOW WHAT IT WAS.
FLIP
A FEW DAYS PASSED SINCE THE UFO UPROAR... CC FINALLY CALMED DOWN.
SEEMS LIKE THE POLICE TOOK CARE OF THE EXPLOSION AT THE LAB AS JUST ANOTHER BOTCHED EXPERIMENT.

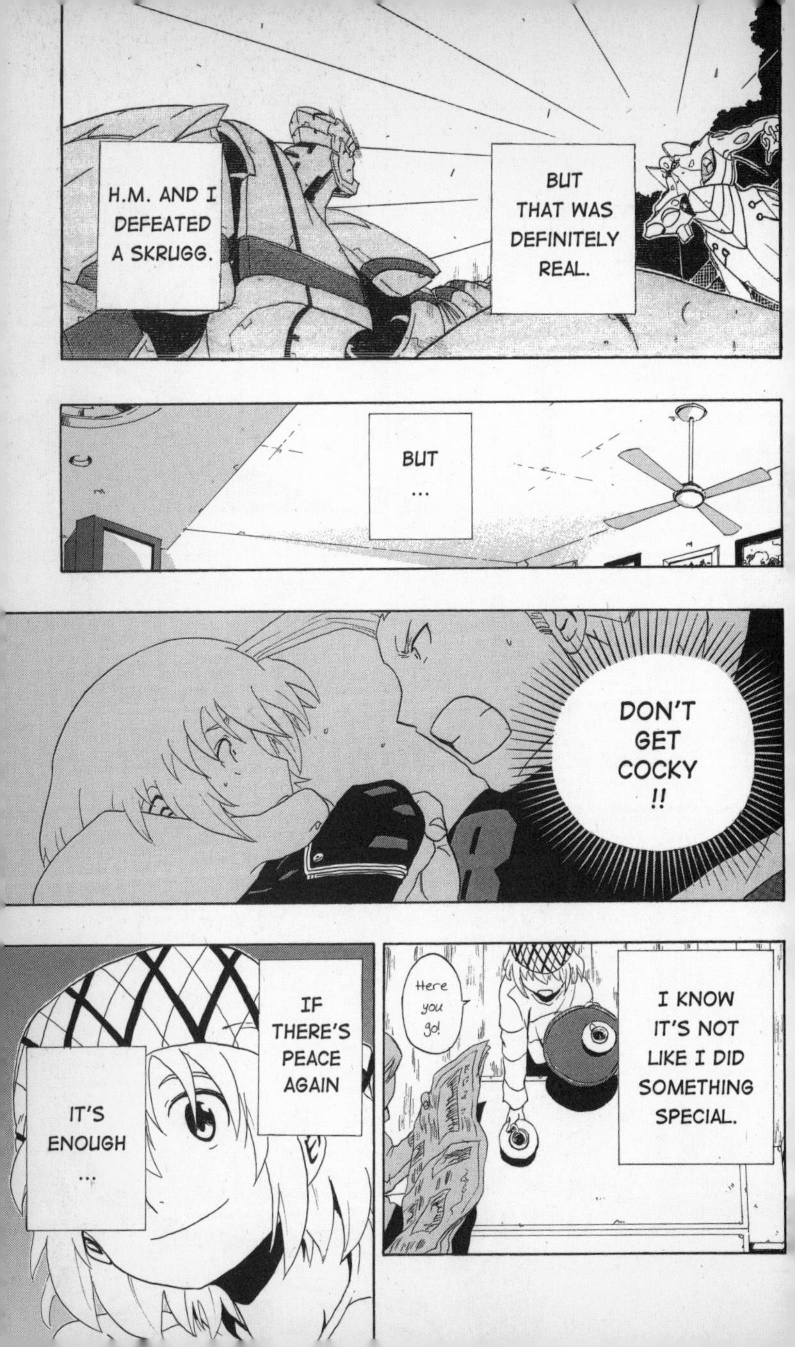
H.M. AND I DEFEATED A SKRUGG.
BUT THAT WAS DEFINITELY REAL.
BUT ...
DON'T GET COCKY !!
I KNOW IT'S NOT LIKE I DID SOMETHING SPECIAL.
Here you go!
IF THERE'S PEACE AGAIN
IT'S ENOUGH ...

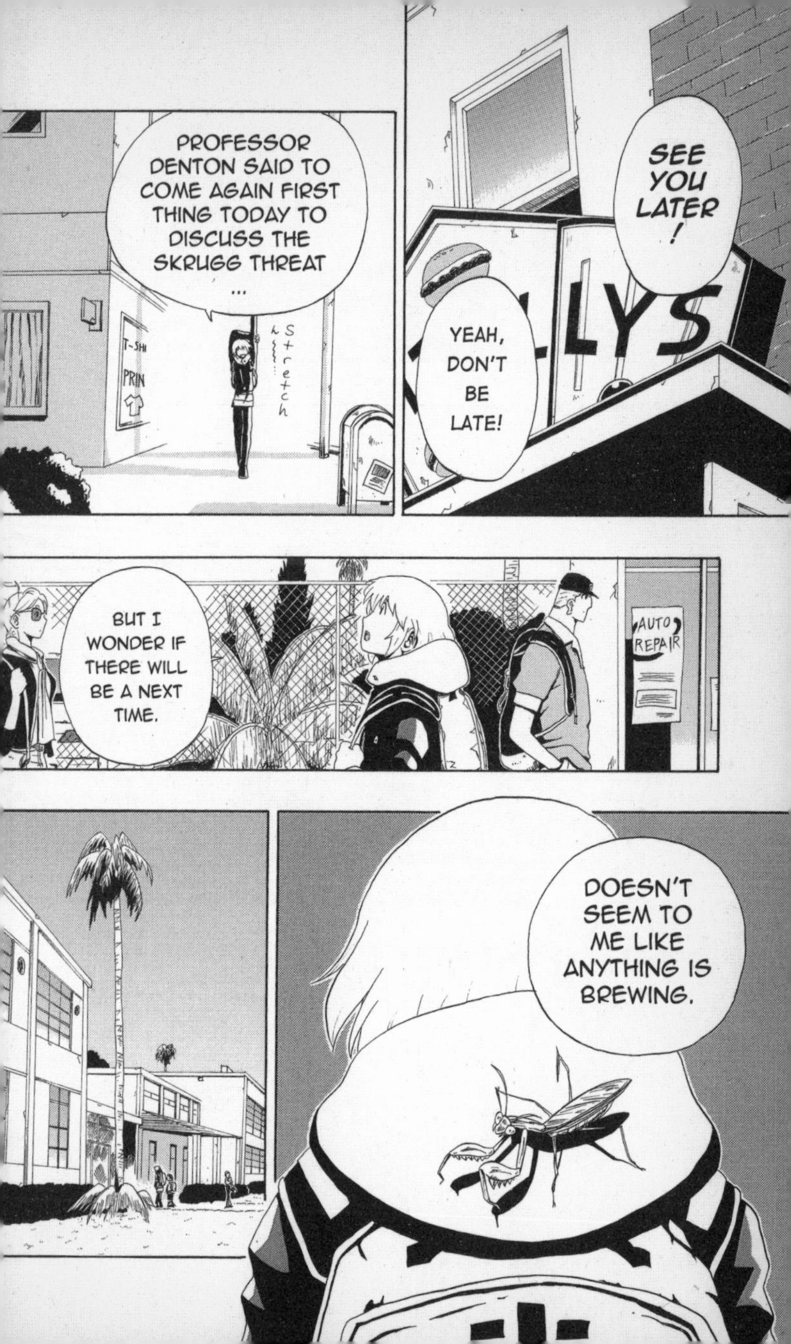
SEE YOU LATER!
YEAH, DON'T BE LATE!
PROFESSOR DENTON SAID TO COME AGAIN FIRST THING TODAY TO DISCUSS THE SKRUGG THREAT ...
Stretch
AUTO REPAIR
BUT I WONDER IF THERE WILL BE A NEXT TIME.
DOESN'T SEEM TO ME LIKE ANYTHING IS BREWING.

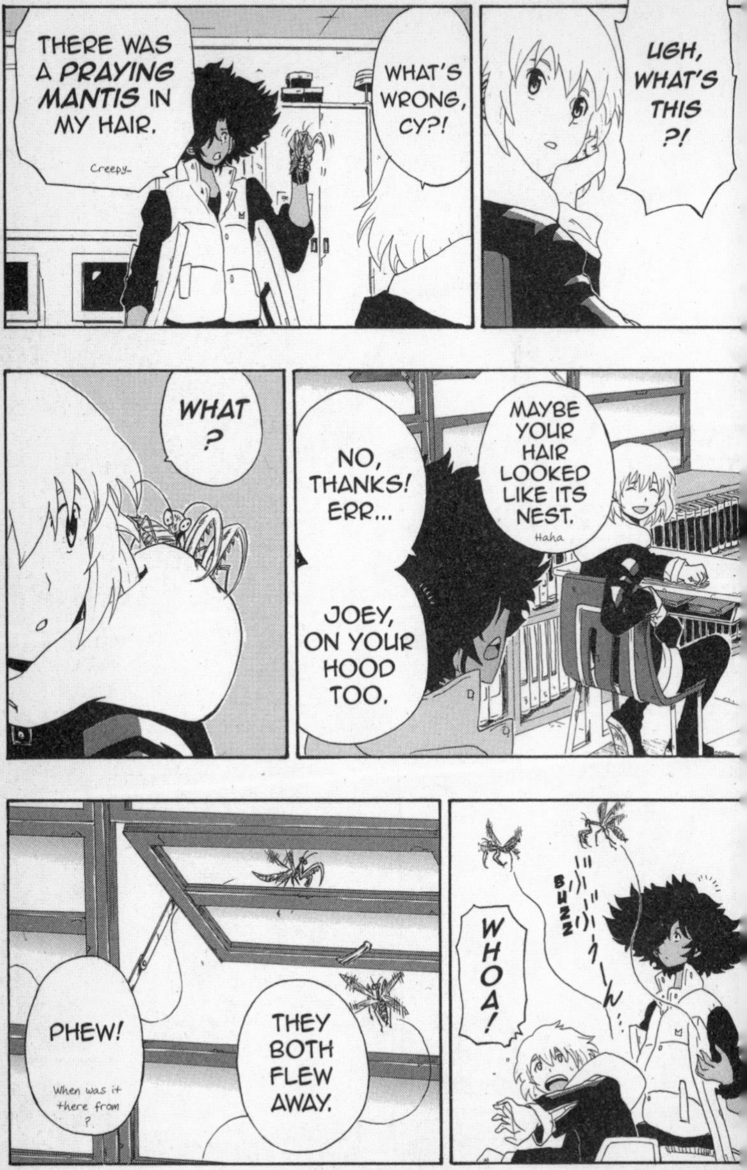
UGH, WHAT'S THIS ?!
WHAT'S WRONG, CY?!
THERE WAS A *PRAYING MANTIS* IN MY HAIR.
Creepy-
MAYBE YOUR HAIR LOOKED LIKE ITS NEST.
Haha
NO, THANKS! ERR...
JOEY, ON YOUR HOOD TOO.
WHAT ?
BUZZ
WHOA!
THEY BOTH FLEW AWAY.
PHEW!
When was it there from ?

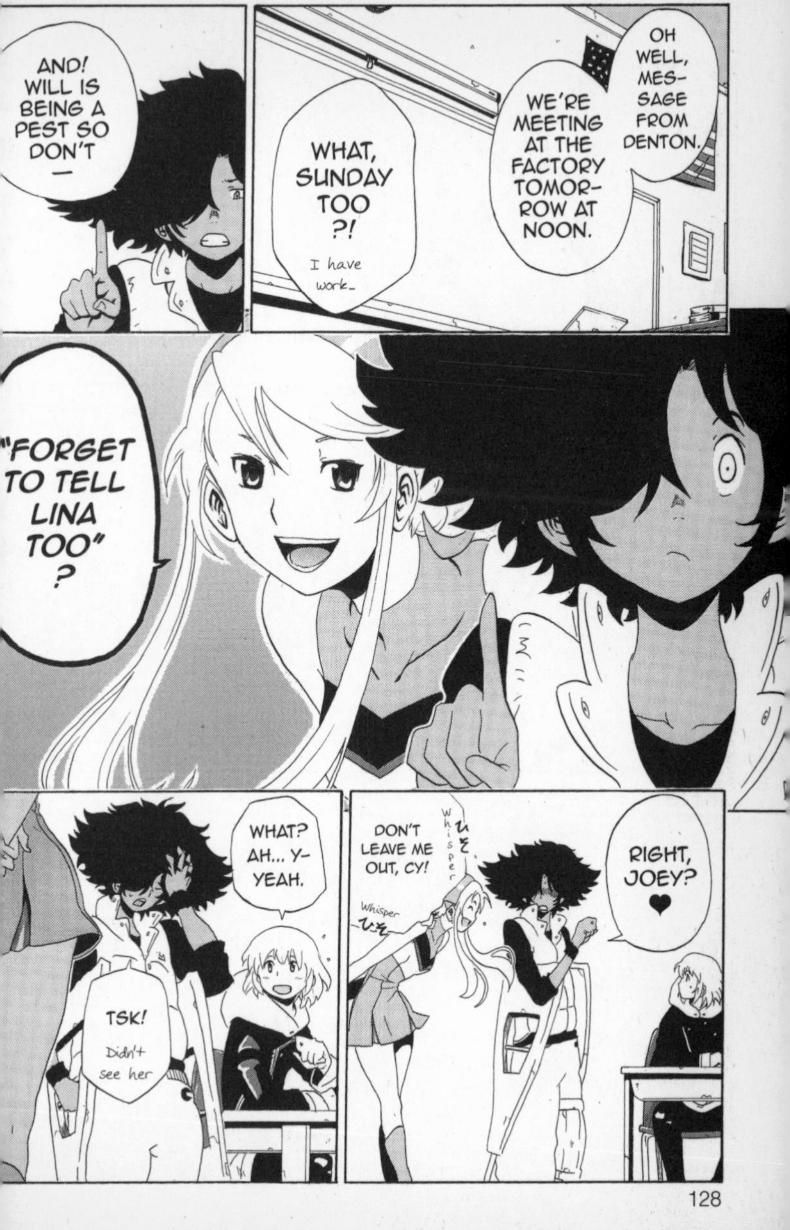
OH WELL, MES-SAGE FROM DENTON.
WE'RE MEETING AT THE FACTORY TOMOR-ROW AT NOON.
WHAT, SUNDAY TOO ?!
I have work...
AND! WILL IS BEING A PEST SO DON'T —
"FORGET TO TELL LINA TOO" ?
RIGHT, JOEY? ♥
Whisper ひそ
DON'T LEAVE ME OUT, CY!
Whisper ひそ
WHAT? AH... Y-YEAH.
TSK!
Didn't see her

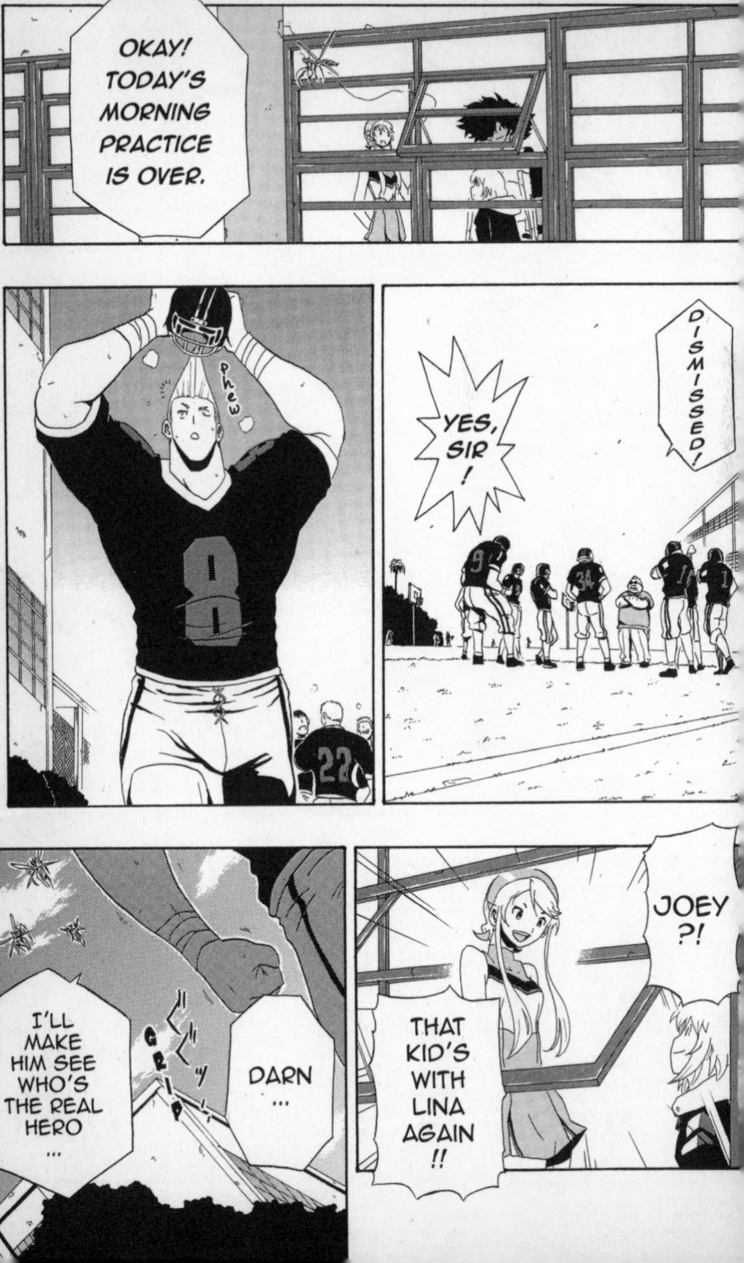
OKAY! TODAY'S MORNING PRACTICE IS OVER.
DISMISSED!
YES, SIR!
phew
JOEY?!
THAT KID'S WITH LINA AGAIN!!
DARN ...
GRIP
I'LL MAKE HIM SEE WHO'S THE REAL HERO ...

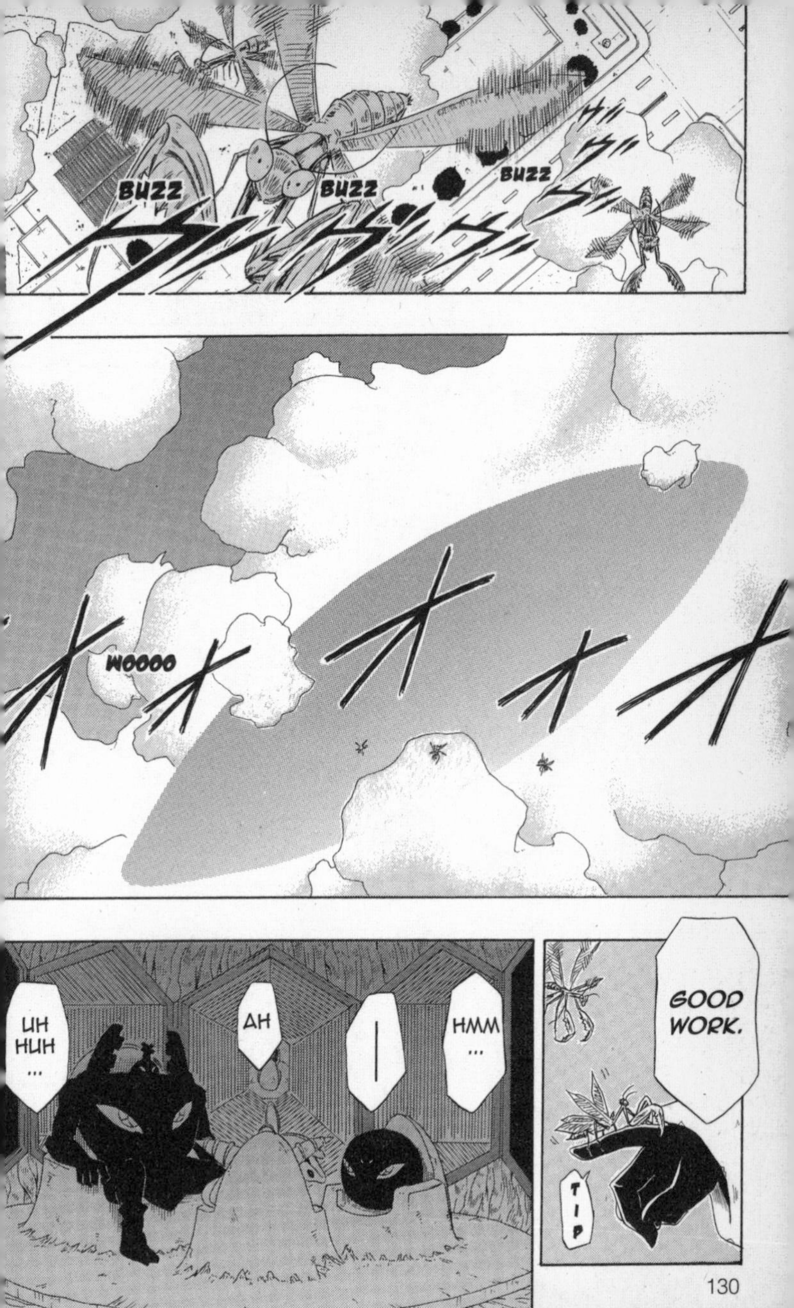
BUZZ
BUZZ
BUZZ
WOOOO
GOOD WORK.
TIP
HMM ...
|
AH
UH HUH ...

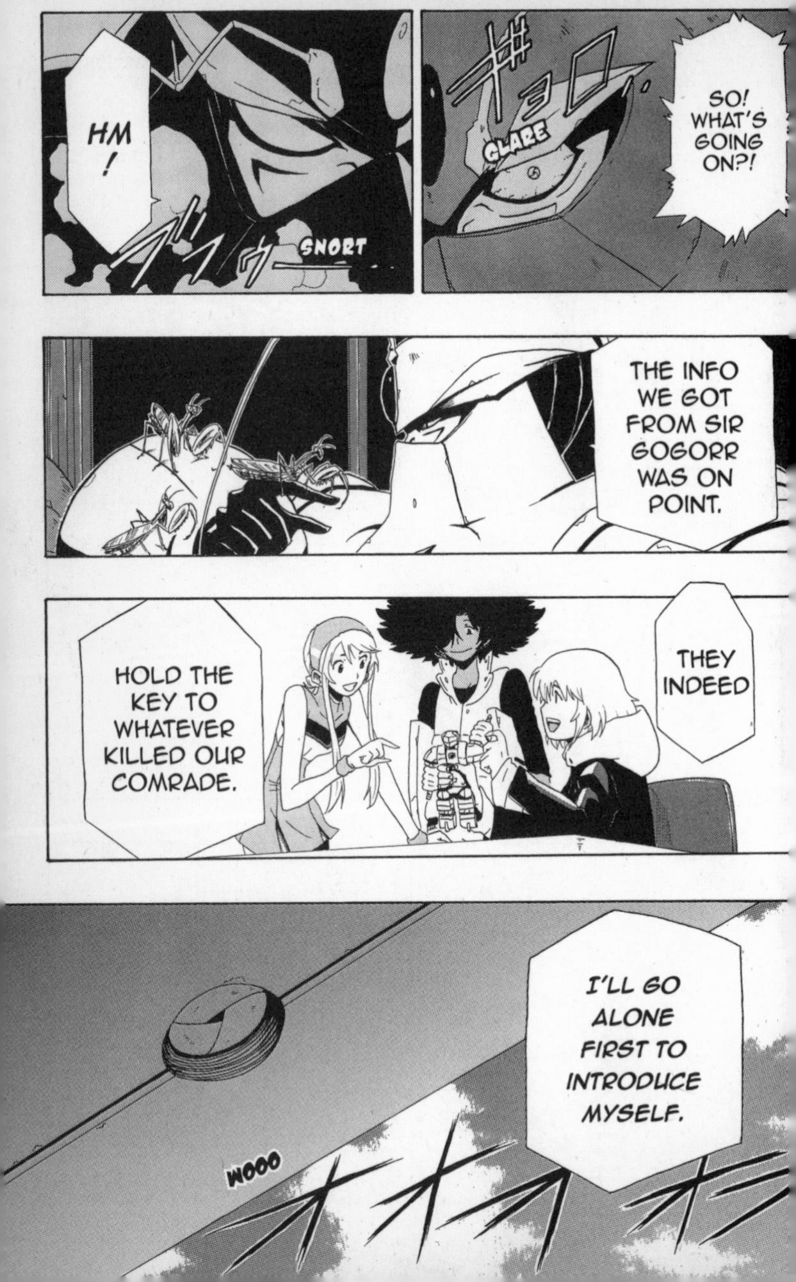
ギョロ
GLARE
SO! WHAT'S GOING ON?!
HM!
SNORT
THE INFO WE GOT FROM SIR GOGORR WAS ON POINT.
THEY INDEED
HOLD THE KEY TO WHATEVER KILLED OUR COMRADE.
I'LL GO ALONE FIRST TO INTRODUCE MYSELF.
WOOO

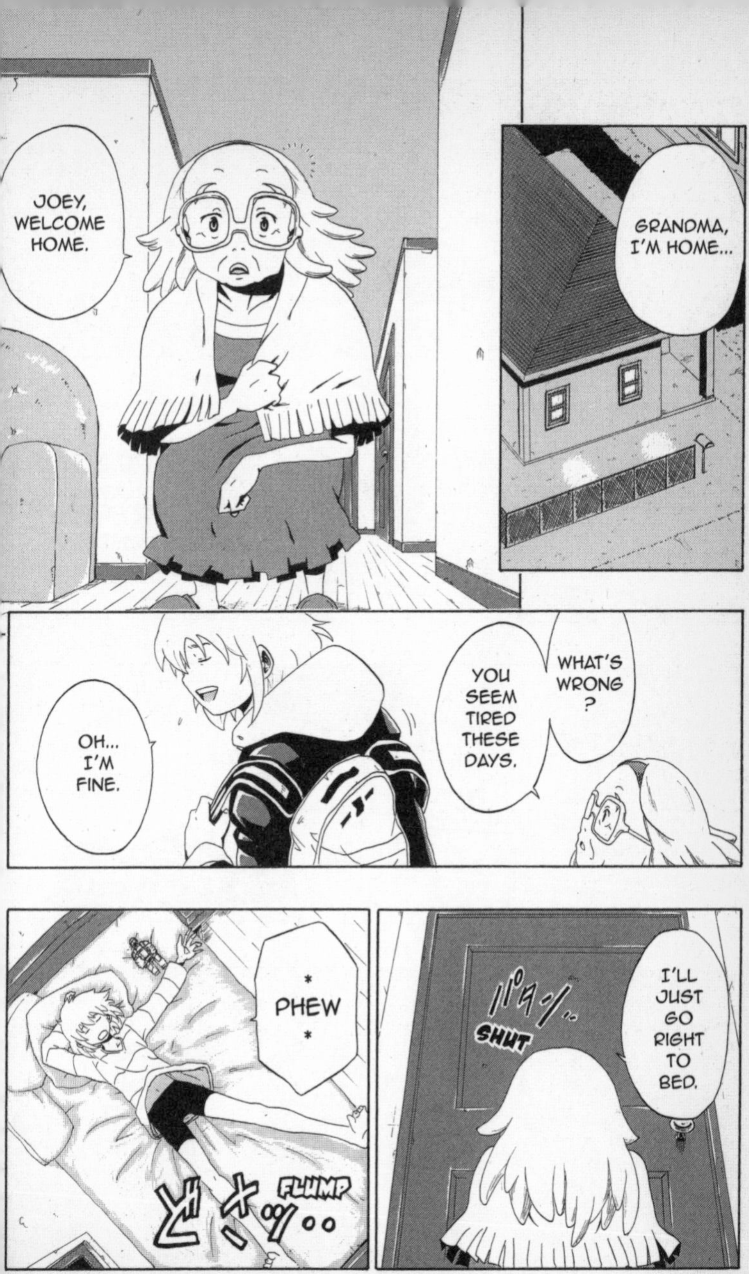
GRANDMA, I'M HOME...
JOEY, WELCOME HOME.
WHAT'S WRONG ?
YOU SEEM TIRED THESE DAYS.
OH... I'M FINE.
I'LL JUST GO RIGHT TO BED.
SHUT
* PHEW *
FLUMP

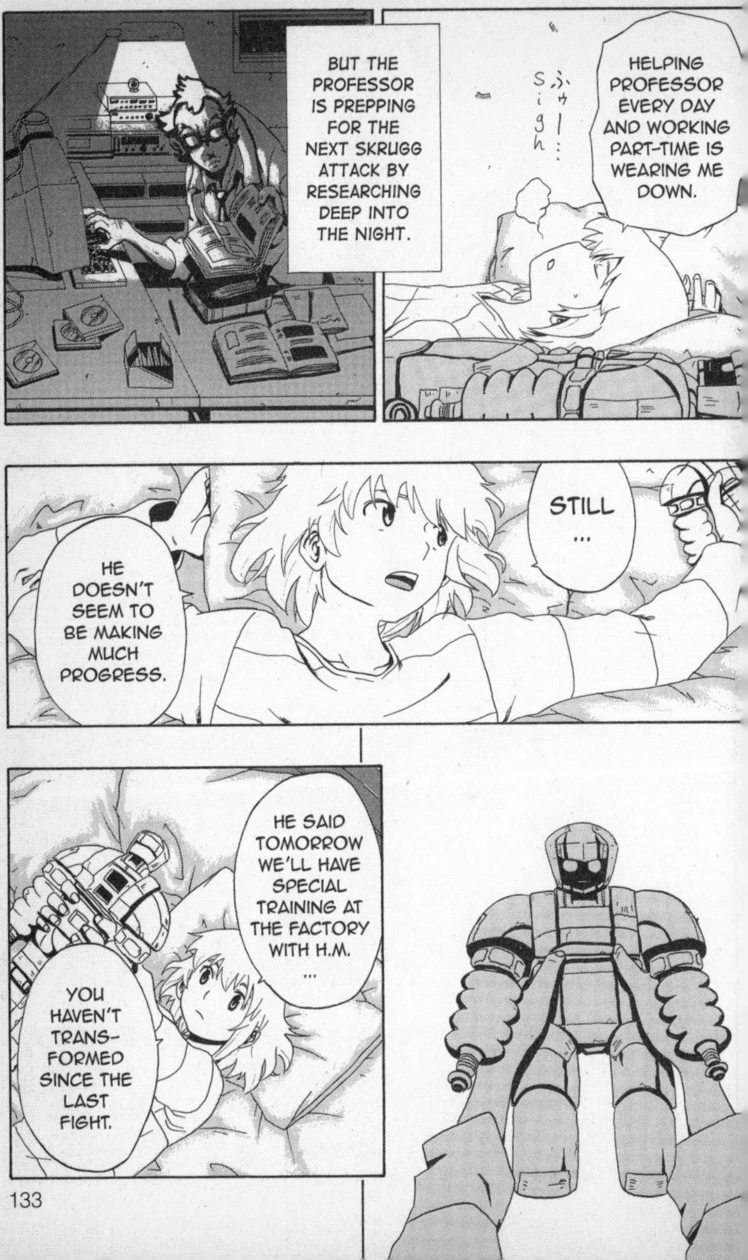
HELPING PROFESSOR EVERY DAY AND WORKING PART-TIME IS WEARING ME DOWN.
ふぅー…
Sigh
BUT THE PROFESSOR IS PREPPING FOR THE NEXT SKRUGG ATTACK BY RESEARCHING DEEP INTO THE NIGHT.
STILL ...
HE DOESN'T SEEM TO BE MAKING MUCH PROGRESS.
HE SAID TOMORROW WE'LL HAVE SPECIAL TRAINING AT THE FACTORY WITH H.M. ...
YOU HAVEN'T TRANS-FORMED SINCE THE LAST FIGHT.

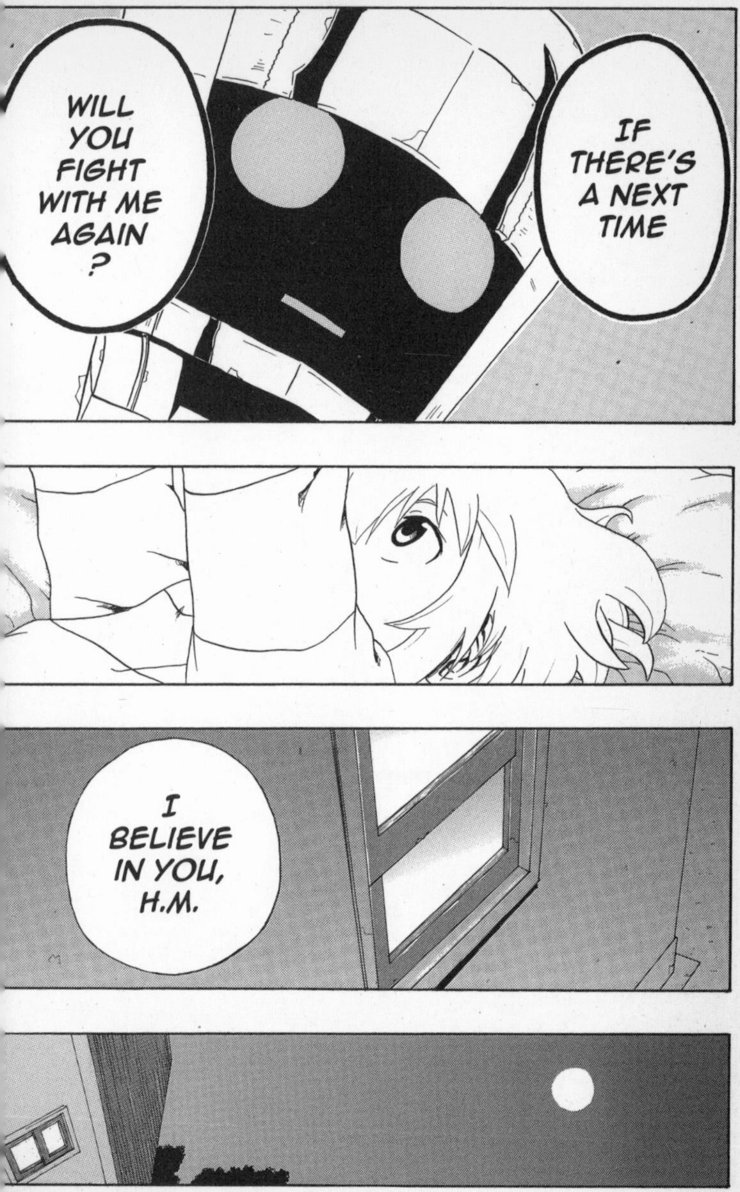
IF THERE'S A NEXT TIME
WILL YOU FIGHT WITH ME AGAIN?
I BELIEVE IN YOU, H.M.

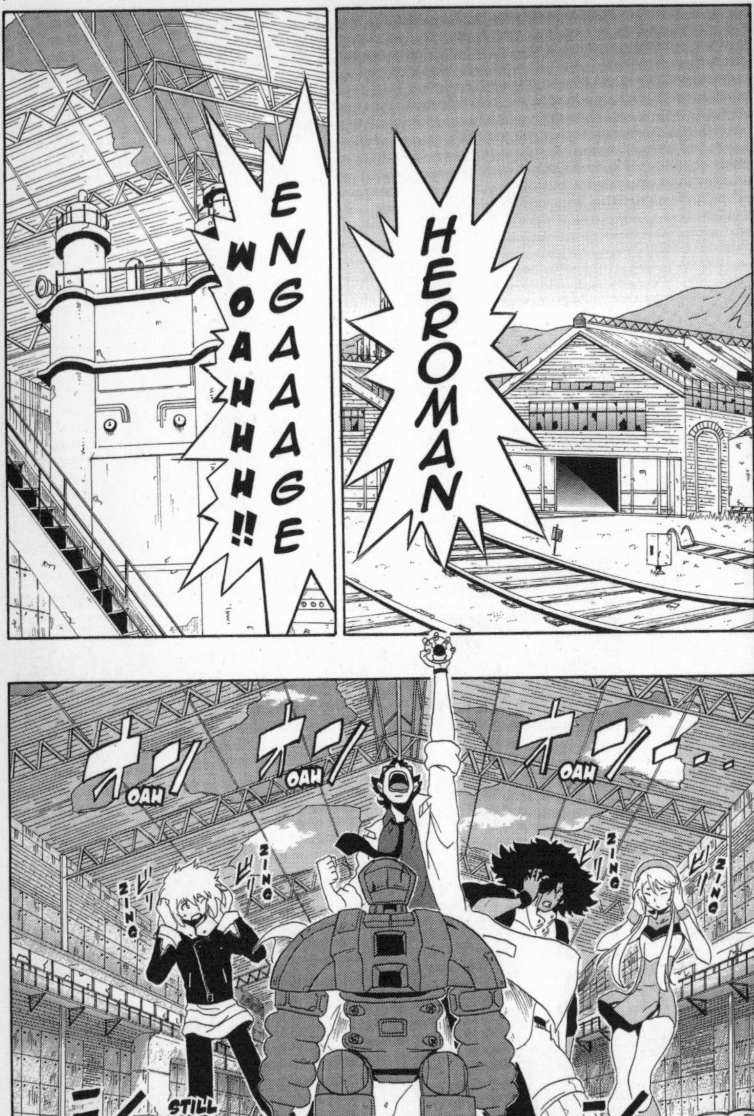
HEROMAN
ENGAAAAGE
WOAHHH!!
OAH
OAH
OAH
ZING
ZING
ZING
ZING
STILL

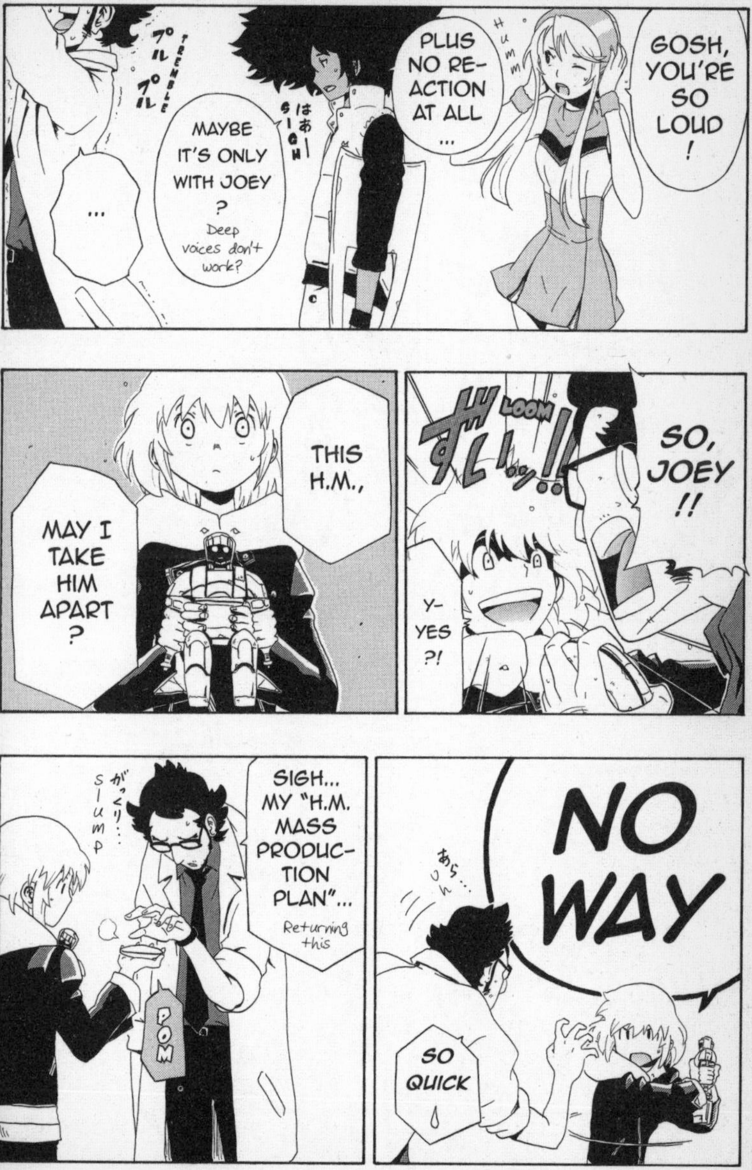
GOSH, YOU'RE SO LOUD!
Humm
PLUS NO RE-ACTION AT ALL ...
はあー
SIGH
MAYBE IT'S ONLY WITH JOEY?
Deep voices don't work?
プルプル
TREMBLE
...
SO, JOEY!!
LOOM
Y-YES?!
THIS H.M.,
MAY I TAKE HIM APART?
NO WAY
あら…
SO QUICK
SIGH... MY "H.M. MASS PRODUCTION PLAN"...
Returning this
がっくり…
SLUMP
POM

HEROMAN

THEN CAN I AT LEAST EXAMINE A TRANS- FORMED H.M.?!

OH ...

THAT, YES.

CRACKLE

ENGAGE!!

FLASH

CRAKLE CRAKLE

CRAKLE

CRAKLE

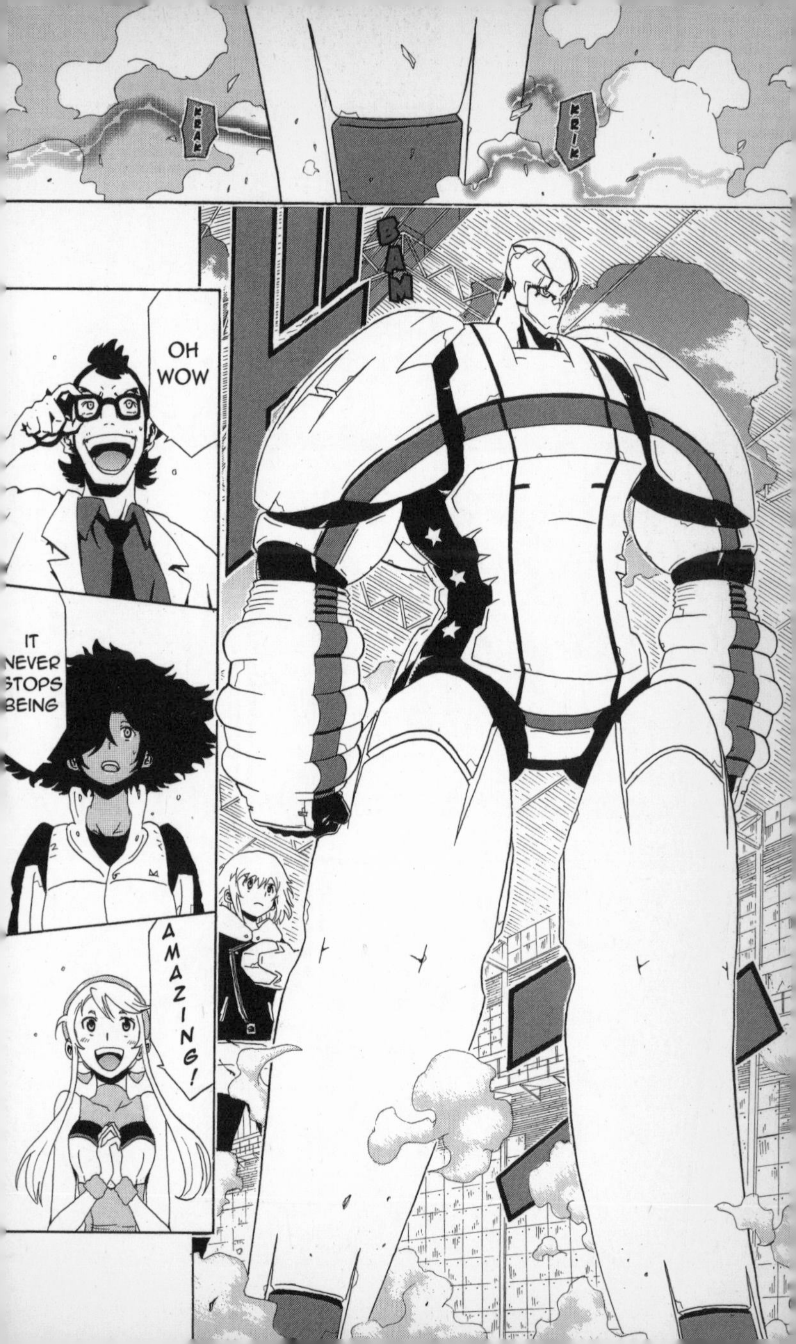
KRIK
KRAK
BAM
OH WOW
IT NEVER STOPS BEING
AMAZING!

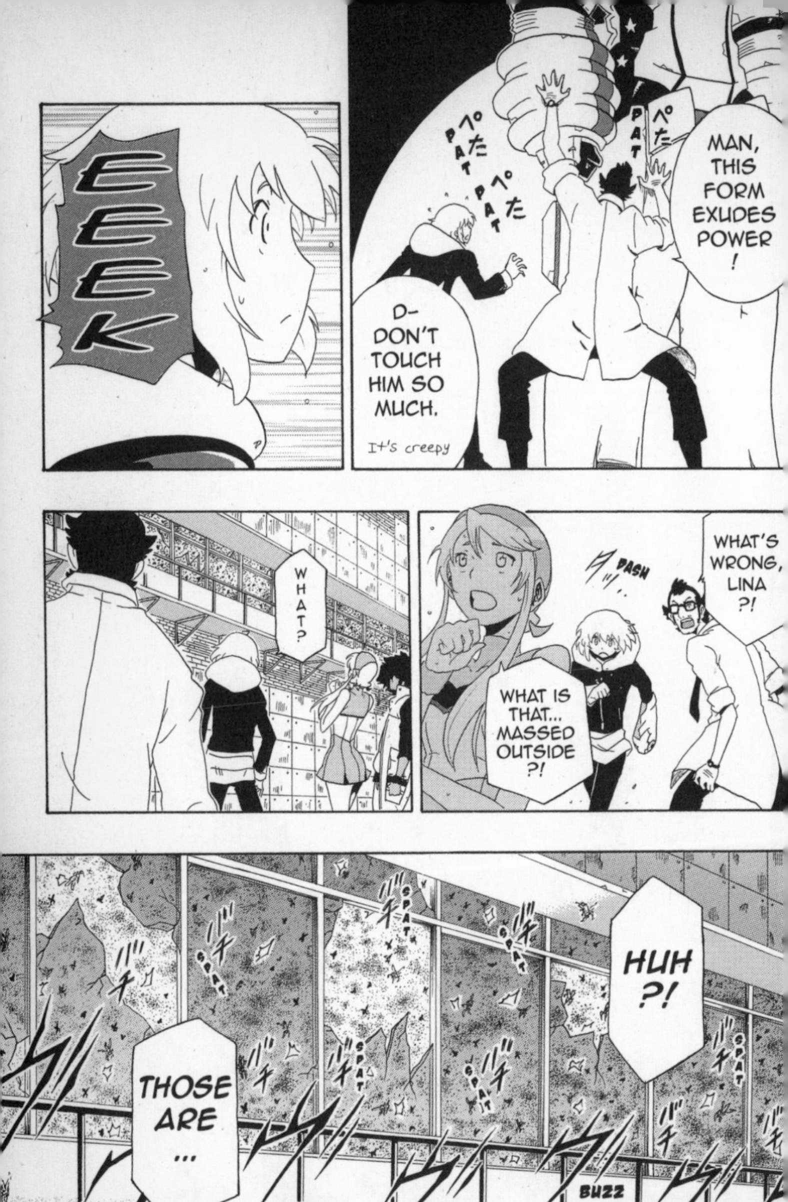

ぺた PAT
ぺた PAT
ぺた PAT
MAN, THIS FORM EXUDES POWER!
D-DON'T TOUCH HIM SO MUCH.
It's creepy
EEEK
WHAT'S WRONG, LINA?!
DASH
WHAT IS THAT... MASSED OUTSIDE?!
WHAT?
HUH?!
SPAT
SPAT
SPAT
SPAT
SPAT
SPAT
THOSE ARE...
BUZZ
BUZZ
BUZZ
BUZZ

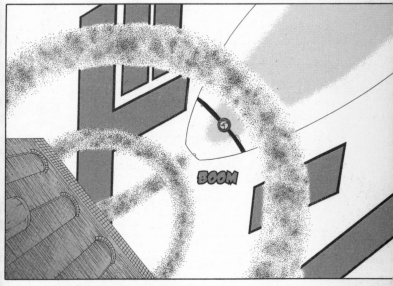

BOOM

KPANK

FWEEE

KSHHH

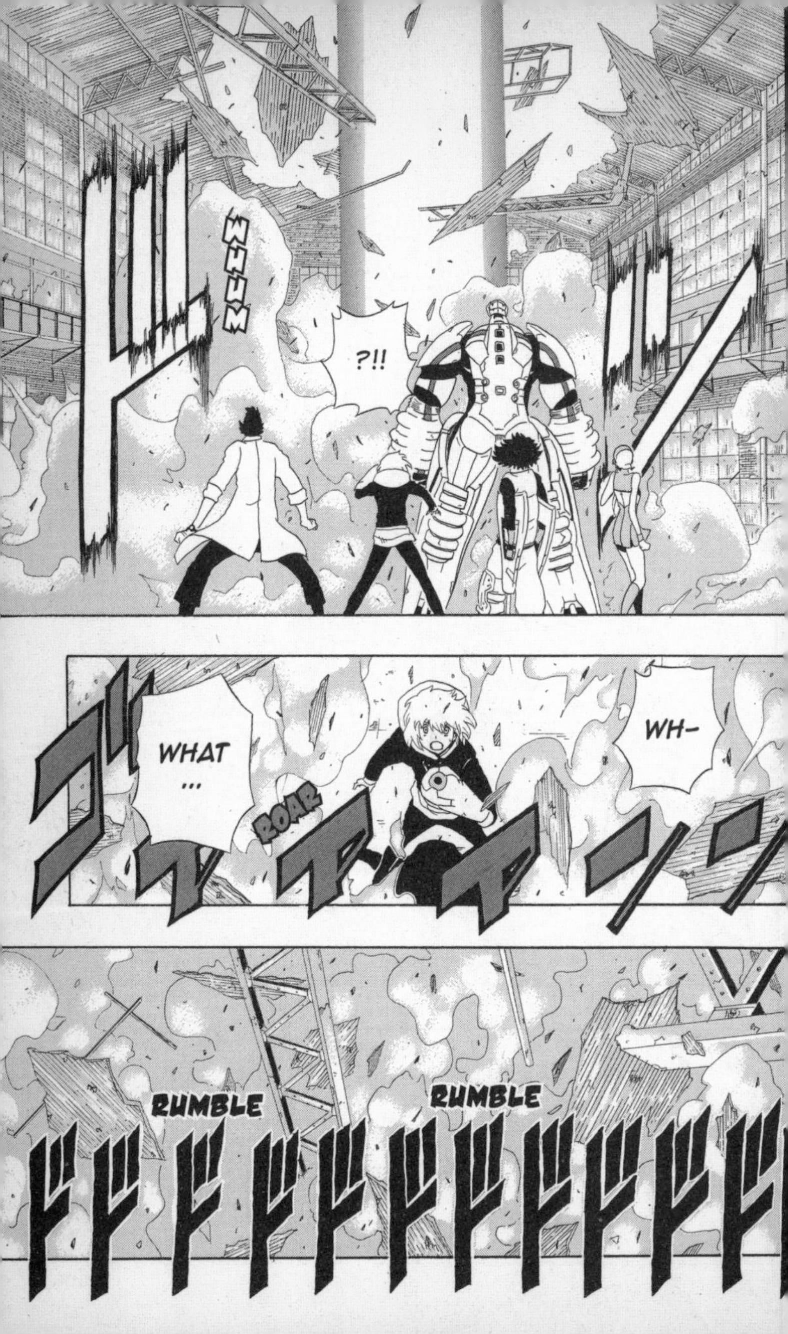
WHUMM
?!!
WH-
WHAT ...
ROAR
RUMBLE
RUMBLE

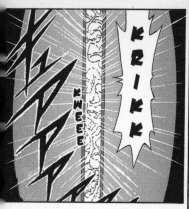

KRIKK

KWEEE

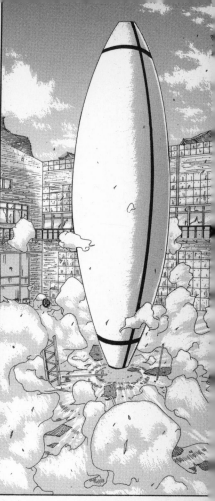

?!!

EEEE

EEEE

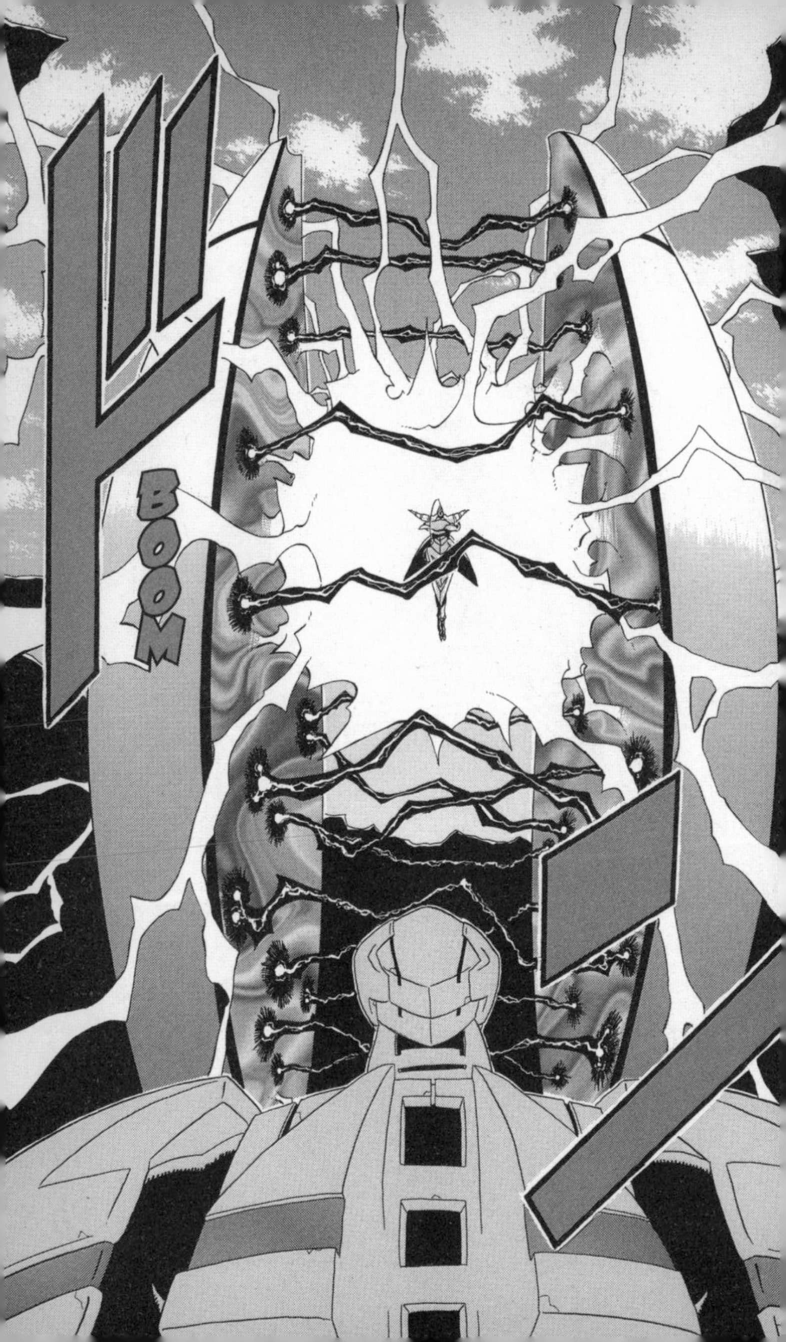
BOOM

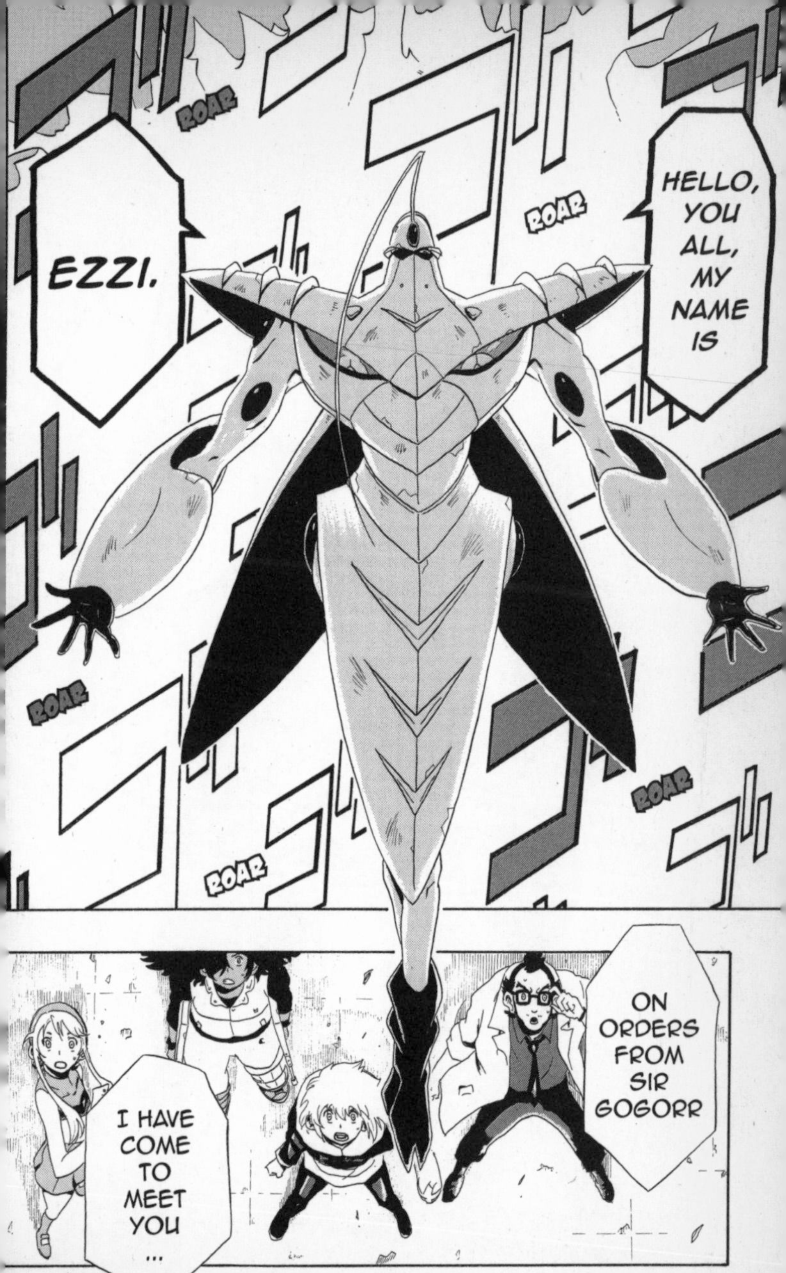
HELLO, YOU ALL, MY NAME IS
ROAR
ROAR
EZZI.
ROAR
ROAR
ROAR
ROAR
ON ORDERS FROM SIR GOGORR
I HAVE COME TO MEET YOU ...

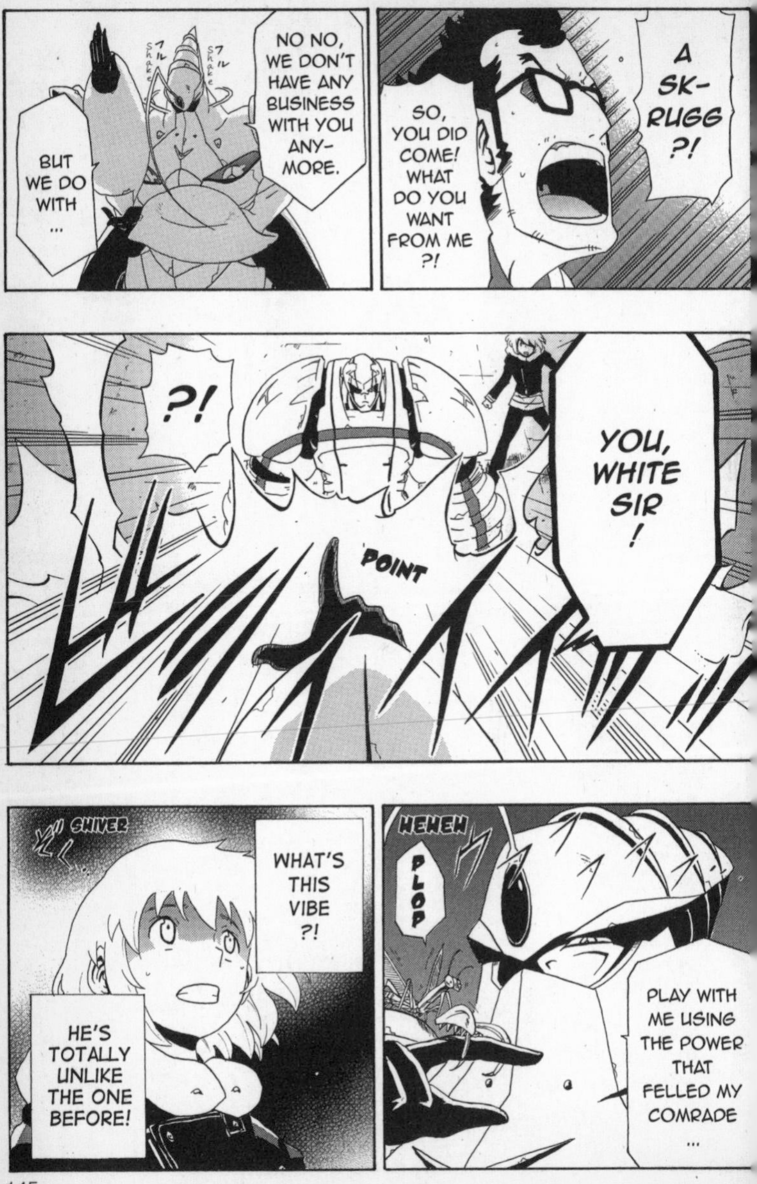
A SK-RUGG?!
SO, YOU DID COME! WHAT DO YOU WANT FROM ME?!
NO NO, WE DON'T HAVE ANY BUSINESS WITH YOU ANYMORE.
BUT WE DO WITH ...
YOU, WHITE SIR!
POINT
?!
HEHEH
PLOP
PLAY WITH ME USING THE POWER THAT FELLED MY COMRADE ...
SHIVER
WHAT'S THIS VIBE?!
HE'S TOTALLY UNLIKE THE ONE BEFORE!

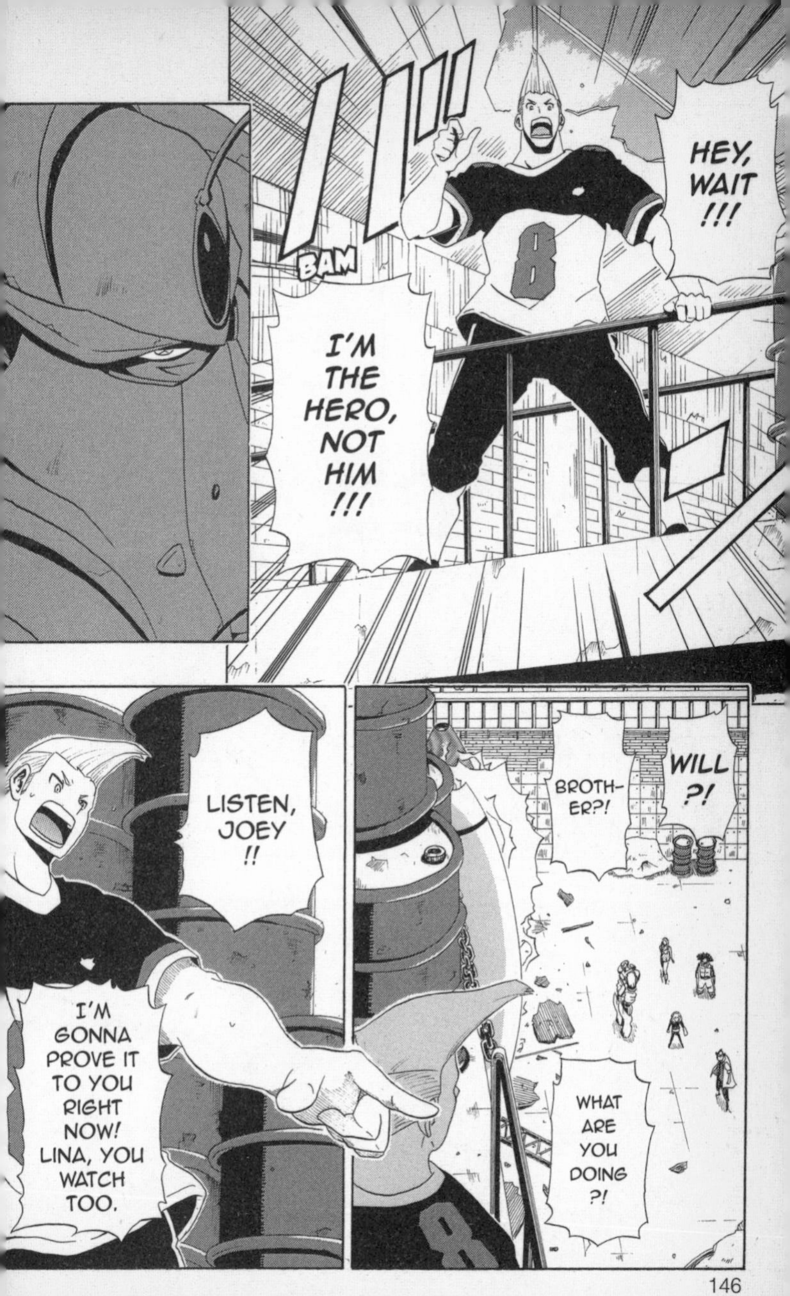
HEY, WAIT !!!
BAM
I'M THE HERO, NOT HIM !!!
WILL ?!
BROTHER?!
WHAT ARE YOU DOING ?!
LISTEN, JOEY !!
I'M GONNA PROVE IT TO YOU RIGHT NOW! LINA, YOU WATCH TOO.

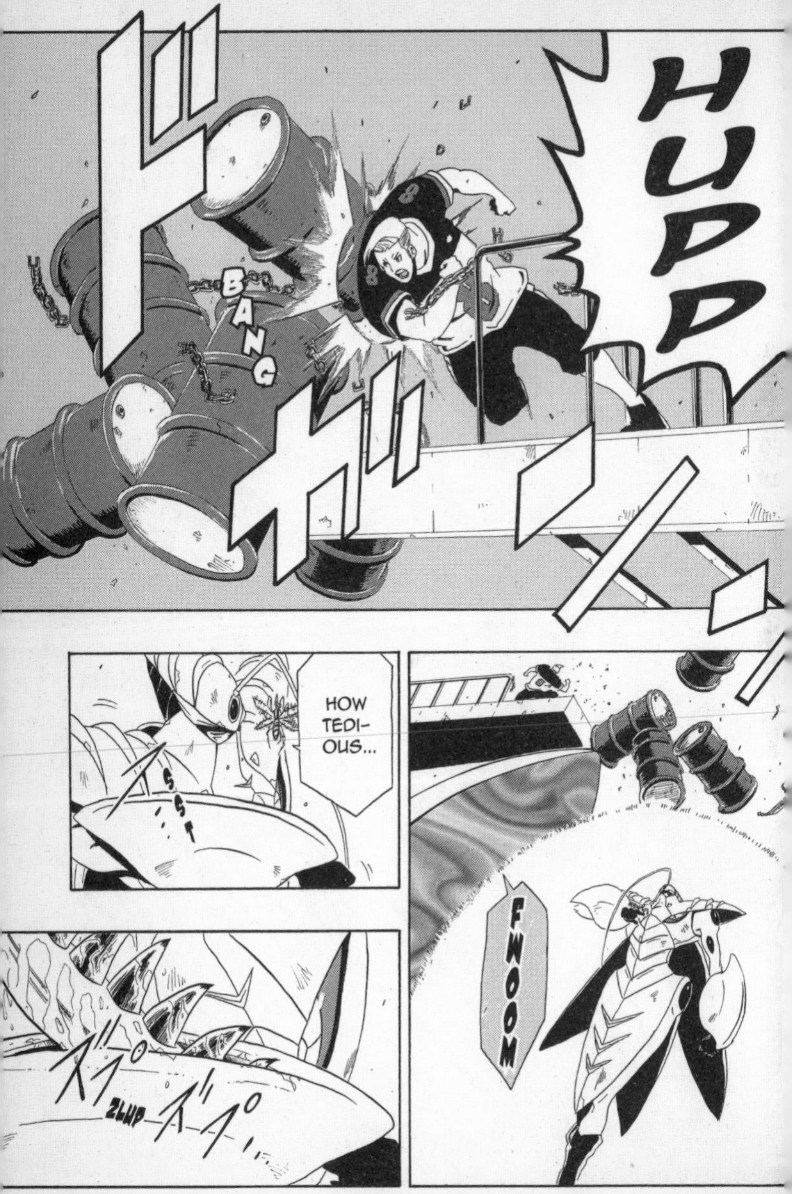
HUPP
BANG
FWOOM
HOW TEDIOUS...
SSST
ZLUP

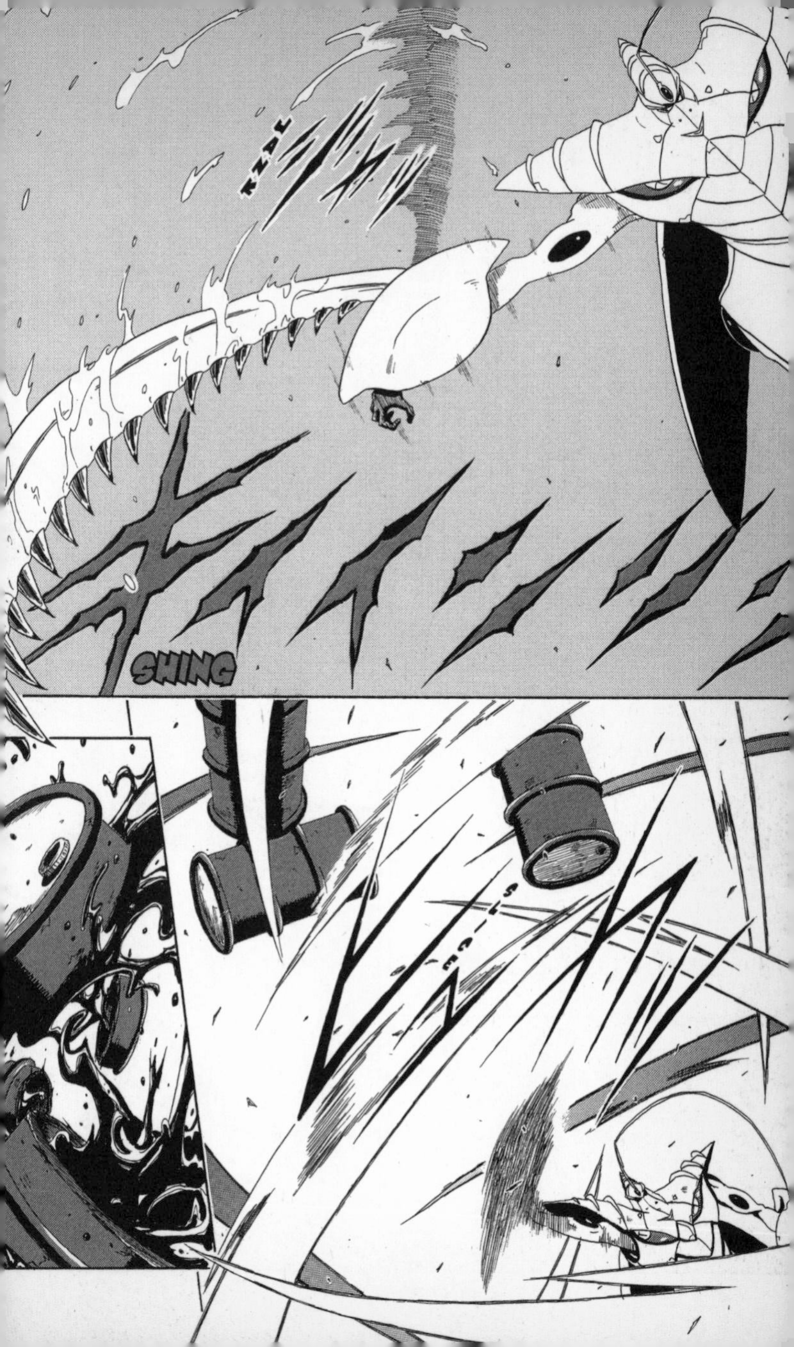
KZAK
SHING
SLICE

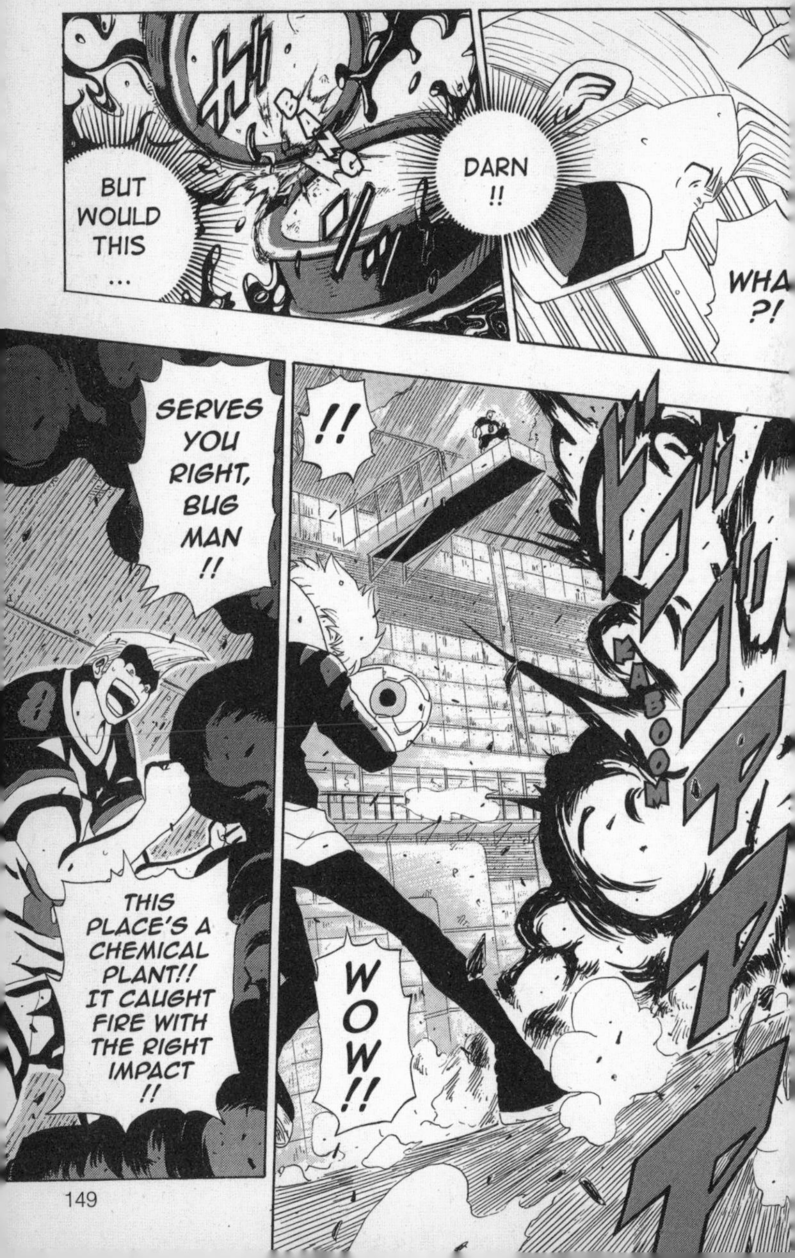
WHA ?!
DARN !!
BANG
BUT WOULD THIS ...
KABOOM
!!
SERVES YOU RIGHT, BUG MAN !!
WOW!!
THIS PLACE'S A CHEMICAL PLANT!! IT CAUGHT FIRE WITH THE RIGHT IMPACT !!

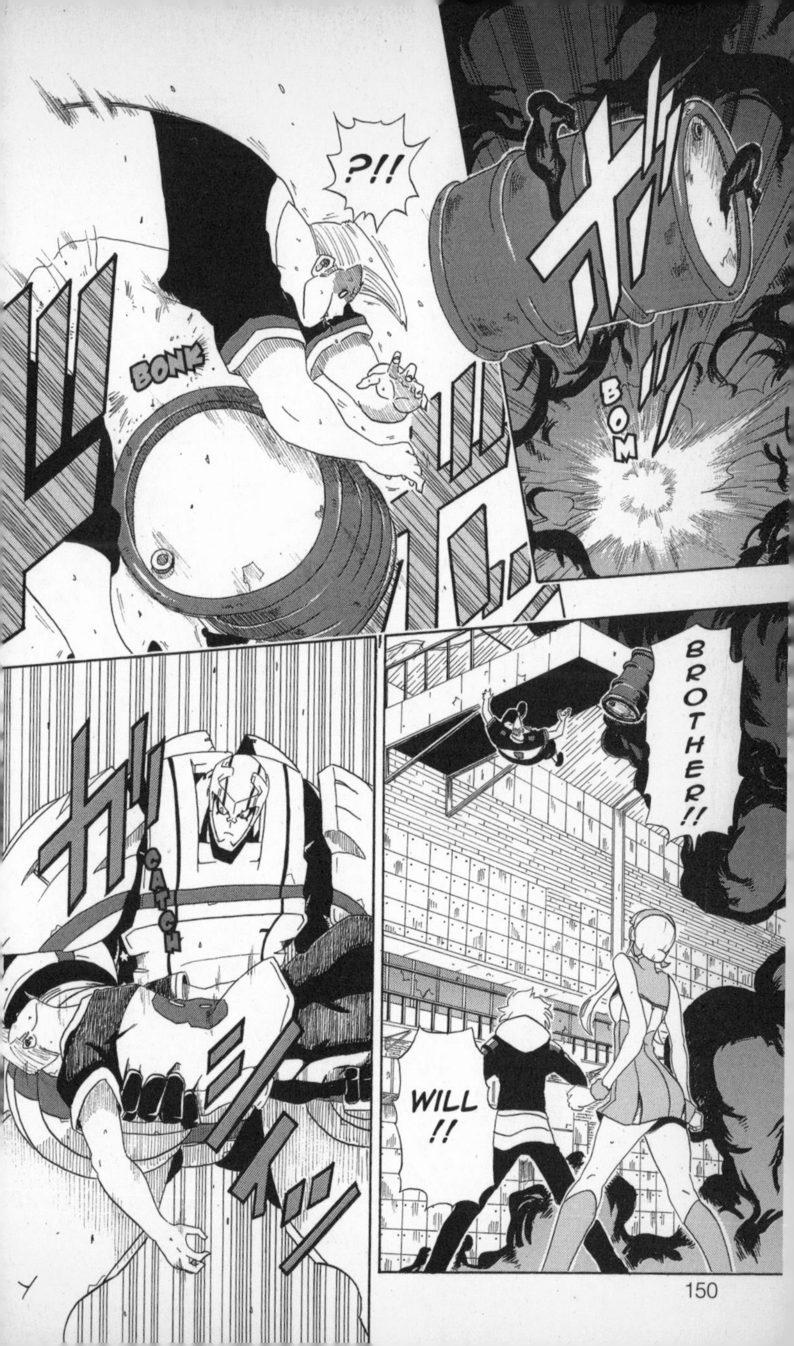
BOM
?!!
BONK
BROTHER!!
WILL!!
CATCH

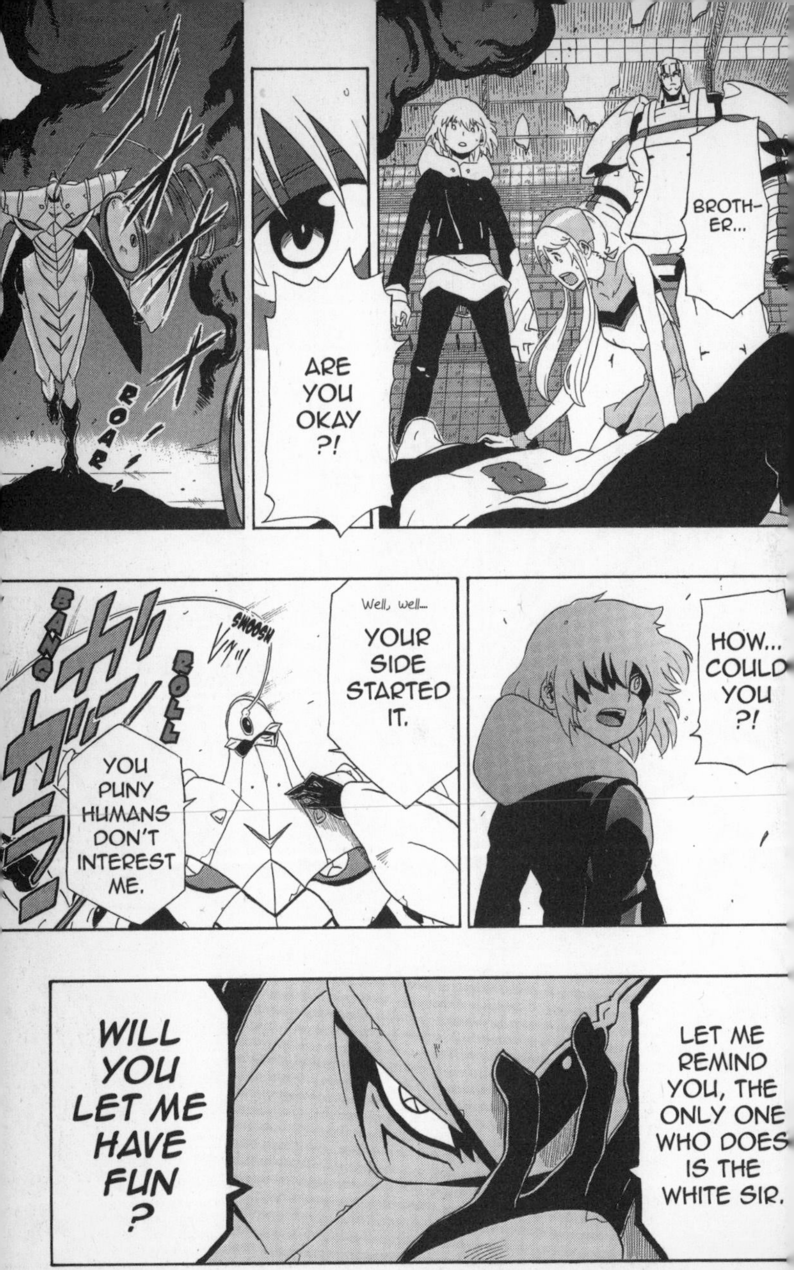
BROTHER...
ARE YOU OKAY ?!
ROAR
HOW... COULD YOU ?!
Well, well...
YOUR SIDE STARTED IT.
SHOOSH
ROLL
BANG
YOU PUNY HUMANS DON'T INTEREST ME.
LET ME REMIND YOU, THE ONLY ONE WHO DOES IS THE WHITE SIR.
WILL YOU LET ME HAVE FUN ?

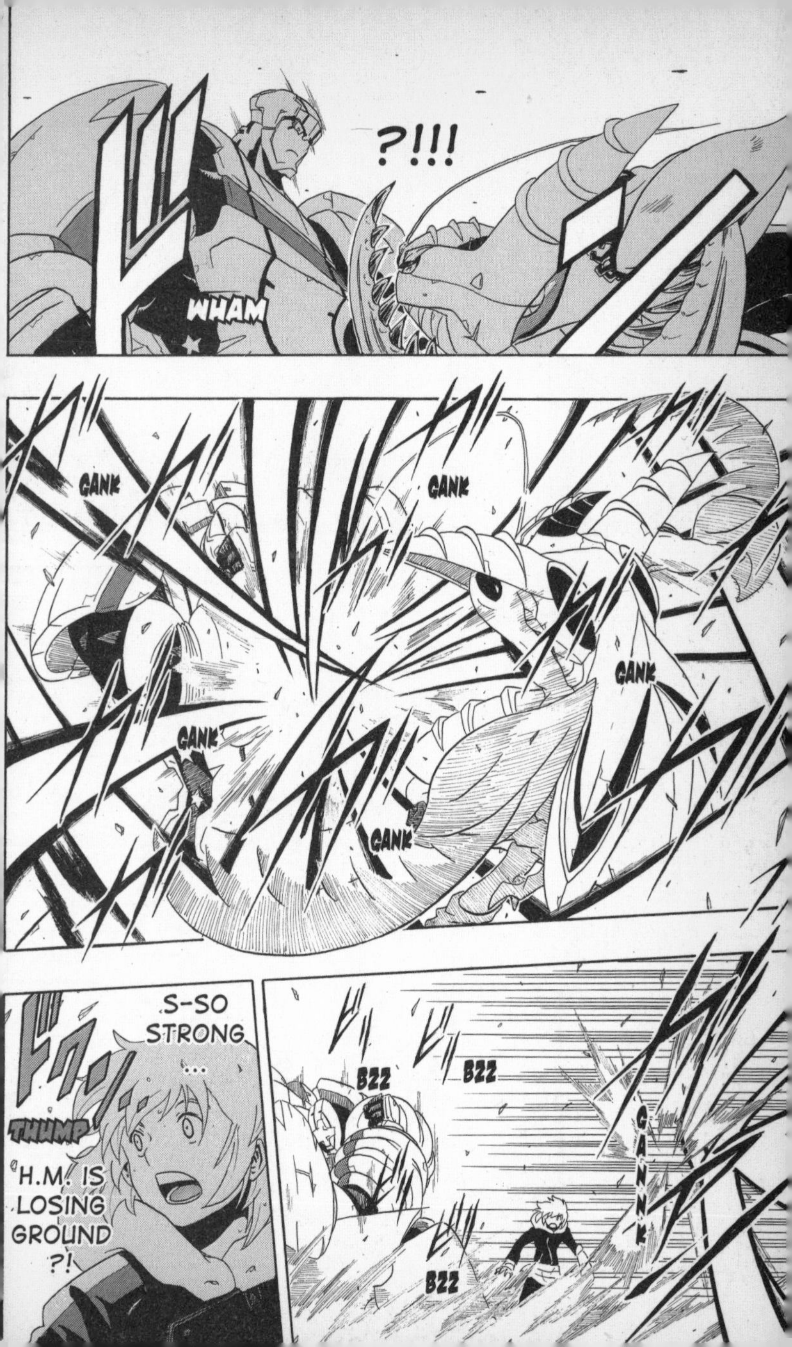
?!!!
WHAM
GANK
GANK
GANK
GANK
GANK
GANNK
BZZ
BZZ
BZZ
S-SO STRONG...
THUMP
H.M. IS LOSING GROUND?!

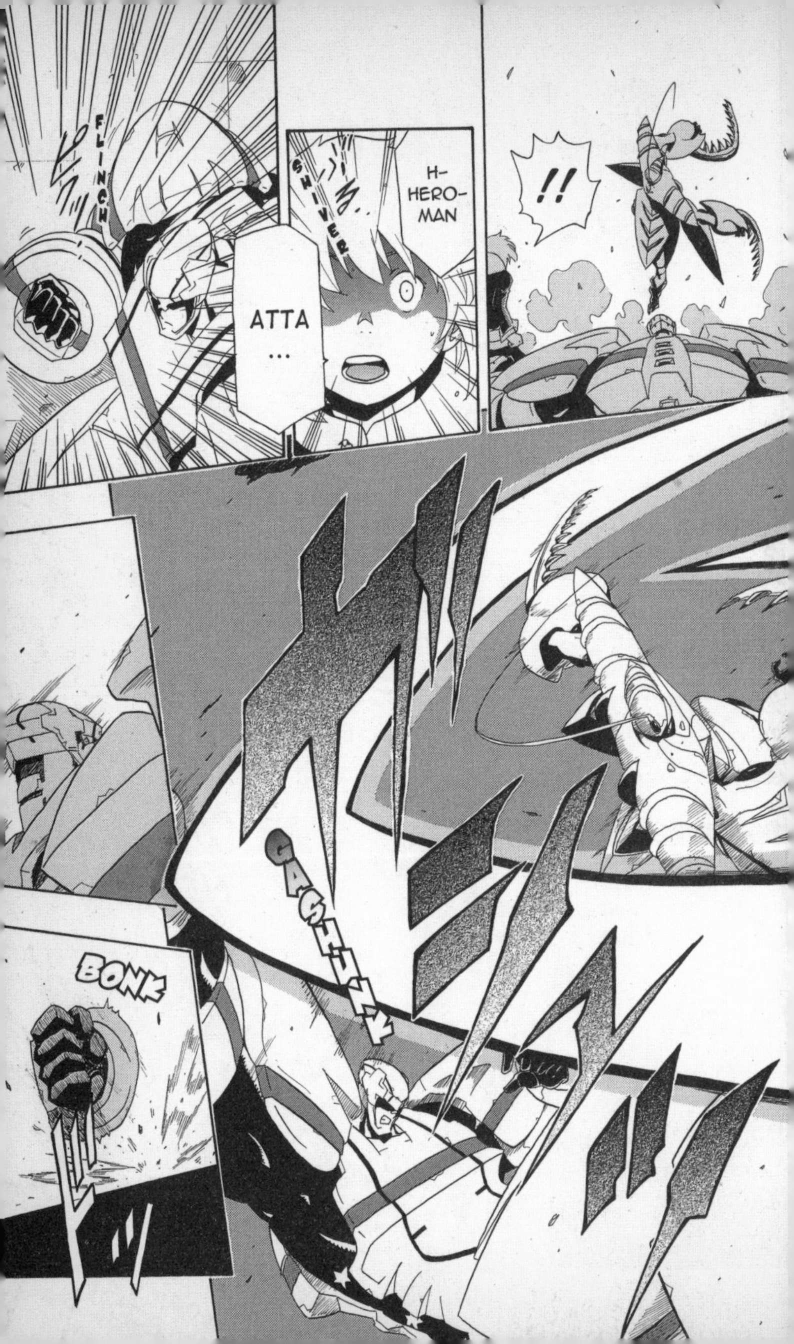
!!
H-HERO-MAN
SHIVER
ATTA ...
FLINCH
GASHUNK
BONK

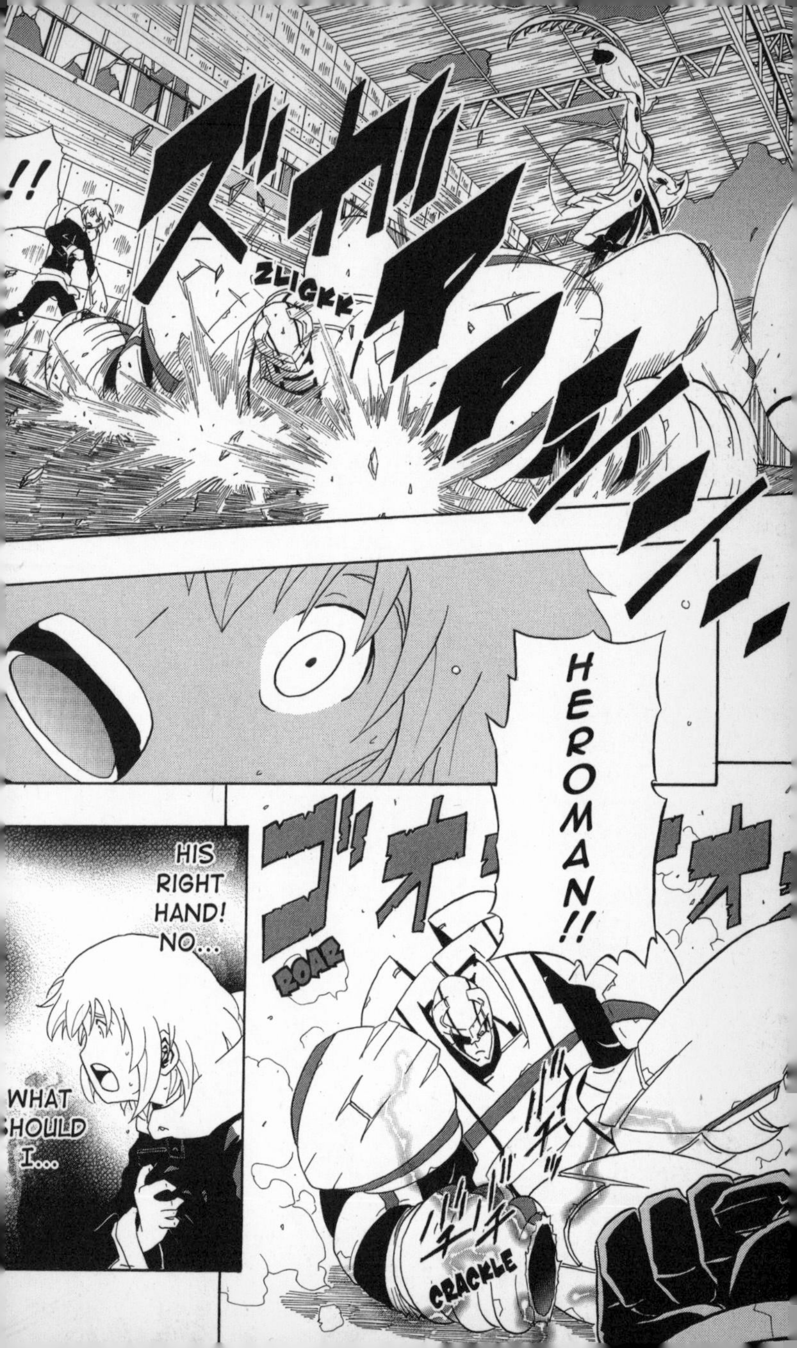
!!
ZLIGKK
HEROMAN!!
ROAR
CRACKLE
HIS RIGHT HAND! NO...
WHAT SHOULD I...

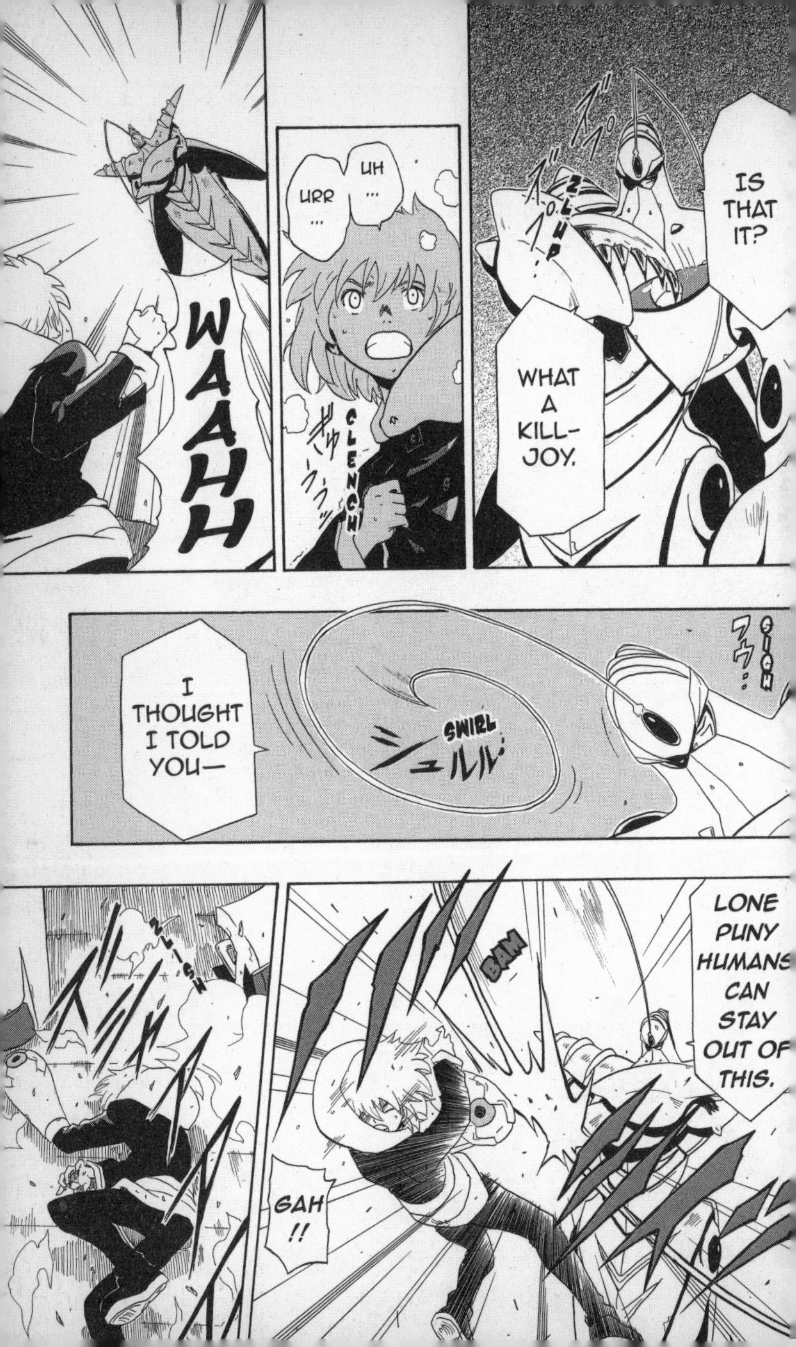
IS THAT IT?
ZLURP
WHAT A KILL-JOY.
UH ...
URR ...
CLENCH
WAAHH
SIGH
SWIRL
I THOUGHT I TOLD YOU—
LONE PUNY HUMANS CAN STAY OUT OF THIS.
BAM
GAH !!
ZLISH

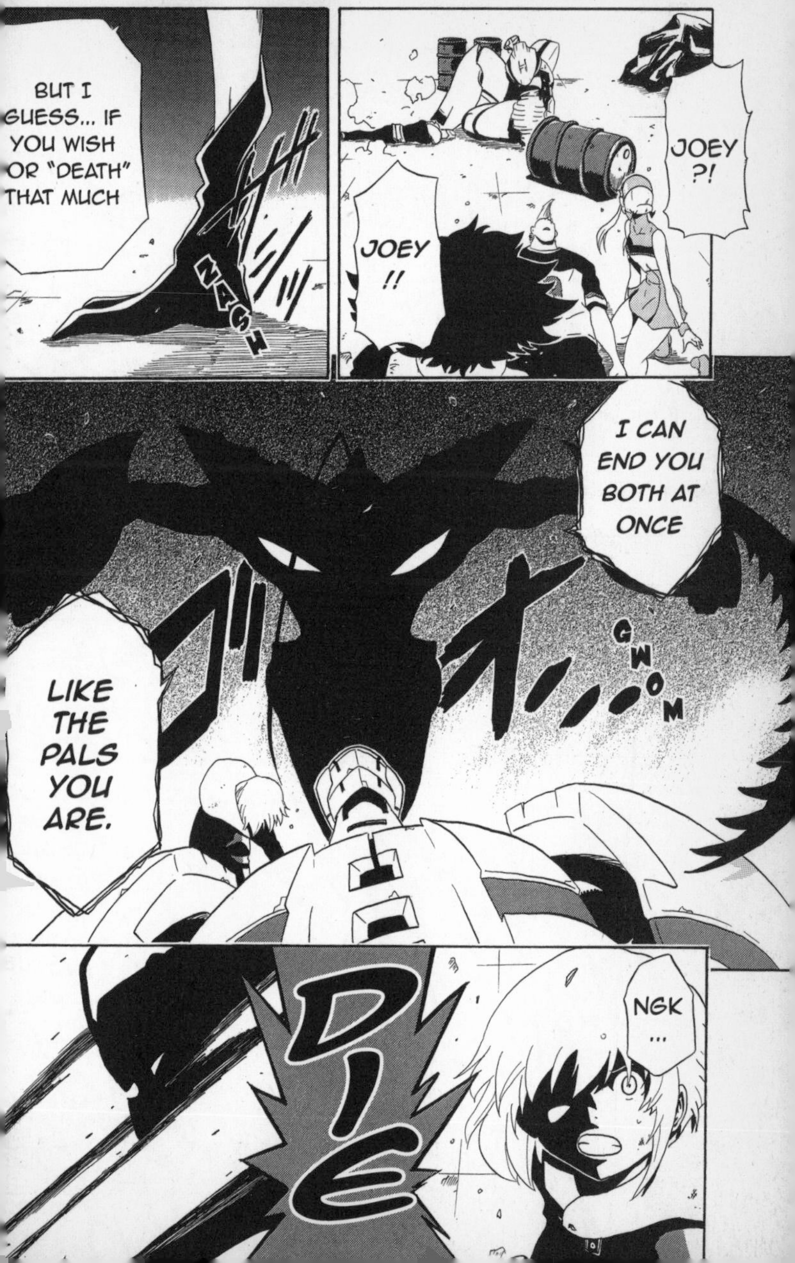
JOEY ?!
JOEY !!
BUT I GUESS... IF YOU WISH OR "DEATH" THAT MUCH
ZASH
I CAN END YOU BOTH AT ONCE
LIKE THE PALS YOU ARE.
GWOOM
NGK ...
DIE

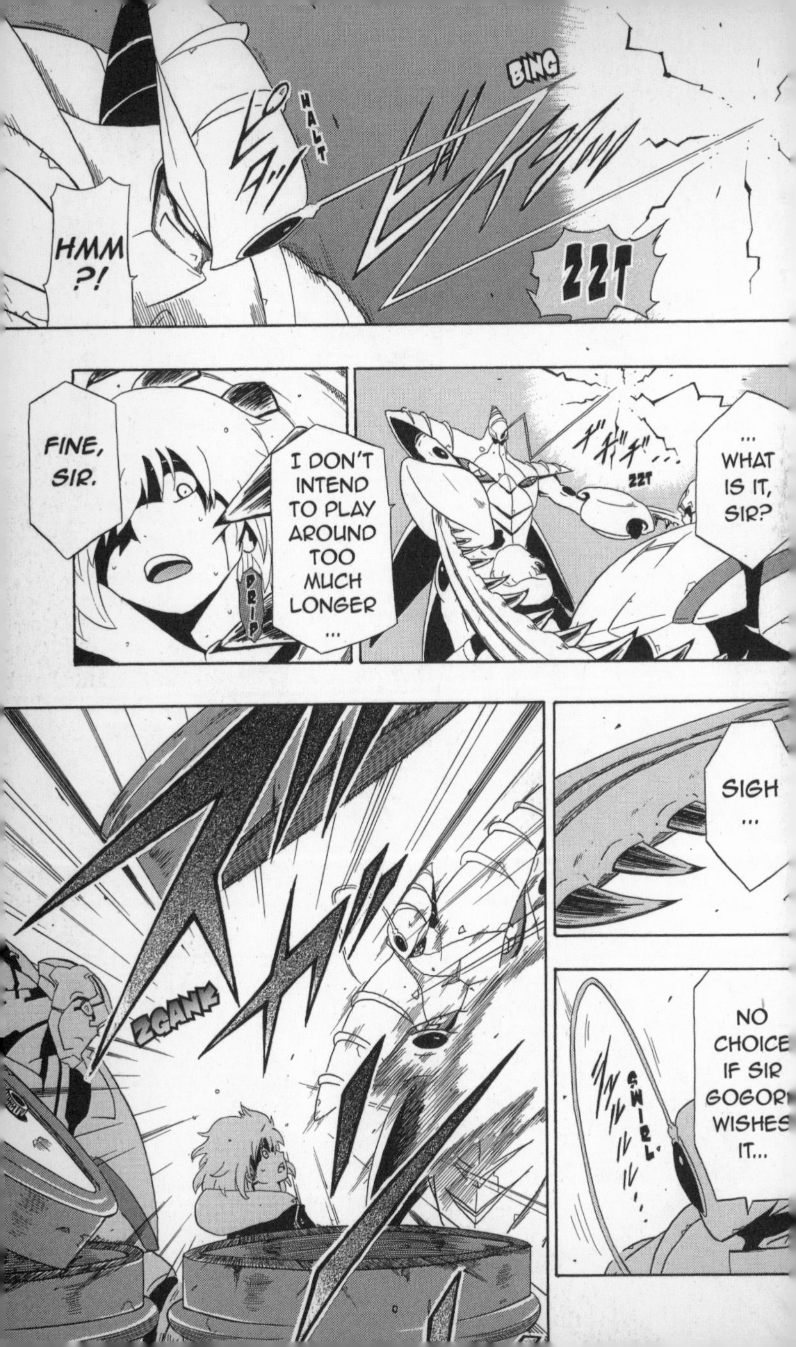
BING
HALT
ZZT
HMM ?!
... WHAT IS IT, SIR?
ZZT
I DON'T INTEND TO PLAY AROUND TOO MUCH LONGER ...
FINE, SIR.
DRIP
SIGH ...
NO CHOICE IF SIR GOGORI WISHES IT...
SWIRL
ZGANK

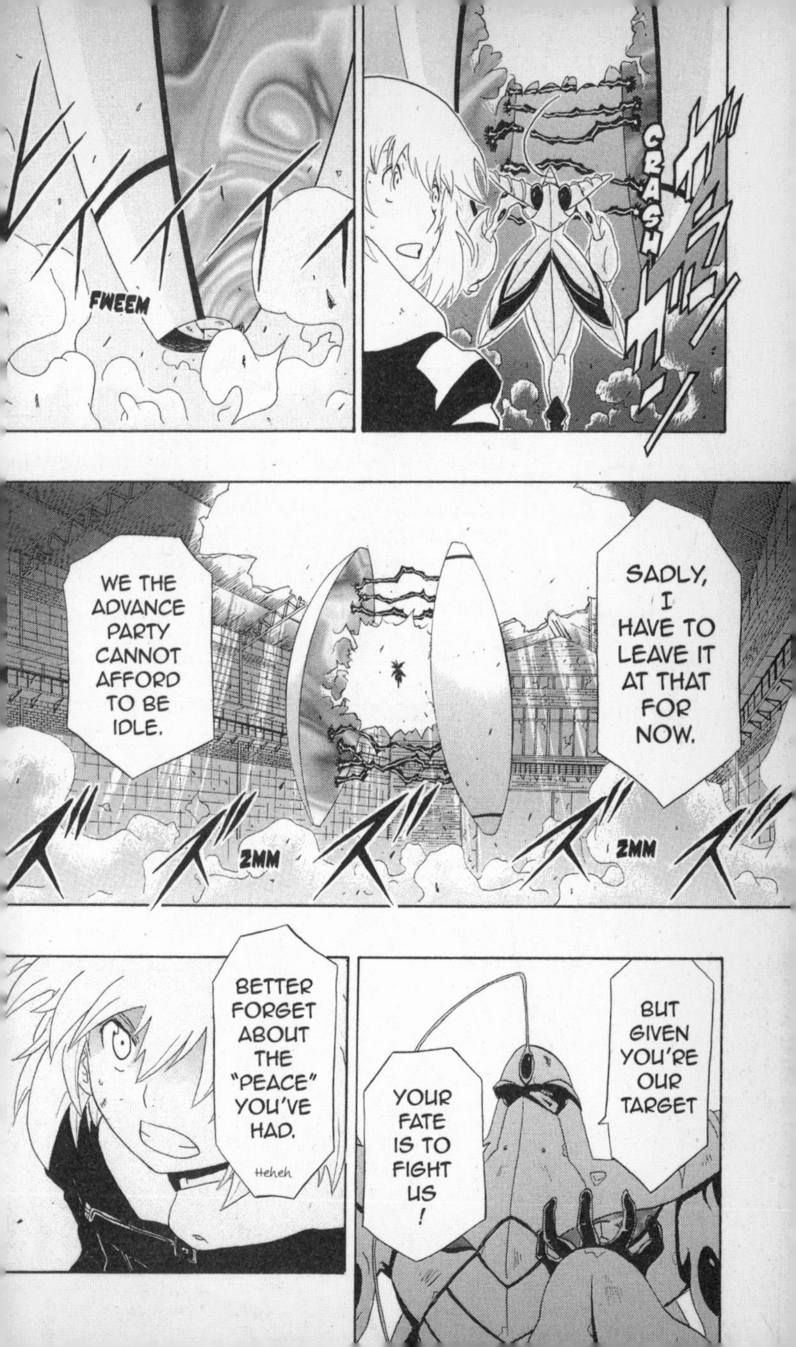
CRASH
FWEEM
SADLY, I HAVE TO LEAVE IT AT THAT FOR NOW.
WE THE ADVANCE PARTY CANNOT AFFORD TO BE IDLE.
ZMM
ZMM
BUT GIVEN YOU'RE OUR TARGET
YOUR FATE IS TO FIGHT US!
BETTER FORGET ABOUT THE "PEACE" YOU'VE HAD.
Heheh

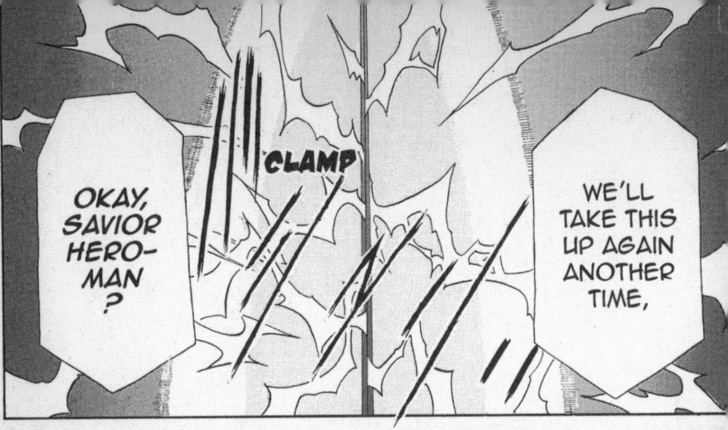
WE'LL TAKE THIS UP AGAIN ANOTHER TIME,
CLAMP
OKAY, SAVIOR HERO-MAN?
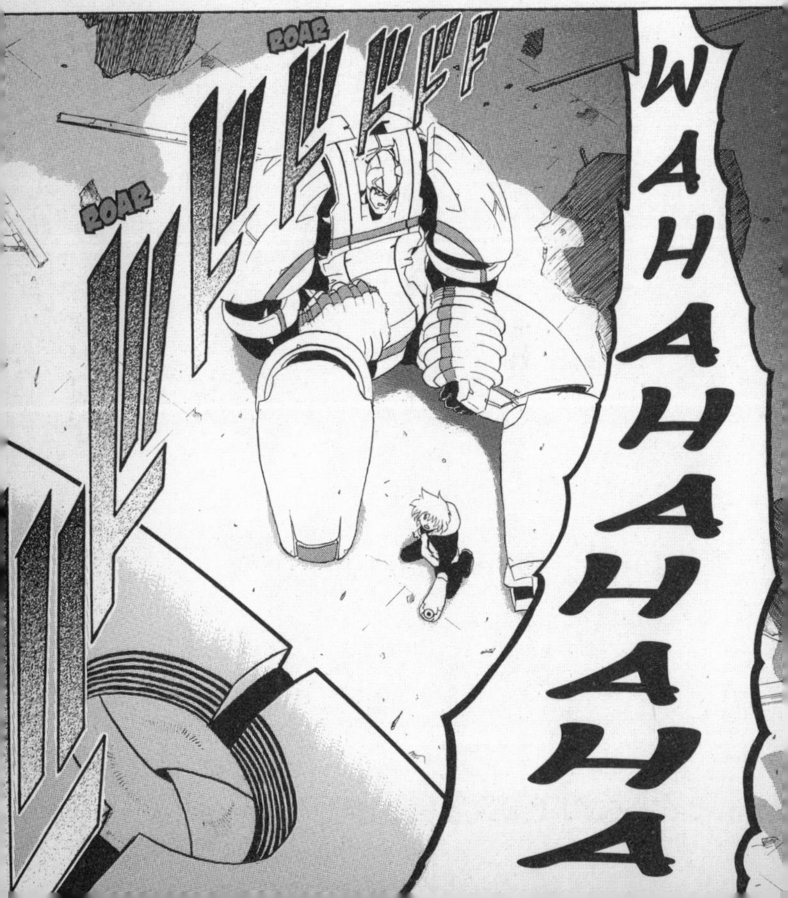
WAHAHAHAHA
ROAR
ROAR

HEROMAN

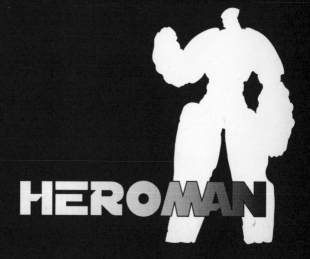

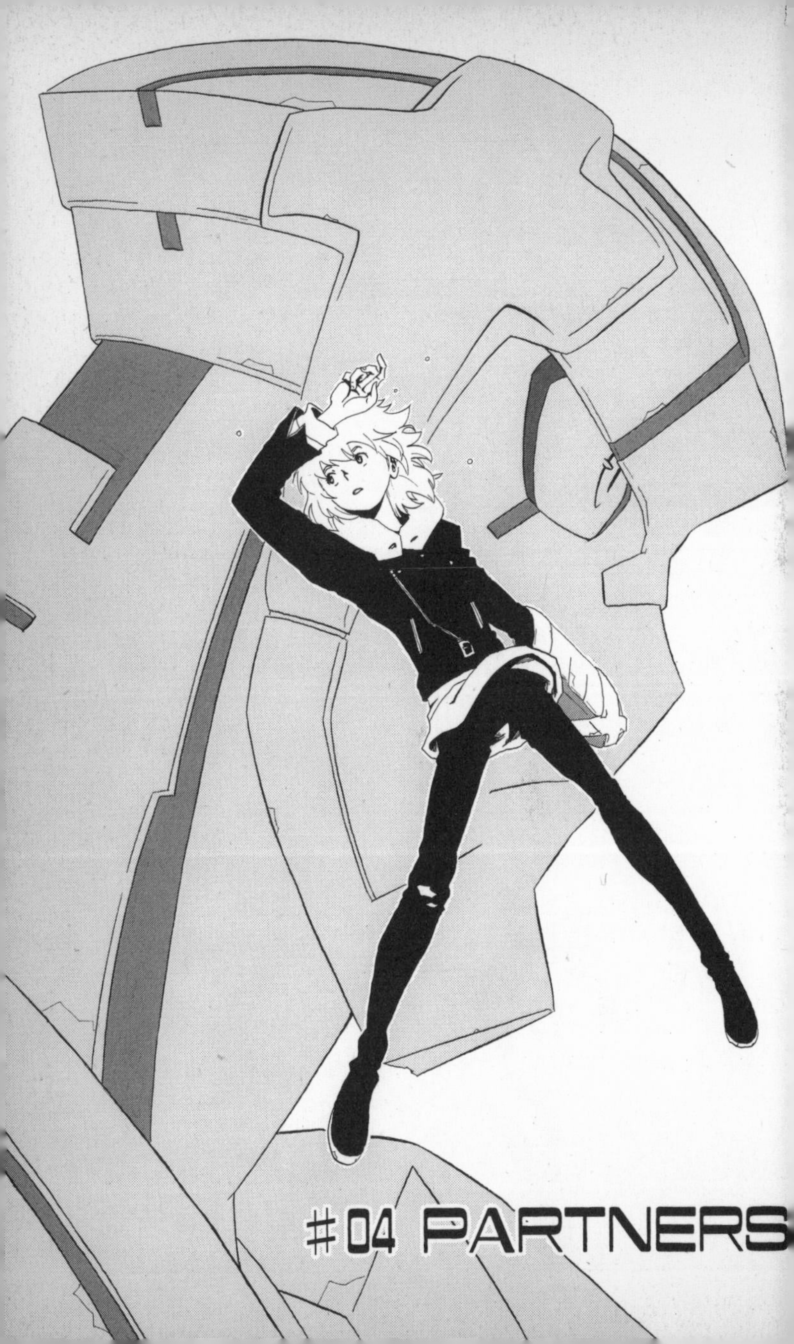

#04 PARTNERS

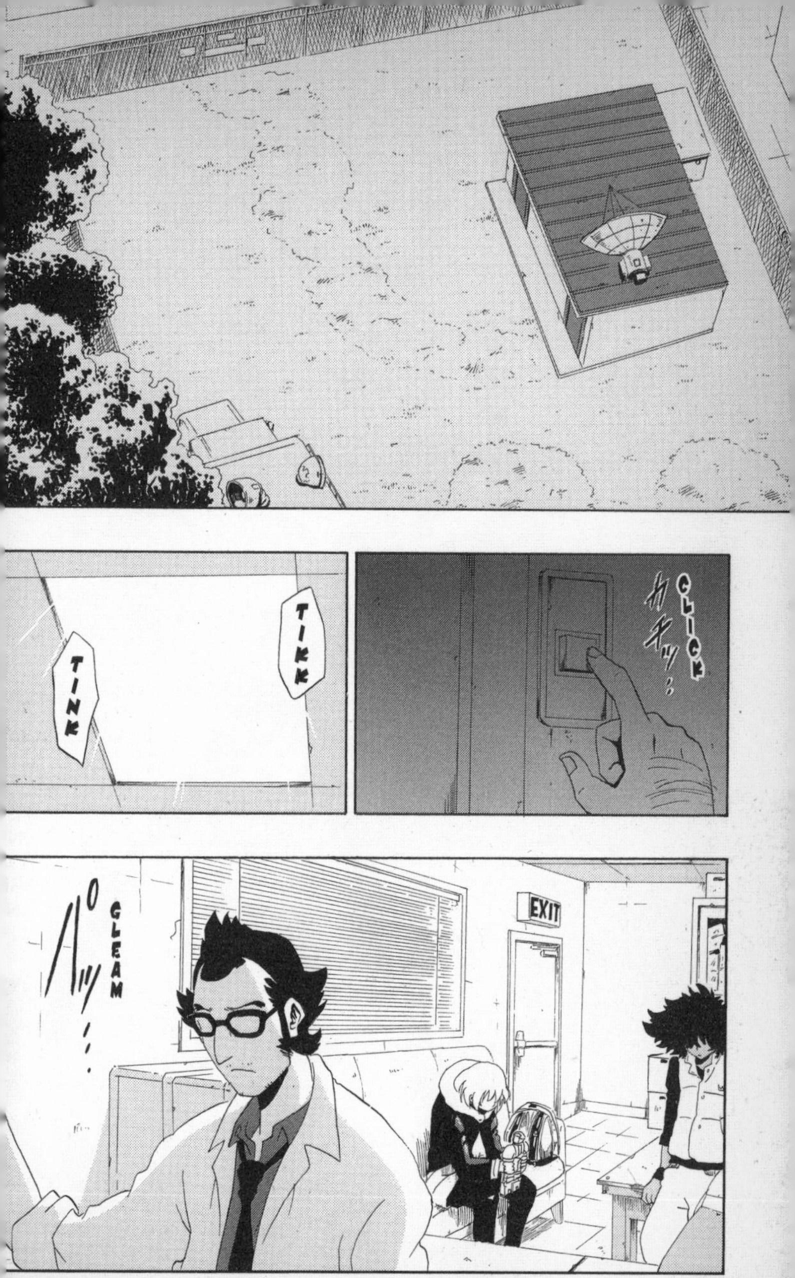
カチッ
CLICK
TIKK
TINK
パッ
GLEAM

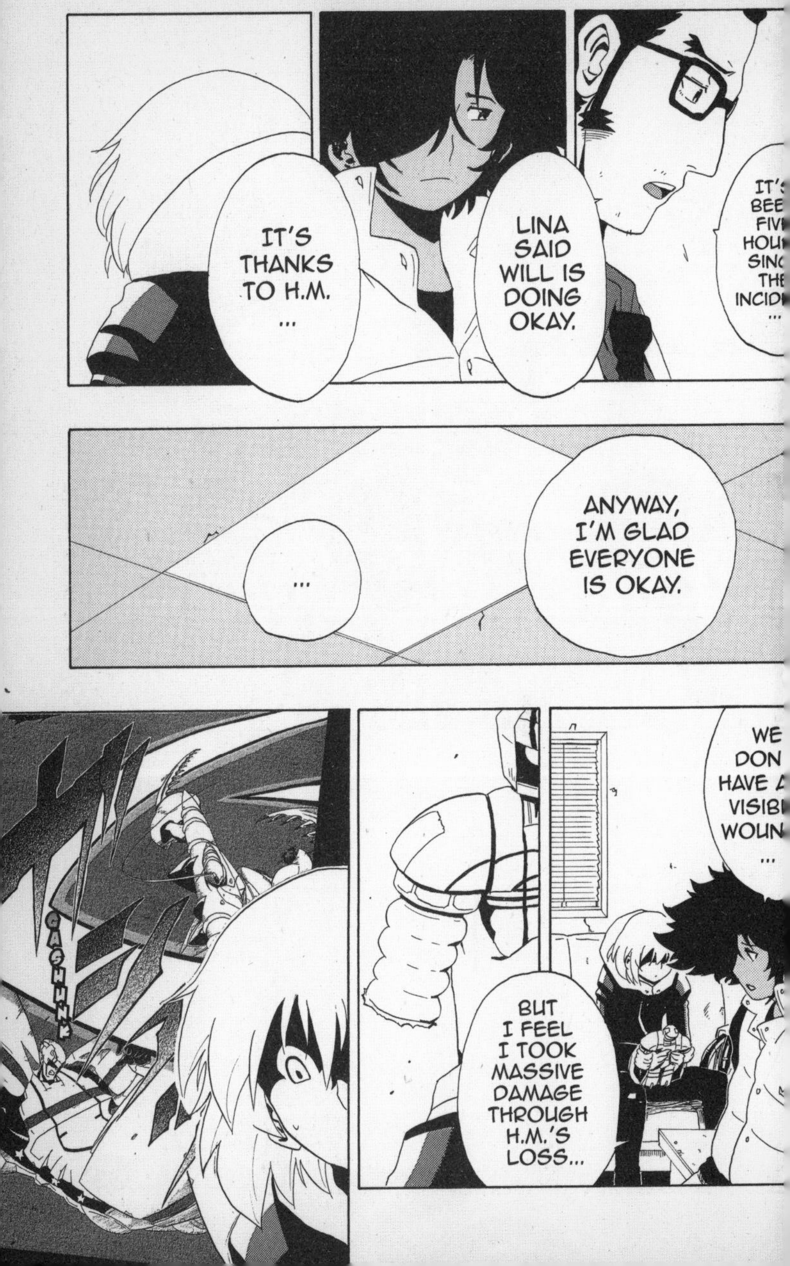
IT'S BEE FIV HOU SINC THE INCID ...
LINA SAID WILL IS DOING OKAY.
IT'S THANKS TO H.M. ...
ANYWAY, I'M GLAD EVERYONE IS OKAY.
...
WE DON HAVE A VISIBL WOUN ...
BUT I FEEL I TOOK MASSIVE DAMAGE THROUGH H.M.'S LOSS...
GASHUNK

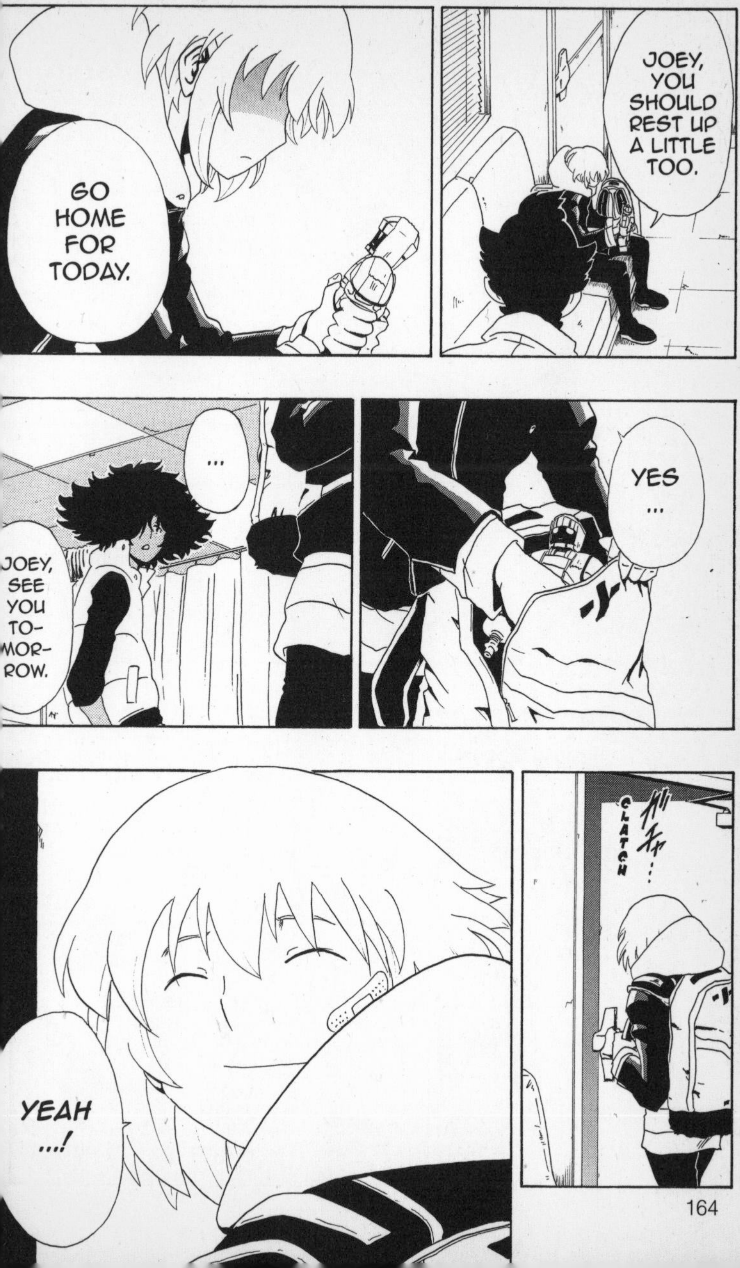
JOEY, YOU SHOULD REST UP A LITTLE TOO.
GO HOME FOR TODAY.
YES ...
...
JOEY, SEE YOU TO-MORROW.
CLATCH
YEAH ...!

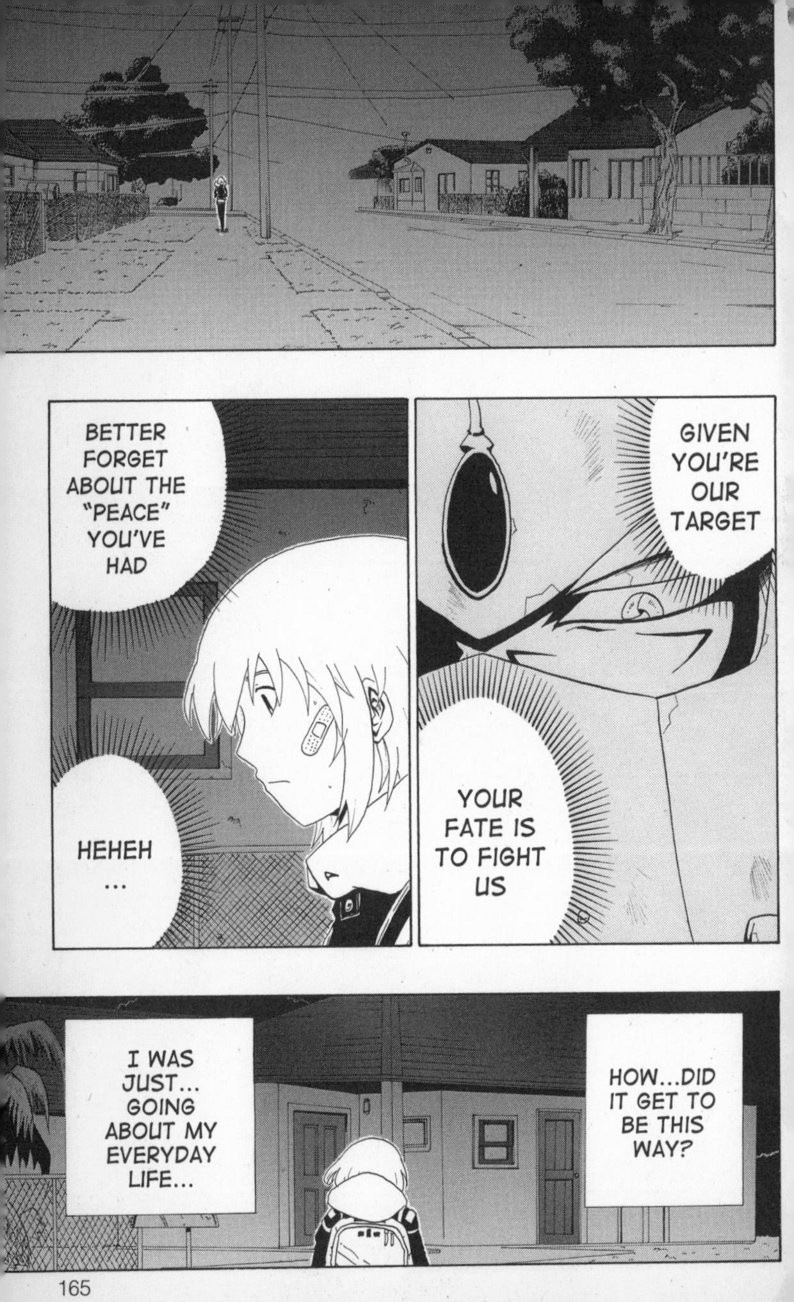
GIVEN YOU'RE OUR TARGET
YOUR FATE IS TO FIGHT US
BETTER FORGET ABOUT THE "PEACE" YOU'VE HAD
HEHEH ...
HOW...DID IT GET TO BE THIS WAY?
I WAS JUST... GOING ABOUT MY EVERYDAY LIFE...

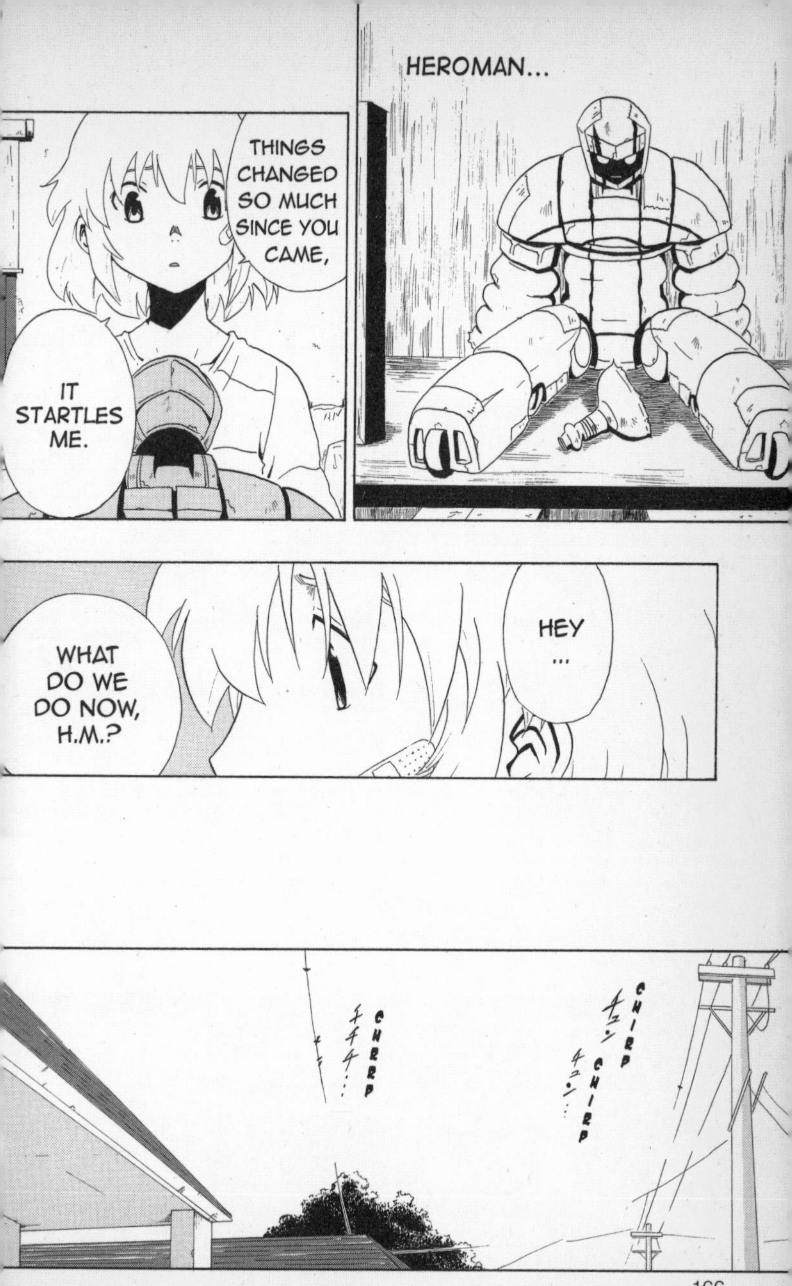
HEROMAN...
THINGS CHANGED SO MUCH SINCE YOU CAME,
IT STARTLES ME.
HEY ...
WHAT DO WE DO NOW, H.M.?
CHIRP CHIRP
CHIRP

BEEN A WHILE SINCE YOU WOKE UP THIS EARLY.

I'VE DECIDED TO START TAKING MORNING SHIFTS AGAIN ...

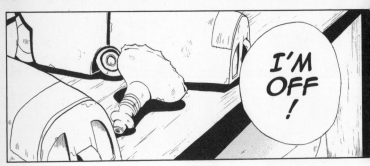

I'M OFF!

I'VE CHOSEN TO

DISTANCE MYSELF FROM H.M.

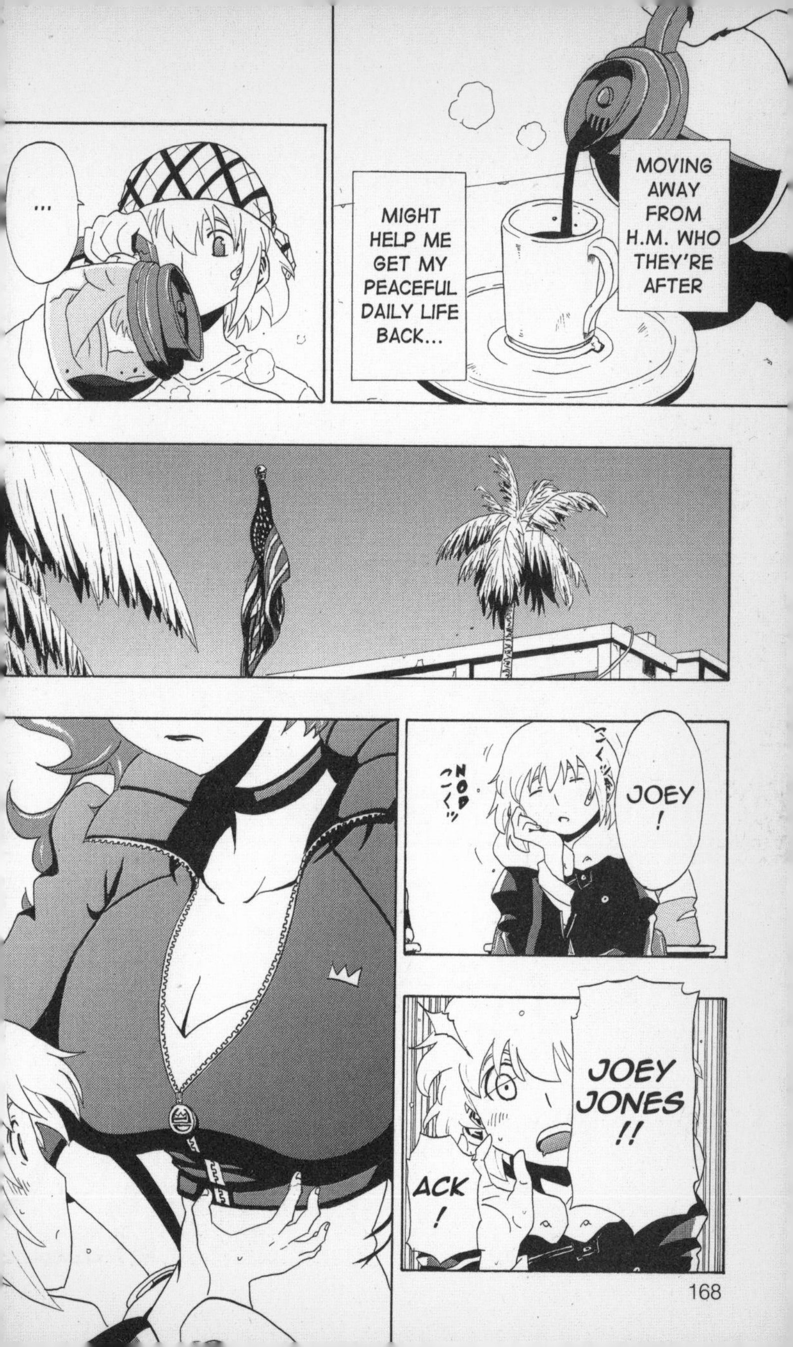

MOVING AWAY FROM H.M. WHO THEY'RE AFTER
MIGHT HELP ME GET MY PEACEFUL DAILY LIFE BACK...
...
JOEY!
NOD
JOEY JONES!!
ACK!

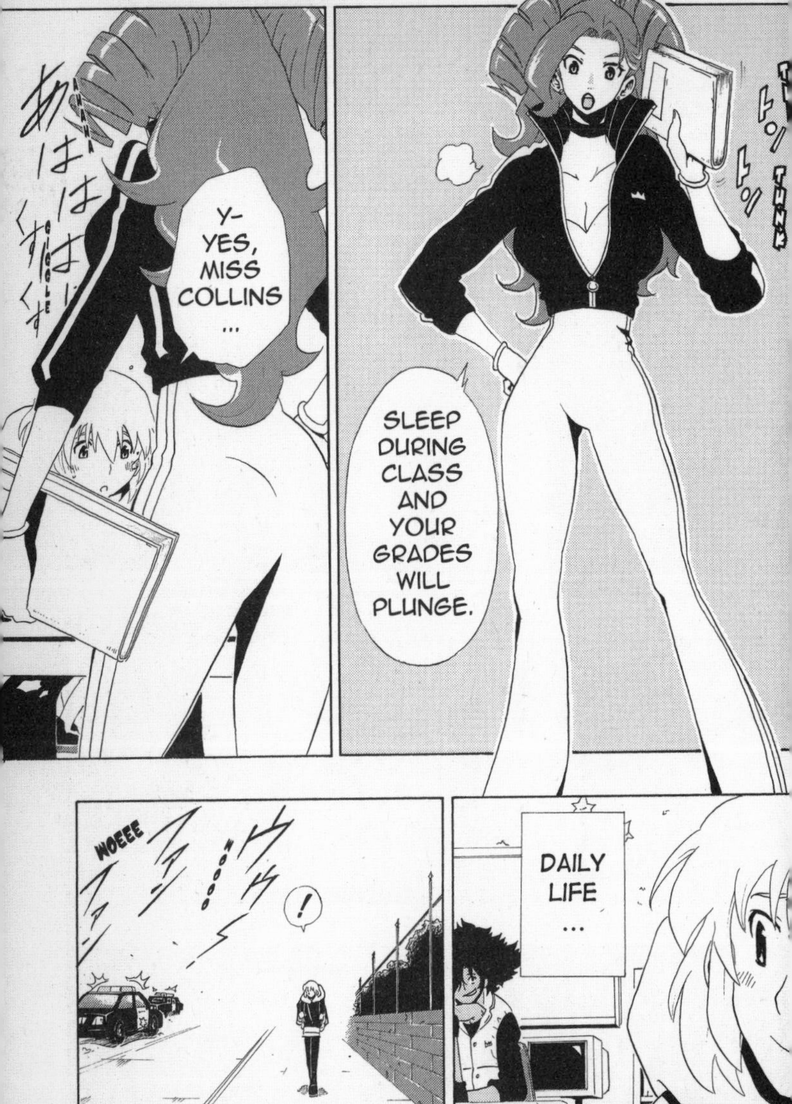
トッ トッ
THUNK
SLEEP DURING CLASS AND YOUR GRADES WILL PLUNGE.
Y-YES, MISS COLLINS ...
あははは
AHAHA
くすくす
GIGGLE
DAILY LIFE ...
ウウ
WOOOO
ファンファン
WOEEE
!

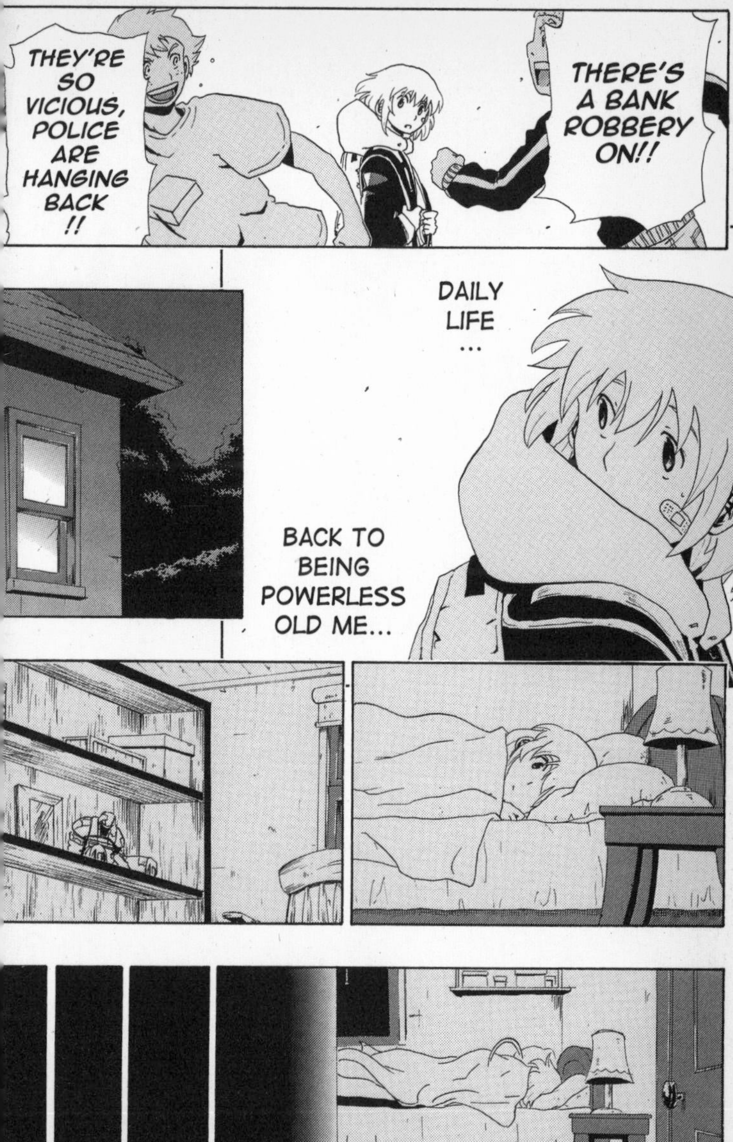
THERE'S A BANK ROBBERY ON!!
THEY'RE SO VICIOUS, POLICE ARE HANGING BACK !!
DAILY LIFE ...
BACK TO BEING POWERLESS OLD ME...

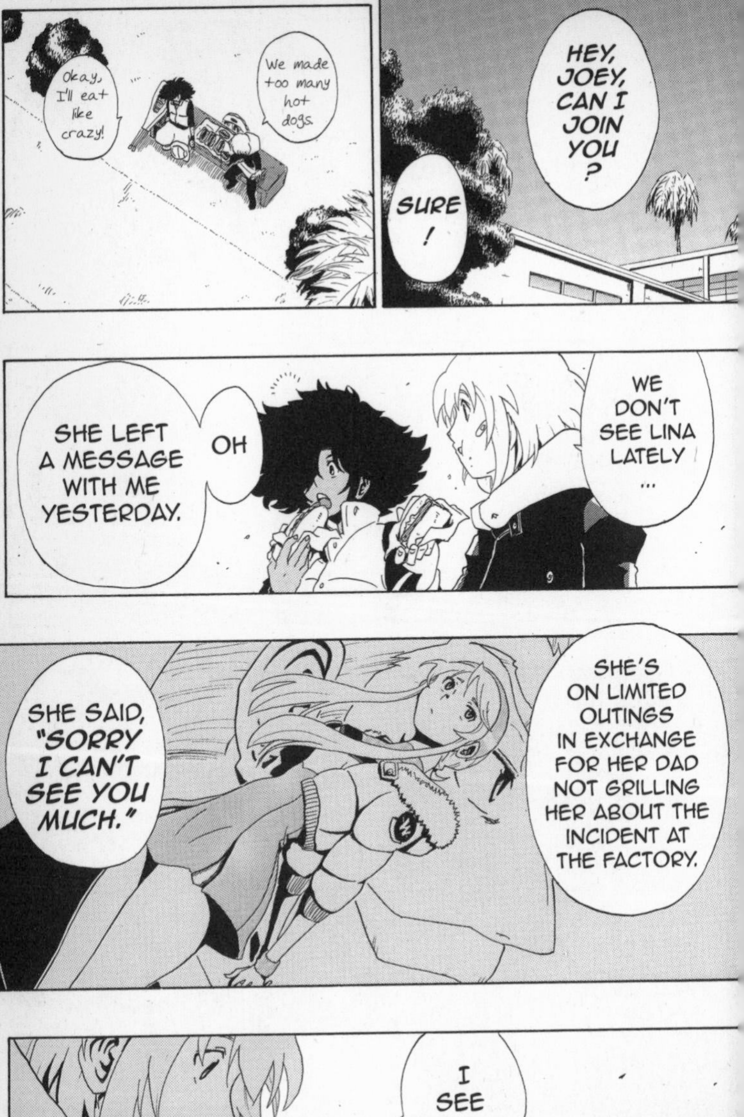
HEY, JOEY, CAN I JOIN YOU?
SURE!
We made too many hot dogs.
Okay, I'll eat like crazy!
WE DON'T SEE LINA LATELY ...
OH
SHE LEFT A MESSAGE WITH ME YESTERDAY.
SHE'S ON LIMITED OUTINGS IN EXCHANGE FOR HER DAD NOT GRILLING HER ABOUT THE INCIDENT AT THE FACTORY.
SHE SAID, "SORRY I CAN'T SEE YOU MUCH."
I SEE ...

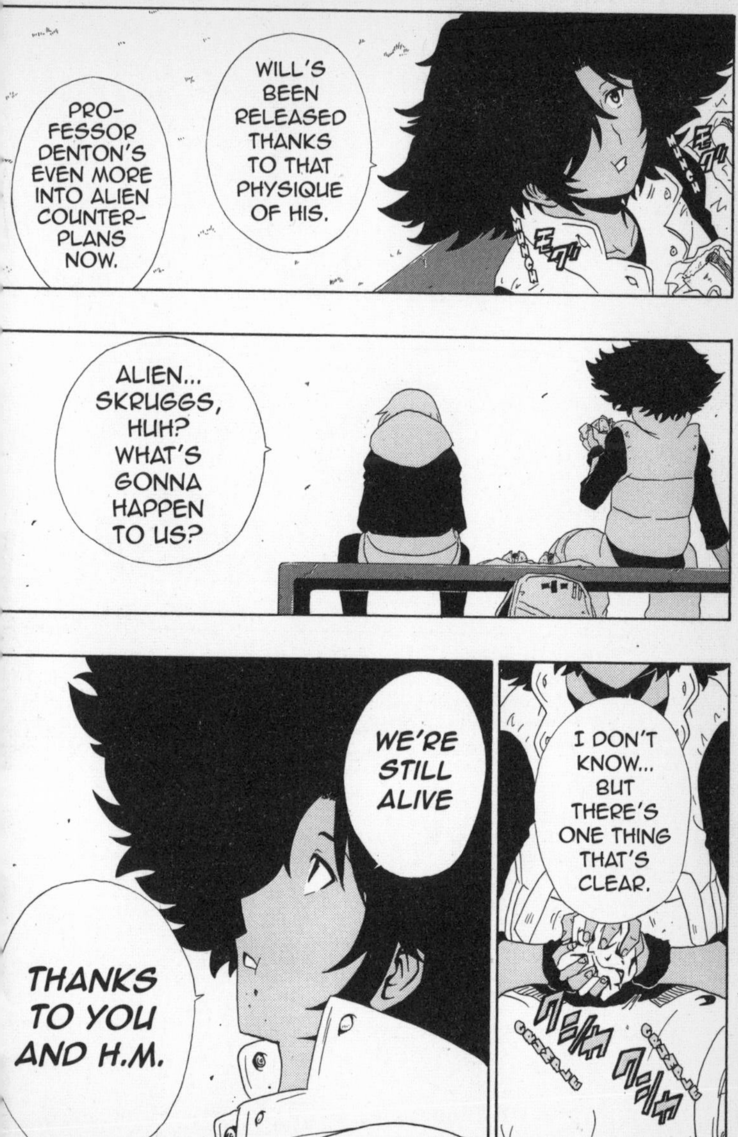
WILL'S BEEN RELEASED THANKS TO THAT PHYSIQUE OF HIS.
MUNCH
MUNCH
PRO-FESSOR DENTON'S EVEN MORE INTO ALIEN COUNTER-PLANS NOW.
ALIEN... SKRUGGS, HUH? WHAT'S GONNA HAPPEN TO US?
I DON'T KNOW... BUT THERE'S ONE THING THAT'S CLEAR.
WE'RE STILL ALIVE
THANKS TO YOU AND H.M.

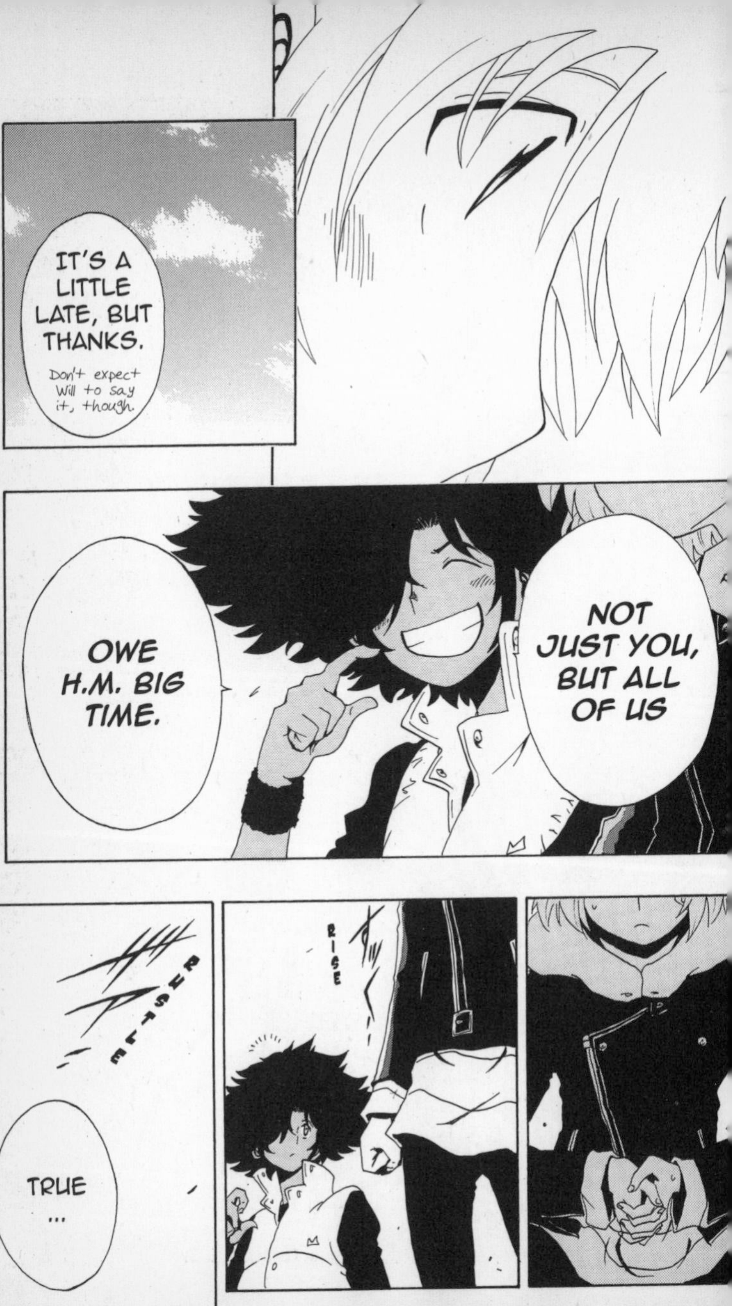
IT'S A LITTLE LATE, BUT THANKS.
Don't expect Will to say it, though.
NOT JUST YOU, BUT ALL OF US
OWE H.M. BIG TIME.
RISE
RUSTLE
TRUE ...

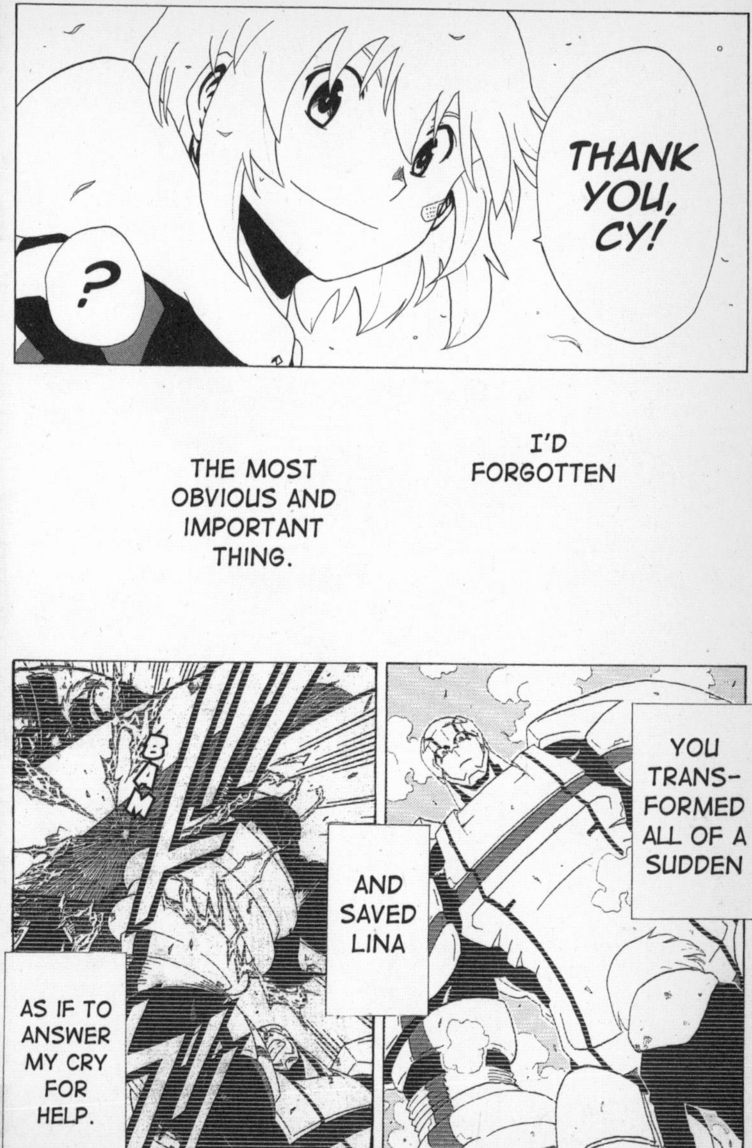
THANK YOU, CY!
?
I'D FORGOTTEN
THE MOST OBVIOUS AND IMPORTANT THING.
YOU TRANS-FORMED ALL OF A SUDDEN
AND SAVED LINA
BAM
AS IF TO ANSWER MY CRY FOR HELP.

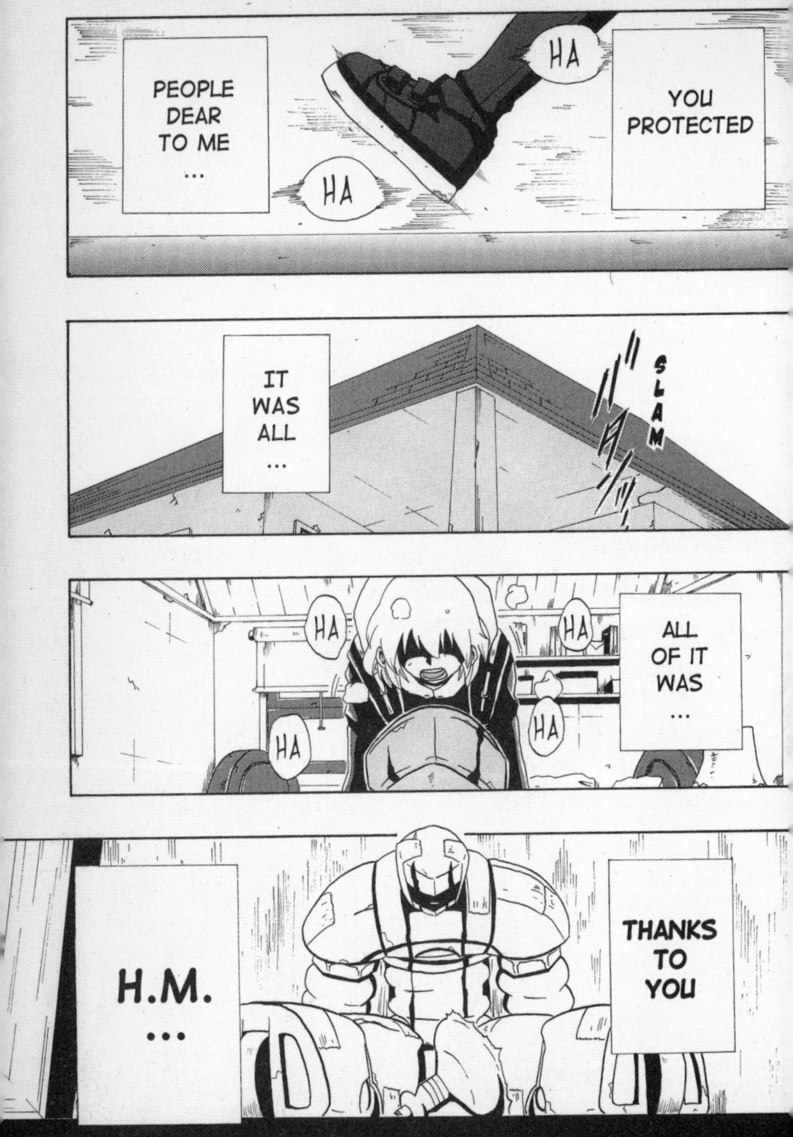
YOU PROTECTED
HA
HA
PEOPLE DEAR TO ME ...
SLAM
IT WAS ALL ...
ALL OF IT WAS ...
HA
HA
HA
HA
THANKS TO YOU
H.M. ...

I'M SORRY, H.M. ...

PRECIOUS HERO, WEREN'T YOU.

YOU WERE MY

YOU'RE THEIR TARGET NOW AND IN A PINCH ...

SINCE YOU SAVED US,

IN THAT CASE IT'S MY TURN TO HELP AND FIGHT WITH YOU.

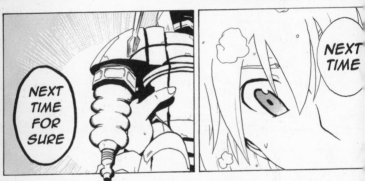

NEXT TIME FOR SURE

NEXT TIME

WE'LL FIGHT AS ONE,

HERO-MAN!

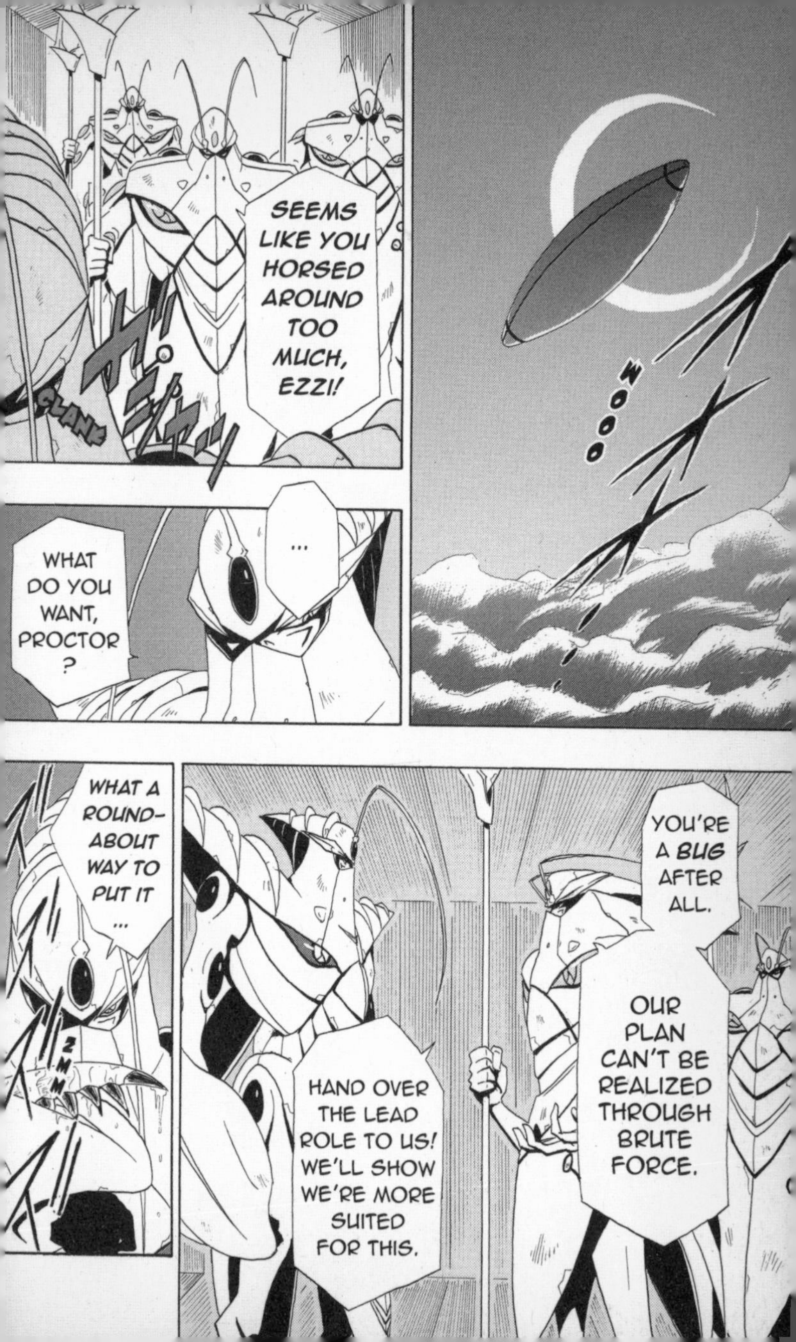
WOOOO
SEEMS LIKE YOU HORSED AROUND TOO MUCH, EZZI!
CLANK
...
WHAT DO YOU WANT, PROCTOR?
YOU'RE A BUG AFTER ALL.
OUR PLAN CAN'T BE REALIZED THROUGH BRUTE FORCE.
HAND OVER THE LEAD ROLE TO US! WE'LL SHOW WE'RE MORE SUITED FOR THIS.
WHAT A ROUND-ABOUT WAY TO PUT IT ...
ZMM

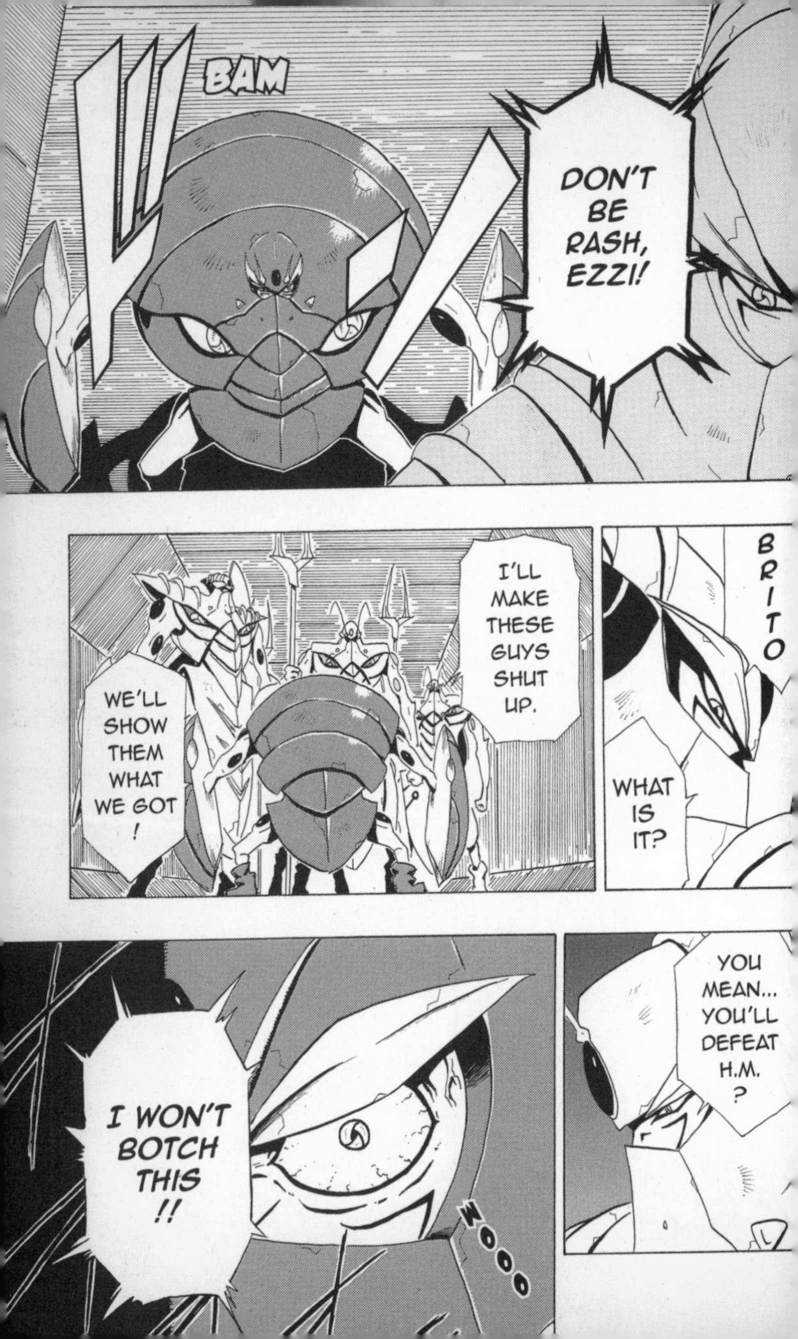
DON'T BE RASH, EZZI!
BAM
BRITO
WHAT IS IT?
I'LL MAKE THESE GUYS SHUT UP.
WE'LL SHOW THEM WHAT WE GOT!
YOU MEAN... YOU'LL DEFEAT H.M.?
I WON'T BOTCH THIS!!
WOOO

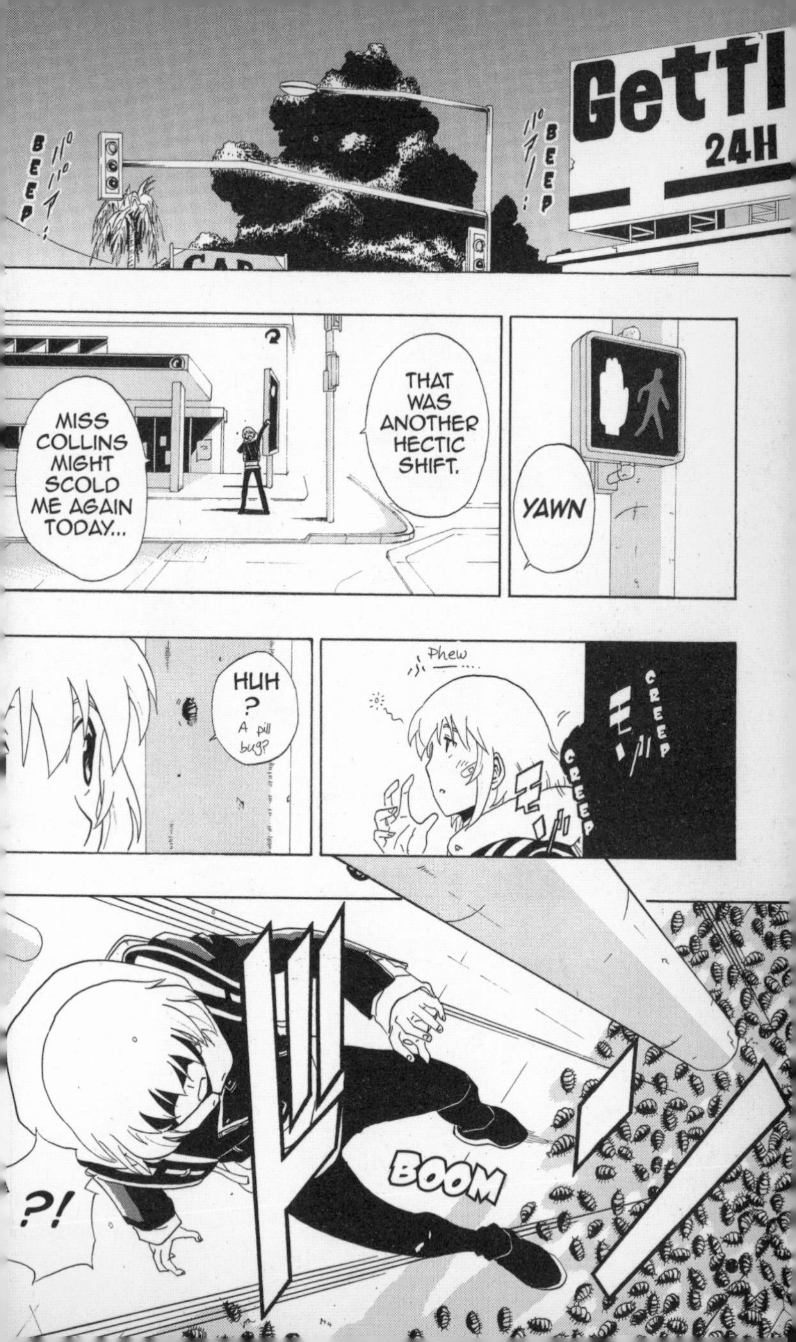
BEEP
BEEP
24H
YAWN
THAT WAS ANOTHER HECTIC SHIFT.
MISS COLLINS MIGHT SCOLD ME AGAIN TODAY...
Phew...
CREEP
CREEP
HUH? A pill bug?
BOOM
?!

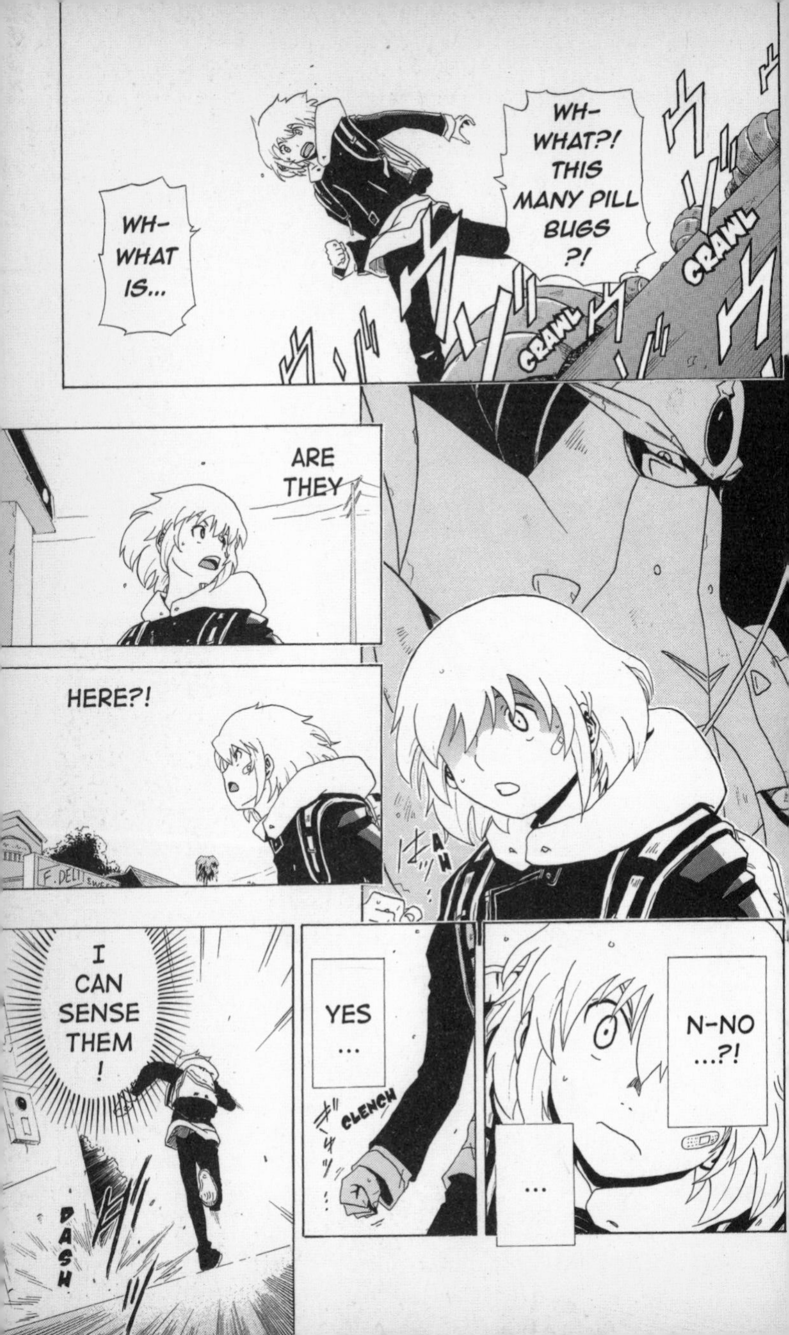
CRAWL
WH- WHAT?! THIS MANY PILL BUGS ?!
CRAWL
WH- WHAT IS...
AH
ARE THEY
HERE?!
N-NO ...?!
...
YES ...
CLENCH
I CAN SENSE THEM !
DASH

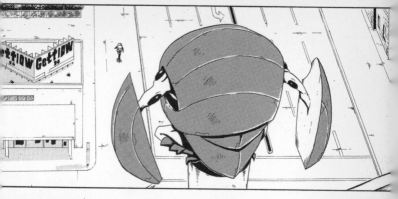

HE CAUGHT ON!

JOEY?

WHY'S HE GOING THE OPPOSITE WAY FROM SCHOOL?

HUH?!

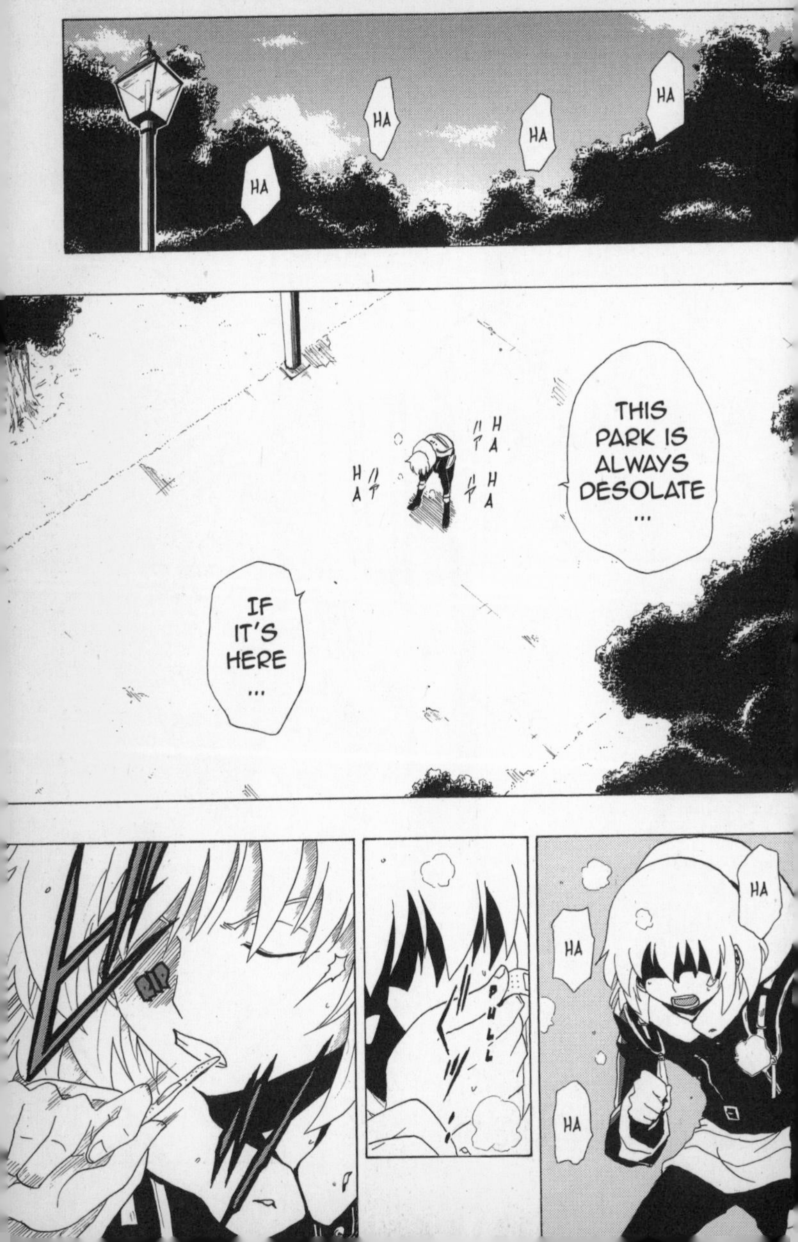
HA
HA
HA
HA
THIS PARK IS ALWAYS DESOLATE ...
HA HA
HA HA
IF IT'S HERE ...
HA
HA
HA
PULL
RIP

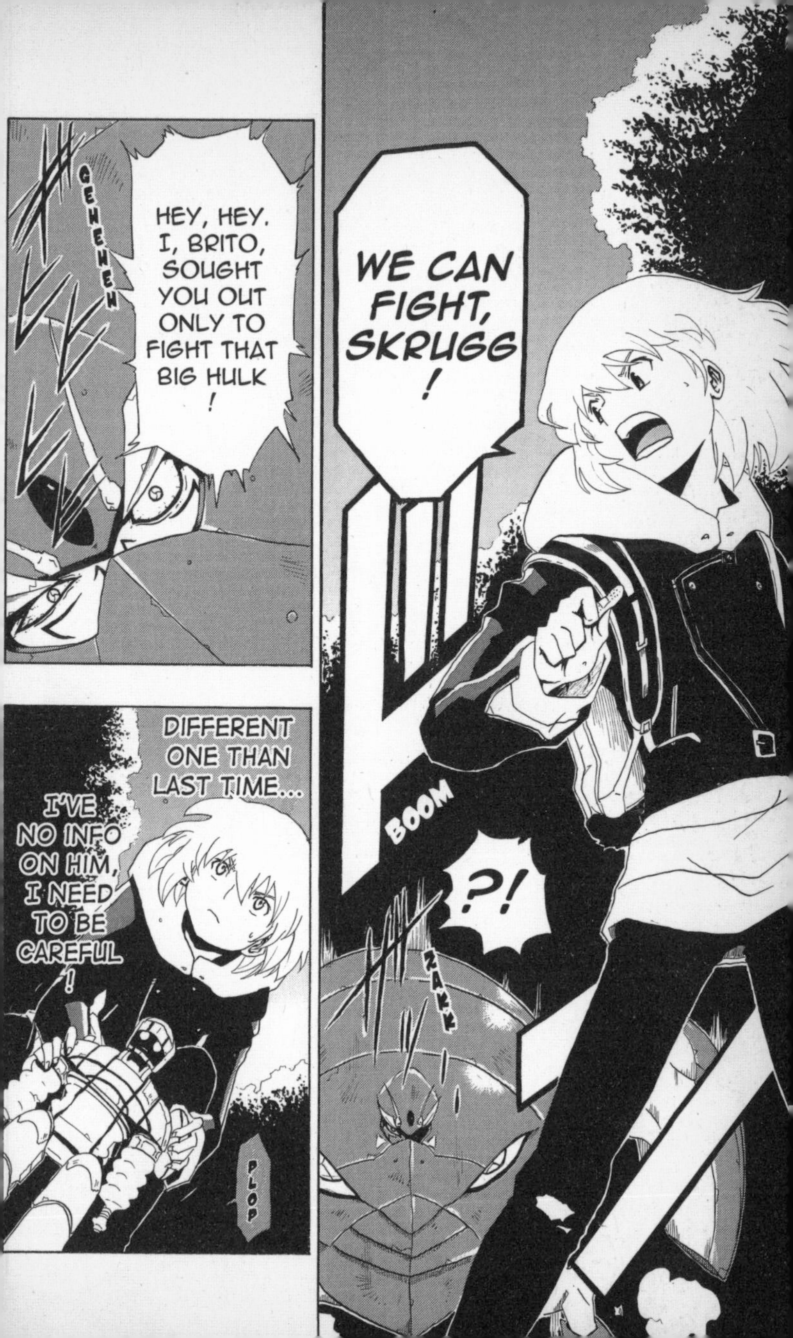
WE CAN FIGHT, SKRUGG!
BOOM
?!
ZAKK
GENENEN
HEY, HEY. I, BRITO, SOUGHT YOU OUT ONLY TO FIGHT THAT BIG HULK!
DIFFERENT ONE THAN LAST TIME...
I'VE NO INFO ON HIM, I NEED TO BE CAREFUL!
PLOP

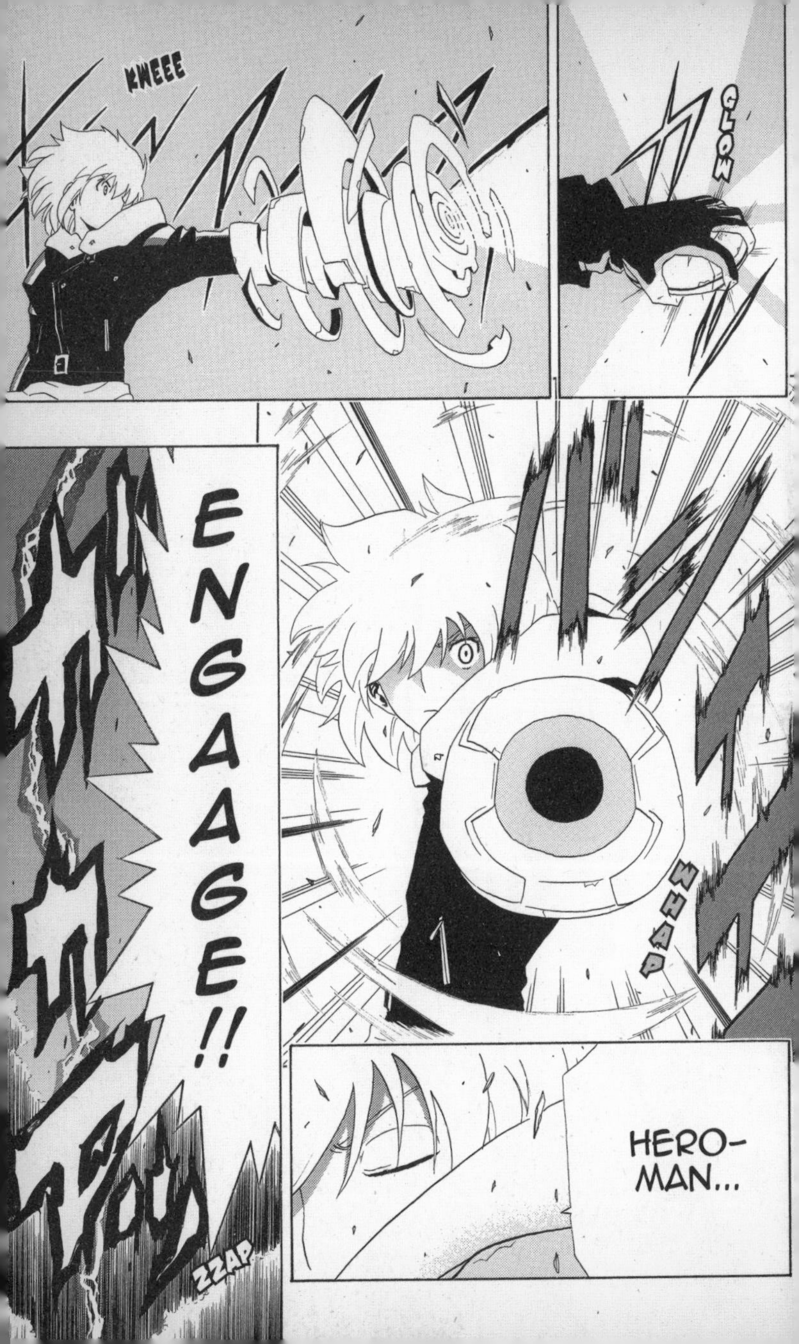
GLOW
KWEEE
WHAP
HERO-MAN...
ENGAGE!!
ZZAP

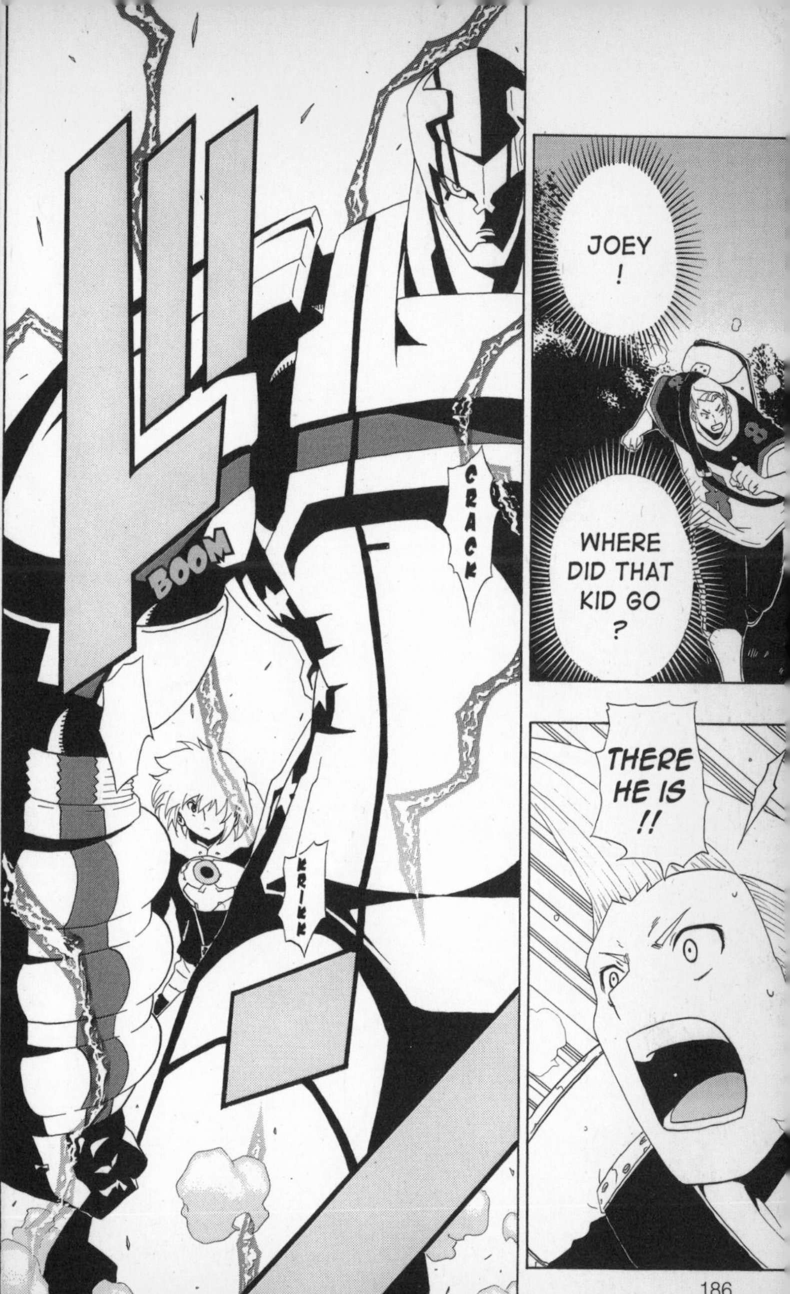
JOEY !
WHERE DID THAT KID GO ?
THERE HE IS !!
BOOM
CRACK
KRIKK

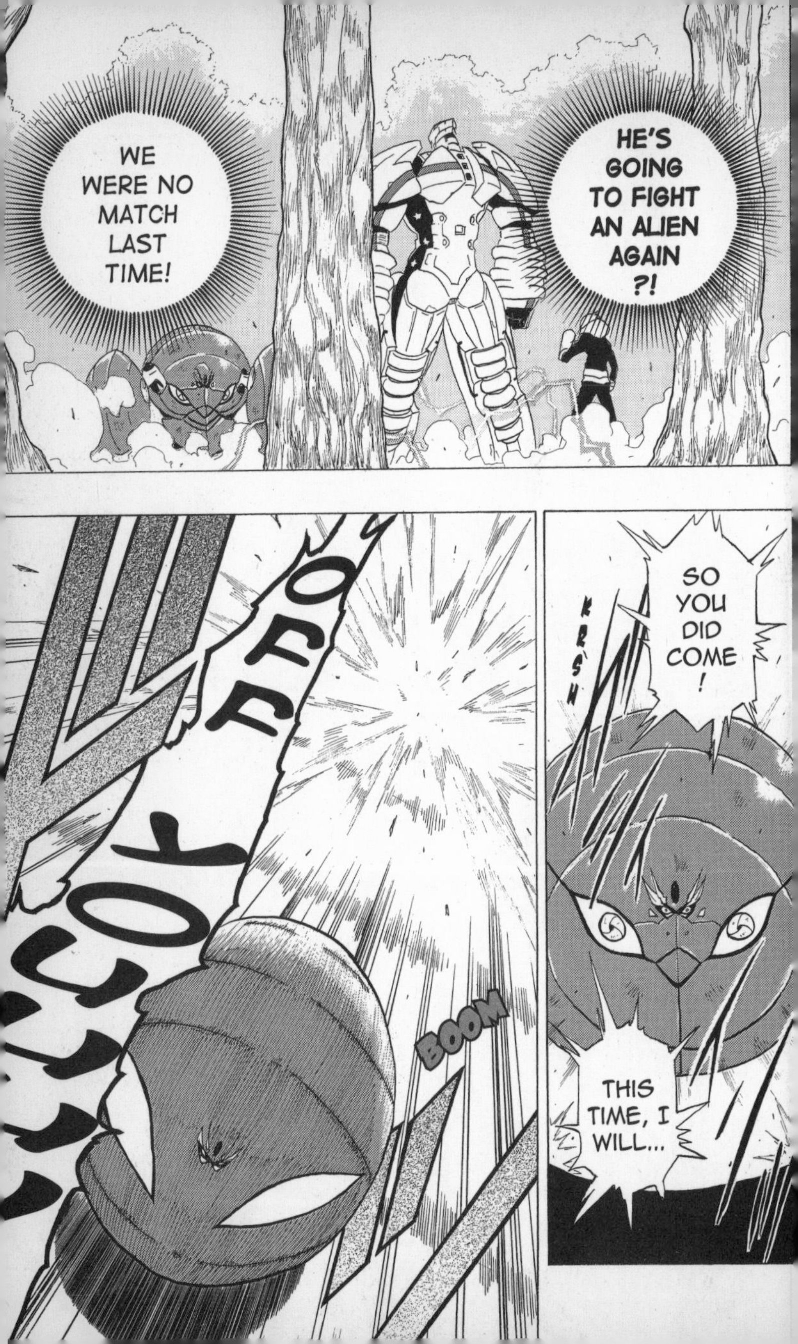
HE'S GOING TO FIGHT AN ALIEN AGAIN?!
WE WERE NO MATCH LAST TIME!
KRSH
SO YOU DID COME!
THIS TIME, I WILL...
BOOM

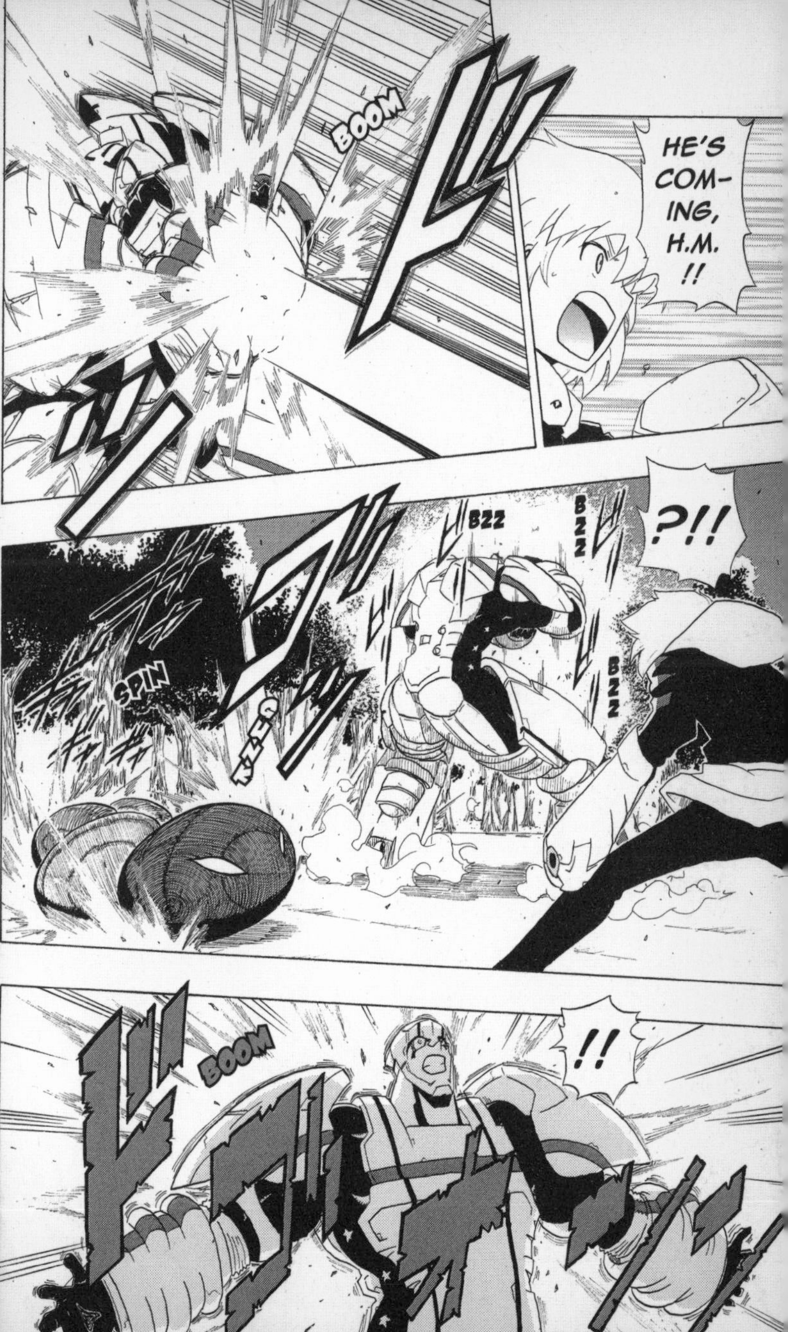
HE'S COM- ING, H.M. !!
BOOM
?!!
BZZ
BZZ
BZZ
SPIN
!!
BOOM

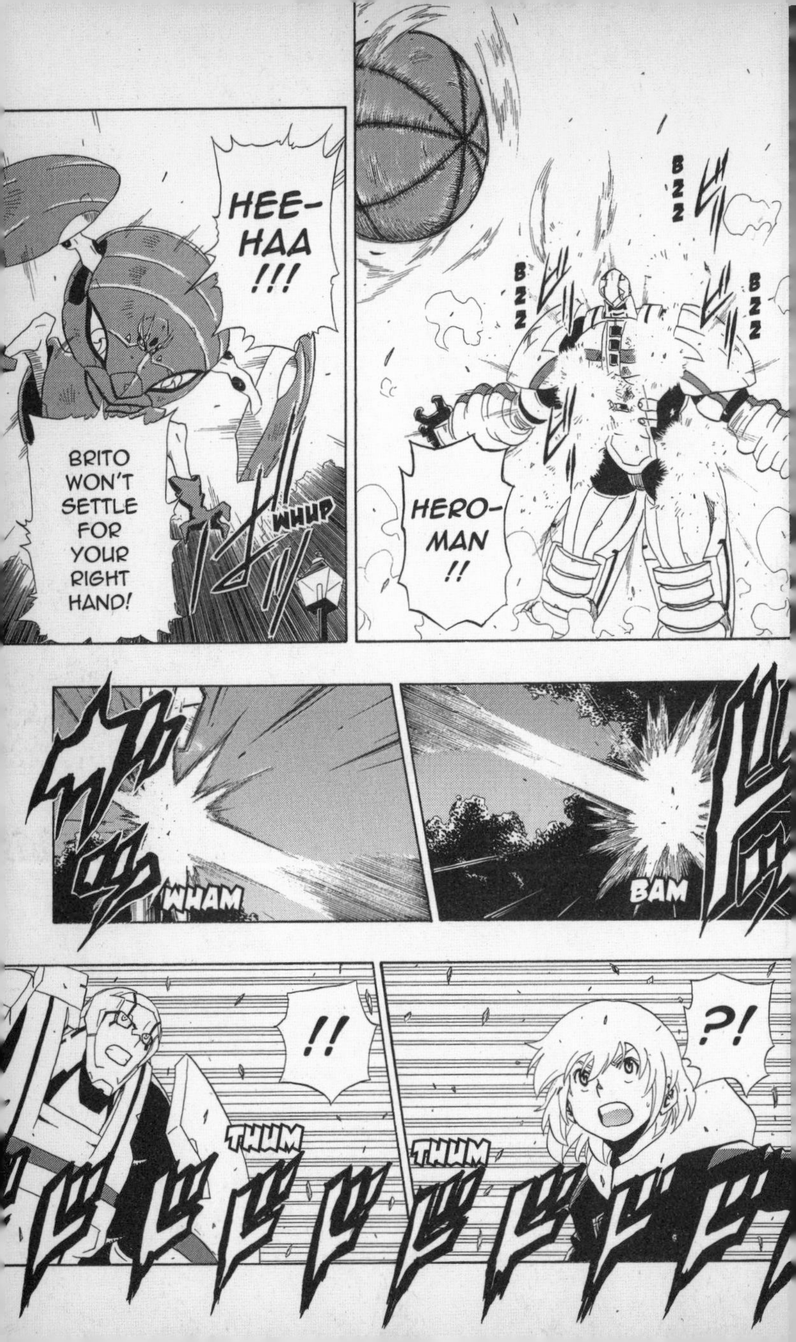
BZZ
BZZ
BZZ
HERO-MAN!!
HEE-HAA!!!
BRITO WON'T SETTLE FOR YOUR RIGHT HAND!
WHUP
BAM
WHAM
?!
THUM
!!
THUM

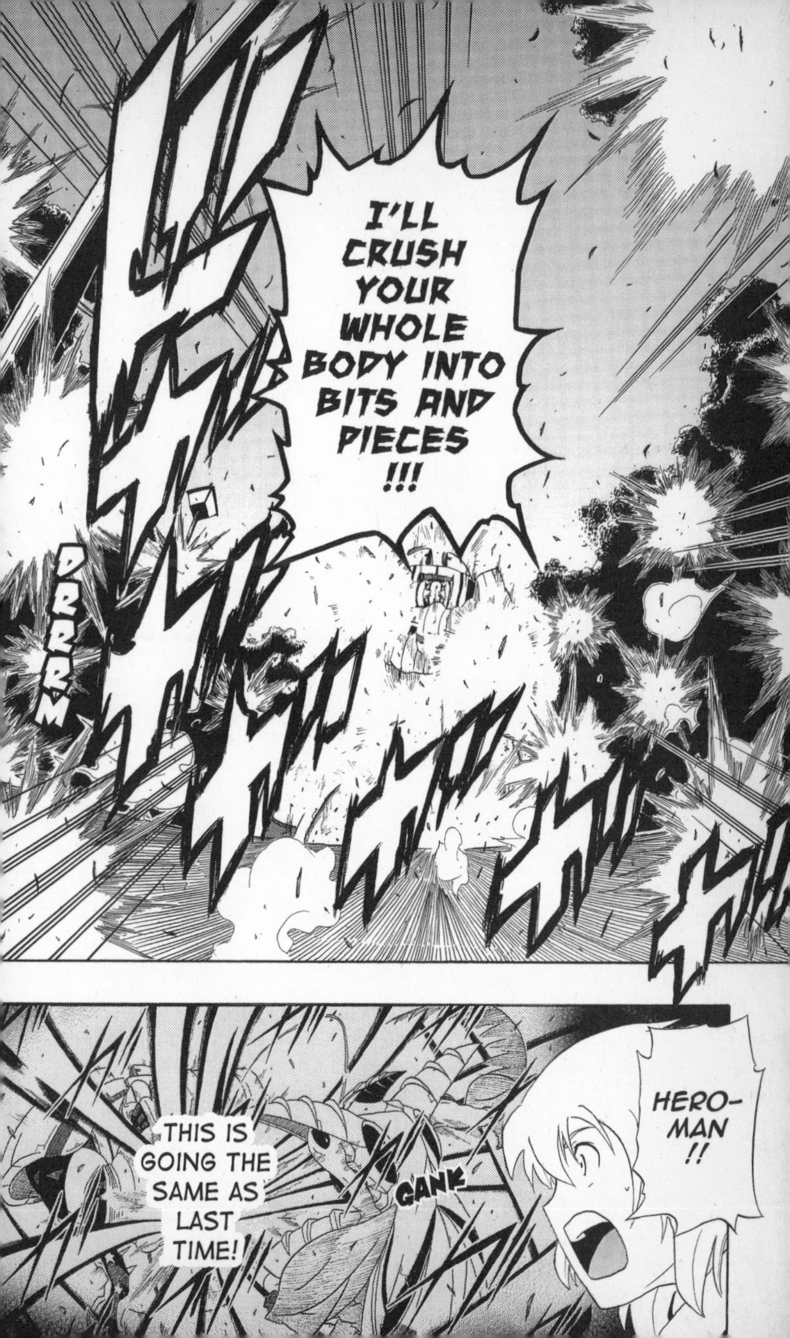
I'LL CRUSH YOUR WHOLE BODY INTO BITS AND PIECES !!!
DRRRM
HERO-MAN !!
GANK
THIS IS GOING THE SAME AS LAST TIME!

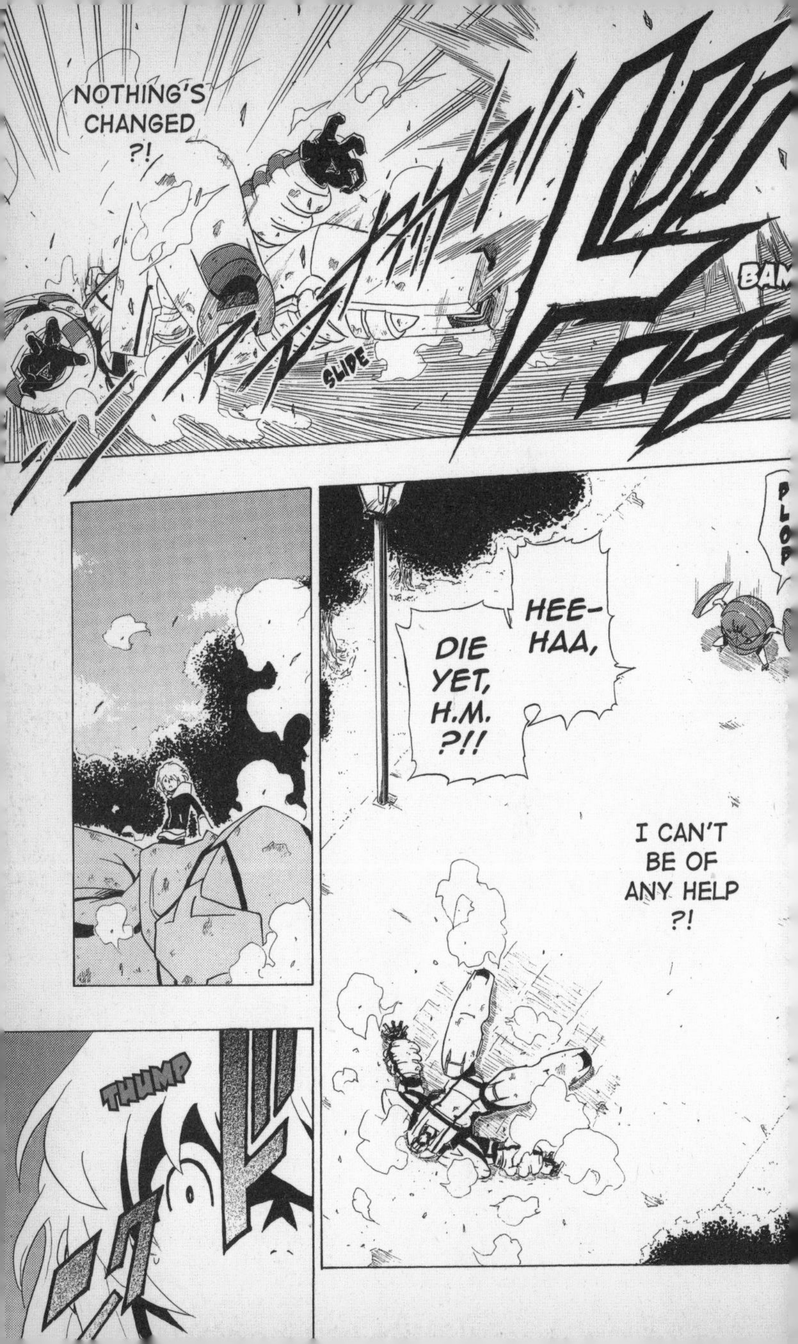
BAM
NOTHING'S CHANGED ?!
SLIDE
PLOP
HEE-HAA,
DIE YET, H.M. ?!!
I CAN'T BE OF ANY HELP ?!
THUMP

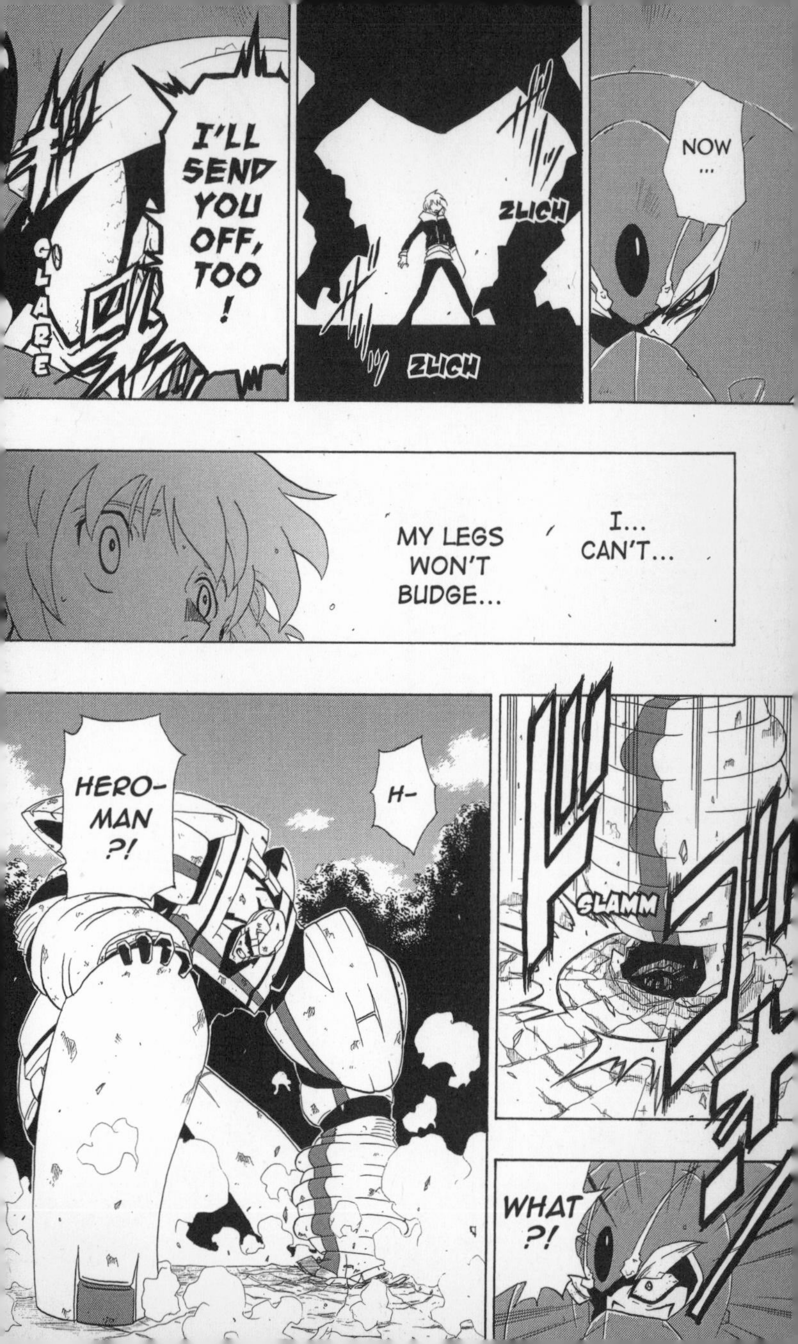
NOW ...
ZLICH
ZLICH
I'LL SEND YOU OFF, TOO!
GLARE
I... CAN'T...
MY LEGS WON'T BUDGE...
SLAMM
WHAT ?!
H-
HERO-MAN ?!

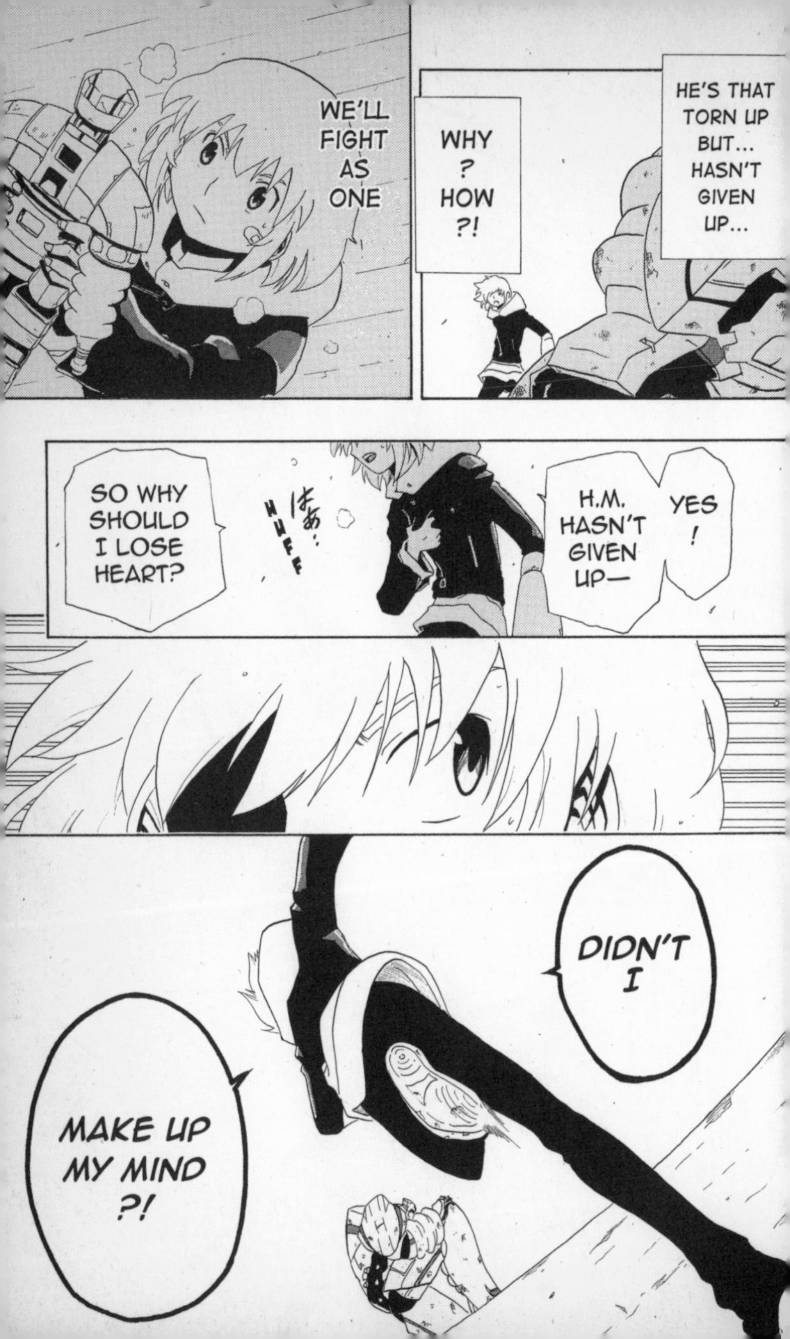
HE'S THAT TORN UP BUT... HASN'T GIVEN UP...
WHY? HOW?!
WE'LL FIGHT AS ONE
YES!
H.M. HASN'T GIVEN UP—
はぁ HUFF
SO WHY SHOULD I LOSE HEART?
DIDN'T I
MAKE UP MY MIND?!

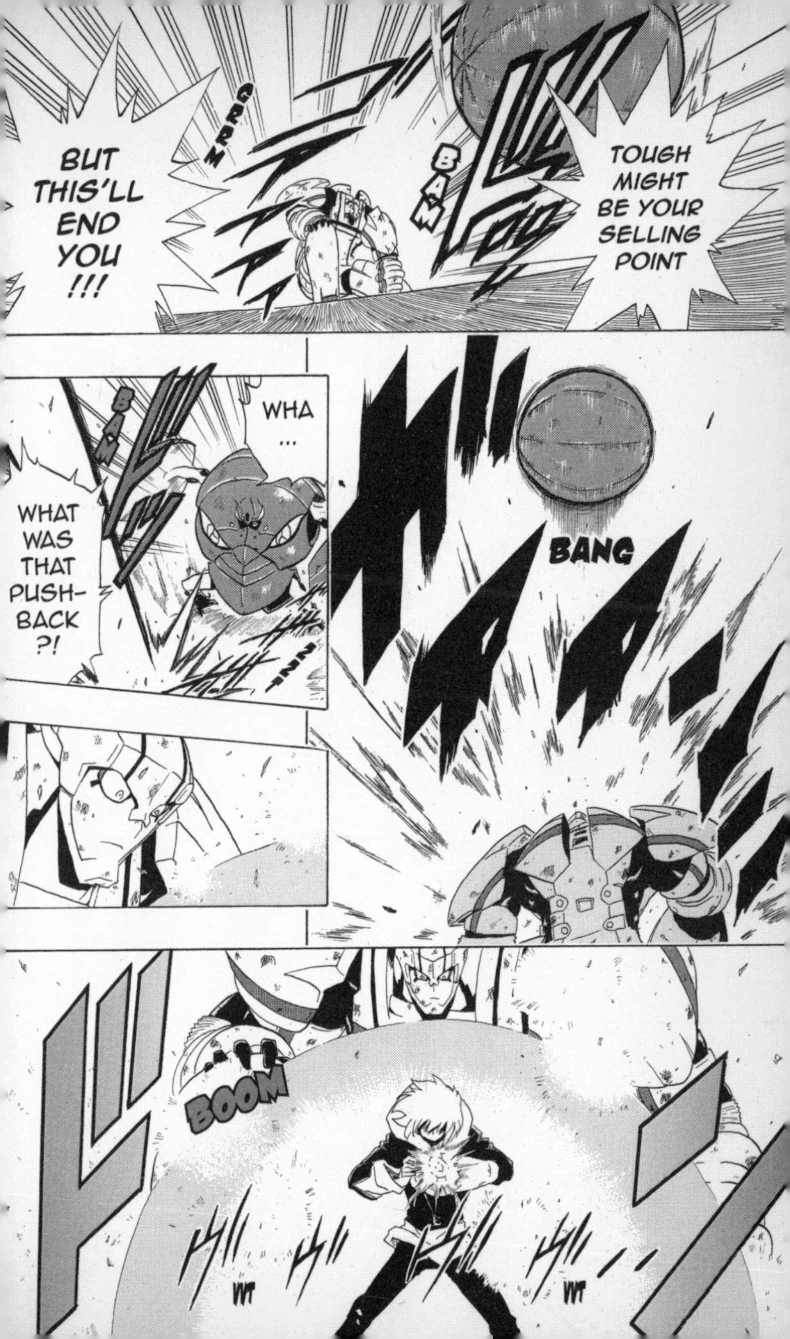

TOUGH MIGHT BE YOUR SELLING POINT
BAM
GRRM
BUT THIS'LL END YOU !!!
BANG
WHA ...
BAM
WHAT WAS THAT PUSH-BACK ?!
BOOM
VVT
VVT

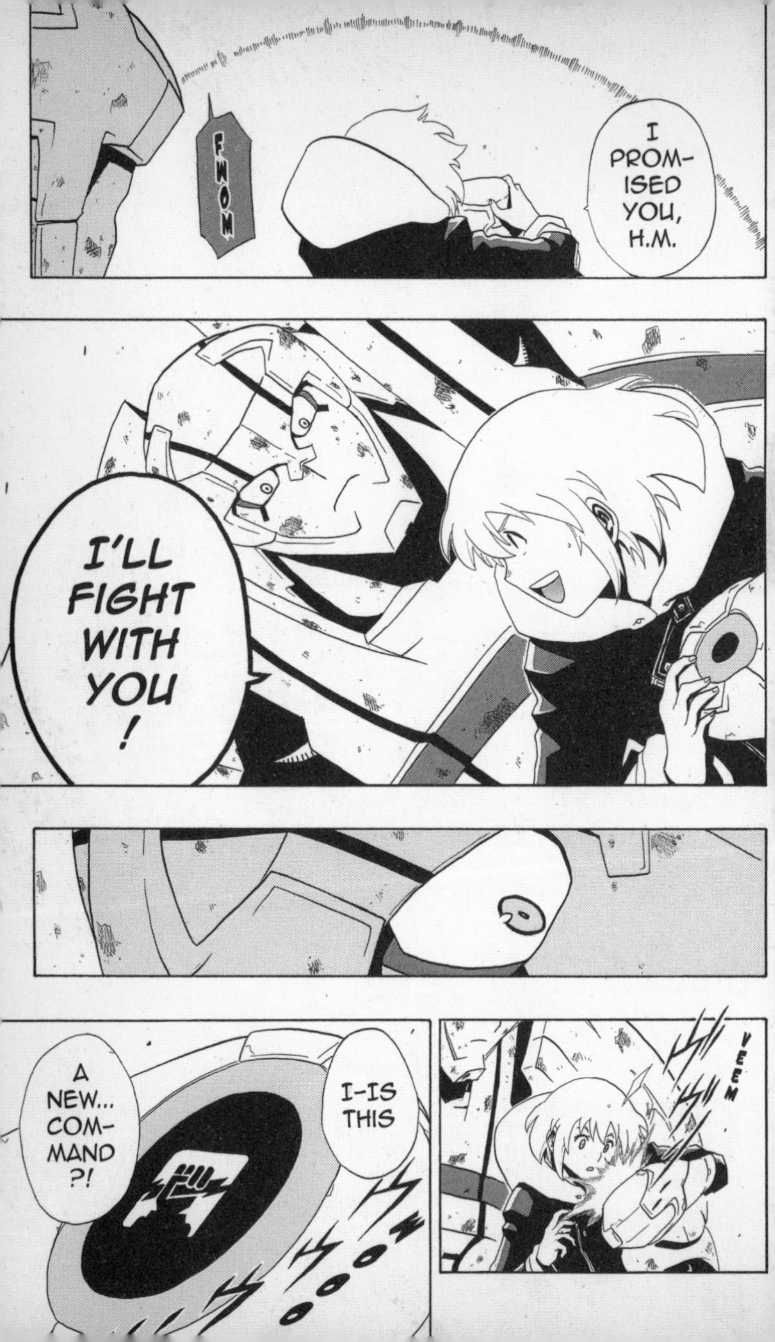
I PROM-ISED YOU, H.M.
FWOM
I'LL FIGHT WITH YOU!
VEEEM
I-IS THIS
A NEW... COM-MAND?!
WOOOO

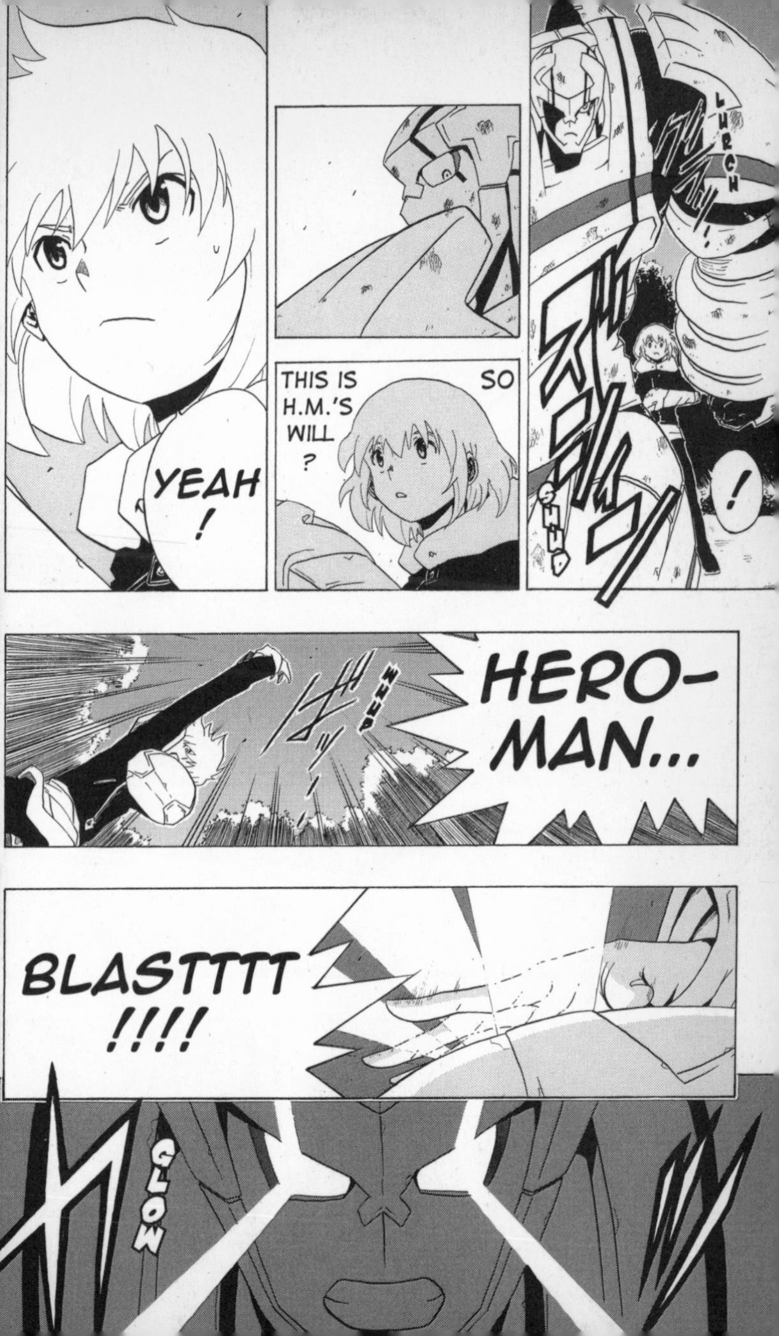
LURCH
!
SHUD
!
SO
THIS IS H.M.'S WILL ?
YEAH !
WHUD
HERO-MAN...
BLASTTTT !!!!
GLOW

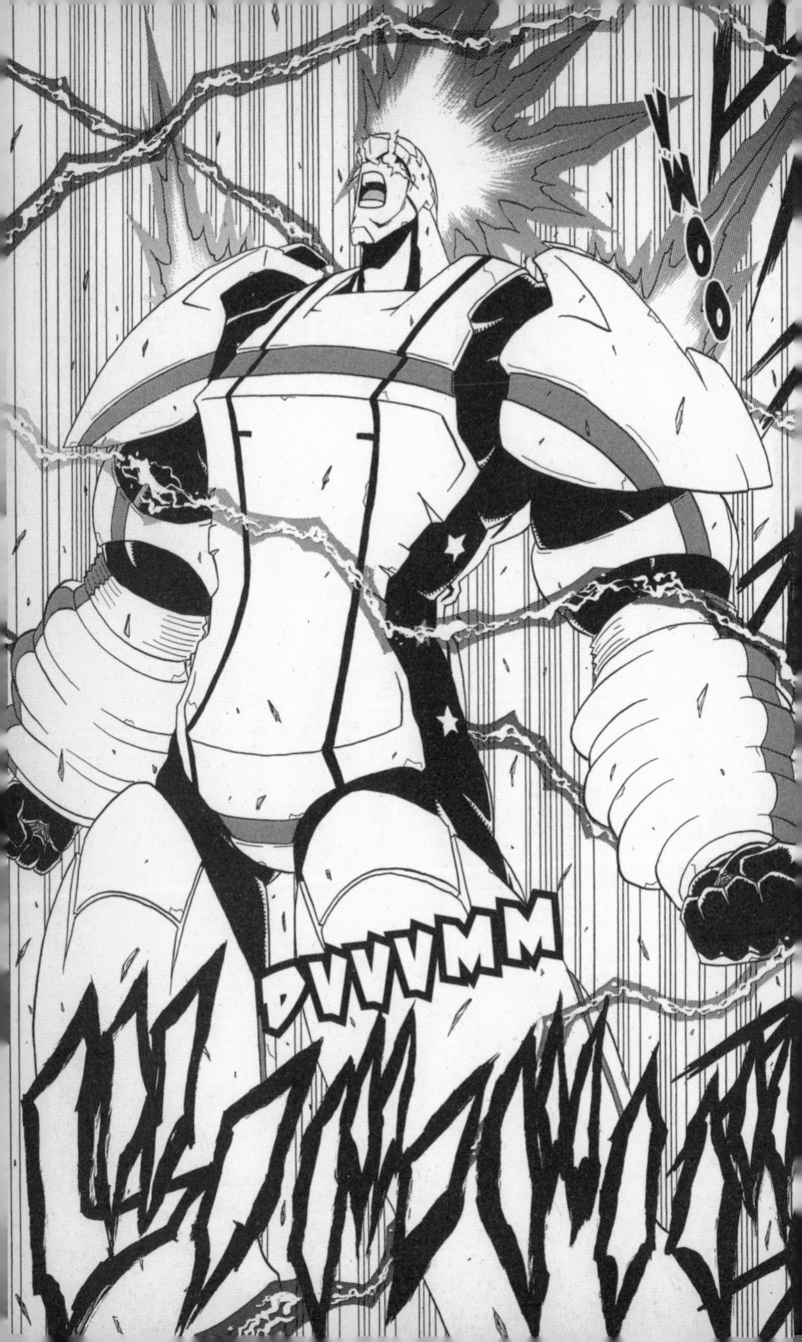
VWOOO
DVVVMM

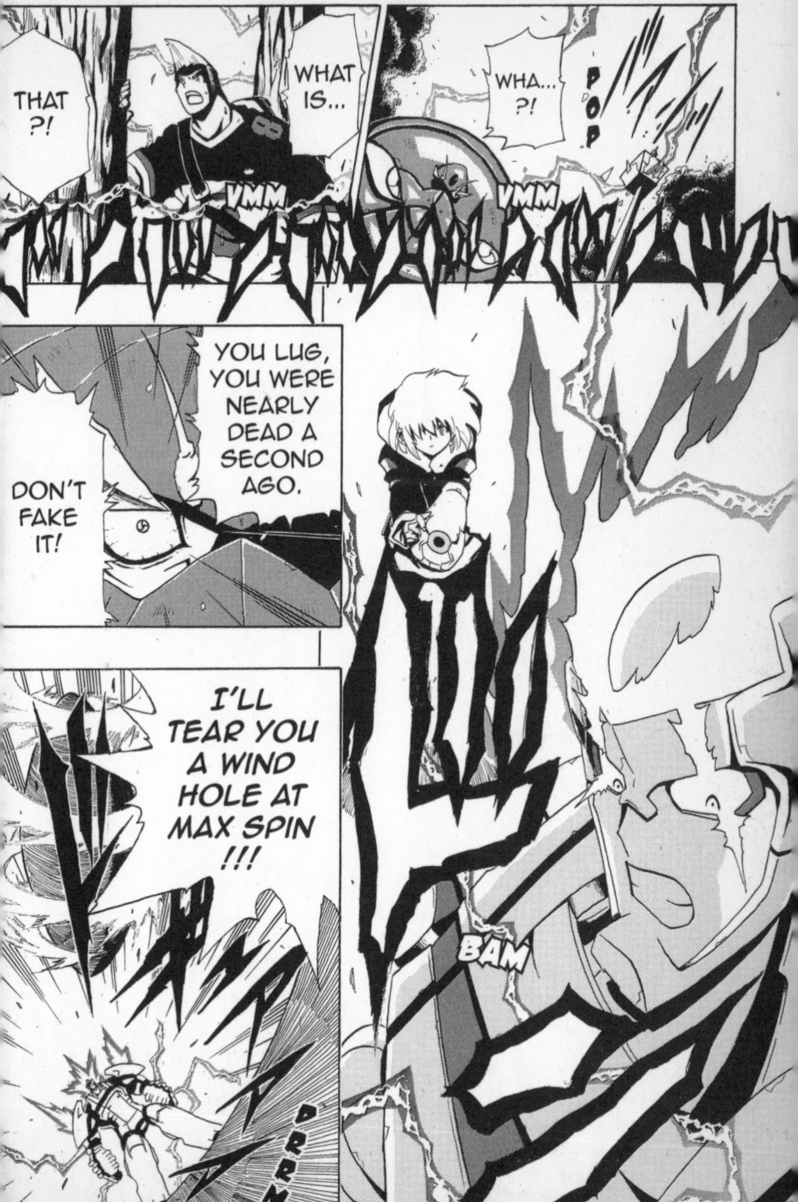
WHA...?!
POP
VMM
WHAT IS...
THAT ?!
VMM
BAM
YOU LUG, YOU WERE NEARLY DEAD A SECOND AGO.
DON'T FAKE IT!
I'LL TEAR YOU A WIND HOLE AT MAX SPIN !!!
DRRM

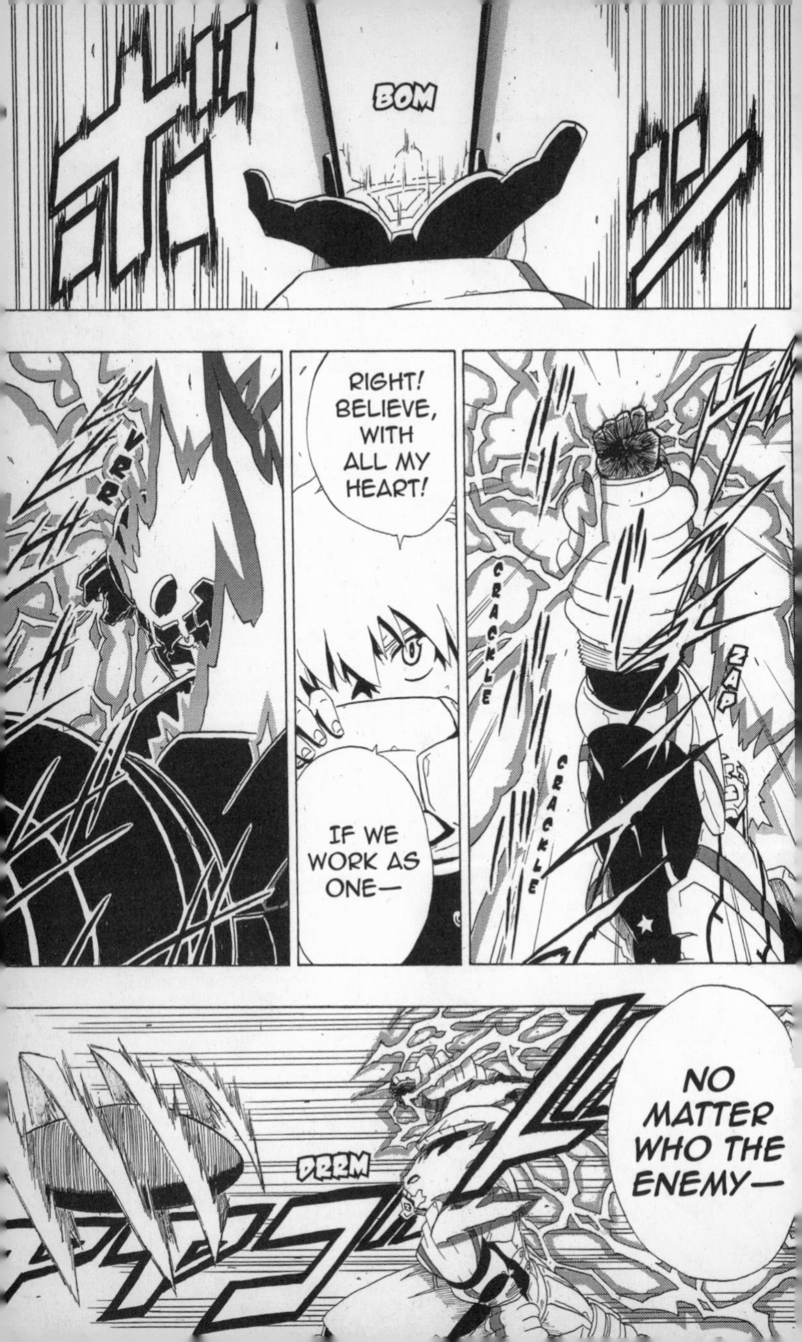
BOM
CRACKLE
ZAP
CRACKLE
RIGHT! BELIEVE, WITH ALL MY HEART!
IF WE WORK AS ONE—
VRR
NO MATTER WHO THE ENEMY—
DRRM

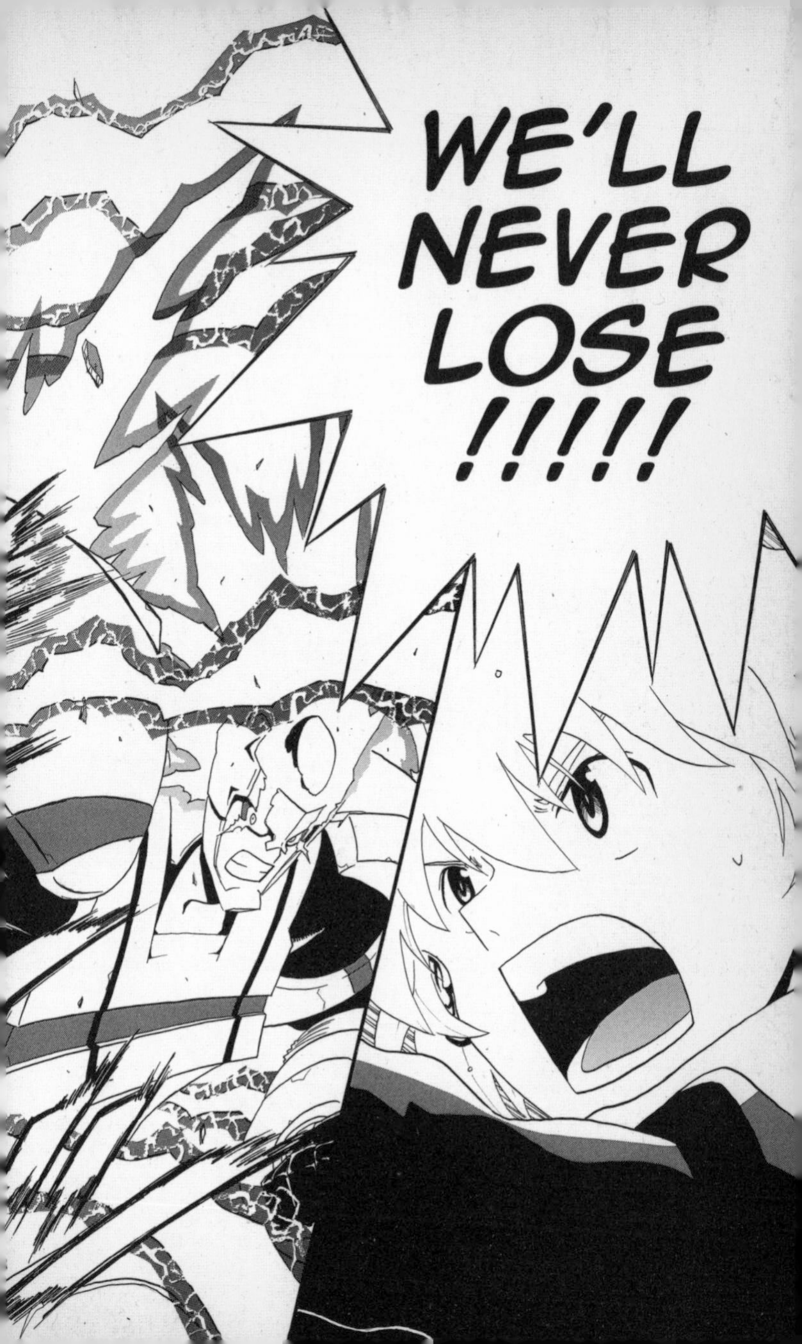
WE'LL NEVER LOSE !!!!!

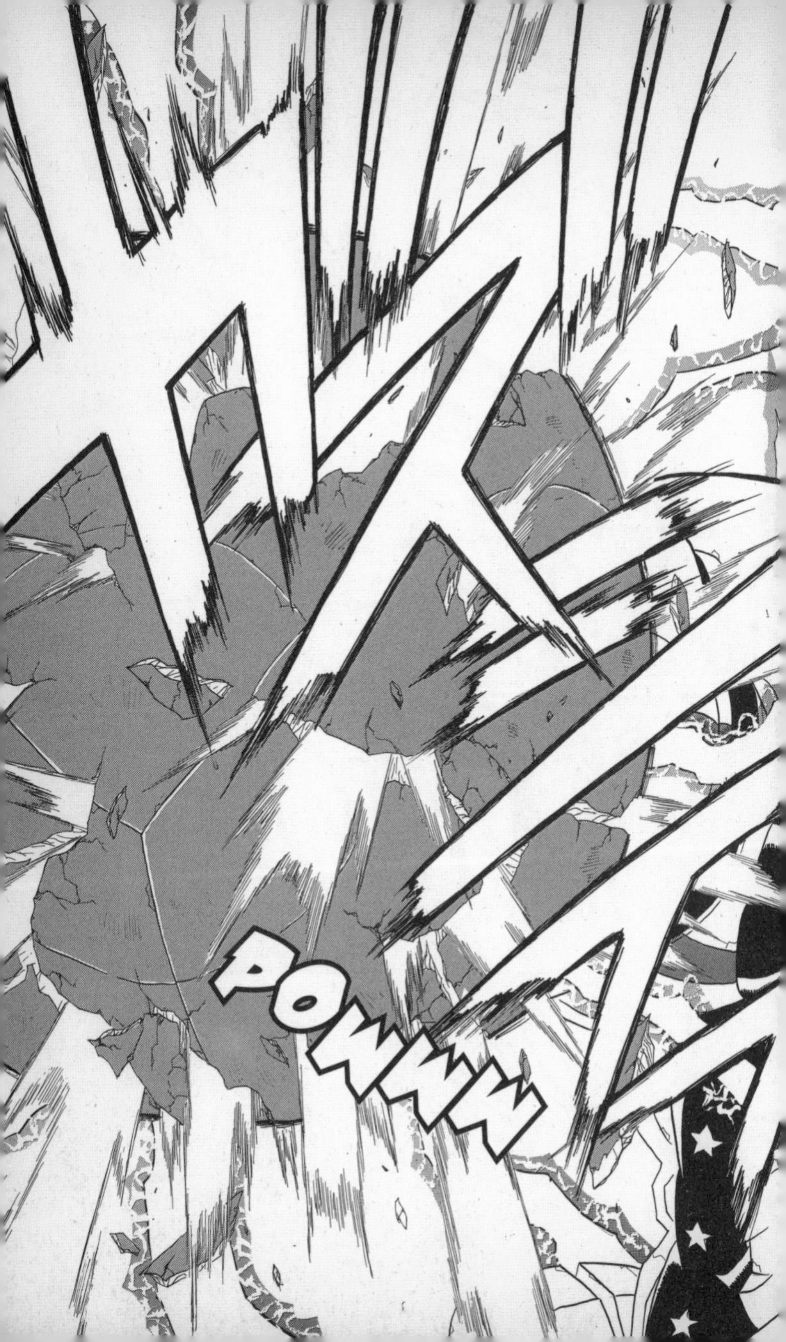
POWWW

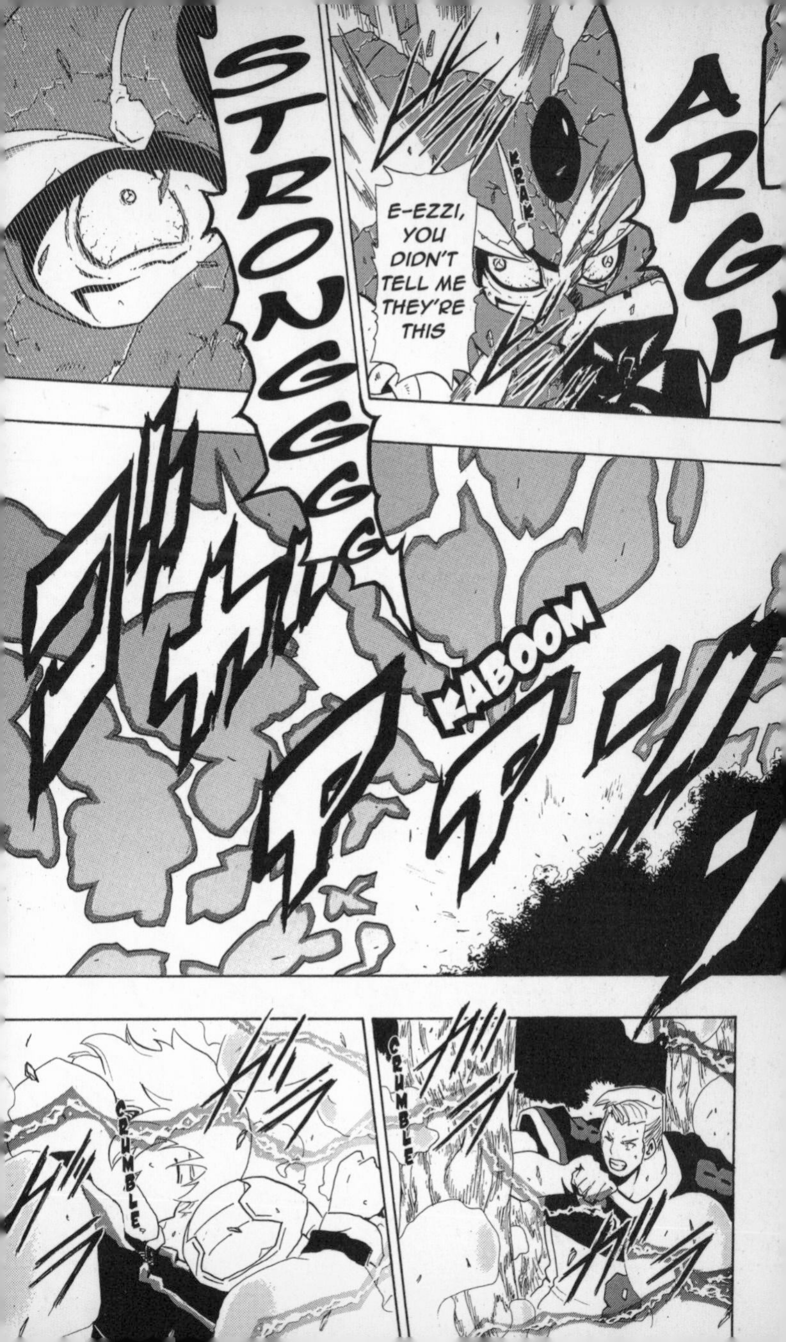
ARGH
KRAK
E-EZZI, YOU DIDN'T TELL ME THEY'RE THIS
STRONGGGG
KABOOM
CRUMBLE
CRUMBLE

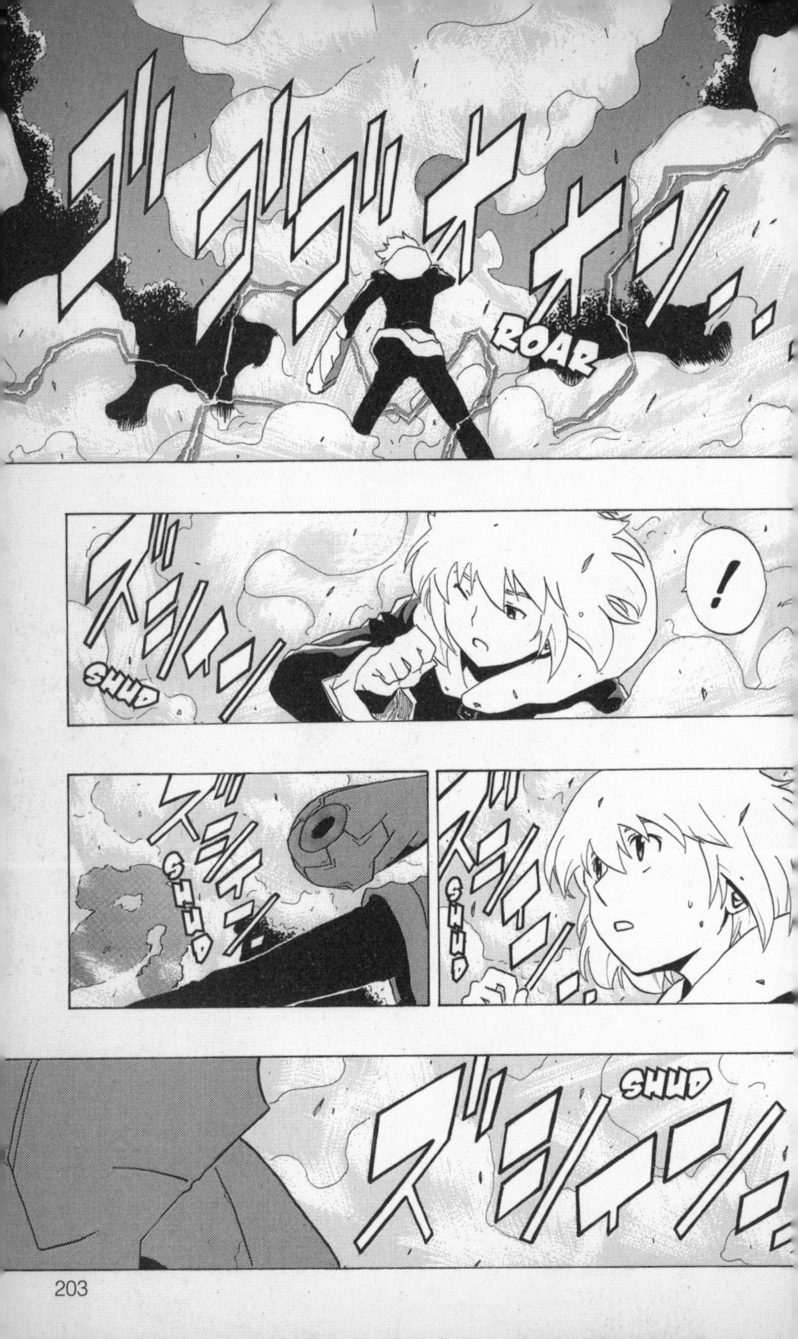
ROAR
!
SHUD
SHUD
SHUD
SHUD

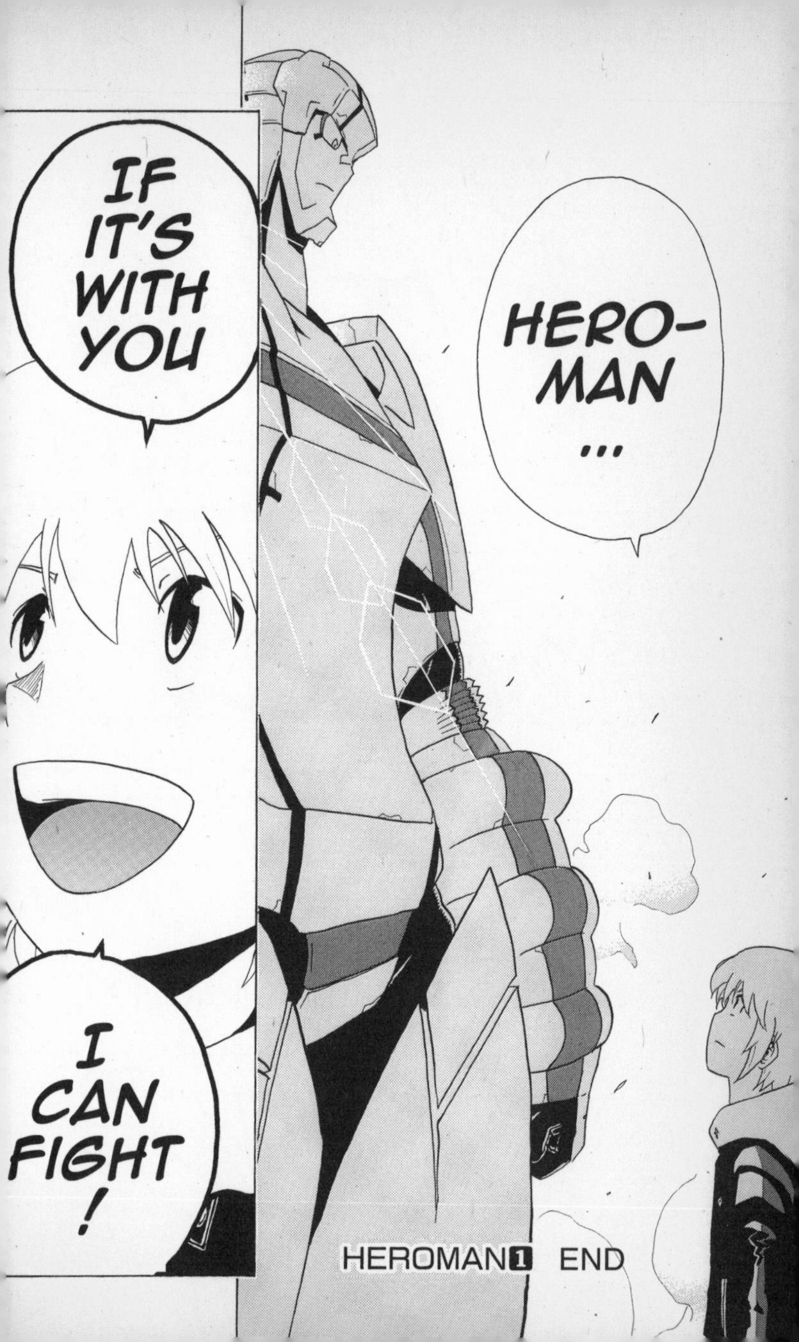
HERO-MAN ...
HEROMAN 1 END
IF IT'S WITH YOU
I CAN FIGHT!

VOLUME 2
COMING THIS
DECEMBER!

HEROMAN